THE POLITICS OF THE BOOK

# THE POLITICS OF THE BOOK

A STUDY ON THE MATERIALITY OF IDEAS

FILIPE CARREIRA DA SILVA

MÓNICA BRITO VIEIRA

THE PENNSYLVANIA STATE UNIVERSITY PRESS | UNIVERSITY PARK, PENNSYLVANIA

Library of Congress Cataloging-in-Publication Data

Names: Carreira da Silva, Filipe, author. | Brito Vieira, Monica, author.
Title: The politics of the book : a study on the materiality of ideas / Filipe Carreira da Silva, Monica Brito Vieira.
Other titles: Penn State series in the history of the book.
Description: University Park, Pennsylvania : The Pennsylvania State University Press, [2019] | Series: Penn State series in the history of the book | Includes bibliographical references and index.
Summary: "Explores several classic works of social and political thought, examining how the history of their publication materially affected their meaning and reception over time. Case studies include works by Durkheim, Mead, Marx, Du Bois, and Weber"—Provided by publisher.
Identifiers: LCCN 2019004849 | ISBN 9780271083421 (cloth : alk. paper)
Subjects: LCSH: Sociology literature—History and criticism—Case studies. | Political science literature—History and criticism—Case studies. | Books—Political aspects.
Classification: LCC HM585.S5237 2019 | DDC 809/.933552—dc23
LC record available at https://lccn.loc.gov/2019004849

Copyright © 2019 Filipe Carreira da Silva and Monica Brito Vieira
All rights reserved
Printed in the United States of America
Published by
The Pennsylvania State University Press,
University Park, PA 16802-1003

The Pennsylvania State University Press is a member of the Association of University Presses.

It is the policy of The Pennsylvania State University Press to use acid-free paper. Publications on uncoated stock satisfy the minimum requirements of American National Standard for Information Sciences—Permanence of Paper for Printed Library Material, ANSI Z39.48-1992.

TO

FERNANDO

BRITO

I slowly love the friends who are sad with five fingers on each side.

The friends who go crazy and are sitting, closing their eyes,

with the books behind them burning for all eternity.

I don't call them, and they turn deeply

within the fire.

—We have a painful obscure talent.

We've built a place of silence.

Of passion.

HERBERTO HELDER, *Aos Amigos*

CONTENTS

Acknowledgments | ix

Introduction | 1

1  *Elementary Forms* and the Cultural Durkheim | 17

2  A Classic with No Author: G. H. Mead's *Mind, Self, and Society* | 43

3  The Dialectic of Dissent: Marx's *1844 Economic and Philosophic Manuscripts* | 62

4  When Souls Came to Matter: The Many Lives of Du Bois's *The Souls of Black Folk* | 97

5  A Work in Translation: Weber's *The Protestant Ethic* | 135

6  Prophets and Princes: On the Editing and Translation of Tocqueville's *Democracy in America* | 157

Conclusion | 201

Notes | 207
References | 223
Index | 251

ACKNOWLEDGMENTS

The idea behind this book first came up over coffee with Patrick Baert near Market Square, Cambridge, in 2010. Patrick was putting together a special issue on new approaches to the study of classical authors for the *Journal of Classical Sociology*. He needed a contribution from us, which he suggested should focus on George Herbert Mead and the history behind *Mind, Self, and Society*. This would eventually lead to the 2011 publication of "Books and Canon Building in Sociology: The Case of *Mind, Self, and Society*" in the *Journal of Classical Sociology* 11 (3): 356–77. A revised version of this appears here as chapter 2. This was our first attempt at exploring the impact of material forms on meaning production. Research time spent in Chicago and Jerusalem around this time proved pivotal for development of the original idea.

As soon as we saw some potential for turning this into a monograph, Penn State University Press was our top choice for a publisher. In time, it would reveal itself to be the ideal home to see our initial idea through to publication. As we show in the book, editors are main players in the development and production of a book. Our deepest expression of gratitude is owed to our editor at Penn State, Patrick Alexander, for his enthusiasm about the book project and his unfailing support and expert advice over the years. Our thanks extend to Alex Vose, his editorial assistant, who has been instrumental in making sure that we stay organized and focused on deadlines. We would also like to thank the reviewers for the time and effort they invested in the manuscript and the helpful comments and suggestions that resulted from their expert scrutiny.

Funding is of the essence for undertaking archival research. Special thanks are owed to the British Academy for the Small Research Grant (SG132730) that enabled us to dig into archival materials spread across various collections and locations. This grant allowed for the hiring of research assistants at various stages—namely, Alice Schneider, Elise Nelson, and Marta Castelo Branco. Their linguistic and archival skills proved critical for our chapters on

Tocqueville, Weber, and Durkheim. We would also like to thank the archivists who helped us negotiate our way through different collections. Without their guidance and help with locating and compiling the relevant sources, this book would not have been possible. Thanks to the Special Collections Research Center, Joseph P. Regenstein Library, University of Chicago; the George Allen and Unwin Archive, University of Reading; the Harvard University Archives; the Harry Ransom Humanities Research Center, University of Texas; the Bavarian State Library, Munich; and the Oxford University Press Archives, Oxford. This book also owes much to the staff at the University Library in Cambridge and the University Library in York, where much of the research and writing of the book took place.

The testing of ideas requires community. We have been lucky to find this in our colleagues at York and Cambridge, as well as in those peers who participated in the various seminars and conferences where we presented materials for the book. We also want to record our thanks to our students, against whom we tested many of our arguments in their early stages, and to those in academia who commented on the many versions of the manuscript. Chapter 2 is based on a paper on Mead presented in Cambridge during the lunch seminar in 2013–14. In August 2015, we organized a session on the books that made sociology at the World Congress of the International Sociological Association in Yokohama, Japan. It was there that our paper on Du Bois's *The Souls of Black Folk*, now chapter 4, was first presented. In 2014–15 and 2015–16, respectively, we used this paper as the source material for the two-session module "Performance and Power" in the Advanced Social Theory paper in Cambridge and a two-hour lecture in the sociology PhD program at the Institute of Social Sciences of the University of Lisbon, with which we collaborate closely. For their generous feedback, we would like to thank those in Yokohama and our students over the years. Finally, we would like to extend our gratitude to the participants in the RC16 Sociological Theory Conference of the International Sociological Association held in June 2016 at Selwyn College, Cambridge, where an early draft of chapter 6 was presented, and to the participants in the Annual Congress of the American Sociological Association held in Montréal, Canada, in August 2017, where we presented the final draft of chapter 4. To the colleagues who patiently read the manuscript and/or commented on it, in part or in full, we express our gratitude for generously sharing their time and knowledge: S. N. Eisenstadt, Donald N. Levine, Terry N. Clark, Marta Bucholc, John Holmwood, William Watts Miller, Tim Stanton, Richard Armstrong, Emily Charnock, Marta Soler Gallart, Manuel Villaverde Cabral, Jeffrey C. Alexander, and Dan Silver.

But it all starts and ends with families. Ours might not exactly know what we are up to most of the time, yet they know of its importance for us and provide the unfailing emotional support that is so critical for thinking and writing. We thank Afonso, the little Achilles, for reminding us of when it was time to close our books and of the wonder of discovering books anew. Thanks would be a very small word for what we owe our families. This book is dedicated to one of them in particular, Fernando Brito, whom we miss dearly and from whom we learned the love of books.

INTRODUCTION

This is a book about books. It is also an argument about the physical form of the book as a primary site of struggle over its interpretation and legacy. Interpretation and appropriation exist in a reciprocal and dynamic relationship; the sense that is made of a text impacts the process of building on it and vice versa. Neither, however, is independent of the particular form the text takes. Hence the stakes are high in determining who comes to shape such a form and to what extent.

As a book about the politics of bookmaking, this is not your usual politics book. The book focuses not on books as vehicles of purportedly political arguments but on books as material forms mediating and constituting meaning—books as objects to which, and through which, things can be done to shape possible future uses. We will therefore concentrate here on the performativity of the medium, or how the objectification of the text in a particular artifact form has the potential to shape our experience of it, not only in terms of its physicality or sensorial qualities but also in terms of its meaning and iconicity, or what the book comes to stand for. In so doing, our analysis sees the form a text takes as having agentic qualities. But this is still, for the most part, a derivative type of agency, dependent on the agency of humans. This is here understood as the problem-solving capacity of the human actors involved in the production, circulation, and interpretation of texts—authors, publishers, editors, translators, interpreters, and theory builders—which can be more oriented toward the past, the future, or the present and involves the continual development of their reflective intelligence (see Emirbayer and Mische 1998, 970–71). Each chapter of the book will speak of the role of these agents in exploring the powerful melding of medium and meaning.

Of all the books we could have examined in this book, we selected a group of texts that at some point or another have been regarded as "classics" of social thought. Given their status as "classics," much has been written about these works and at least as much has been constructed upon them. Their constituent parts—ideas, concepts, and arguments—and their logical structure have been taken apart and reconstructed on many occasions. Debates about their interpretation and legacy have been intense and are ongoing. We will not enter into these debates here, at least not directly. This book proposes to look at these works from a different perspective. It investigates the story behind the books themselves.

What can be gained from adopting this stance? The answer seems far from obvious. To many, focusing on the book as object misses the point of our engagement with these works, their ideas, and their enduring relevance and is therefore in need of further justification. For us, this can be justified in two ways. First, regarding the complex and close interplay between material form and meaning production, we suggest that texts are products of an embodied mind—a mind that makes sense of itself and the world through association with the body, notably in the very physical and sensuous act of writing. In this sense, discursive practices are always already material, and our understanding of theory as theorizing, as practice rather than outcome, can emerge only through examining their interplay. Writing, for one, is not a disembodied act. It is rather a physical act of craft, committing ideas and words to a physical medium, working them out through it. Their relationship to material form is one of mutual entailment rather than mere externality (Barad 2003, 822). Hence just as it would be wrong to reduce meaning to form, conceiving meaning apart from form would be equally disingenuous. Second, if texts are embodied forms, and if form affects and is even constitutive of meaning, then there is a very literal sense in which producing a book can be "meaning making." It is, therefore, to be expected that the struggle over the meaning of a text, and the possibilities of creative development it opens up, will sometimes become a struggle over its particular and specific physical embodiments.

As the overall purpose of this book begins to emerge, the conclusion seems to follow that this is either a history of social thought, through the history of the books that made it, or an exercise in descriptive bibliography, looking at these books as objects and describing them painstakingly as such, with a view to producing a sociology of texts, one that shows how changing form affects meaning. We would say it is not fully either. History deals with processes over time and often takes on a linear or teleological quality. But this book does not offer a systematic diachronic analysis of the evolution of the material form(s) taken by the classical texts of social theory, not even when this analysis is circumscribed to the Anglo-Saxon world.[1] In the majority of these chapters, the approach adopted is synchronic, and we will be dealing rather with snapshots or slices of history being deliberately singled out to allow for a more in-depth examination of the forces mediating media transmutations. These are the object of descriptive bibliography, which tends to ignore what we wish to bring to the fore—that is, the agents responsible for them, as well as the implications of their actions. These agents are the protagonists of the politics of the book. Books are mobile physical outlets certain agents use to project meaning. Sometimes this comes in the form of a disciplinary project; on other occasions, it has a more distinctively political character. Books are often battlegrounds where war is waged, their pages offering support for agents' maneuvering to show how certain claims are indefensible, for attacking or even demolishing opposing arguments, for making targeted criticisms, in short, to win an argument against adversaries. Our analysis of the book is genealogical insofar it is concerned with discussing certain key historical junctures at which agents—by commenting, reviewing, editing, introducing, or translating the book in question—fought one another over what it stands for.

BOOK MATTERS

Texts are embodied entities. The materiality of texts and, in particular, of books, as a specific material form of textual transmission, is integral to the analysis presented in this book. In a culture overwhelmingly focused on the mind and its products, materiality is easily marginalized. However, the physical embodiment of texts is integral to the process of objectification whereby thought comes to divide itself from itself to become more self-reflexive and more widely transmissible. The shared origin of text and textile in the Latin *texere* (from the Latin *textus*, a tissue, in turn derived from *texere*, to weave) is a powerful reminder of materiality as an emergent quality of texts. Taken literally, it speaks of the centrality of textiles to the material history of texts and their circulation. Paper was, after all, originally made from cotton rags gathered from hemp and flax clothing. Metaphorically, however, the meaning of the term *text* extended in ways that left its materiality behind. *Text* is now typically used to refer to the book or other written or printed work regarded in terms of ideational content rather than physical form. The rich vocabulary of cloth is still in use, of course. But rather than referring to any concrete material embodiment—textile or otherwise—it describes the labor of composition—that is, writing, understood as the verbal activity of spinning the web of words that forms a text. However, in a text, such spinning is never mere mental play: it is always instantiated in specific media; it is a physical process. In other words, in a text, work and medium are intimately entwined. Words do not form a text *apart* from the particular material form in which they are incorporated but *through* it.

There are two main reasons the textual object itself is worthy of inquiry in a book about classics of social and political thought. First, given the complex interplay between form and content, the textual object can provide privileged access to thinking or theorizing as an activity rather than as a thing. Second, given how form impacts textual meaning, analyzing the textual object can open a door to multiple ways in which form can be deployed to construct meaning, thus providing parameters within which the book can be understood. And meaning can be made of layer upon layer of editorial signs.

It all begins with the choice of format. A work that is awarded the honor of a hardback prestige edition is often admitted to the pantheon of classics. Similarly, a work that is republished as a paperback once its hardback edition passes the commercial test is sanctioned for its popularity, its classic status, or both. A paperback edition conveys multiple meanings. The first is purely economic: in short, better price. The second concerns the relationship of the reader to the book, as an object that is lighter, more portable, easier and more intimate to use. Finally, the scholarly paperback published in a renowned series conveys editorial selectivity by scientific peers and, by that very fact, constitutes the work as a classic, addressed primarily at a knowledgeable university public. Mass production may not, therefore, necessarily rob the work of its aura. On the contrary, its paratextual meaning may be synonymous with canonization.[2]

That editorial practice regarding issues such as format, typography, design, binding, and layout can profoundly affect the ways texts might be read makes such a practice a likely battleground for those seeking to control texts, their identity, and their meaning. At its most extreme, such a battleground can become a field of vicious dispute. John Locke famously hinted at this when he reflected on the effects of the division into chapter and verse of the texts forming the Bible.[3] The division of the Bible into a series of aphorisms, he explained, not only detracted from the overall coherence of God's Word. It made it fit for appropriation for sectarian purposes, with textual fragmentation paving the way for fragmentation of the commonwealth along religious and political lines. From the decoupage of the text to the evisceration of the reading public, Locke saw a disquieting continuity. There could hardly be a more compelling reason to think that matter matters and take the materiality of the text seriously.

PARATEXTS

The struggle over the books of the sociological canon may be far less contentious, but not necessarily less intense. Paratexts are normally one of its epicenters. As the prefix, "para-," indicates, the term *paratext* refers to a series of devices surrounding the main text that form the frame through which it comes to be viewed—that is, received and interpreted. Besides formatting and typography, paratexts include both things within the book (technically known as the peritext) such as title, author's name, front and back covers, jacket blurbs, index, footnotes, table of contents, foreword, dedication, preface, introduction, frontispieces, and illustrations and things outside the book (technically known as the epitext) such as commentaries, interviews, and reviews. All these mediate the book to the reader, making it present to them. But here as elsewhere presentation is not a question of mere display through a transparent screen; it is, rather, a representation, involving construction.

Paratexts do things. They act on the text, constructing it as such or such by identifying it, contextualizing it, presenting its defining features and purposes to the target audience. They generate meaning beyond the borders of the text and shape the production of meaning by/from it. This gives them a paradoxical quality that is, again, already signaled by the prefix "para-," signifying simultaneously proximity and distance, similarity and difference, interiority and exteriority, a boundary, or both sides of the boundary line at once divided and connected by it (J. Miller 1979, 219).

Gerard Genette captured the liminal quality of the paratext perfectly: "More than a boundary or a sealed border, the paratext is, rather, a threshold"— that is, "a zone between text and off-text, not only of transition but also of transaction" (1997, 1–2). Such a threshold—or in-between area, as it were— constitutes a kind of ownerless *res nullius*, which is up for grabs, free to be owned by anyone seeking to influence the text's production of meaning or looking to drive it in particular directions.

Genette attributed this role primarily to the author, whom he saw invested in protecting the text's integrity or correct interpretation. As such, Genette reserved a specific function to the paratext—that is, "to ensure for the text a destiny consistent with the author's purpose"—and excluded from paratexts anything for which the author or their associates (namely, posthumous editors, perpetuating the author's intentions) did not accept responsibility (1997, 407). Behind this understanding of the paratext lies a conception of the identity of the text as fundamentally fixed and immutable, and of the paratext as the instrument allowing the text to be adapted to new eras, ideally without betraying authorial meaning and intentions (9).[4] However, as Genette admits, not all paratexts are crafted by the author or controlled by them, and not all editors and publishers who craft paratexts are primarily, or even committed at all, to the centrality of the author's viewpoint, to "the paratextual performance" that "sustains it, inspires it, anchors it" (408). Their intervention in what Philippe Lejeune describes as a pivotal "fringe of the printed text which in reality controls one's whole reading of the text" (1975, 45) may follow from from a radically different conception of the text, the paratext, and their uses—and of what may enhance, impede, or ultimately block the text's reception. By looking into paratexts—from author-publisher correspondence to titles, prefaces, and introductions—we will primarily inquire about the performativity of these devices, or what they attempt to do to the text. We will also be taking meaning not as something simply inherent in the text but as emerging out of successive interventions in it, notably those having for their target liminal devices that enable "a text to become a book and to be offered as such to its readers and, more generally, to the public" (McKenzie quoted in Genette 1997, 1).

## THE POLITICS OF TRANSLATION

Translations are sometimes included in the broad category of paratexts.[5] However, in this book, we grant them a more autonomous standing. By doing so, we recognize the centrality of language to meaning production. If paratexts are thresholds of textual interpretation, with translation we move decidedly into its midst.

It is true that translation is sometimes conceived of as a purely derivative activity, consisting in a search for word-for-word equivalents, with the purpose of preserving meaning unchanged from source-language text to target-language text. This is translation as ruled by an ideal of neutrality, guarding against any imposition of extraneous meaning or interpretation. Thus conceived, translation is easily relegated to the margins of the original text and hardly justifies independent analysis. However, translation is never, or even primarily, just a linguistic act. As Peter Ghosh rightly points out, translation is rather a "conceptual act" focusing on the transfer of concepts, their meaning and point, between different, and often alien, contexts—linguistic, temporal, geographical, and cultural (2001, 59–63). As such, all translation presupposes a gap, and the bridging of this gap—if it is to produce intelligibility—will always require paraphrase or interpretation. This gap also accounts for the politics of translation, in the sense that, as Kari Palonen correctly observes, it creates a playroom, as it were, "for alternative translations as well as a built-in conflict between the users of the 'original' and those using a translation" (2003, 16).

The translation theorist André Lefevere explores the political dimension of translation further. The translator, he claims, thinks primarily in terms of two grids—the grid of concepts and the textual grid, which "in their interplay, may well determine how reality is constructed for the reader, not only of the translation, but also of the original" (1999, 75–76). Translation is, therefore, a form of rewriting, and this rewriting is responsible for the way in which the receptor culture constructs "images" and "representations" of both author and text. The study of these rewritings is critical, according to Lefevere, because they "play an analyzable part in the manipulation of words and concepts which, among other things, constitute power in a culture" (1985, 241). The contexts, modes, and purposes of such rewritings are multiple. However, Lefevere proposes that we analyze them by looking into "controlling factors," which he articulates through the notion of "patronage." Patronage refers here to "any power (person, institution) that can further or hinder the reading, writing or re-writing of literature" by acting not as a repressive force but as the main producer of knowledge and discourse (1992, 15). Decisions about particular translation choices and about what to translate are chief components of this power.

When dissecting the cultural power of translation, Lefevere focuses on two main aspects. The first refers to the ways in which translators deliberately manipulate texts to advance their own ideology or that from which the patronage springs. The second aspect refers to how translators pour texts into dominant discourses to secure their acceptance (1990, 88, 57). *Manipulation* is a term too normatively invested to be of analytical use to us here. It predetermines what it needs to establish. Translators are best understood as agents, whose agenda and perspective must be considered in determining what goes on in translation. If translation is always a transport or a transfer, translators—alongside authors, editors, and publishers who define the parameters within which translators work—are key gatekeepers of what gets presented to the target audience and how. Translating a text, and doing it in one way rather than another, can strongly impact its subsequent reception, use, or interpretative appropriation. It is, therefore, unsurprising that prominent theorists and commentators become involved, either directly or indirectly, in translating works and even in formulating the criteria translation should follow. What is at stake in their work, and in the translation wars that often follow, is one of the driving questions behind certain chapters of this book.

THE RATIONALE AND STRUCTURE OF THE BOOK

In each chapter, the reader will find a self-enclosed genealogy of a given book. We offer genealogies of six books: *Mind, Self, and Society*, by G. H. Mead; the *1844 Economic and Philosophic Manuscripts*, by Karl Marx; *The Souls of Black Folk*, by W. E. B. Du Bois; *The Protestant Ethic and the Spirit of Capitalism*, by Max Weber; *The Elementary Forms of Religious Life*, by Émile Durkheim, and *Democracy in America*, by Alexis de Tocqueville. All these books are theoretical texts. Albeit not necessarily for the same reasons, or at the same time, all of them have also been regarded as sociological classics. Similar claims were, of course, made in other academic disciplines about each of them. So as to avoid offering six disparate histories, with little or no relation to each other, we focus on the reception of these works in postwar American sociology, arguably the most influential national sociological tradition of our time.

As theoretical texts, it is easy to take these books as containers for arguments or a tightly knit set of propositions. However, the focus of our analysis is not on what these texts say, on how they say it, or indeed on how they do things in and through saying it the way they do. Although this angle of analysis is not entirely absent, our interest lies primarily in the intertwining of *content* and *form* in theoretical writing, as perhaps in all writing, and in particular in the transformations that occur as such writing is organized and printed in a book form. This means we turn our attention to publishing and the forms of editorial composition that made these texts and their reception possible. This results in a change of protagonists when our study is compared with the common study of social or political "thought."

The six genealogies we offer often, but not always, begin, still, with the figure of the author. They sometimes, but not often, seek to ascertain that author's intentions. And they hardly ever probe the arguments that lie behind the text's propositions. Our research has rather as its main characters a collective of agents—including publishers, editors, translators, and commentators—who we show to be engaged in a complex process of book*making*, whereby texts are not simply reproduced from established originals but actively shaped by and through a series of decisions about the manner in which one might reproduce and make sense of them. Because these agents do not act in a vacuum, to make sense of their action and of the effects (intended, unintended, or a combination of both) it produces, we need to work outside the normal confines of so-called intellectual history, to look more broadly into writing genres and their statuses; technologies of publication and their cultural meanings; patronage relationships; political structures and unfolding political events; intellectual and editorial networks; surprising affiliations and disaffiliations between editors and editors and commentators, within and across countries; and the long shadow cast by academes and professional institutions.

In many of our analyses, albeit to different degrees, the attempt to separate authorial composition and revision from editorial and compositorial interventions will prove infinitely more complex than perhaps anticipated. This is not solely explained by the weakness of earlier editorial practices, which often failed to show what the editor had done and what the documentary evidence was. To assume this much is to assume too much. It is to assume, for instance, the material fixity of the text and the unambiguity of the available textual "evidence." It is also to assume that even in the face of ineradicable ambiguity, a book can be produced without privileging one particular "version" of the work over another. It is to take the eventual choice between "versions" as something that can never be "neutral" or non-value-laden. The truth, however, is that all these assumptions have little or no basis in reality. As we hope to show by exploring the forces, mechanisms, events, agents, and indeed the accidents that have helped *make* (and sometimes also *unmake*) the texts under analysis, the social life of texts, even of the "systematic" texts yielded by core social disciplines, is far more complex and unsettling than their present physical existence betrays. Even this is far from settled, however: just as a definite version of a text is a near impossibility, so it is equally impossible that a definite *edition* of the text and apparatus is ever produced. To think otherwise is to deny the constructedness of the book—any book.

The interplay between the construct (form) and content defines how we approach our six theoretical texts. We are, however, less interested in assessing the legitimacy of the constructions we anatomize, or in evaluating the quality of the editorial practices underpinning them (a judgment that would in many cases be anachronistic, as guided by modern scholarly and editorial criteria), than in what publishers, editors, and translators were *doing* (or, at least, *attempting to do*) in offering the reading public a new version of the text under consideration. In taking editorial action, broadly conceived, as *meaning-producing* action, we explore each of the six books as a material object as much as the text printed on its pages, especially where this has been significantly recomposed. The assembling of the book is taken as a space of struggles within which agents confront each other, directly or indirectly, with different means and ends, according to their different position in a field of forces that can be disciplinary and/or more explicitly political.[6] These struggles take a variety of forms: from struggles about the "true" meaning of the work; to struggles between scientific rigor and advocacy; through struggles within and between academic disciplines about who and what constitutes legitimate disciplinary knowledge and whether and how it should be recovered and inform new research; and the internal and external struggles *of* and *about* books intent on explaining the present and fashioning the future. Given the breadth and depth of the struggles at stake, it is often the case that the fight for the book starts and often takes on a particular intensity in the liminal devices that mediate the relation between text and reader. In the books we examine, this is especially true of the introductions.

Introductions are used to prime the reader, who will then venture forth to read the rest of the text with a set of expectations and preunderstandings guided, if not controlled, by the writer of the introduction. This is why our analysis pays special attention to such introductory texts as framing devices after which the text may be read that also seek to "reenact" the text by tuning it to resonate with contemporary audiences. Introductions are immensely valuable for us in that they allow us to chart the changing meanings that later readers have been instigated to make of a text from the immediacy of their own historical circumstances. Central to a study of the politics of the book, the writers who use of the book's introduction to advance their own interpretation, if not their own interests or agendas, often in conflict with each other, are nonetheless but one set of agents of book production who are often ignored behind the towering figure of the author.

Many hands and minds go into the making of a book. Lead editors, we will see, may be effectively led by other, perhaps more important, figures (notably, commentators), just as they may double as the writers of the introductory materials that offer a window onto the text. Their interventions in the physical form of the book may be multiple and, as we shall also see in the analysis of our six books, of great consequence. Sometimes critical interventions happen already at the assembly stage and involve decisions as to what to include and in what order. Understanding the influence of assembly, and any constructed connections, on the production of meaning, we hope to show, is no less important than examining the ways in which paratexts construct and contest a text's authority, identity, and meaning. In like manner, a new rendition, perhaps even a new translation, of a key concept may radically alter the ways in which readers come to understand this concept's relationship to other concepts and the world, and the world itself. Reworkings of the text and its organization may range from the most subtle and sophisticated to the most crude. If the line between engaging with and exercising power over a text can be thin, and sometimes impossible to maintain, the transition from power to violence betrays itself more readily. This much is apparent in the acts of mutilation we will encounter, whereby passages or whole chapters deemed dispensable or simply inconvenient are simply excised from the body of the text, leaving other passages and chapters deprived of their relatedness backward and forward. Interventions need not be so drastic, however, to produce effects. As a matter of fact, here as elsewhere, subtlety can be more effective. Neither need interventions be restricted to interventions in the book. Sometimes, interventions are rather on the book. Some of the agents we examine will be seen to have written works of commentary themselves or developed programs of empirical social-scientific research inspired by the "classics" they edit, translate, or make. What such intellectual interventions share, however, is a definite orientation toward the ideas in these books.

In the books we examine, these ideas typically take the form of theories of society, politics, or both. It is therefore all too easy to reify these theories, to conceive them as free-floating entities, the meaning of which depends entirely on the reader's hermeneutic abilities. But since thinking exists by taking form, and survives over time by reforming itself, one would miss one of its most important aspects if one sidestepped the forms of its composition as well as the modes of its embodiment and circulation. For what a social or political theory is taken to mean and entail emerges out of the dialectic between form and content afforded by different media, notably the book as a physical object, one that is performed by concrete epistemic communities in specific historical conditions. Limited by these are, for instance, the technologies of publication as well as the parameters of editorial practice, with the "authoritative" form of the scholarly edition being redefined over time and paperback originals, ranging from the popular to the scholarly, progressively becoming the main form of a text's circulation. Some of the texts we will be examining will have known both forms, scholarly hardback/paperback and mass-market paperback editions, albeit not necessarily at the same time. Whether we follow one, the other, or both physical forms, and our choice of specific exemplars, will be determined by two main factors. The first is their availability and/or prominence in the period covered in the chapter. The second factor is the role played by the particular agent (author, editor, translator, commentator) we are exploring in the text's production and dissemination. As we focus less on "theory" as an abstract, disembodied, purely cognitive affair than on theory conception, production, communication, reception, and reutilization as a set of materially embodied practices, the contexts that we deem relevant for the study of social and political thought will inevitably expand themselves. If, as we contend, form matters, the history of ideas cannot be told apart from the form they take—how these permutations of form came about; how and why they became the focus of disputes; and how they have helped shape academic disciplines and the world itself—these are the objects of study.

This means, in short, that we conceive of the human and nonhuman elements present in our dealings with theory books as including (1) the book, a plethora of materials ranging from paper handwritten or typed manuscript notes and galley proofs to the various editions and formats of the book and e-book as such where ideas are inscribed as text; (2) the author, a person to whom we grant authorial control to the effects of those ideas and that can be an individual person, an individual at the center of a collective, or a purely fictive persona; (3) the translator, an individual whose intellectual and emotional investment in the work often overflows translating the ideas and arguments in the book into full-blown commentary and editorial curatorship of the book; (4) the publishing house, a commercial enterprise where editors work with authors, translators, reviewers, and literary agents, as well as typographers and graphic designers, as to put the book into production and accompany its commercial life; and (5) the commentator, typically a scholar whose academic success partly depends on researching, writing, and teaching about the text/author in question in sites such as the book's paratexts and epitexts, as well as lecture rooms, academic journals (including book reviews), scientific congresses, and periodical literary reviews. In each of our case studies that follow, we explore one or more of these aspects as we analyze the politics of that particular book. The combined result is less a revisitation of the canon wars of the 1980s, which opposed the traditionalists' nostalgic praise of the value of classic works to the multiculturalists' strident pleas for inclusion of the long-silenced voices of the marginalized, than a clearer understanding of how form matters in the struggles over meaning that structure social and political theorizing.

We begin with Émile Durkheim's *The Elementary Forms of Religious Life*, a work that has received increased attention among sociologists since the 1990s. Pivotal here has been the commentary by Jeffrey C. Alexander, whose strong program in cultural sociology can be directly traced back to the "cultural" Durkheim of *Elementary Forms*. Our genealogy of the book—centered around the figure of the commentator, not the author—allows us to present our approach vis-à-vis alternative genres in the history of social and political thought. In chapter 2 we discuss what counts as an author. We focus on *Mind, Self, and Society*, whose purported author—G. H. Mead—was not involved in its creation, nor did he ever express the wish to have it published. And yet it was through this fabricated amalgamation of texts of plural authorship that "Mead, the sociological classic" was constructed, in a skewed process of disciplinary canonization that has reduced Mead's contributions to a problematic and unrepresentative fraction of his oeuvre. We then turn our attention to a book that, strictly speaking, is not a book—or, at least, was not originally conceived for publication, much less in a book form. Karl Marx's *1844 Economic and Philosophic Manuscripts* originated as notebooks. However, as the notebooks were assembled into *one* book—indeed into *the* book that was meant to offer the long-awaited key to Marx's philosophical system—heterodox Marxist circles felt ready to use the greater power that comes with legitimacy. They had now what they needed to unleash a dialectics of dissent driven by the concept they made interchangeable with the *1844 Manuscripts*—that is, alienation. This was a dialectics intent on defeating, rather than simply convincing, opponents and on seeing the world's political landscape radically transformed in its wake. Chapter 4 discusses Du Bois's *The Souls of Black Folk*. Partly compiled of previously published pieces, this is a book the author had to rewrite himself, finding the right combination of tone, form, and metaphor to confer upon assorted materials the kind of continuous legibility expected of a book. One such metaphor is the idea of a double consciousness, which has come to stand for the "multicultural Du Bois" sociologists have been rediscovering since the 1990s. As we explain in this chapter, however, this is but the latest of various, often contradictory, meanings, that have been ascribed to the book, as successive editions appeared during the twentieth century, traversed academic disciplines, and helped negotiate political fault lines. In chapter 5 we move away from the figure of the author to consider the role of the translator-interpreter. The book under analysis is Max Weber's *The Protestant Ethic and the Spirit of Capitalism*. Its translation into English by the young Talcott Parsons in 1930 lies behind the sociological canonization of Weber in Anglo-Saxon academia. Weber's *The Protestant Ethic* is a well-known case of creative tension between translation and reception: the Weber we have come to know in the English language, perhaps *the* sociologist regarding "disciplinary" questions about the formation and standing of sociology as a discipline vis-à-vis philosophy, religion, historiography, and politics,[7] is also a Weber now known to be strongly "mediated" by Parsons's own conceptual apparatus and categories. In our chapter, we look into the translation in an oblique way. We take as our starting point the work Parsons was primarily engaged in as he immersed himself in the translation of Weber: his DPhil dissertation. This makes it possible to see more clearly the ways in which the translation of Weber's book served as a catalyst for Parsons's own getting to grips with Weber's sociological theory of capitalism and his employment of ideal types as part of a broader strategy of concept formation. Our final book is Tocqueville's *Democracy in America*, a withering classic among sociologists but still a foundational text in neighboring political science. This allows us to explore the twin processes of canonization *and* decanonization. Traversing academic disciplines, one finds an influential but little-known group of new and repeat editors-translators-commentators from different ideological persuasions whose work in and on Tocqueville's book helped frame his arguments and the conditions for accessing them anew over the course of the twentieth century.

By bringing together in one volume the connected histories of these six books, we build on Roger Chartier's claim that there is no "order of discourse" without an "order of books" (1994, ix). Our aim is to promote an expanded understanding of the history of social and political scholarship by engaging in the history of the books in which it has been materially embodied and by which it has been materially shaped. In so doing, we move beyond the dominant conceptualization of the production and reception of scholarship as something dealing primarily, perhaps even singularly, in abstractions or "ideas" and of its proper history as a "history of ideas" unfolding in the ethereal and disembodied real of "great" thought. In particular, we operate within a distinctive approach to theory construction. This differs from other approaches to the history of ideas insofar as our object is not individual intentions or the contextual factors (say, institutional constraints or professional networks) within which ideas were created but the written media through which those ideas were circulated and their authors attained the recognition of their peers. We understand ideas, texts, and the discourses in which they participate as taking form and indeed as coming into existence, in the proper sense of the word, as they become physical realities and are inscribed in certain material forms—books, for example. It is to these forms, and the book form in particular, that we attend in what follows. This is no case of reification or fetishism of the object. We rather contend and hope to document vigorously that the collective process of construction and communication of the material bearings of texts is an integral part of the process of construction of their meaning.

Again, we resort to Chartier, who rightly observes that books are "objects whose forms... command the uses that can invest them and the appropriations to which they are susceptible" (1994, ix). In both their verbal and nonverbal dimensions, such forms are, more or less intentionally, constructed by a multiplicity of agents, whose diverse positions and diverse dispositions in the processes of cultural production and political struggle we reconstruct to make sense of the ways in which they configured the engagement with the text by successive generations of readers. These are normally agents acting alongside, above, or beyond the author and in whose power it is to mediate between readers and texts whose identities and whose meanings they are also always already enacting through their mediatory practices. In looking at their work and, in particular, at how their interventions in the book form have effected (or, at least, tried to effect) meaning, we will be confronting contemporary readers with the constructedness of their encounter with the text, any text. This constructedness, we intimate by our choice of books, is brought up to a new level when it aims at the production or reproduction of canonicity, of books meant to determine and radically change the ways in which we perceive, orient ourselves, and act in the world. In focusing on the material and social contexts in which social and political discourse takes form and sees itself being reconfigured, we show that a vital dimension of the history of the production, communication, and reception of texts is being inevitably missed when their material bearings—or, we should perhaps say, their material enactments—are taken as irrelevant "matter," self-evident or stable over time. The medium is here no mere transparent carrier of content. It is rather the case that the act of giving a text its material form involves a set of practices that are generative of, not merely incidental to, that text's meaning, status, and identity. For this reason alone—if not only for this reason—book matters deserve more than passing notice even among specialists in the history of "thought."

CHAPTER 1

# ELEMENTARY FORMS AND THE CULTURAL DURKHEIM

*Les formes élémentaires de la vie religieuse* (*The Elementary Forms of Religious Life*) was Émile Durkheim's last monograph. In June 1912, 1,650 copies of the first edition were printed. The editor was Félix Alcan, a well-known French Jewish publisher and scholar. Between 1912 and 2012, the work was translated in twenty-three countries in a total of fifty-six editions. Profoundly influential in anthropology during the twentieth century, this work is the animating force of today's "new Durkheim."

INTRODUCTION

When giving texts their material form, agents of different ideological persuasions and disciplinary affiliations operate within a number of specific narrative genres with fundamentally distinct epistemological assumptions and theoretical-methodological implications. This plurality of narrative genres characterizes the history of modern social thought. As "visions of the sociological tradition" (Levine 1995),[1] they help frame how sociologists have approached particular authors and texts. Émile Durkheim's last book, first published in 1912 under the title *Les formes élémentaires de la vie religieuse* and translated into English in 1915 as *Elementary Forms of the Religious Life* (hereafter *Formes* and *Elementary Forms*, respectively), is no exception. Throughout the twentieth century, each narrative genre has ascribed a fundamentally different meaning to *Elementary Forms*.

One such narrative genre is contextualism. Contextualist interpretations are distinctive in that they subordinate the cognitive dimension of the work to other kinds of orientations (e.g., ideological, religious, or socioeconomic). From such a perspective, *Elementary Forms* is a product of bourgeois ideology, offering an instrumentalist picture of social order. Changes in Durkheim's orientation are then attributed to reasons exogenous to the theory and research of sociology. In American academia in the 1960s, contextualism was often associated with neo-Marxist views. A case in point is Alvin Gouldner's "structural" reading of Durkheim. In the introduction to *Socialism and Saint-Simon*, Gouldner sees Durkheim "converging" with the materialism of Marx as Durkheim rejects the theological explanation of values as "divinely given and thus without a developmental history" (Durkheim 1958, 24) and predicates the existence of social values on the interaction between concrete persons. But Durkheim's theoretical convergence with Marx should not be taken as a sign of ideological convergence. On the contrary, Gouldner portrays Durkheim as the quintessential conservative defender of bourgeois class interests against the working-class movement of his time (see also Gouldner 1970, 119). Thus *Elementary Forms* becomes an expression of Durkheim's class interests. In the 1960s, Gouldner was hardly alone in his contextualist approach to Durkheim. Before Gouldner, Irving Zeitlin and Peter M. Blau offered similar "structural" readings. The former saw in Durkheim expressions of "a conservative and authoritarian ideology that dominated his entire sociological system," *Elementary Forms* included (Zeitlin 1968, 241), while the latter found in Durkheim's structuralism—in particular, his emphasis on concrete group pressures—an alternative to Parsons's structural-functional emphasis on the structuring effect of values through internalization (Blau 1960).

If one adopts a positivist perspective, *Elementary Forms* becomes a repository of scientific outputs. Positivist accounts typically assume the form of an optimistic narrative about the accumulation of knowledge. Progress is made as we move from insufficient or uncertain knowledge toward more robust, certain science. From this perspective, interpreting *Elementary Forms* becomes an exercise in mining it for contributions to the progress of the discipline. The earliest example of such a positivist narrative of the sociological tradition that mentions *Elementary Forms* is Park and Burgess's *Introduction to the Science of Sociology* (1921, 35, 193–96). For Park and Burgess, the main contribution of the work is the concept of "collective representation." They adapt a portion of the conclusion in which Durkheim discusses logical thought to create a section on "Collective Representations and Intellectual Life." This was the first segment of *Elementary Forms* and the only one of any of Durkheim's works to figure in a sociology textbook in America, and it is framed as an exemplar of a "social realist" position.[2] A decade later, in *Emile Durkheim and His Sociology*, Harry Alpert recuperates the realist versus nominalist framework in order to assess Durkheim's contributions. For Alpert, *Elementary Forms* is but the final expression of Durkheim's lifelong attempt to supersede the nominalist-realist divide, and as such, it is the most elaborate contribution to that mission one can find in his oeuvre (Alpert 1939, 160–63). Despite its contributions to the sociology of knowledge (55), *Elementary Forms* is narrowly classified as belonging to Durkheim's writings on "religious sociology" (49).

From a pluralist perspective, *Elementary Forms* is an exemplar of a theoretical approach or school of thought. Pluralist narratives see the history of sociology as the sum of multiple independent theoretical approaches, neither converging nor progressing toward a future single position or paradigm. While some commentators emphasize the role of dialogue in the development of these multiple strands (Levine 1995), others see the differences separating these traditions as insurmountable. The archetypal example of the latter kind of pluralism is Pitirim Sorokin's *Contemporary Sociological Theories* (1928). Here, Sorokin depicts *Elementary Forms* as a representative work of the "sociologistic" school of thought. His evaluation of the work is mixed at best. Sorokin praises Durkheim's sociologistic explanation of religious symbols and conceptual knowledge but criticizes the underlying conception of an exterior collective mind as one-sided and reductionist (1928, 466).[3] Following Sorokin's interpretation but replacing "sociologism" with "organicism," Don Martindale sees *Elementary Forms* as a work representative of the "organismic" sociological tradition. Unlike Sorokin, however, Martindale is sensitive to the development of Durkheim's thought. Since "during the course of his development, Durkheim's underlying organicism grew ever more pronounced" (1981, 89), Martindale presents *Elementary Forms* as the most articulate expression of Durkheim's organicism. Concretely, Martindale locates it in a new and distinct phase of Durkheim's work that began in 1898, a phase characterized by a "more idealistic conception of the social group, with more emphasis on 'collective representations' and by adventurous speculation concerning the social origin of morals, values, religion, and knowledge" (Benoit-Smullyan quoted in Martindale 1981, 89).

From a humanist perspective, *Elementary Forms* contains a valuable moral lesson. Humanist narratives distinguish themselves by equating the history of sociology with a sociological canon of classic texts. Such a canon contains intellectual and moral achievements that present-day readers ignore at their peril. Robert Nisbet's *The Sociological Tradition* (1966) and Raymond Aron's *Main Currents in Sociological Thought* (1965–67) illustrate two accounts of the history of sociology in this vein (see Coser 1971).

Nisbet analyzes the classic works of the sociological tradition in search of the "unit-ideas" contained in them. Such a careful study of sociology's unit-ideas promises to unveil the discipline's most valuable and enduring statements. Nisbet considers *Elementary Forms* under the unit-idea of "community" (2004, 86). He rejects any fundamental difference between early and late Durkheim and notes that *Elementary Forms* shares a "social metaphysic with all of Durkheim's writings," including posthumous works and articles in *L'Année Sociologique*. Nisbet insists that all Durkheim's writings reflect "a methodology rooted in the conviction that . . . all human behavior above the level of the strictly physiological must be regarded as either emanating from, or else sharply conditioned by, society: that is, by the totality of groups, norms, and institutions within which every individual human being consciously and unconsciously exists from the moment of his birth" (86–87).

Likewise, Aron discerns no discontinuity in Durkheim's work. Rather, all of his writings offer variations on the same central humanist plea for rationalist individualism. For Aron, however, Durkheim's emphasis on the collective was at times at the expense of the individual, both epistemologically and politically. The most glaring example of this was *Elementary Forms*, which Aron found profoundly unappealing, owing to his liberal-conservative persuasion (and the place it afforded religion in regulating democratic passions), hence his incensed humanist indictment: "It seems to me absolutely inconceivable to define the essence of religion in terms of the worship which the individual pledges to the group," for this would "inspire in men a fanatical devotion to partial groups, to pledge each man's devotion to a collectivity and, by the same token, his hostility to other collectivities." Aron concludes, "To suggest that the object of the religious feeling is society transfigured is not to save but to degrade the human reality which sociology seeks to understand" (1967, 66).

From a synthetic perspective, *Elementary Forms* illustrates a stage in the development of Durkheim's ideas. Narrative accounts of the history of social thought in this genre tend to employ painstaking textual exegesis in order to detect implicit processes of theoretical convergence among a number of authors. In so doing, theoretical syntheses promote a reorganization of the theoretical landscape of a discipline from an earlier stage marked by conflict between partially correct approaches to a future stage characterized by a theoretical consensus around a new paradigm or research program. The first synthetic figuring of *Elementary Forms* is Talcott Parsons's *The Structure of Social Action*, where it represents the culmination of Durkheim's theoretical convergence with Weber while transitioning from an early positivist emphasis on adaptation to a mature voluntarist position where he considers normative factors as well (1937, 343ff.). Jürgen Habermas, in his two-volume sociological treatise *The Theory of Communicative Action* (1984–87), construed *Elementary Forms* as an antiutilitarian icon. Despite the significant differences separating Parsons's and Habermas's synthetic narratives, *Elementary Forms* performs the same role in both—that is, it signals a key developmental stage in Durkheim's thought away from positivism and toward subjectivity (Parsons) or intersubjectivity (Habermas). Indeed, *Elementary Forms* occupies a key position in the "paradigm change" (Habermas 1984, 399) that interested Habermas—the linguistic turn in the social sciences of the 1970s and 1980s. He considers Durkheim's theory of religion in order to complete the program of reconstruction of "symbolically mediated interaction and action in social roles" (43) pursued by George Herbert Mead. Mead's explanation, however, only holds for ontogenesis.[4] According to Habermas, if one seeks an explanation for the phylogenetic transition from symbolically mediated to normatively guided interactions, one needs to turn to *Elementary Forms*. In the footsteps of Parsons's "voluntaristic" reading of Durkheim, Habermas also sees an early Durkheim, still tied to the "tradition of the philosophy of consciousness," who provides an ultimately circular explanation of the origins of the sacred and thereby the meaning of moral authority: "The moral is traced back to the sacred, and the sacred to collective representation of an entity that is itself supposed to consist of a system of binding norms" (50). The way out of this conundrum involves a paradigmatic change on Durkheim's part away from the paradigm of consciousness and toward intersubjectivity. Nowhere is this paradigmatic change clearer than in *Elementary Forms*. This crucial work opens up a path for Durkheim that "points in the end to a clarification of the symbolic structure of the sacred and to a non-positivistic interpretation of collective consciousness" (51).

Given this plurality of narrative genres, it is anything but obvious why today's sociological commentary on Durkheim and the empirical exploration of his insights are overwhelmingly dominated by the "cultural Durkheim." In fact, as late as 1970, very few sociologists in America paid attention to *Elementary Forms*.[5] Today, however, it is Durkheim's most influential book for sociologists in America and elsewhere. *Elementary Forms* became the central totem of culturalist readings of the French master, helping transform

"Durkheim," once the master analyst of modernization, into the "cultural Durkheim" celebrated in the pages of national newspapers for his sociology of moral life that enables us to become more aware of the myths and beliefs that bring us together as a community.[6] Paul Vogt is correct when he writes that "knowledge of Durkheim and his books is a full part of the definition of what a sociologist is in America" (1993, 227), but this evades the more important question of why *Elementary Forms* became synonymous with Durkheim, who in turn became the "cultural analyst par excellence" in the late twentieth century but not before.

In this sociological treatise on religion focusing on the case of totemism in Australia, some have found the promise of a positive scientific inquiry of religion as real, whereas others have seen a vision of a more culturalist model of secular society. We explore these changes in the book's meaning (as well as the meaning of its author and the sociological project associated with his name) by analyzing the dialectic between form and content through the actions of a number of key human agents. All these agents share the same orientation toward the book as a meaning-making project. Given their cultural orientations, material interests, and institutional affiliations, however, these agents not only collaborate with or reflect on but actively contest one another over what the work stands for. The politics of *Elementary Forms* becomes ever more salient at key historical junctures, as this collective of agents intervenes either *in* the text and its material form or *on* the text's reception through critical reviews or commentary.

The author occupies a central position in this collective of agents. Our interest lies in how Durkheim's theorizing about religion developed as he worked on this editorial project. Durkheim's authorial control over the work, however, was never absolute. This much is clear from the case of the English translation, a project triggered and led not by Durkheim but by the translator, Joseph Ward Swain, in conjunction with the editor, Cecil A. Reynolds. Durkheim was relegated to the position of consultant on the translation work and the main editorial decisions. Such a focus on the figure of the editor, whose commercial motivation is often entangled with noncommercial considerations, will lead us to consider the role of publishing houses more generally. In the case of *Elementary Forms*, the Anglo-American collaboration between Allen and Unwin in the United Kingdom and the Free Press in the United States is seen to have played a key role in supporting this editorial project throughout most of the twentieth century. Publishers collaborate closely with another type of agent: translators. In fact, the catalogs of these two publishers include the first two English translations of *Elementary Forms*;

both the original Swain translation and the 1995 translation by Karen E. Fields appeared in the United States as a result of this collaboration. Besides authors, editors, and translators, there is yet another agent whose actions are oriented toward the book. Commentators offer readings of the text, often creatively exploring the world-making potential of books. However, because commentators are typically not directly involved in the politics of the book, whoever undertakes a methodologically narrow study of the history of the book can neglect commentators. As we will show by reference to Durkheim's *Elementary Forms*, such neglect can seriously limit our understanding of struggles over the work's meaning.

In what follows, we will show the extent to which the latest iteration of these struggles was shaped by the actions of one commentator—Jeffrey C. Alexander. Our choice is justified by the fact that Alexander's writings and teaching not only played a key role in proposing a new reading of Durkheim's work but also deal explicitly with the discipline's processes of canon formation in general. Thus Alexander is a particularly self-conscious agent whose efforts to propose a new research program can be construed as part of his more abstract, metatheoretical reflections about how disciplines deal with their pasts.

## ALEXANDER'S CULTURAL DURKHEIM

Arguably the most influential American interpreter of Durkheim since Talcott Parsons, Alexander's commentary is in many respects an exploration of themes first laid out by Parsons. The voluntarist theory of action as an alternative to the utilitarian model of society developed by Parsons in *The Structure of Social Action* (1937) and, prior to this, in his doctoral dissertation on Sombart and Weber (1927/1928–29) serves as the general background theme for Alexander's reading of *Elementary Forms* in the four-volume *Theoretical Logic in Sociology* (1982–83). In the second volume, dedicated to Marx and Durkheim, *Elementary Forms* is depicted as the most accomplished expression of Durkheim's "voluntaristic theory of order" (1982–83, 2:469). This conclusion is the outcome of one of the most methodical exegeses ever performed on Durkheim's writings and one of the most productive as far as an empirical research program is concerned. Today's cultural Durkheim is the direct result of this endeavor.

Like *Structure* fifty years before, *Theoretical Logic* is an exercise in theoretical synthesis.[7] It is a monumental effort aimed at generating a synthesis of the main contributions of a series of seminal thinkers to one central problem: how action relates to order. Each thinker's interpretation is framed by this general goal.

Alexander presents Durkheim's movement from materialist sociological theory in *Division of Labor in Society* (1893) toward an idealist, subjective, and spiritual model from the mid-1890s onward as a demonstration of his thesis that in the late Durkheim one finds a seminal contribution to the timeless problem of action and order. One direct consequence of this interpretation is a dramatic change in the relative position of *Elementary Forms* in Durkheim's oeuvre.

According to Alexander, there is not one but two Durkheims. There is the materialist Durkheim of the middle period and the mature idealist Durkheim. Separating these two periods is a key intellectual breakthrough, which Alexander reconstructs by means of an exhaustive analysis of all Durkheim's writings and personal correspondence.[8] Properly understood, this breakthrough offers a valuable alternative to dominant utilitarian, positivist models in the social sciences. Durkheim's crucial shift from materialism to idealism occurred immediately following the publication of *Division of Labor* in 1893 (2014), which concluded with his endorsement of an instrumental explanation of the nature of modern law and socialist regulation and culminated with *Suicide*, completed in 1896 and published in 1897 (2005). In less than three years, Durkheim moved decisively toward subjectivity. As textual evidence of this shift, Alexander offers two brief review articles Durkheim published the same year as *Division of Labor*: the articles written in 1894 that were to be published as *The Rules of Sociological Method* (1966) the following year and the 1894–95 lectures on socialism and *Suicide*. In these writings, Alexander contends, we find overwhelming evidence that Durkheim had "effectively reversed the logic of his earlier work" and "embarked upon an idealist path" (1982–83, 2:220).

Alexander reconceives Durkheim's sociology of religion in the light of this crucial shift. It was the "momentum created by this earlier shift that led him to find in the anthropology of religion the more voluntaristic vocabulary he so urgently sought. The subjective model of association was already in place by early 1894" (1982–83, 2:236). Thus Durkheim's basic explanation of religion is a direct consequence of his more general, presuppositional abandonment of materialism in favor of idealism rather than a separate line of research (Lukes 1973). Crucially it does not evolve in any significant way between 1898, when Durkheim wrote his first essay on religion, and 1912, the year *Elementary Forms* was published. The only change is the theory's degree of sophistication and the wealth of empirical data employed to support it. The essential insight remains the same. Certainly *Elementary Forms* emerges from Alexander's reading as Durkheim's final, most accomplished statement on religion but also, more fundamentally, on a voluntarist theory of secular life.

As with Parsons's, Alexander's synthesis has given rise to an empirical research program aimed at applying the lessons of the classics in the study of contemporary social and political life. In the years following the publication of *Theoretical Logic*, Alexander made use of two books to position his neo-Durkheimian "strong program" vis-à-vis both the sociological establishment of the 1980s and contemporary intellectual movements—namely, cultural studies. The first is the popular textbook *Twenty Lectures* (1987). There is no chapter on Durkheim as such, but the chapter on the hermeneutic tradition covers some of the themes and authors Alexander later included in the genealogy of structuralism on which cultural sociology was grounded. Partly because of its pedagogic intent, *Twenty Lectures* offers a pluralist narrative of the sociological tradition, in which it is a clear departure from *Theoretical Logic*. But Alexander's admiration for Parsons's synthetic efforts remains unchallenged. The anti-Parsonian movement of the 1970s—encompassing a disjointed combination of symbolic interactionists, conflict sociologists, and the like—had become the sociological establishment of the 1980s. As a result, sociology could no longer conceive of culture as an independent causal variable. The time was ripe for a cultural sociology. This is the theme of Alexander's next book, *Durkheimian Sociology* (1988), a collection of essays for which *Elementary Forms* "functions as a model for explaining central processes in secular social life" (11).

From this point onward, Alexander ceased to comment on the sociological tradition at large and focused exclusively on exploring the "secular relevance of Durkheim's religious sociology" (1988, 193; see also Alexander and Smith 2005). The central goal had been to develop a strong program in "cultural sociology" (Alexander and Smith 2001) as an alternative to "materialist" approaches such as Pierre Bourdieu's "sociology of culture." Most of the themes explored by Alexander and his associates' strong program in cultural sociology are explicitly political and deal with representation. Against the backdrop of *Elementary Forms*, representation is shown to provide the crucial mediation between individual interaction and social order—that is, the process through which subjectivity is transferred from immediate association to the ideational order that governs future acts in such varied cases as the Watergate scandal, the civil sphere, cultural trauma, the election of President Obama, or the Egyptian democratic revolution of 2011 (e.g., J. Alexander 2010).[9] This is, in brief, the origin of the "cultural Durkheim," arguably the most influential appropriation of the French master in the social sciences today and one of the few explicitly oriented toward exploring the implications of Durkheim's sociology of religion vis-à-vis secular phenomena.

In what follows, we document Durkheim's crucial "shift toward subjectivity" (J. Alexander 1988, 15n1), on which the "cultural Durkheim" is premised, by following the book from its origins with Durkheim to its circulation and reception in the English translation. This enables us to better appreciate how the "cultural Durkheim"—that is, the mature Émile Durkheim and the seminal interpreter of cultural traditions as hermeneutically construed by Alexander—has always been profoundly imbricated in the history of Durkheim's final book.

### WRITING *LES FORMES ÉLÉMENTAIRES*

There is no doubt that Durkheim is the author of *Formes*. Yet it would be wrong to infer from this that *Formes* is the work of a solitary genius. In fact, of all the sociological classics, Durkheim's oeuvre was most thoroughly a collective production (R. Collins 2005, 101; see also Besnard 1979, 1983; Fournier 2014). In no other book is this clearer than in *Formes*. *Formes* is, to a large extent, the product of the Durkheimian movement in the sense that it was a collaboration oriented toward the development of a theoretical approach and an empirical program of research into social and religious phenomena. A key institutional platform of the Durkheimian movement was *L'Année Sociologique*. This new journal provided Durkheim and his associates with an outlet in which to publish programmatic statements and major pieces of research, including the essay on his core theory of religion, "De la definition des phénomènes religieux" ("Concerning the Definition of Religious Phenomena"; 1899), which appeared in the journal's launch issue. As soon as Durkheim's theory began to circulate in the pages of *L'Année*, however, news of a pathbreaking ethnographic study of totemism in Australia reached Paris, shaking the Durkheimian sociological program to the core. In the following decade, the Durkheimians' answer to the challenge set by Baldwin Spencer and Francis Gillen's *The Native Tribes of Central Australia* (1899) would take many forms, but none as definite and encompassing as *Formes*.

Behind the print publication of *Formes* in 1912, there lay a five-year research period culminating in the draft of the eventual work, a lecture course on religion and its origins in 1906, and another five years to produce a final manuscript, essentially complete in 1911 and published in early 1912. To begin with, it is widely agreed that Durkheim's treatment of religion throughout the 1880s and early 1890s was "largely formal and *simpliste*" (Lukes 1973, 240). What is less clear is when and why Durkheim's theorizing began to shift toward the formulation that would eventually be inscribed in the pages of *Formes*. In what follows, we propose an account that takes the materiality of Durkheim's theorizing seriously. This account is a collaborative endeavor, combining some of the most recent historically minded scholarship on Durkheim's process of writing *Les formes élémentaires de la vie religieuse: Le système totémique en Australie* (e.g., Jones 2001; W. Miller 2012) with our own archival research on its translation and reception in the English-speaking world. By tracing the evolution of successive drafts of Durkheim's work, we will show how Durkheim's theorizing emerged from the dialectic between form and content. Such textual comparison enables us to appreciate Durkheim's exceptional moment of intellectual creativity.

Consider the successive beginnings attributed to Durkheim's crucial "new" understanding of religion. Some authors, such as Alexander, point to the 1899 essay "Concerning the Definition of Religious Phenomena," others to the 1902 essay on totemism (e.g., Jones 2001, 48), and still others to the 1906–7 lecture course on religion (W. Miller 2012). We believe all these writings constitute successive steps in the development of Durkheim's theorizing, each featuring significant advances toward the definite formulation of his ideas in *Formes*. Common to these writings, *Formes* included, is the ethnographic evidence provided by Spencer and Gillen's *The Native Tribes of Central Australia*. What changes is Durkheim's way of making sense of this material vis-à-vis competing approaches.

While there is no doubt that the 1899 essay inaugurated a new way of thinking about ancient religion, it remains riddled with contradictions. As Durkheim would later concede in *Formes*, one such contradiction was to simultaneously posit the universal character of the dualism of the sacred and the profane while conceptualizing the sacred as an energy able to permeate everything, leaving nothing profane. No less important, the theory this essay outlines is still insufficiently voluntaristic, to adopt Alexander's vocabulary. In fact, Durkheim's model follows James Frazer's largely rationalist and utilitarian conception of taboo in *Totemism* (1887). As a result, religious beliefs are here defined solely in terms of their obligatory character, as Durkheim would later lament in a footnote in *Forms* (1995, 44n68). In his essay on totemism, Durkheim (1902) expands his understanding of the nature of religious beliefs. This analytical shift responds to Frazer and Baldwin Spencer's utilitarian interpretation of the Intichiuma, a ritual practice of an Australian aboriginal people called the Arunta. Frazer and Spencer read the Arunta ritual as a completely rational system of cooperative magic, arguing that the function of totemism was economic. Durkheim finds in Robertson Smith's earlier theory of totemism (1889), which emphasized both the joyful nature of the earliest religious rituals and the socially integrative function of such rituals, a way of superseding Frazer and Spencer's utilitarian interpretation. In particular, as Robert Alun Jones suggests (2001, 51–52), this enables Durkheim to shift his analysis from the negative aspects of the cult, such as taboos and interdictions, to more positive practices, such as feasts and communal sacrifices, thus taking a significant step toward his mature understanding that the obligatory character of religious beliefs arises from the fact that they belong to the group that enforces them on its members. But not until his 1906–7 lecture course does Durkheim realize that stating that religion and society were originally fused together in totemism, as he did in his 1902 essay, is a mistake. In the beginning, these two aspects were separate. This suggests that the entanglement between sacred and profane is a historical development and that one should be able to disentangle them analytically. As William Watts Miller stresses (2012, 235), this is what Durkheim sets out to do in the 1906–7 lecture course as he makes two important theoretical breakthroughs: the novel understanding of the idea of "effervescence"[10] and the idea that the sacred and the profane operate in two different times. In the previous year, Durkheim described the French Revolution as a "creative era" during which "effervescence and collective enthusiasm" took on a "religious character" (1905, 382). Around the same time, other Durkheimians were tackling the problem of how exceptional events such as the French Revolution and routine moments are related. In an essay on the collective representation of time, Henri Hubert explored the nature and structure of calendars (1904). This was also a concern of Durkheim's nephew, Marcel Mauss, in his essay *Seasonal Variations of the Eskimo* (1906). Partly due to this collaborative work, Durkheim expands his conception of effervescence. No longer limited to exceptional periods, effervescence is now conceived of as occurring also in normal times as exceptional events become embedded in collective memory through recall in calendar rites. This idea of the dual times of the sacred and the profane appears prominently in the lecture course on religion, in which Durkheim applies it to Australia in a further revised version of his theory.

As a result of these successive modifications to his thinking, Durkheim was in a position to resolve the contradiction he incurred in the 1899 essay and to articulate a more fully voluntaristic, nonutilitarian theory of religion. The idea of a double temporality regarding the dualism between sacred and profane enables Durkheim to resolve his earlier paradox, and he is now able to account for the source of the energy of the sacred in exceptional effervescent times while explaining why it does not spread everywhere at routine times. But also, and not least, this is a way of tackling the external problem posed by

Spencer and Gillen's Australian ethnography. It makes it possible to concede that the totemic group might lack importance in ordinary times yet also assert that it remains the center of socioreligious life thanks to its preeminent role in the great communal rites, social renewal, and effervescence of special times (W. Miller 2012, 239). This is, in brief, the immediate intellectual context that frames Durkheim's writing of his last major monograph.

Durkheim began writing the draft of the final text in the spring of 1908.[11] In writing up this draft, he kept to the basic plan he had laid down in his 1906–7 lecture course. This constitutes a draft of the final text, and after an introduction, Durkheim outlines the material of what would become book 1, 2, and 3's opening two chapters on a negative cult and on sacrifice as a rite associated with the positive cult. The draft includes a brief conclusion on what makes religion "eternal" (Durkheim 1975, 122). The final text arrived at the desk of the editor, Félix Alcan, on February 3, 1912, as certified by the contract signed by Durkheim on that date at 108 Boulevard Saint-Germain. Durkheim received the final proofs of the manuscript "around May 20."[12] The work, titled *Les formes élémentaires de la vie religieuse. Le système totémique en Australie*, was published in June 1912 (Borlandi 2012, 284). Over these four years, Durkheim drew on, expanded, and revised his 1906/1907 lecture course in order to produce a manuscript that is, in several key respects, profoundly different from the original draft.

Drawing on Miller's meticulous intertextual analysis (2012, 235–40), we will now discuss the changes made by Durkheim. Some of them involved adding new material, others interweaving existing passages in new contexts, still others the removal of certain segments of the text. Durkheim's attempt at making sense of religion in a thoroughly sociological fashion unites this composition. His theorizing on religion was a decade-long process involving regular oral and written communication with other members of the Durkheimian group, the preparation and delivery of lectures on the topic, individual consultation of a vast set of documentation, and finally, writing up a draft intended for publication. The changes Durkheim made to the final draft in late 1911 and early 1912 were the last steps of this process, offering precious textual evidence of the way Durkheim's theorizing evolved until the moment before submitting the manuscript to the editor.

The first type of change involved expanding his earlier account. In book 3, after the analysis of sacrifice Durkheim added several new passages on rites. He also expanded the overall conclusion to the work. Theoretically, this results in a new concept of the rite as a fundamentally social phenomenon. This new concept is absent from the draft. Durkheim began by transferring a seemingly unimportant remark about two different aspects of a rite from the end of the draft to the new chapter that follows: "The profound moral efficacy of the rite determines belief in its physical efficacy, which is illusory" (1975, 122). Once relocated, this statement functions in an entirely different way. The physical act of reinscribing this statement in a different position in the text reflects a sudden expansion of Durkheim's reasoning regarding what is entailed by a rite, providing Durkheim with the conceptual basis on which to distinguish different kinds of rite. Concretely, he uses it to characterize one particular type of rite, which he designates as the mimetic rite: "The moral efficacy of the rite, which is real, has driven belief in its physical efficacy, which is imaginary" (1976, 359).[13] This type is then contrasted with the dramatic rite, to which Durkheim attributes crucial significance. Dramatic rites, also known as representative or commemorative rites, are of exceptional importance as they require no belief whatsoever in their physical, material efficacy. For the believer, they function in a purely representative way—that is, their efficacy is purely social or moral. This crucial advance in Durkheim's theorization of religion as a fundamentally social affair is the product of his writing up the final manuscript of *Formes*. It is absent from the draft, and only appears in the work. In between was Durkheim's sensuous involvement with the text, through which his understanding evolved in significant ways.

A second type of intervention by Durkheim in the text returns us to the etymology of the word "text" and its textile imagery. By comparing the draft with the work, one can see Durkheim weaving together different segments of text on the elementary forms of thought along the whole body of the work, where he applies these highly abstract neo-Kantian philosophical categories to specific aspects of religious experience.[14] Crucially, Durkheim's sensuous interweaving of statements across the manuscript occurs exactly when he decides to provide a sociological answer to the philosophical question of the nature of knowledge, the most abstract and ambitious purpose of *Formes*. A fuller appreciation of Durkheim's textual interweaving while composing *Formes*, however, requires us to go beyond the intertextual context of the draft and the work to consider the earlier 1903 essay "Primitive Classification" (Durkheim and Mauss 1903).[15] Between this essay and the draft, Durkheim introduced the new idea that the origin of logical and conceptual thought lies in the creative energy of effervescent times. Yet it is between the draft and the work that Durkheim made the most significant changes. In the centerpiece of both the draft and the work, Durkheim discusses the idea of an elementary "force," "energy" or "power." How this elementary category manifests itself is then interwoven into chapters 3 through 5, on rites, in book 3. Durkheim considers successively three categories of the understanding: time (which Kant had described as a "form of intuition"), causality, and creativity. As to the problem of time, Durkheim's sociological answer begins by noting that social life does not proceed in a linear, constant pace. Rather, in any given community, there are markedly different rhythms with periodic upsurges of energy. Durkheim finds the solution to account for this apparent contradiction in rites. Rites, he explains, offer an experiential space in which this elementary energy or force is renewed periodically. Durkheim then discusses causality. He offers a description of social life that works according to an underlying logic. Again, he resorts to the idea of an elementary energy to describe the nature of the forces at work in the necessary connections between the different elements of social experience. Finally, Durkheim considers creativity. This turns out to be of crucial importance for Durkheim's argument as a whole. Social change, in both its sacred and profane dimensions, proceeds by means of a constant process of re-creation of its basic structures and institutions through effervescent energies.

All these different types of change show Durkheim's thinking evolving significantly as it is successively inscribed in the essay, in the draft, and eventually in the work. With each reinscription of Durkheim's thought comes a set of changes to Durkheim's thought itself. Rather than a single early "shift toward subjectivity" in the mid-1890s, our analysis shows that this shift occurs gradually, through a number of crucial developments, as Durkheim's theorizing is put into writing for different purposes, but most importantly for the publication of *Formes*. This is neither a plea for intentionalism nor a retreat toward contextualism. Instead, we believe there is much to be gained from a greater appreciation of how thinking often operates in sensuous ways. The sensuousness of the late Durkheim's theorizing is at its peak when most abstract. For Durkheim, thinking about ways of rendering Kant's epistemology amenable to sociological analysis was not only an intellectual challenge but also a creative, tactile process. More generally, it is apparent that the writing up of *Formes* and its subsidiary materials for almost a decade enabled Durkheim to position himself in some of the intellectual debates of the time, contributing to the early institutionalization of sociology in French academia, achieving greater clarity about his means and purposes, and eventually articulating, as rightly emphasized by Alexander and his associates in recent years, one of the most potent antiutilitarian theories of the twentieth century.

On February 7, 1912, the final version of the work reached Félix Alcan, and the book was published under the title *Les Formes élémentaires de la vie religieuse. Le Système totémique en Australie*, with 647 pages and a folded ethnographic map of Australia at the end of the book.[16] The publication of the work in its definite form (at least, the first and last edition published during

Durkheim's lifetime) might lead us to think that, through this particular inscription, Durkheim's theory achieved a fixed, stable status requiring from the interpreter only a set of hermeneutic skills to make sense of the text. However, the print publication of *Formes* in 1912 is but the first of a long line of inscriptions of the late Durkheim's ideas on religion and epistemology. These ideas were periodically reinscribed, sometimes in translation, over the next century. With each reinscription, changes were made to the typographic form through which these ideas are presented to the reader, translation choices were made as to the best way of rendering Durkheim's French text into foreign languages, paratexts were written to frame the scope of hermeneutic possibilities used to approach the work, and critical commentary was produced to explore the implications of these ideas.

## FROM *LES FORMES* TO *ELEMENTARY FORMS OF THE RELIGIOUS LIFE*

Commentary over the meaning of the late Durkheim in the social sciences and the humanities throughout the twentieth century has always returned to the book, either in materialistic terms (as in commentaries that reduce meaning to the external factors of its production) or in idealistic terms (in which meaning is assumed to exist independently of the material conditions of its existence). Despite its attempt at reconciling detailed textual exegesis with close attention to contextual factors, Alexander's critical commentary of *Formes* falls closer to the second pole. Few, however, seem to have considered the possibility that the meaning of the book could also have emerged, in important ways, from the dialectic between content and form integral to its making. This partly explains Alexander's genealogy of influence of *Formes* during the twentieth century, which locates the meaning of the work within a grand theoretical synthesis toward subjectivity. By following the book, however, we can arrive at a different kind of genealogy. Such a genealogy is explicitly aimed at reconstituting the politics of the book—that is, the struggles over the meaning of the work and its author, including those in which Alexander was involved. We begin by briefly recounting the creation of the first English translation.

Shortly after its publication in French, there were plans to translate *Formes* into English. The translation originated in Durkheim's desire to have the work circulate among an international readership and the persistent efforts by Joseph Ward Swain, a young American student of Durkheim's who acted as translator and a literary agent of sorts. That Swain, an Episcopalian from

South Dakota, had to reconcile the work of translation with his own doctoral research[17] did not benefit the quality of the translation. Yet if it were not for Swain's efforts, not only in seeking out alternative publishers when the original ones abandoned the project but also in conducting many of the negotiations with the publishers, the whole project would probably have floundered.

The correspondence exchanged between Swain, on behalf of Durkheim, and Cecil A. Reynolds, managing director of the publishing house George Allen and Unwin in Oxford, offers valuable evidence of the sequence of events surrounding this editorial project.[18] Durkheim and Swain's first choice, however, was not Allen and Unwin but an American publisher, Macmillan, in New York. Macmillan, however, turned down the project. They replied that *Formes* was "a work which could be published in England to much better advantage than in the United States,"[19] and recommended Allen and Unwin as an alternative, noting they are "the publishers of an important series in Philosophy and Religion" and "perhaps in as good a position as any publisher to handle this book." Durkheim's original plan to address an American readership was thwarted, but Swain was not to be dissuaded so easily. Following the American editor's advice, he approached Allen and Unwin in October 1914. Swain began by informing them that he had studied with Durkheim in Paris during the past year, that Durkheim gave him permission to translate the book, and that he had already completed a first draft translation of a portion of it. Before going any further, however, Swain wished to see whether some sort of arrangement in regard to its publication could not be made in advance. To persuade Allen and Unwin, Swain took the initiative to briefly present the character and scope of the book to be translated, along with the draft of his translation of the introduction, the conclusion, and the table of contents. This, he assured the editor, would be sufficient to show that the book

> is in no way a highly technical treatise on the phenomena of primitive religions, but is rather an attempted interpretation of them. While [f.2] it is true that a certain amount of space is necessarily devoted to the description of these phenomena, this is not at all the primary purpose of the work. As is clearly set forth in the pages I am sending you, M. Durkheim's object is to study these religions in order to seek in a scientific manner the origin and nature of religion in general. The book, then, is an exposition of his thought in regard to what he calls «Sociologie Religieuse» and the summing up of the work, not only of M. Durkheim himself, but also the entire school of French sociologists who have been publishing [in] *L'Année Sociologique* for

the past 15 years. In fact, this book will undoubtedly long remain the classic exposition of this sociological theory of religion.

In France this sociological thought of M. Durkheim is recognized as one of the two most important currents of contemporary thought, the other current being that developed by M. Bergson. From my own experience at the Sorbonne, I am able to state that the work of Durkheim there is regarded as equally important with that of Bergson. So knowing the success of English translations of Bergson's writings, it has seemed to me that there is a need for a translation of Durkheim as well.[20]

Reynolds replied the next day, showing interest in the project and asking for more details. Swain explained that the portion of the translation he had sent them was all he had done and that he had not completed the translation as yet. At present, Swain explained, he has translated about half of the book and offered to send Allen and Unwin the rest of what he has translated to date. This he did on October 26, with the accompanying note:

> I am sending you under another cover another chapter of my translation of Professor Durkheim's book, "The Elementary Forms of Religious Belief." As I have already explained to you, I consider this chapter one of the most important in the book, so it has seemed to me that it will aid your Reader greatly in forming an opinion of the book. Also, since it is written in a somewhat different style from the chapters I have already sent you, where considerable space was necessarily given to a technical description of the phenomena of the Australian religion, it will aid in showing that the book is not a mere technical treatise, but rather an attempted explanation of these elementary phenomena.
>
> I have as yet received no reply from the Felix Alcan Company in Paris, but as soon as I do, I will let you know what they say.
>
> Yours very truly,
> J. W. Swain [pencil addition: MA Harvard, BA Columbia]

This is important for several reasons. First, it shows that the title of the work in translation was still undecided. Second, it introduces the figure of an external reader who would play an important yet critical role in the translation process. Third, it shows the Swain's continuing efforts to persuade Allen and Unwin of the potentially wide appeal of the work.

Between November 1914 and March 1915, there was a voluminous amount of correspondence between Swain and the publisher. First, the external reader was consulted to give his opinion of the quality of the translation. He noted that there were "various solecisms" but that these were "trivial matters" that could be easily adjusted when the translation was completed. Reassured with this answer, Swain proceeded and concluded the translation sometime in late 1914. Durkheim read the translation in early 1915 and was very satisfied with it, telling Swain that "any changes he might want to make would be so slight that they could easily be marked in the proofs."[21] On February 4, 1915, Swain sent Allen and Unwin his translation. As it transpired, Durkheim was intent on reversing the original order of the title and subtitle in French. Maybe because he thought *Elementary Forms* would not be an appealing title to the Anglo-American public, Durkheim's first choice was *Totemism*.[22] However, Durkheim's title of choice was not to be. This is because of the intervention of John Henry Muirhead, the reader hired by Allen and Unwin. A well-known British philosopher whose main interests revolved around religion and morals (e.g., 1892), Muirhead notes that "Totemism" might lead to a confusion with James Frazer's book with the same title, and that it would be preferable to retain the literal translation of the French title: "The Elementary Forms of the Religious Life." Hence the English translation of the work was christened.

If Muirhead's suggestion avoids an unfortunate confusion with Frazer's book, it does little to prevent Swain's own unfortunate translation choices.[23] Just as the correct translation of *c'est la vie!* is not *that's the life!*, but *that's life!*, the title of Durkheim's major work should not have been translated, even in the name of literalness, as *The Elementary Forms of the Religious Life*, but as *The Elementary Forms of Religious Life*. Swain's quest for literalness will have important implications for how the work was rendered into English, starting with the title but extending well beyond it. At the dawn of the twentieth century, literalness was thought equivalent to accuracy, and readers were expected to hear not only foreign words but foreign structures "through" their own language. For instance, to read an English-American translation of the Bible was partly seen as an exercise of the readers' Greek syntax (Glassman 1981, 48). Likewise, Swain's translation of *Elementary Forms* made generations of English-speaking readers exercise their French syntax and even vocabulary, as Swain populated the text with false cognates (Fields 2005, 160–65).

Printed in Plymouth, Devon, at the printing presses of William Brendon and Son, the English translation of Durkheim's *The Elementary Forms of the Religious Life* is said to be "just out" in the *Review of Politics, Literature, Science and Art* of October 16, 1915 (120, no. 3129, 381). Sold at fifteen shillings,[24] its first print run was 1,000 copies, 250 of which were exported to the United States, where the book was distributed by Macmillan. For eighty years, this was the introduction for thousands of English-speaking students to the work of the late Durkheim—or, better still, to the last work of Durkheim as the "late Durkheim" was still years to come.

The periodization of Durkheim's writings, his canonization in sociology and anthropology, and the relationship between his contributions and those of other classics would be the object of much dispute among commentators after 1945. It is likely that Swain's quest for literalness had some impact in the reception of Durkheim's final work in the Anglo-American context. The sheer variety of interpretations, however, seems to suggest that this did not determine per se the reception of *Elementary Forms*. Rather, the hermeneutical encounters between the work and commentators, who as a rule read French and most probably consulted both the original and the translated versions of the work, seem to have been shaped by a much wider set of factors. These included personal research interests, disciplinary affiliations, national traditions, and broader ideological and epistemological orientations. As these multiple factors influenced one another and interacted with contextual circumstances, the specific narrative forms of the sociological tradition with which we began this chapter gradually emerged. Such narrative forms can be seen to operate in the case of the critical commentary of *Elementary Forms* in this period. Since the 1990s, however, this plurality of narrative genres around Durkheim seems to have given way to the relative predominance of one particular genre—Alexander's synthetic narrative of the "cultural Durkheim." We now turn to this particular vision of the sociological tradition.

### ELEMENTARY FORMS TODAY

Today commentary on *Elementary Forms* no longer refers to Swain's 1915 translation. In the 1990s and early 2000s, two new editions and translations of Durkheim's last work appeared, rapidly establishing themselves as the authoritative entry point to the work in English-speaking countries: Karen E. Fields's 1995 translation for Free Press and Carol Cosman's 2001 abridged translation for Oxford University Press. These new editions have gradually come to function as outlets or platforms through which interpreters have advanced claims regarding the relative importance of *Elementary Forms* (and Durkheim). Alexander, who established the cultural sociology program around it, by and large spearheads critical commentary on the work today.

Both the new translations and Alexander's interpretation, however, were made possible by the developments in Durkheimian scholarship discussed above but also by broad intellectual movements and new disciplinary orientations. We will now discuss whether they have been able to critically reflect on this or merely reproduce it (and transfer it to the text). In any case, the fact remains that, taken together, these developments in the reception and edition of the work mark a new phase in the social life of *Elementary Forms*.

By and large, the reception of *Elementary Forms* in America has been anything but a success story. In the 1950s and 1960s, the general view of the work was that it had become marginal and an overlooked text (Morrison 2003, 399). Even the paperback reprint of the work in 1965 did not seem to make much difference, at least in sociology. Since between the late 1960s and the early 1980s sociologists, especially critical sociologists, predominantly worked with antinormative modes of theorizing, *Elementary Forms* remained out of sight. There were those, of course, who paid attention to the work, such as Robert Alun Jones, Edward Tiryakian, Robert Bellah, and Edward Shils. These figures may have been important in American sociology at the time, but for the most part, they also remained isolated thinkers without significant followings. If for many anthropologists *Elementary Forms* constituted a key foundational text, only in the early 1990s did its canonization in sociology gather pace (Smith and Alexander 1996, 587).[25]

Key to this evolution was the advent of the "new Durkheim studies" of the 1970s (e.g., Clark 1968, 1973; Lukes 1973; Birnbaum 1976; Filloux 1977; Jones 1977). Crucial in this regard was the new journal *Études Durkheimiennes*, founded in 1977 under the tutelage of Philippe Besnard. In 1972 Steven Lukes published the magisterial *Émile Durkheim: His Life and Work*. Lukes's pathbreaking intellectual biography emerged from extensive empirical historical research (including interviews with many of Durkheim's relatives, archival research, and unpublished sources—namely, letters and manuscripts) and from a "new" understanding of Durkheim's work as a whole. Lukes's study opened the way for a new generation of Durkheimian scholars who revolutionized our understanding of the French master's collaborative network, institutional mode of operation, and intellectual development. The subsequent opening of archives also provided new data about Durkheim's life and work, and the impetus for new analyses of the work he produced under the complicated intellectual and social conditions surrounding the emergence of sociology in France. As a result, since the 1970s, Durkheimian studies have steadily proliferated around, besides Lukes himself, Marcel Fournier, Philippe Besnard, Robert Alun Jones, Massimo Borlandi, and W. S. F. Pickering.

In addition, the rise of broad intellectual movements such as poststructuralism, postmodernism, and cultural studies between the 1970s and 1990s signaled the exhaustion of modernist ways of thinking and a general swing in the social sciences and humanities toward hermeneutics, semiotics, and cultural analysis broadly construed. In this intellectual climate, homogeneous and rigid conceptions of society and human agency came increasingly under critical scrutiny. A greater concern with the social life of things ensued in an attempt to supersede the modernist chasm opposing materialist and idealist approaches.

The politics of the book were deeply affected by these developments. Their protagonists, which include the commentators of and the editorial agents behind the 1990s editions of *Elementary Forms*,[26] drew on these developments in their interventions. Consider Fields's 1995 translation of *Elementary Forms*, the first translation of the work since Swain's. Fields explicitly positions her translation against Swain's (Fields 1995, li–lxi). While the former translation is depicted as a modernist representative of the quest for literalness, Fields praises the postmodern hermeneutic license of the translator-interpreter. For Fields, a translation is both a product and a process. As a product, it cannot help but appear to be what it cannot possibly be—the text itself, but in a different language.[27] Certainly, the writer can craft this appearance, whether by employing idiomatic language or by making the author sound foreign. Whatever the appearance, however, a text cannot move by itself; it must be rebuilt. As a process, every translation is a reconstruction, and every translator works like an artisan, not a medium (Fields 2005, 166). The meaning of the work is dramatically transformed not only because of the changes in context described above but also as a result of this new rendering of the text into English—thus a change in both content and form.

It is a change in content insofar as Fields's translation offers a new interpretation of Durkheim. The first sign of this is the title itself. Swain's odd title *The Elementary Forms of <u>the</u> Religious Life* was (finally) replaced by the correct *The Elementary Forms of Religious Life*. More generally, when compared with Swain's, Fields's translation is characterized by its more contemporary use of language as well as her conscious attempt to make her translation reflect (and promote) emerging understandings of the message of *Elementary Forms* and its place in contemporary sociology.

It is a change in form as the 464-page Free Press edition has little or nothing in common with the previous material incarnations of the work. Crucial in this regard are this edition's paratexts. The 1995 edition has a long scholarly introduction by Fields herself, in which the reader is introduced not only to issues of language and translation but to the relative contribution of this work to the understanding of Durkheim as a whole. She seeks to broaden the readership of the work to include "American postmodernist theorizers of discursive practices and representations," since in her view, "dead ancestors should stay dead to us unless pleasure and excitement come from getting to know them" (1995, xxiii). A jazz enthusiast, Fields compares reading *Elementary Forms* to listening to Wynton Marsalis's "translation" of the "old work" of Duke Ellington. In both instances, the "case for studying old works needs to be made now, partly through the manner of their presentation" (xxiv). Fields's "manner" of presenting *Elementary Forms* to a new generation, as she notes in the introduction (xxiii–xxiv), is not simply a matter of recoding words from one grammatical system to another. It involves, as she rightly points out, recoding texts from one semantic context to another. It involves carrying the letter of the text and the spirit of the original to the linguistic-cultural context of reception. And, we might add, it is also a matter of reassembling material signifiers from one specific typographic form into another. Indeed, the "manner" in which Fields chose to present *Elementary Forms* to a new generation includes a solid paratextual apparatus. This edition contains hundreds of editorial notes;[28] the ethnographic map of the original French edition, absent from Swain's 1915 edition, providing the reader with a spatial visualization of the ethnographic materials discussed in the text so as to clarify and reinforce their significance; and a comprehensive index, which adds to the scholarly quality of the work as a whole. As a result of these changes in content and form, the Free Press 1995 edition of *Elementary Forms* marks a watershed in the social life of the book. Closely aligned with postmodernist understandings of the philosophy of translation, and accompanied by a robust scholarly paratextual apparatus, this new incarnation of the work provides material support to the "cultural Durkheim" of the 1990s.

This material support also came in the form of an abridged, student-oriented edition. In 2001 Oxford University Press (OUP) published yet another new translation of *Elementary Forms*. This abridgment, translated by Carol Cosman and covering approximately 75 percent of the original text, was commercialized in the Oxford World's Classics series, the leading world book series of trade paperbacks in literature and social science. The paratexts of this edition are clear about the intent to position the work within dominant intellectual movements in the social sciences today. In the introduction, Durkheim scholar Mark S. Cladis, who is responsible for the critical apparatus of this edition, frames the text within his communitarian, culturally sensitive secular lenses (1992, 1999). Invoking Richard Rorty's pragmatic emphasis on vocabularies, Cladis praises Durkheim for having articulated "a powerful vocabulary for articulating the normative, communal aspects of modern, democratic societies—the vocabulary of religion." Not unlike Alexander's emphasis on public performance and deep cultural scripts, Cladis goes on to argue that one "finds religion wherever public, normative concepts, or rites are employed. Religion, then, pervades traditional and modern—even postmodern—societies." He concludes, in an unmistakably voluntaristic, collectivist tone, "The upshot of this, morally and epistemologically, is that human life is, in a significant sense, life together. This is Durkheim's response, and challenge, to a long tradition of Cartesian, individualistic thought" (2001, viii).

Independent of these editorial initiatives, Alexander's critical commentary on Durkheim draws on very much the same interpretative-hermeneutic intellectual movements. The fact that Alexander was not associated with these new translations and editions does not mean, however, that he has been impervious to them. In a review of Fields's translation for the *American Journal of Sociology*, Alexander and Philip Smith make the reasons for their endorsement clear (Smith and Alexander 1996). They point to three major factors explaining the emerging centrality of *Elementary Forms* for mainstream sociology in this period (587–88). First, there was a broad swing in the discipline as a whole toward cultural analysis. This general intellectual movement has seen hermeneutics, semiotics, and related interpretative perspectives become more central to contemporary sociological theory. Second, sociologists taking inspiration from *Elementary Forms* proved able to make use of Durkheim's visionary ideas in the context of a changed intellectual climate. The third reason for this discontinuity in the social life of *Elementary Forms* refers to the ways in which contemporary scholars have interpreted it. Whereas previous experience emphasized objectivist readings, later interpretations are said to have detected a decisive epistemological break in the middle-period Durkheim. Smith and Alexander's enthusiastic endorsement of Fields's work of translation is a strong indication of how closely aligned their intellectual interventions around the work are. While Swain's literal, "stilted, convoluted late-Victorian tones" "embody and reinforce the image of Durkheim, the scientist and philosopher," "Fields's reworking of the text gives to *Elementary Forms* a Geertzian tenor. Here Durkheim becomes the virtuoso interpreter of cultural life, the translator of traditions." Crucially, they assure us, Fields's Durkheim "reads like a daring and imaginative theorist rather than a pedantic relic of 19th century positivism" (1996, 590). Cosman's abridgment (2001, xxxvi) goes even further in the attempt to bring the text up to date by retaining all the passages on "topical issues, for example the role of women in religion," while purging the text of "dated controversies" and "the more antiquarian aspects" of Durkheim's thought. A battle between past and present understandings of the work is being waged in the pages of *Elementary Forms* today, the victors defining much of the reception of the text in the coming years.

## CONCLUSION

Neither an imaginative postmodern theorist nor a pedantic relic of a bygone era, the hitherto ignored facet of Émile Durkheim we have uncovered in this chapter is that of an author committing his ideas to a physical medium, and working them out through it. Given this perspective, Durkheim's theorizing on religion and epistemology emerges as the product of an embodied mind. The reconstruction of his ten-year-long sensuous process of writing the collection of texts from which *Formes* originated alerts us against readings that try to locate *the* crucial breakthrough in any one of those steps. Rather, *Formes* emerges from our study as the destined location of the path Durkheim took in the company of his numerous associates, before his students, and in the solitude of his studio. Until the very end, Durkheim continued to theorize through the physical act of crafting the manuscript for publication. Once published, *Formes* (soon afterward, *Elementary Forms*) gained a life of its own. In time, it became a totem for interpreters keen to use Durkheim's legacy to push for certain research agendas and disciplinary projects.

Twentieth-century commentary on *Elementary Forms* took many forms. Either a product of bourgeois ideology, a repository of scientific outputs concerning collective representations, an exemplar of sociologism, a classic statement on community, or the key developmental stage in Durkheim's thinking away from positivism, the politics of the book has taken the work to mean fundamentally different things over the years. Each perspective on the meaning and importance of *Elementary Forms* and its author to sociology, anthropology, and religious studies had to establish itself against a number of competing others. From these struggles over the meaning of the work emerged explorations of different facets of Durkheim's message, from his political persuasion and methodological lessons to his theoretical contributions. Founded on mutually incompatible epistemological assumptions, some of these visions of the sociological tradition are fundamentally at odds with one another. Together, they offer an overview of some of the main strategies of theory-building employed in the discipline in the twentieth century.

Despite how commentators have construed *Elementary Forms* in various and mutually contradictory ways, they all share one thing. They have all taken the book for granted. Primarily interested in the ideas inscribed in its pages, commentators were more likely to pay attention to Durkheim's intentions, biographical circumstances, career interests, and broader contextual factors such as ideology, intellectual traditions, academic disciplines, or socioeconomic conditions than to the dialectic between form and content as a source of meaning. As a result, none of these narrative accounts examines *Elementary Forms* as we have proposed—that is, the material expression of Durkheim's theorizing on religion and epistemology that, far from being constant, changes with each subsequent embodiment (and implied rereading). If we take the materiality of the text seriously, however, a new approach to theory-building emerges. This new approach is more sensitive not only to the ways in which Durkheim's theories were actually produced but also to the distinctly political character of the struggles over their meaning.

A crucial new theme of research emerges from this perspective, which we explore in the remainder of this book. Durkheim's quest for the sacred unveils the sacred properties of objects in the secular domain. This is the case of objects endowed by human agents with special properties, both abstract objects, such as an idea one holds dear, and physical ones—say, a classic book. Alexander's genealogy of structuralism has unveiled a "subterranean" line of research from Saussure to Geertz exploring the late Durkheim's attention to culture, here equated with the deep structures of meaning that frame human agency (e.g., J. Alexander 1987, 281–329; 2001). Cultural sociology is the hermeneutic exercise of describing how agents work the binaries (civil versus uncivil, authentic versus artificial, etc.) that structure discourse.[29] Our own genealogy expands beyond a semiotics of the late Durkheim's theorizing whose primary focus is discourse. As Durkheim repeatedly emphasizes, physical things are part and parcel of the social world, as imbued with meaning as concepts or theories.[30]

Texts are important. But texts are always the product of an embodied mind, whose activity is always irrevocably embedded in the world of things. Hence Durkheim's semiotics of the sacred-profane calls for the adoption of an inclusive approach to the study of texts, starting with the text in which it finds itself inscribed.[31] As materiality is found to be integral to the construction and articulation of meaning and to affect interpretative responses, to study a text apart from the ways in which it has been physically woven and rewoven is to lose sight of a critical aspect of its being in time.

CHAPTER 2

## A CLASSIC WITH NO AUTHOR

## G. H. Mead's *Mind, Self, and Society*

George Herbert Mead's most famous work, *Mind, Self, and Society: From the Standpoint of a Social Behaviorist*, is a compilation of student notes and unpublished manuscripts. Edited with an introduction by Charles W. Morris, it was first published by the University of Chicago Press after Mead's death in 1934. The book presents Mead's intersubjective conception of the self in a lively and accessible style. In the 1960s, *Mind, Self, and Society* played a key role in the establishment of symbolic interactionism and in Mead's subsequent inclusion in the sociological canon. The book has been translated into several languages, including Japanese, French, German, Spanish, and Italian. A second edition, annotated by Daniel R. Huebner and Hans Joas, was published in 2015.

INTRODUCTION

Founding fathers and classic texts are the main protagonists of a certain way of viewing the history—and thereby defining the identity—of different disciplines in the social sciences and the humanities. However, the relationship among authors, texts, and authorial-textual achievement is arguably a complex one, and it has produced a vast literature and heated debates over the last few decades. It is by achieving a classical standing that a text contributes to an author's canonization as one of the discipline's greats. But despite the agentic and individualistic connotations of the "author" concept, it is not always possible to trace exemplary texts back to a determinate author who can be posited as their source. Texts can become classics in their own right, even when their authorship is loosely collective, doubtful, or unknown. There can be a relative autonomy of texts with regard to their authors. We will discuss one such extreme case in this chapter. The text is *Mind, Self, and Society*, and the author is George Herbert Mead.

The placing of an author name on a text has momentous consequences for the way in which that text is understood and evaluated. This is because the mere suggestion of "authorship" triggers sweeping and relatively unexamined views on literary property, the origins of a text, and the identity of the person accountable for it. *Mind, Self, and Society* is a unique site for questioning these assumptions about the relationship among authors, texts, and authorial-textual achievement. In it, the naming of an individual as the author conceals questions of the utmost importance regarding who counts as an author. Yet this circumstance did not prevent that text from being retrospectively named the foundational text of a distinctive sociological approach and turned into a sociological classic (Camic 2008, 326). Alongside books such as Erving Goffman's *The Presentation of Self in Everyday Life* (1959), Howard Becker's *Outsiders: Studies in the Sociology of Deviance* (1963), and Herbert Blumer's *Symbolic Interactionism: Perspective and Method* (1969), *Mind, Self, and Society*—a monograph edited by Charles Morris and published by the University of Chicago Press in 1934—has come to be regarded as one of the seminal texts responsible for establishing symbolic interactionism as a distinctive sociological tradition.

Sociological classicality will always be dependent on the dialectic between the value of a text and the richness of its interpretative appropriation. Yet as Peter Baehr rightly stresses, not "all classics follow the *same* pattern in attaining their status" or "become classics for the *same* reasons" (2002, 119; our emphasis). As we will see, the singular process through which *Mind, Self, and Society* achieved a classical standing throws much-needed light onto the complexities of the process of canon formation in sociology. But before we embark on the analysis of our case study, a couple of preliminary remarks are in order.

To begin with, the canonization process of an author or a text as a "sociological classic" bears some resemblance to certain religious rituals, from the Roman Catholic Church's process of beatification to ancient sacred totemism. The core meaning of the word *canon* is "rule" or "measure," and it became quickly entangled with the notion of authority, a normative sense of *canon* that was strongly reinforced by its application to a church edict or, more generally, to the group of texts accepted as "authentic" or "sacred" by a particular religion. If it is true that sociological canonical texts, unlike theological ones, are neither determined by decree nor set once and for all but rather introduced to an ongoing critical colloquy by means of reader appropriation and social diffusion, it is also clear that in creating a common frame of reference, they allow for the emergence of a more unified interpretative community akin to a religious community with a gospel. More important to our purposes here, perhaps, the "tangible form" of the totem that Durkheim describes in *Elementary Forms*, which allows the "intangible substance" (i.e., its spiritual force, or "mana") to be represented (1995, 201), stands close to the idea of the sociological classic as a symbol, with the totem as a symbol of the mana and the sociological classic as a symbol of sociology's own identity. Second, such a symbolic condensation of meaning in a classic makes it something akin to an icon.[1] An icon, from this perspective, is an object whose aesthetic shape conveys meaning. Consider the example of William Shakespeare, perhaps the most important Western cultural icon. When one is confronted with the name "Shakespeare" (or with his portrait), the meaning conveyed far surpasses that of an especially gifted writer who lived in the British Isles during the seventeenth century—it represents the apex of English literature; it is the embodiment of the English language itself with all the awe, amazement, and emotional identification this implies. Yet this meaning is conveyed not through a linguistic or cognitive process but through a sensuous experience. It is through a "feeling consciousness," a concept Jeffrey C. Alexander retrieves from Mead, that one can be iconically conscious: "It is to understand by feeling, by contact, by the 'evidence of the senses' rather than the mind" (J. Alexander 2008, 782). Sociological classics are, similarly, iconic symbols that perform the important functions of creating frames of reference, providing legitimization, and securing knowledge transmission.

Despite the lasting resonance of the notion of "feeling consciousness," Mead did not become the iconic symbol of symbolic interactionism through his essay "The Social Character of Instincts," where he introduced the concept and which forms one of the chapters of a book he came close to publishing in 1910 (the book was eventually abandoned by Mead, not uncharacteristically, with the galley proofs in his possession).[2] It was rather through a posthumous work, *Mind, Self, and Society*, that Mead would come into the limelight and achieve the classical status that makes him an attractive choice for authoritative peer citation. It is then to the history of this second, more influential work that we turn in the remaining part of the chapter.[3] After examining the way in which the book came into being, we will concentrate on two episodes in the history of its reception by sociological circles, first in the United States and then in Europe, while also assessing how the peculiar story of the book's formation both governed and affected this reception. The protagonists of these episodes are Herbert Blumer and Jürgen Habermas, arguably the two most influential actors in the process of the disciplinary canonization of G. H. Mead.

## FABRICATING *MIND, SELF, AND SOCIETY*

The best way to start is with a flash-forward—that is, with a glimpse into the way in which, every year in classrooms around the world, freshmen sociology students are introduced to the reading of *Mind, Self, and Society*. The text is normally described as the most representative exemplar of the work of George Herbert Mead, the founding father of symbolic interactionism and of microsociology generally. As for Mead himself, he is often presented as someone who was much more at ease with teaching than with putting his ideas in writing. As a result of this attitude toward writing, students are told, he published very little. Against this background, the book *Mind, Self, and Society* emerges as the almost-perfect solution to an unfortunate situation that might have otherwise deprived us of contact with Mead's ideas. Due to the felicitous initiative of a group of former students led by Charles W. Morris,[4] two sets of student notes were taken from Mead's course on advanced social psychology in the late 1920s and subsequently gathered into a book made available to the public. This story of the students' actions has been reproduced time and again ever since the first wave of posthumous publications of Mead's writings in the 1930s.[5] Very few articles or books on Mead have questioned this narrative.[6] But while it is the case that some students made extensive efforts to collect notes of some of Mead's most popular courses, the fact is that this particular "mythology" (Skinner 1969) of the bringing of *Mind, Self, and Society* into being does not accurately describe what happened. To demythologize it, another, more rigorous history must be told.

In the original copy of the transcript of the social psychology course from which *Mind, Self, and Society* was created, a mysterious note, written on the last page, reads, "Reported by W. T. Lillie."[7] Who was W. T. Lillie? Was he one of the students attending Mead's course? After all, these notes are listed in the Mead Papers Archive at the University of Chicago as "student notes," and all the literature agrees that *Mind, Self, and Society* was created from them. But why would a student use such an awkward expression? One's doubts are confirmed as one examines the list of students enrolled in that course: there is no one with that name.[8] If Lillie was not a student, who was he?

Let us return to the book for a moment to begin unraveling the mystery. In the preface to *Mind, Self, and Society*, Charles Morris explains that George Anagnos, a former student of Mead, found that industrialist Alwin C. Carus, despite never having studied under Mead himself, proved willing to "provide the means necessary to employ persons to take down *verbatim* the various courses." To this Morris adds that "the whole is by no means a court record, but it is certainly as adequate and as faithful a record as has been left of a great thinker's last years" (Mead 1934, vi). Precious additional information about how *Mind, Self, and Society* was put together is found in the correspondence exchanged between Charles Morris and Henry and Irene Tufts Mead (the son and daughter-in-law of G. H. Mead).[9] In the letters, Morris informed the Meads of the existence of stenographic notes in Carus's possession and asked them whether they were willing to pay for them, in which case he could use them to assemble a book. The Meads, who were interested in having George Herbert's ideas published in book form, agreed to pay the amount requested. Finding himself in possession of copies of Carus's stenographic transcript (made by W. T. Lillie, a former University of Chicago business undergraduate, from Mead's winter 1928 course on advanced social psychology), Morris set out to compile and edit *Mind, Self, and Society*.

Editors sometimes take controlled liberties for the sake of readability. They may, for instance, advise changing the order of materials or even adding new materials that might contribute to a deeper understanding of the text. As a rule, however, such changes are agreed upon with the author, or if that is impossible, they are meticulously brought to the reader's attention as resulting from an editorial decision, whose rationale is then explained. Unfortunately, however, Morris failed to observe these basic rules of scholarship. This editorial failure, we will see, would have far-reaching consequences for the reception of Mead's ideas. A systematic comparison between *Mind, Self, and Society* and the copies of Carus's notes at the Mead Papers Archive at the University of Chicago reveals the extent of the creativity of Morris's editorial work. Significant materials were omitted. Mead's typically short sentences were rewritten into long-winded ones. And more than a fifth of the volume was taken from a 1930 set of student notes typed between six months and two years after they had been taken and possibly, as a result of this elapsed time, altered in their rewriting. To give an example, all of chapter 11 of *Mind, Self, and Society*, which Morris entitled "Meaning," is taken from this latter set of notes, albeit also rather freely assembled from different parts of them.

What is more, the chapter contains two contradictory accounts of the notion of "meaning," which the note taker warned Morris was something he (the note taker) could not attribute to Mead and might instead be a result of his own lack of clarity. Morris's distortions are magnified by the fact that once a "clean copy" of his edited version of the 1928 notes was finished, he never used the original again, as he decided to work instead from further retyping and the 1930 typed notes. This decision is, for instance, responsible for Morris's misidentification in the book's preface of the course as being from "1927."[10]

Another glaring example of Morris's editorial license, and one that would have momentous consequences for the interpretation of Mead, is the decision to introduce the label "social behaviorism" both in the title and in part 1 of *Mind, Self, and Society*. "Social behaviorism" is Morris's term, not Mead's. Mead never used this term to describe his ideas. Nevertheless, it became the standard depiction of Mead's strand of behaviorism as opposed to more positivistic, externalist types of behaviorism such as the one espoused by John Watson, Mead's colleague at the University of Chicago.[11] As we shall see in the next section, this editorial decision in particular had substantial theoretical consequences: it provided supporters of a more hermeneutically sensitive sociology, such as Herbert Blumer, with a seemingly authoritative argument against those who wished to read Mead in a different light (see, e.g., Blumer 1980).

The fact that *Mind, Self, and Society* has all the outward appearances of being a book and has been treated as such by generations of practitioners and students has conferred upon it an elusive air of finality, authenticity, textual authority, and authorial control. However, from the history of its production, it is clear the text is marked by a "radical instability."[12] This is a book that resulted from the assemblage of words uttered by Mead at different times, before different audiences, with different illocutionary forces, and one that is punctuated by the addition—or perhaps better, the intrusion—of yet more words from various external provenances: from the students, the stenographer, and the editor himself. Such plural "writing" turns the published text into an almost collective enterprise, and it explains both the murkiness surrounding the book's authorship and the inflections of the language in which it is written. Mead's control over the published text was none—in striking contrast to the editor's, whose license entirely justifies, but has rarely prompted, considerable skepticism about the received image of the book's author. The modern paradigm of single authorship is hardly applicable to this work, but it looms very large in the imaginations of those who have read *Mind, Self, and Society* (or who even just vaguely know of it). If the proper name on the cover of a text is normally taken to encapsulate an account of its origins and who may be responsible for it, such a straightforward attribution of meaning, intention, and responsibility must surely be suspended when it comes to *Mind, Self, and Society*.

It is not only that Mead delivered the different lectures from which the book was assembled with no understanding that they might be put together posthumously in the form of a book. He—who had always been so careful about what to publish, about whether to give his output to print—had no say in the decision to transform a peculiar material (*lecture notes*) into the volume that would make his reputation. This aspect is worth stressing, because within the modern authorial paradigm, not all kinds of speech are equated with authorship, and not all the author's discursive activity is considered to be an equally worthy subject of scholarly discussion. If anything, lecture notes, which today are commonly thought of as the raw material for (at best) textbooks, fare quite poorly on this "authorial" scale. There are reasons for this. For one, in Western culture—and academic culture in particular—the written word is privileged over the spoken word, as it is thought to allow for greater control, rigor, and reflexivity, as well as time for doubt and critical engagement on the part of readers. It does not, therefore, come as a surprise that Niklas Luhmann should associate the emergence of philosophy with that of writing: with "the formation of cities, cities for writing, and *writing* for *philosophy*" (1995, 354; our emphasis). Behind this association lies the idea that the externalization involved in writing invites greater reflexivity, eliciting the writer to turn back on his or her own previous ideation, question it, and take it apart; this is much less the case with the spoken word, whose immediacy precludes reflection. It is true that our civilization was shaped by a handful of canonic figures who wrote nothing and yet exercised great intellectual influence—chief among them is Socrates, whom many credit as the founder of Western philosophy. But it is also true that we know Socrates from written discourses featuring him as protagonist: the "Socratic dialogues," which became a subgenre in their own right in antiquity. This did not happen by accident. When detached from the immediate context that defines the spoken word by being fixed in writing, ideas gain an added life-span and a new capacity for circulation by virtue of becoming communal resources, constantly subject to de- and recontextualization, appropriation, and reappropriation by "an audience which extends in principle to anyone who can read" (Ricoeur 1981, 139). In other words, the written word has the benefit of becoming reading material as well.

*Mind, Self, and Society* embodies the paradoxes of a culture marked by moments of constructed crossover between the spoken and the written word. The text that would lead to Mead's canonization is a text that, like the ones in which Socrates is protagonist, testifies to the dialogical nature of thinking as put into play in a process of interaction, which is also one of immediately reciprocal orientation—this time not in the streets and households of Athens but in the modern university classroom. *Mind, Self, and Society* springs (with much questionable mediation, as we have seen) from words uttered in the classroom before mixed cohorts of graduate and undergraduate students—an apt context for rehearsing ideas in a more casual way (as Mead, who was known to suffer from writer's block, would probably have preferred) and for conveying them in a pedagogical style that typically combines simplified argumentation with rhetorical intention for the audience's persuasion. One possible way to conceive of the difference between teaching and writing is in terms of a distinction between intentional and reflexive thought. One would think the former less effective than the latter in communicating with the expert audience of the academic journal or academic monograph, under the guise of which *Mind, Self, and Society* would first circulate. After all, the stylistic qualities of "classical texts" are a decisive factor in their capacity to stand out, set themselves apart from the ordinary, and persuade. In an almost paradoxical yet intelligible way, the great appeal of *Mind, Self, and Society* seems to lie in its violation of contemporary academic writing conventions: it speaks to us in a fluid, almost conversational tone, which contrasts strikingly with the much denser style of Mead's written works and has survived Morris's long-winded insertions. This enhanced accessibility of the volume has contributed greatly to its wide reception, social transmission, and diffusion. What the work loses by not being grounded in a more systematic method of argumentation or responding to alternative arguments (thought about other authors' thoughts is almost absent), it gains in suppleness.[13] *Mind, Self, and Society* also seduces readers with its liveliness, its almost face-to-face quality, and the devices it deploys to embody abstract ideas in examples and therefore have a forceful impact on a less-specialized audience. Chief among these devices are reassuring repetition, almost pictorial illustration, and movement back and forth from the empirical to the historical-philosophical argument. For all its editorial flaws, *Mind, Self, and Society* has become a "vital" classic—a text that is continuously read and reflected on. And in assuming this quality, it is living proof that the reasons and processes that make a text a "classic" can be very different indeed.

## THE RECEPTION OF *MIND, SELF, AND SOCIETY*: THE CASE OF HERBERT BLUMER

While style matters, since "textuality" is also rhetorical performance, the fact remains that it is through the process of reception (Jauss 1970) that texts attain recognition and ultimately achieve their classic standing. Cultural resonance, textual suppleness, and reader appropriation (Baehr 2002, 125) are key contributing factors to the success of this process. That is, the text must be able to continue to "speak to" readers; it must invite their responses throughout time; it must not offer full closure but rather lend itself to profitable interpretation and reinterpretation in markedly different epochs, cultural milieus, and situations: it must be continuously appropriated by different readers, either with a view to integrate it positively into their own texts, theories, and research projects or in order to reopen controversy and distance themselves critically from it. In what follows, we will turn to a few especially relevant episodes in this process of the appropriation of *Mind, Self, and Society*—a process that was in no way smooth and cumulative.

In early 1931, when Mead fell seriously ill (he would die in April of that year), he realized the need to find someone to replace him in the instruction of his advanced social psychology course, the same course that would serve as the basis for *Mind, Self, and Society*. Mead's choice was the young sociologist Herbert Blumer, on whose dissertation committee he had served. Mead knew Blumer well. Blumer was a Chicago sociology graduate (he had done a PhD with Ellsworth Faris on the topic of method in social psychology) and had taken several of Mead's courses. This opportunity to succeed Mead in teaching his by now celebrated social psychology course seems to have been a consequential point in Blumer's definition of himself as a scholar of the human condition (Morrione 2004, 181).

And it would in retrospect prove to be the key stepping-stone to a long and influential career. In postwar American sociology, Blumer was one of the few sociological theorists who developed a consistent alternative to Talcott Parsons's structural functionalism.[14] That alternative was *symbolic interactionism*, a term coined by Blumer himself in the 1930s (Blumer 1937) that would, in due course, appropriate Mead as its "founding father." Later, in the 1960s, Blumer's *Symbolic Interactionism: Perspective and Method* (1969) became the standard theoretical and methodological presentation of the central tenets of this hermeneutically sensitive sociological approach.[5] Symbolic interactionism, according to Blumer, is premised upon three basic ideas: first, human beings act toward things on the basis of the meanings that those things have for them; second, the meaning of such things arises out of the social interaction between social actors; and third, these meanings are handled in and modified through an interpretative process (Blumer 1969, 2). Blumer then distinguishes a number of "root images" on which symbolic interactionism is grounded. First, there is the nature of human societies. Societies, according to symbolic interactionism, are made not of structures or abstract systems but of "people engaging in action" (7). Second, social interaction emerges from engagement between actors, not from external factors imputed to them. Mead's distinction between "the conversation of gestures" and "the use of significant symbols"—that is, between nonsymbolic and symbolic interaction—is presented as the inspiring source of this second root image of symbolic interactionism. Third, objects are defined as anything that can be indicated or referred to—that is, human social life is a process in which objects are being created, transformed, or cast aside (12). Fourth, human beings are conceived of as acting organisms. But contrary to the then prevailing Parsonian conception of human behavior as a response to a certain number of factors (income, education, etc.), symbolic interactionism suggests "a picture of the human being as an organism that interacts with itself through a process of making indications to himself" (14). Fifth, human action is understood as individuals fitting together their different lines of action through an interpretative process—hence "joint" or collective action. Sixth, responding to criticisms that Mead's work was inadequate to address macrosociological issues as raised, for instance, by Merton (1968), Blumer presents the notion of "interlinkage of action," the last "root image" of symbolic interactionism: at a more general level than joint action, Blumer points out, people's actions are organized at the level of the whole society in a way that is not to be reduced to external factors or subsumed into an overarching structure (1969, 17).

Blumer always emphasized the American roots of this approach, from classical American philosophical pragmatism (C. Tucker 1988; see also Shalin 1986) to the Chicago-style sociology in which he had been educated. The role played by Blumer's image of Mead in this narrative was pivotal. Mead's intentions, and especially Mead's social psychology as presented in *Mind, Self, and Society*, were systematically presented as a crucial legitimizing element of Blumer's version of symbolic interactionism: he quoted extensively from this text, presenting it as the chief intellectual reference of the Chicago school of sociology. Blumer went as far as presenting his theoretical proposals as if these represented Mead's opinions: for instance, he begins one of his most cited papers by stating that his "purpose is to depict the nature of human society when seen *from the point of view of* George Herbert Mead" (1966, 535; our emphasis). In this case, like many others, authorial legitimation follows the (more or less artificially construed) route of iteration.

Besides signaling the beginning of Blumer's long intellectual career,[16] the biographical circumstance that led him to see himself as Mead's "appointed successor" had an important consequence for his reading of *Mind, Self, and Society*. The fact that this book had been assembled from notes from the very same course that made him Mead's intellectual heir helps explain why Blumer never seriously addressed any of the many editorial issues that plague the book. He was more interested in controlling its interpretation, with a view to also governing a certain tradition of scientific inquiry, than in questioning what he (Blumer) was interpreting in the first place. In what surely is one of sociology's greatest ironies, Blumer, the creator of one of sociology's earlier and most accomplished social constructionist approaches,[17] failed to adequately address the constructed nature of his view of the discipline's past.[18] Instead, Blumer's account of his early Chicago days, despite contributing greatly to Mead's canonization, often amounted to little more than a self-serving mythology—a blind spot in his otherwise brilliant analysis that cost him greatly, for it did not pass unnoticed by his critics,[19] who were all too aware of the rhetorical spin Blumer put on the construction of the disciplinary controversies he was involved in (Mills 1942).

Blumer also reads Mead in two distinct senses. Besides interpreting Mead's words for social-scientific purposes, he creates (under the pretense of "discovering") another "Mead," the inspiring figure of symbolic interactionism. Blumer's double reading results, as almost without exception happens in the process of reception, from his own theoretical agenda and, more unusually, in this case from the particular biographical circumstances connecting him to Mead. Both of his prior conditionings lead to a problematic, unquestioning acceptance of the limitations of *Mind, Self, and Society* as the privileged entry point into Mead's thinking.

These limitations were first systematically exposed in the 1970s. Critics of Blumer, such as Clark McPhail and Cynthia Rexroat (1979), came to offer a new, more historically minded view of Mead's influence on symbolic interactionism. Drawing "primarily upon Mead's articles" and other writings by Mead himself instead of "student lecture notes, e.g., 1934 [i.e., *Mind, Self, and Society*]," McPhail and Rexroat were among the first to move beyond Morris's volume and seriously question Blumer's "Mead." In the wake of the historicist revival of the 1960s and 1970s, the next decades would witness a complete revolution in this regard, with the publication of various journal articles and academic monographs offering rigorous historical reconstructions of Mead's life and work. One of the central topics of this literature—the complex network of influences linking symbolic interactionism, American philosophical pragmatism, and the Chicago school of sociology—has only been subject to sound historical scrutiny from the 1970s onward.[20] Mead's actual influence on his colleagues of the sociology department, for instance, has been questioned, and in the process, the place Blumer reserved for Mead in the 1930s Chicago school of sociology has been exposed as a case of his own backward projection of Mead's later centrality in the tradition articulated by that school—symbolic interactionism.[21]

Still, Blumer's role in Mead's canonization should not be diminished. His use of Mead's ideas helped found and develop a consistent alternative to Parsons's structural functionalism, and by appropriating Mead to construct it, Blumer contributed actively to a redefinition of the sociological pantheon with the inclusion of his former teacher. Whereas Parsons can be said to have exerted a crucial influence in canonizing Weber and Durkheim through his 1937 *The Structure of Social Action*, as we shall see, it is due to Blumer's work that Mead started to earn a place in the canon as the founding father of symbolic interactionism. The cost of this "positioning" (Baert 2012) was a significant blurring of the purported founder's work by the discourse around it. Blumer's very selective appropriation of Mead's ideas, drawn overwhelmingly from a single textual source—*Mind, Self, and Society*—resulted in a limited appreciation of the range of Mead's contributions to contemporary social theory. But this effect can be seen more clearly when we follow the history of the reception of *Mind, Self, and Society* across the Atlantic to postwar Germany.

## *MIND, SELF, AND SOCIETY* IN GERMAN SOCIAL THEORY

The elevation of a text to "classic" status is highly dependent on its capacity to allow for multiple readings and adoptions in different contexts. *Mind, Self, and Society* illustrates this through its key role in attempts to bridge the traditional anglophone/continental divide. Although its first German translation dates from 1967,[22] copies of the original version were available in Germany well before, since 1945. This fact helps account for the second encounter between German idealism and American pragmatism. The first encounter took place in the second half of the nineteenth century with the reception in the United States of the idealism of Hegel, Humboldt, and Fichte and occurred chiefly through the "Metaphysical Club," a conversational club formed in 1872 in

Cambridge, Massachusetts, by Peirce, James, and others (Menand 2001). At least part of the second German-American encounter took the form of the reception of Mead's ideas in Germany.[23] The relevance of Mead's reception in postwar Germany stems from the fact that it was a German intellectual current—German idealism—that, along with Darwinism, made the strongest impact on the first generation of pragmatists. In this light, it is of added significance to examine how German social thinkers tried to reestablish—in completely different social and political conditions from those of America at the end of the nineteenth century—the intellectual connection between "their" sources of German idealism and American pragmatism.

The bridge was first re-created by Arnold Gehlen, a cultural conservative with ties to the Nazi regime. In the 1950 edition of his *Man: His Nature and Place in the World* (1940), Gehlen uses the naturalistic theory of action he finds in *Mind, Self, and Society* to overcome Cartesian body-soul dualism, a goal he shares with the American pragmatists.[24] Despite selectively overlooking the pragmatists' emphasis on democracy as a way of life and the thoroughly intersubjective character of Mead's theory, Gehlen's interpretation of Mead had the merit of putting *Mind, Self, and Society* on the reading lists of 1950s German philosophy students. One of these students, Karl-Otto Apel, would play a pivotal role in the history of the reception of this book in Germany, for it was Apel who, in Heidelberg in the early 1960s, introduced *Mind, Self, and Society* to his friend and colleague Jürgen Habermas (Habermas 1985, 76–77).

Together with Blumer, Habermas is one of the sociological theorists who has done the most to explore Mead's contributions to contemporary sociology. Again, like Blumer, Habermas appropriates Mead's ideas to build his own sociological theory, but from a new horizon of preoccupations and the critical tradition of which he is a part. Habermas, unlike Blumer, is a critical theorist who wishes to reconnect functionalism with symbolic interactionism in order to build a communicative theory of society (see also Joas 1993, 141).

By tracing the role played by *Mind, Self, and Society* in Habermas's interpretation of Mead at the beginning of the second volume of *The Theory of Communicative Action* ([1981] 1987)—Habermas's magnum opus and a crucial work in the process of Mead's canonization—one gains a clearer understanding of the somewhat hazardous history of this particular book and the theoretical implications of Morris's editorial work for sociology.

*The Theory of Communicative Action* revolves around a classic sociological theme, the societal shift toward modernity. According to Habermas, modernization entails a process of rationalization that is better captured if one distinguishes between the "system" component of societies (market economy and the state bureaucratic apparatus) and the "lifeworld" (culture, society, and personality). Each author Habermas discusses in the work is said to have made a significant contribution to the sociological understanding of this process of societal rationalization, from one perspective or another. For instance, Weber is credited with having created the tradition of the critique of rationalization, a tradition later developed by Lukács and the Frankfurt school. This Marxist tradition equated the rationalization of society with the reification of consciousness. As a result, this conceptual strategy is, for Habermas, marred with paradoxes, or "aporias," of the paradigm of consciousness that impose the need for a paradigm change. The first contribution toward this paradigm change comes, in Habermas's view, from "Mead with his communication-theoretic foundation of sociology" (1987, 1); the second, complementary contribution (as we have seen in the previous chapter) is Durkheim's theory of religion. Thus, with a stroke of the pen, Mead is placed not in a second tier but right alongside the original triumvirate of sociological greats. "Mead and Durkheim belong, like Weber," Habermas writes at the opening page of volume 2, "to the generation of the founding fathers of modern sociology" (1).

Because in *The Theory of Communicative Action* Habermas's Mead is for the most part the author of *Mind, Self, and Society*, it is through this text that Mead's canonization as one of the discipline's greats continues to take place. Habermas's interpretation of Mead's social psychology in part 5, volume 2 of *The Theory of Communicative Action* is arguably one of the most detailed and competent readings ever produced on that aspect of Mead's theorizing. In little more than one hundred pages, Habermas scrutinizes all major aspects of Mead's social psychology; confronts it with the theories of several other authors, including Wittgenstein and Durkheim; compares his interpretation of Mead with that of others (such as Tugendhat's); and draws important lessons for contemporary social theory. Yet Habermas's interpretation of Mead is severely limited by two different problems.

The first is related to Habermas's misunderstanding of the authorial status of *Mind, Self, and Society*. Habermas reads this text as if there were an author with absolute authorial control over it, that author being, of course, George Herbert Mead: "Mead presented his theory under the rubric of 'social behaviorism' *because he wanted* to stress the note of criticism of consciousness" (Habermas 1987, 4; our emphasis); "*Self* and *society* are the titles under which Mead treats the complementary construction of the subjective and social worlds" (25; his emphasis); "Mead was fully aware, however, that in going from the individual to society, [*Marked in the text by the break between parts 3 and 4 of MSS.*] he would have to take up once again the phylogenetic viewpoint that he had already adopted in explaining symbolically mediated interaction" (43; our emphasis). These passages suffice to illustrate the point we are making: Habermas draws a number of conclusions from portions of *Mind, Self, and Society* that he takes as representing Mead's ideas, whereas they exclusively reflect Morris's editorial decisions or insertions (decisions that we can sometimes safely say are at odds with Mead's original intention). This problem is aggravated by a second but entirely connected one: the centrality Habermas concedes to *Mind, Self, and Society* in his interpretation of Mead's work. Despite being aware of the posthumous nature of this text and the existence of other published writings by Mead on topics that interested him, Habermas resorts overwhelmingly to this text at the expense of Mead's own writings: of the sixty-three citations of Mead in *The Theory of Communicative Action*, fifty-two come from *Mind, Self, and Society*. There is also the question of Habermas's peculiar interpretative framework and the ways it leads him to overlook aspects of Mead's thought that could prove very useful in dealing with Habermas's preoccupations. Habermas reads Mead, as well as all other sociological classics, from the perspective of his distinction between "system" and "lifeworld." From the imposition of this dual interpretative framework results a limited (and rather predictably one-sided) appreciation of Mead's thinking. Mead is credited with having cleared the way for a communicative conception of rationality essential for the analysis of the process of rationalization of the lifeworld, but the ability of Mead's communicative social theory to account for the reproduction of society as a whole is readily dismissed. This is how Habermas arrives at his "second, more radical reservation" concerning Mead's theory of society: its allegedly hopeless *idealistic* character, deemed unable to address issues related to the "material reproduction of society" such as economics, warfare, and politics (1987, 110). Hence he sees the need to complement Mead's communicative social theory, which is useful for the study of the "lifeworld" (namely, its "personality" component), with a functionalist analysis, which in Habermas's structurally bipartite view is the only realistic theoretical approach to the "system" dimension of modern societies.

Mead's alleged idealism, however, is as much a consequence of Habermas's peculiar interpretative framework as it is of the undue prominence of *Mind, Self, and Society* in the reception of Mead's ideas. The theoretical fruitfulness of Habermas's analytical lens is accompanied by a conceptual rigidity that precludes the degree of historical learning that other, less categorical frameworks would allow for. Habermas appropriates Mead through his distinction between "system" and "lifeworld," a binary framework that opposes instrumental versus communicative types of rationality and action.

In such a scheme, the theoretical space for other types of action, or for an overarching conception of action such as the one proposed by Joas (drawing on the pragmatism of Peirce, Dewey, and Mead), is very limited. In addition, Habermas has a peculiar strategy of theory construction: he constructs opposing poles of theoretical positions, selects certain elements from each pole, highlights their complementarity, and then reassembles them into a new, synthetic theoretical proposal. Such an instrumental reading of the past has inevitable costs: he learns considerably less from those of the past than he would if he read them more in their own terms. Also as a result of this strategy, Habermas's ability to question his beliefs and theoretical presuppositions by confronting himself with them diminishes. No less impoverishing is the imposition of external, artificial categories upon the work of past authors. Mead is reckoned an idealist only insofar as he is assessed according to Habermas's theoretical benchmark. Once Mead is recontextualized in the progressive era of American philosophical pragmatism, one realizes there is no systematic neglect of materialist issues on Mead's part: besides the philosophy of science and social psychology, Mead is responsible for a systematic treatment of moral and political issues underpinned by questions of war, urbanization, and international relations, among others (see, e.g., Silva 2008). But to appreciate this, one needs to take into account the entire corpus of Mead's writings and not limit oneself to *Mind, Self, and Society*.

The early history of *Mind, Self, and Society* helps put into perspective Habermas's reading of Mead as an idealist thinker. As Peter Baehr rightly observes, whenever a founding is invoked, a legitimation claim is never far behind (2002, 5–39). *Mind, Self, and Society* was from the start constructed as the crib of Blumer's symbolic interactionist program, whose main focus is interpersonal intimacy—a theme not central to Mead's original analysis.[25] Just as Blumer used Mead's authority to sanction his research agenda, so did he turn to Mead when he wanted to confront the dominant functionalist approaches as to the best ways to study society. The methodological focus of symbolic interactionism on qualitative, ethnographic case study research was erected upon a theoretical perspective that stressed the importance of a symbolic understanding of social action and was polemically contrasted with the quantitative, survey-based sociology emerging on the East Coast that became dominant after 1945.[26] In other words, Blumer placed *Mind, Self, and Society* right at the center of a key disciplinary controversy between symbolic interactionists and functionalists. By anchoring his methodological insights on Mead's analysis in *Mind, Self, and Society*, Blumer found an original source of legitimation for his approach vis-à-vis the dominant functionalism of the time. But while Blumer and his followers were thereby keeping Mead alive, they were also rendering him suspect in the eyes of mainstream sociology, which, from the 1930s onward, was dominated by a structural functionalist type of analysis.[27] It is no surprise then that the mainstream turned to Europe in search of its founding fathers: Marx, Weber, and Durkheim (e.g., Mills 1959). It was only after the mid-1960s—a decade of social upheaval, generational conflict, and culture wars—that symbolic interactionism gained a reinvigorated cultural resonance and a new generation of practitioners began to question the nature and limits of the existing sociological canon. As a result, Mead's name gradually made it into social theory textbooks and sociological treatises (e.g., Coser 1971). That this canonization occurred mainly through *Mind, Self, and Society*, which was so instrumental to Blumer in his controversy against the functionalists, helps explain Habermas's depiction of Mead as an idealist. But Habermas's inability to go beyond this previously construed cleavage attests to the limitations of his sources and theoretical strategy.

CONCLUSION

While Blumer and Habermas were pivotal in construing Mead's work as a sociological classic, the current generation of Mead scholars has attempted to strike a balance between historical rigor and theoretical creativity. Much like the "new Durkheim studies" of the 1970s, the protagonists of the "new Mead studies"—first Hans Joas (1985) and Gary Alan Cook (1993) and more recently Filipe Carreira da Silva (2008), Daniel Huebner (2014), and Jean-François Côté (2015)—have all resorted to intensive archival research in order to circumnavigate the poor editorial fate of Mead's oeuvre. As we write, there is still no complete critical edition of Mead's writings, nor is there any plan to publish one. This regrettable situation, however, has not prevented the recent "Mead renaissance" in sociology and other social and human sciences, most notably in history, psychology, and philosophy (e.g., Joas and Huebner 2016). Even in the natural sciences, we find evidence of this revival of interest in Mead's ideas. For instance, cultural neuroscience (the study of how culture and environments shape our brains and our perceptions of ourselves) has turned to Mead's pioneering theory of the social self for inspiration. This renaissance has taken place not because of but despite *Mind, Self, and Society*, which continues to obfuscate the true scope of his contributions. In fact, if one continues to rely on *Mind, Self, and Society*, Mead's renaissance of late will be short lived and do no justice to the actual extent of his contributions.

Paradoxically, the new edition of *Mind, Self, and Society* has only made things worse. Published by the University of Chicago Press and annotated by Joas and Huebner (Mead 2015), it is presented as the work's "definitive edition." Instead, this revised reissue of Morris's volume provides the definitive demonstration of the radical instability that characterizes *Mind, Self, and Society*. The editors opted to reissue a "slightly revised" version of the text originally edited by Morris in the 1930s, dropping the original subtitle (*From the Standpoint of a Social Behaviorist*), correcting obvious typographical errors, and completing the bibliographic references (Joas 2015, ix–x). This editorial option is justified by the argument that "no collection of Mead's articles . . . can replace the synthesis of his thinking that we find in the text of *Mind, Self, and Society*." Such a claim is obviously unwarranted, first of all, because it reifies rather than questions the long-held misapprehension that Mead's thinking can be "synthesized" through one of his undergraduate courses, designed with obvious didactic purposes and covering only a tiny segment of his social theory. More serious than taking the part for the whole, however, is ignoring the fabricated nature of the text.

As we have seen, the text of *Mind, Self, and Society* has no discernible relationship with George Herbert Mead apart from the fact that it originates from his lectures. Mead exerted no control over its editing or publishing. He expressed no wish to have his lectures published posthumously. This is understandable, as Mead regularly published the results of his work in a variety of outlets, from academic journals to collected volumes. This rather extensive and varied corpus of writings is what one should read if one wishes to gain access to his thinking (e.g., Mead 2011). Commentators today resort to *Mind, Self, and Society* to illustrate minor points only (e.g., Shalin 2011; Côté 2015). In the absence of an unequivocal relationship between text and author, to rely on *Mind, Self, and Society* as an access point to Mead's thinking—however revised and annotated that edition may be—remains fundamentally problematic. Actually, the more thorough the critical edition of the text, the more evident its problematic character as an entry point to Mead's ideas becomes.

The 2015 University of Chicago Press edition includes an impressive one-hundred-page appendix resulting from Huebner's exhaustive archival research on the historical circumstances involving the creation of *Mind, Self, and Society* in the early 1930s (Huebner 2012, 2014). Details such as the identity of W. T. Lillie—the stenographer who took the notes that would ultimately form the bulk of *Mind, Self, and Society*—have finally been revealed (Huebner 2012, 144n29), as well as answers to fundamental questions such as the extent to which Mead was directly engaged in conducting experiments, calibrating mechanical apparatuses, and dissecting neurological specimens (Huebner 2014, 40ff.). Huebner's meticulous historical research is at its best when applied to the origins of *Mind, Self, and Society*. The appendix provides a comprehensive, chapter-by-chapter analysis of the original sources used by Morris as well as the passages that he eventually selected for deletion. Proving that paratexts sometimes perform unintended functions, Huebner's systematic reconstruction of the sources of *Mind, Self, and Society* ultimately results in a methodical deconstruction of the text's legitimacy as an introduction to Mead's theorizing. As Huebner correctly emphasizes, his research has exposed a rather complex social process resulting from a "particular temporal sequence of actions that were given direction (or changed direction) at identifiable moments because someone found or read particular texts" (137). Despite bearing the name "George Herbert Mead" on its cover, *Mind, Self, and Society* emerges from Huebner's research as a fabrication, "the work of different individuals who created physical materials for disparate purposes within their own social situations" (136).

*Mind, Self, and Society* is, in other words, the ultimate example of a classic with no author. It derives its legitimacy from its ex post facto association with "Mead, the sociological classic." The latter, in turn, is largely a by-product of the sociophysical assemblage that goes by the name of *Mind, Self, and Society*, whose conversational and accessible style has ensured its continued position as a vital classic in the field. What the text does not provide, as its latest incarnation definitively shows, is access to Mead's theorizing. This he developed over several decades, motivated by a fundamental commitment to experimental science and democratic politics, and articulated in more than one hundred scholarly publications as well as in numerous reports, public talks, newspaper articles, and lectures. But if the history of *Mind, Self, and Society* shows it needs to be ruled out as a valid access point to its putative author's ideas, by the same token it offers us an important admonition against any simplistic understanding of the relationship between founding fathers and classic texts one might still entertain. If anything, it helps us realize that the link between text and author is all but evident, let alone unambiguous.

CHAPTER 3

## THE DIALECTIC OF DISSENT

Marx's *1844 Economic and Philosophic Manuscripts*

Karl Marx was only twenty-six years old when he wrote the *1844 Economic and Philosophic Manuscripts* in Paris. First published in 1927 under the title "Preparatory Materials for *The Holy Family*" in Moscow, it was only in 1932 that they were published in German for the first time in two simultaneous editions: the MEGA (*Marx-Engels-Gesamtausgabe*) I edition and the Landshut-Mayer edition. In 1956, the *1844 Manuscripts* were first translated into English, and soon afterward, in 1962, a French translation was released. The textual source of the "existentialist" young Marx, the *1844 Manuscripts* would ignite a dialectic of dissent among nonorthodox left-wing circles in academia and beyond until the fall of the Berlin wall in 1989.

### INTRODUCTION

Of all of Marx's works, none is as surrounded by mystery and controversy as the *Economic and Philosophic Manuscripts of 1844* (hereafter *1844 Manuscripts*). Their late, politically charged discovery, their content, and their form—their original form but also the forms emerging from their printed versions—have combined to elevate a work of complex and inconclusive meaning to quasi-mythical status. It is often not a myth's narrative content but its capacity for symbolic condensation and intensification that gives it its unique mythical quality. So it has been with the *1844 Manuscripts*. From the mid-1950s onward, they were given shape and significance by being made into *the* work of the young and untamed philosophical Marx and into the locus of his theory of human alienation and the promise of our redemption from it. Read in this way, the *1844 Manuscripts* were meant to create the perceptual order from which sense could be made of our wretched condition and the seeming discord in Marx's opus.

There is hardly a better illustration of the excitement and turmoil the *1844 Manuscripts* generated than Marshall Berman's vivid firsthand account in *Adventures in Marxism* (1999). The year 1956—a year that began with the sensational news of Nikita Khrushchev's speech denouncing Stalin's crimes and ended with the Suez Crisis and the Hungarian uprising against the Soviet Union—saw the first English translation of the *1844 Manuscripts* by Martin Milligan for the Foreign Languages Publishing House in Moscow, an edition released three years later in London by Lawrence and Wishart.[1] The translation sent shock waves across the Atlantic, helping energize the "New Left" in the United States (see, e.g., Mills 1959; Jacobs and Landau 1966). Its publication coincided with the emergence of this intellectual movement and provided an invaluable resource in the movement's attempt to separate the "authentic" socialist tradition from Stalinism. Berman recounts how in 1959, as an undergraduate at Columbia University, he was told about this "wild" book, offering "an alternative vision of how man should live," which Marx had written "before he became Karl Marx" (Berman 1999. 6).

The book, Berman was told, had been deliberately "kept secret for a century." But it had now finally emerged. Any aspiring young Marxist had to read it. Rites of passage are often not painless, however. Hence, handily, the text was not readily available. The Columbia bookstore—"the fools"— did not have it. One had to find one's way to the secret book. Berman would eventually find his copy. Striding south on Broadway to Greenwich Village, he headed to the Four Continents Book Corp., a Fifth Avenue bookstore that acted as the official distributor of Soviet publications, but not without wondering whether the USSR, which sent its tanks to Budapest the same year the English translation was released, would be willfully distributing the book if it were really as dangerous as it promised. As Berman would soon learn, he was not the first to make this pilgrimage. The staff knew exactly what he wanted. To their surprise, the cryptic little book had become one of their best sellers. Berman was unfazed by their lack of enthusiasm. There he was before the object of his desire. He describes the somewhat strange composite text in detail: "a collection of three youthful books, divided into short essays," whose titles "appeared to be provided by twentieth-century editors in Moscow and Berlin." The text was not intact, therefore, but the book itself made for a quite handy and intimate cult object: "midnight blue, nice and compact, a perfect fit for a side pocket in a 1950s sport jacket." As he leafed through the book in the bookstore, he entered a quasi-religious ecstasy: "Suddenly I was in a sweat, melting, shedding clothes and tears, flashing hot and cold" (Berman 1999, 7). At the register, it seemed almost sacrilegious that such a precious, world-changing thing should cost only fifty cents. Berman bought twenty copies, barely able to contain his excitement over going out and spreading the word "that would both rip up [people's] lives and make them happy" (9).

Berman's account of his discovery of the manuscripts is personal but not unique. It speaks of the experience of many on the left in the postwar generation. Neither is his explicit description of the book as a "Kabbalah" to be dismissed as a rhetorical tic by default (Leopold 2007, 6–7). The surfacing of the *1844 Manuscripts* in book form after more than a century of oblivion felt to many like a miracle. Here was a text delivering Marx's thought before its many distortions under Engels, the banner of Marxism and Marxism-Leninism. It provided the missing link in Marx's philosophy. It presented the principled ground of his critique of political economy. It spelled out the onto-ethical integrating logos of Marx's entire project. If there was a text capturing the essence of Marx, this was it. To these people, the *1844 Manuscripts*, offered the long-lost key to his thought and required corresponding veneration.

#### WHAT IS THERE IN A NOTEBOOK?

On the face of things, however, the *1844 Manuscripts* would seem an unlikely candidate for the task at hand. It is true that their reputation would lead one to believe that the *1844 Manuscripts* had always existed as such—that is, as the almost finalized draft of a paradigm-changing book, with a working title, a preestablished arrangement of parts, and a full-fledged argument running throughout. But to treat them as such is only to perpetuate the myth of the printed edition as a neutral medium: transparent and value-free; reproducing, rather than intervening in, the original; and preparatory to, rather than already effecting, textual criticism.

Yet the complex history behind the editing, translation, and publication of the *1844 Manuscripts* shows exactly the opposite.[2] They are a case in point of editing as an interpretation and as an act of creation. They show how various editorial choices can result in the construction of different texts seemingly cut from the same materials. Given how assorted and disjointed these manuscript materials are, much hinged on creating a whole out of the parts and on designing the whole with a particular sense of direction. This implied active editorial mediation between authorial intention and all the available documentary evidence, notably the diverse materials composing the "manuscripts" themselves, for what Marx had left was not a typical "manuscript."

Rather, it was a very different kind of object, and a curious one at that—a handcrafted assemblage of notebooks with an uncommon physical design and anything but an air of finality to them. Fragmentary in nature, the notebooks stubbornly resisted easy interpretation. Their interrelation was not immediately apparent. They broke off at crucial junctures. The handwriting was hard to read, and some of the passages were corrupted or missing. The heavily stylized writing, jammed with complex philosophical concepts (alienation, objectification, species-being, essence, self-realization, to cite but a few), resulted at times in cryptic passages. In sum, the manuscripts presented themselves as a riddle for the editor to work with and work out.

To some extent, these manuscripts were not uncommon. When Marx died, he left behind a trail of assorted writings—some meant for publication, some not—including incomplete manuscripts, rough drafts, and a vast number of notebooks. The nature of the notebooks varies considerably. A few comprise little more than a list of items—addresses, titles of books, and ideas. Most, however, bring together extracts from books Marx read, including some in his own collection. In the latter, literal transcriptions often give way to summaries and syntheses permeated by comments and reflections. On occasion, these sit alongside theses and plans and build up to what begins to look like a rough draft. Such are the *1844 Manuscripts*.

Despite their plurality of form, it would seem easy to dismiss most notebooks as mere copybooks of quotations. Even leading experts on Marx have done so at some point.[3] But Michel Foucault is right to warn us against ready dismissal. These assemblages are "works on the self," Foucault admonishes, and "not imposed on the individual" (1983, 243). By this, he means that they are the product of a mind at work, not a passive mind. To copy suggests passivity in the form of imitation or reproduction of an original. Yet when Foucault stresses the process of self-construction going on here, he highlights the fact that copybooks are things authored by the copier rather than by the writer of what is being excerpted. Such books are, therefore, nonaccidental products of agency. They reflect judgment and a series of choices: of what is worthy of attention, of how the part being lifted is to be sorted out under new thematic headings or grouped together with other parts so that it all makes sense (again), and of the intention with which all this lifting and reorganizing is done. Moreover, in note making—as opposed to mere note-taking—literal copying often coexists with paraphrasing and summarizing, both of which already embed the copier's thoughts. As such, notebooks frequently offer a unique insight into processes of thinking of which there would be little evidence otherwise. These include issues such as the problems that the copier thought needed addressing and his work method, notably his choice and use of sources. On their own, or when juxtaposed with more finished work of the same period, notebooks can reveal how the author read his sources and whether and how these shaped his thinking—what avenues of inquiry they opened and to what extent these were pursued and had an impact on the pursuit of his own arguments. When notes are punctuated by reflections and critical comments, they allow direct access to an author's evolving thoughts and the processes whereby they are taking shape. Some notebooks, especially those including theses and plans, can also disclose the broader intent and direction of an author's project or research program. All of this is *thought-in-process* that can be extracted from examining notebooks.[4] And it is also far more than one would have expected to extract from a humble assemblage of citations.

Although their use was commonplace in Marx's time, not all celebrated authors used notebooks or made them integral to their work processes. But this was certainly not the case with Marx. An avid reader, he made note making, excerpting, and synthesizing part and parcel of his theorizing. For Marx, thinking through problems was as much a cognitive affair requiring concentration and a sense of purpose as it was a sensuous activity involving the paper leaf as its privileged form of material support. The care he took in preserving his notes shows that he deemed them valuable and not meant for mere contingent purposes. For sure, he used the notebooks for a common mnemonic purpose. Marx would return to them to be reminded of arguments he read and even to quote from them rather than the originals. But his notes did more than store information for future usage. Crucially, they were used to articulate thought. Marx's methods of note making, the way he grouped and arranged his notes, therefore expressed as well as shaped his modes of thought and argument. Therein lies their special significance.

In light of Marx's work process, one of the surprising aspects of his scholarship is how late scholars came to engage with his notebooks and how little attention was paid to their form. If true in general, the surprise is even greater when considering the 1844 *Manuscripts*, given the politically charged wars of interpretation in which they have been used as the primary weapon. They mix excerpts, syntheses, critical commentaries, and theses much in the manner of other notebooks Marx produced in Paris at the time. But here such mixing takes on a particular form, not unprecedented, that, for the most part, was lost or transfigured in publication. Yet to a large extent, the manuscripts are the product of their form—that is, their unconventional original physical form and the reinvention of this form in printed versions.

## A WORK OF CRAFTSMANSHIP

To explore this claim, we will need to examine the physical form of the manuscripts in detail. We will start with the manuscripts in their prepublished form. But before we provide a description, a broader categorization is in order. As originally put together by Marx, the manuscripts are a work of craftsmanship. To explain what we mean by this, let us recall Marx's own words in the *Grundrisse*. There, Marx defines craftsmanship as a "form-giving activity," enabling the development of the self and social relations (1973, 301). That this form is always already meaning-bearing is a necessary implication of the fact that "labor is purposeful activity" (311). Indeed, for Marx, labor is a process of objectification in which man gives form to objects such that his intentions and purposes are realized, and in doing so, he also forms himself. It is, therefore, in the object of his labor that man becomes an object "for himself." This also means that man cannot gain self-consciousness except through his externalization in matter that has been worked upon.

To this reciprocal determination of human subject and material object, Marx gives the name *praxis*. Praxis presupposes an internal constitutive relation between the related parts—human subject and material object—rather than a mere external relation, or a relationship of influence, in which the parts remain essentially separate or independent. Sensory experience is an integral part of praxis as a process of mediated self-determination insofar as the sensuous experience is the medium in which human subject and material object meet and determine each other.

Marx's contention that self-consciousness is always dependent on some external object on which man impresses the form of his being and in which he perceives himself as an object offers a window onto the process at work in the composition of the manuscripts. They show that physical making or, in other words, craftwork was an integral part of Marx's thinking: of how he came to understand the thoughts of others, draw ultimate conclusions and realize inherent contradictions, and articulate his own thoughts, ideally beyond those of others.[5] In the manuscripts, Marx's thought, therefore, acquires a visible, almost tactile quality, which gets lost in the printed versions.[6] The curious physical form of the manuscripts is the artifact of an often messy, often clairvoyant, intellectual workshop, in which Marx left room for learning and experimentation. This is also a workshop in which subject and textual object, meaning and form, are in the process of being created and re-created through an ongoing mutually constitutive relationship. Any rigid division between the artisan who labors and the nobleman who thinks—any estrangement of mental from physical labor, substantive content and physical form—has no place behind its doors.[7]

Therefore, it is to be expected that a few interpreters would be tempted to take a look inside. This has most clearly been the case with the late Margaret Fay (1944–1979), a PhD student at Berkeley who from the late 1960s took a keen interest in Marx's *1844 Manuscripts* after reading Herbert Marcuse's *One-Dimensional Man*.

Overwhelmed by the burgeoning literature on the text—the *1844 Manuscripts* were rapidly becoming a sort of "sacred text" for the revisionist, humanist New Left—Fay decided to travel to the International Institute of Social History in Amsterdam to see the object of such polemics and exegetical wars firsthand. There she experienced the strangeness of the manuscripts' original material form. In particular, "the eccentric pagination, the page division and other physical aspects" engaged her intellectual curiosity and gave her "the idea of approaching Marx's text by exploring these unknown features" (Fay 1983, 130). As she explored this approach to understanding the text, Fay became convinced that "any interpretation of Marx's text must take into account these aspects" (131). Yet her work on the meaning-bearing form of the manuscripts was plagued by continuous self-doubt, and her partial conclusions would only be released posthumously. As with Marx's other manuscripts, it would be a long time before other Marx scholars engaged directly with them.

To some extent, Fay's self-doubt was justified. Making inferences about what the author meant and why he did what he did from the incomplete and ambiguous evidence the physical form provides is fraught with difficulty. Fay's ambitious plan, however, was to enter "the controversy over the origins, method and structure of Marx's 1844 theory of alienation" (1983, 136)—the chief controversy surrounding the manuscripts—from this unexplored position. This led her to engage closely with the physical evidence of the first notebook, where the theory is presented. But the challenge was immediately apparent. The notebook presents itself as having been designed by Marx almost like a maze—not very clear or easy to navigate by the modern user. Here is Fay's description:

> It consists of nine double sheets (36 pages), folded in two and sewn together in the middle with a rough thread. The folded edge, which is sewn into the spine, forms the top of each page, so that the pages of this notebook "flip" over, in contrast to most books today with "turn-over" pages, the sides of which are sewn into the spine. The first nine pages of the notebooks are unnumbered and seven of them are blank. On the first (the outermost) page is written *Heft I* (Notebook I); the reverse side is blank. The third page carries a list of 29 bibliographical items, which was clearly a later addition since the date of publication which Marx gives for the first item is 1845. The last 27 pages of the notebook are all written on and carry a Roman numeral in the left-hand corner of the edge sewn into the spine. The written text follows the numbered sequences, but the numbered sequence is not the physical sequence which we find as we turn the pages of the notebook. The pagination of Marx's manuscript can only be explained on the assumption that it originally existed as two self-contained notebooks: the four center double-folio sheets containing pages I through XVI, which we will term the core notebook, and the five outer sheets, which contain the unnumbered pages, and the pages numbered XVII through XXVII. (1983, 136–37)

In the relationship between what she designated the "core notebook" and "outer sheets," Fay found the key to her reinterpretation of the manuscripts. Marx's theory of alienation, she claimed, resulted from his critical engagement not with Hegel, as had been traditionally understood, but with Adam Smith.[8] This, she argued, was clear from the physical evidence of the text. The most striking feature of the core notebook is the division of each page into three columns, each with a different heading ("Arbeitslohn," "Profit des Kapitals," and "Grundrente," respectively). The headings as well as the content of the columns, Fay maintained, were "taken directly from Adam Smith's analysis in *The Wealth of Nations* of the threefold division of the exchange value of commodity" (1983, 133). In turn, in the first of the outer sheets, Fay saw the beginnings of Marx's theory of alienation in an examination of the alienation of land (p. XVII in the original), rather than, as had been commonly believed, in the analysis of the alienation of labor that follows (p. XXII). She insisted that in the physical layout of the text, but also logically, Marx's theory of alienation followed from his engagement with Smith. Contrary to what had been argued, any change between parts did not indicate a break in the argument or a change in direction on Marx's part. It was rather the case that Marx was moving to a different way of presenting his argument—namely, from a method of inquiry to a method of presentation.[9] Linking both parts, Fay concluded, is Marx's dialectical method, in both its negative (i.e., critical) and positive (i.e., reconstructive) aspects. The negative aspect consists in an immanent critique whose object is not reality itself but the attempt to understand it—namely, in Marx's case, classical political economy and, in particular, Adam Smith. Its purpose is to disclose the internal contradictions in the founding work—namely, by physically juxtaposing contradictory passages across the columns—so that it becomes possible to move from the recognition of these contradictions to their supersession. This involved the development of Marx's own analytical concepts—notably, alienation—and interpretative framework and opened up the possibility of a reconstruction of reality.

After decades of neglect, Fay's main interpretative claim—Marx's indebtedness to Smith on alienation—has come under fire (Tribe 2015, 51–54). But her work on the construction of the manuscripts and its relevance for our understanding of what Marx was doing—namely, coming to grips with classical political economy and creating its immanent critique—was pioneering and deeply innovative. Like no other work before hers, it brought attention to how successive selective philological interventions (deletions, changes in form, additions of headings, etc.) leave a lingering imprint on the manuscripts, thus shaping their transmission and reception in intervening decades. The different printed editions of the manuscripts, Fay claimed, generate a marked disfigurement from which the manuscripts and their interpretation have never recovered.

## THE STRANGE LATE BIRTH OF A "BOOK"

Marx would not live to see the publication of the manuscripts. In effect, he most certainly did not want to see them published as he left them. Marx saw what was perhaps a more than usual difference between the draft and the finished work. As the locus of Marx's self-development—of his first foray into classical political economy—it is not even clear that he saw the manuscripts as a draft as such. Had he been confronted with the object produced by his labor after its printing in book form, Marx may well have been opposed to it as an alien being, a power independent of its producer and his intentions, that had now acquired a life of its own.

A prolific writer, Marx published very few books during his lifetime. Volume 1 of *Das Kapital* was a rare but important exception. Upon his death in 1883, many of Marx's manuscripts, notes, and correspondence lay unpublished. Among these sat the now famous *1844 Manuscripts*. Although there is reason to believe that the manuscripts were the object of the contract Marx signed in 1845 with Carl Leske, a publisher in Darmstadt, for the publication of a work entitled "A Critique of Politics and of Political Economy," the work never went to print. Fear of revolutionary associations seems to have led the publisher to cancel the contract in September 1846. Unlike other early writings, however, the *1844 Manuscripts* not only lay unpublished; they were also veiled in obscurity. Their existence was unknown, and their discovery was all the more significant for this. Their publication came rather late, however. It was only in 1932, nearly a century after their original composition, that the manuscripts were first published in full. The first complete English translation had to wait another twenty-four years.

What happened between speaks volumes about the intriguing life of manuscripts and the hopes and hazards of their discovery and publication. Marx's literary executor was Friedrich Engels, who kept Marx's papers after his death. Upon Engels's death in 1898, the papers were entrusted to Marx's daughter, Laura Lafargue, who inherited Engels's estate. Convinced that they had exhausted their contribution to the socialist cause, Laura and her husband, Paul Lafargue, committed suicide in 1911. As a result, Marx's papers were put in the care of the German Social Democratic Party (SPD) archives in Berlin. In 1938, they were sold to a Dutch insurance company, which made them available to the Amsterdam-based International Institute of Social History (IISH), where, for the most part, they remain.

That the manuscripts found themselves deposited there ensured their physical preservation but not necessarily their publication and circulation to a wider public. In fact, the publication of Marx's corpus was always a precarious business. The first failed attempts to publish it took place in Marx's own lifetime, first by the hand of Herman Becker in 1851 and then courtesy of Engels and O. Meissner, the publisher of *Das Kapital*, in 1867. Other attempts followed Marx's death, but they faced opposition from Engels, who harbored hopes of directing a joint edition of his and Marx's collected works. In all these projects, however, the editorial line was the same. It was also pursued years later in the Mehring's 1902 edition, the line stipulating the reissue of previously published works that were now out of circulation. As for the unpublished works, they remained relegated to marginal status and were excluded from any such editorial efforts. It is true that between Engels's death and World War I, part of Marx's and Engels's unpublished work would eventually be sent to print. But the resonance of these initiatives was small. It was not until the Russian Revolution of 1917 that the idea of pursuing a complete edition of their works gained momentum.

The year 1917 proved a decisive turning point in the fate of Marx's corpus. Up to that point, German Social Democrat Karl Kautsky had been unchallenged as the legitimate executor of Marx's and Engels's legacy. But with the growing divide between reformist and revolutionary socialists (Labedz 1962, 18–19), his role came to be contested. The Bolshevik regime needed to bolster its ideological position by constructing itself as *the* representative of orthodox Marxism and by constructing the latter as being at odds with social democracy. Control over the publication and interpretation of Marx's legacy was one of the main means to this end. Hence the regime hurried to place Marx's legacy in new and safer hands. David Riazanov, a historian and a veteran Bolshevik revolutionary, was the man chosen for the job. Riazanov's scholarly credentials were indisputable. Prior to the revolution, while in exile in Germany, he had carried out meticulous research for the German Social Democrats into the history of Marxism (Leckey 1995). The quality of his work elicited an invitation to direct an edition of Marx's writings between 1852 and 1862, which eventually came out in two volumes in 1914. But the Bolshevik Revolution prompted Riazanov's return to Russia, where he joined the Bolsheviks and resumed a more active political role. On Lenin's invitation, he became the founder and director of the Marx-Engels Institute in Moscow. There he took over from Kautsky as the world's leading expert on the Marx-Engels corpus and as Marx's literary executor. In this role, he set up strategic collaborations, notably with the Institute for Social Research in Frankfurt, in order to collect the materials necessary for the first historical-critical edition of the collected works of Marx and Engels.

The editorial plan for this edition, the *Marx-Engels-Gesamtausgabe* (MEGA)—also known as the first MEGA—comprised forty-two volumes divided into four parts or sections. The first section, consisting of seventeen volumes, would bring together the writings of Marx and Engels with the exception of those concerning his major work, *Capital*. Thirteen volumes of the second section would be devoted exclusively to this work and signal its centrality to the whole project. The correspondence of Marx and Engels, including that between them, was to form the third part. Finally, tables of contents (indices) completed the fourth and last part of the edition.

Even if between 1927 and 1935 only eleven of the forty-two volumes came to light, they would significantly broaden access to Marx's work. In particular, Riazanov played a key role in the dissemination of Marx's unpublished work—in particular, some of his early writings. An orthodox Marxist himself, Riazanov had little sympathy for the philosophical musings of the young Marx, which he saw as remnants of bourgeois ideology. However, he was above all a scholar, a painstaking historian of Marxism, who believed that the early writings represented an important stage in Marx's intellectual development that demanded rescue, documenting, and study. Riazanov set to work. In a 1923 communication on the Marx-Engels estate, Riazanov referred explicitly to some new materials he had found in the SPD archives, including the *1843 Manuscripts*. No mention of the *1844 Manuscripts* was made at this point, but four years later, Riazanov released a Russian translation of the first sections as part of the third volume of the *Marx and Engels Archive (Arkhiv K. Marksa i F. Engelsa)*. The sections composed a large part of what would come to be known as the "third manuscript."

This was the first time the *1844 Manuscripts* were made public. Like other early writings now circulating more widely, they faced a hostile political environment. As the Soviet regime hardened under Stalin, so did the version of Marxism associated with it. The early writings challenged monolithic Marxist-Leninist codification, which was now in full sway, and work on Marx's corpus was coming to be perceived as harboring a dangerous counterpower in need of being brought under control by the Communist Party. As such, it should come as no surprise that Riazanov became one of the first victims of the so-called cultural revolution.

In January 1931, as Marx's works were starting to be published, Riazanov was removed from the institute and arrested on charges of collaboration with a Menshevik plot. He would spend the following years in and out of prison, only to be executed in 1938 in a labor camp in Siberia. In time, the elimination of people working on Marx's corpus, including Riazanov and some of his collaborators at the institute, would give way to more subtle techniques of control. As late as the 1960s, the early writings were rendered invisible by being consigned to the unnumbered "Supplement" (*Ergänzungsband*) of the collected *Marx-Engels Werke*, now edited in Moscow and Berlin. Under such a canny editorial hand, their publication could be a cause of their disappearance.

Despite the far lighter hand of the editor, the 1927 edition was already a case in point of how form, or editorial arrangement, may direct interpretation. Because the manuscripts were originally untitled, the choice of the title under which to present them to the public would become contested terrain. Naming the manuscripts was one of the main ways in which claims about their status and meaning were to be made. In their 1927 rendition, the manuscripts came out under the title "Preparatory Materials for *The Holy Family*." This title established a hierarchy between both of the mentioned works, with the *1844 Manuscripts* being denied autonomy and presented as mere building materials for the finished work, *The Holy Family*. Behind the title lay an implausible assumption about the relationship between both works, and this determined the criteria of selection from the manuscripts. Riazanov selected only those sections that bore a seeming relationship with, or seemed to offer a bridge to, the 1845 work—namely, "Private property and labor," "Private property and communism," "How do we stand on Hegel's dialectic," and "Necessity, production, and the division of labor" (Riazanov 1927, 247–86). In the process, the *1844 Manuscripts*' status as a critical analysis of political economy was downplayed.[10]

After their first fragmentary edition and several other even more fragmentary resurfacings, the *1844 Manuscripts* were laid to rest again.[11] Five more years elapsed before the full text was finally sent to print. In 1932, however, the *1844 Manuscripts* were simultaneously presented in two editions. They were the centerpiece of *Historical Materialism: The Early Writings*, a two-volume compilation edited by two social democrat scholars, political sociologists Siegfried Landshut and Jacob-Peter Mayer.[12] Landshut and Mayer's compilation circulated almost simultaneously with volume 3 of the MEGA I. These were not just any editions either. They were competing editions in many respects. Contrasting in framing, form, and nature, the editions had a very different kind of impact too. The MEGA I edition of the manuscripts was primarily a scholarly one aimed at presenting a reliable text.[13] Its impact is explained by the quality of the philological work, which offered a solid basis for most subsequent editions and translations of the work. By contrast, the Landshut and Mayer anthology was far more relaxed in its editorial practices, and it also came to be far more successful in shaping the text's meaning and reception. Meant for a wider readership, this edition was intended to make the *1844 Manuscripts* the cornerstone of the interpretation of Marx. And it was a success. As we shall see, the face of Marxist scholarship changed radically in its aftermath.

The Landshut-Mayer edition is a prime example of how an edition can *make* a work—in this case, the *1844 Manuscripts*. At the most fundamental level, this was achieved by treating the manuscripts as *a* manuscript or an almost finished work advancing a well-articulated theory—that is, a book in the making rather than multiple unfinished notebooks or perhaps even mere preparatory materials. Work began in the SPD archives, with the devoted but occasionally faulty transcription of the manuscripts carried out by Mayer in collaboration with Friedrich Solomon. In 1946, Mayer would write a book on the sociology of film in whose prefatory remarks he confessed, "To a great degree sociologists construct books: they enforce a formalised unity by way of an apparent logic" (1946, 14). His purpose in the 1946 book was to counteract this tendency by laying bare the raw materials out of which his approach to film was built. But this was not to be the case in 1932. Then the construction of a formalized unity prevailed. Landshut and Mayer's original idea was to prepare the manuscripts for separate publication in book form. However, the original project was abandoned, and the manuscripts came to be published as part of a larger anthology of Marx's early works. The manuscripts' fashioning as a stand-alone work presenting a distinct theoretical perspective continued, however, but now it relied on their internal reworking rather than on putting them between covers. This was the kind of reworking that was more effective the less it showed itself. Such a reworking needed to create the *1844 Manuscripts* as if they preexisted their own (editorial) creation.

This involved erasing most traces of editorial construction that made the manuscripts into one object. The editors covered their tracks mainly by way of omission. There is very little concerning the history and composition of the manuscripts in the Landshut-Mayer edition.[14] Any attempts at contextualization are readily abandoned in favor of Marx's own prefatory remarks, which are said to give "all desirable clarity about the context which Marx wanted to make clear with the composition of this book" (1932, 285). The text's original physical form is described cursorily.[15] Although the unique philological challenges the text presented are generally recognized, these are not accounted for in any detail. In particular, no explanation is given of how the published text has been constructed or presented, and the rationale for decisions concerning construction and presentation is largely absent. The suggestion is rather that the text has been published with no editorial mediation, exactly as found: "Our edition brings [together] the manuscript without changes to its assembly" (285). The only clue to the fact that the text might have been rearranged lies in the preservation of the original pagination. This hints at the fact that critical editorial decisions were made, and they may have prepared the text for a particular reception and interpretation.

This is most clearly shown through a comparison with the 1932 MEGA I version (Musto 2015, 233–37). In both 1932 editions, for obvious technical reasons and imperatives of readability, the eccentric form of the original manuscripts is domesticated. But it is also for reasons beyond those immediately apparent. First is the assumption that a serious work takes on (or is amenable to) a fixed book form and the corresponding requirement that the printed book should produce order where it is lacking. However, this conflicts with Marx's understanding of theory as theorizing (i.e., self-correcting thought in movement) and his criteria of success as, as in Gareth Stedman Jones's words, "not a matter of finishing a book, but of proving a set of propositions" (2007, 152). Second is the production of this particular text under the assumption of authorial intentionality—that is, that it was Marx's intention to deliver a critique of political economy (Rojahn 2002, 33; Musto 2009, 391). This assumption translates itself into the composition of the text. As such, like the Landshut-Mayer edition, the MEGA I also begins with a "preface" extracted from the third notebook. Besides providing an overview of Marx's work in the *1844 Manuscripts*, the "preface" seemingly supports the treatment of the manuscripts as a book, insofar as Marx refers explicitly to "a work" and to the analysis of Hegel's philosophy in notebook 4 as its "closing chapter." The positioning of a preface at the front therefore produces an almost immediate "book effect." It suggests order and intent, directing readers to a conception of the manuscripts as a work—a critique of political economy—following a definite and prearranged order. The organization of the notebooks in the MEGA I furthers this impression by treating them as if they were distinct chapters into which the text was originally divided. But if both 1932 editions fashion the manuscripts after a work with a certain intentionality and directionality, they differ as to what the latter might be. The introduction by the editor of the MEGA I edition, albeit also succinct, reconstructs the genesis of the text, and the arrangement of the notebooks follows for the most part their original physical organization with the necessary adaptations to a new medium. The body of the text comprises three notebooks (numbered 1, 2, and 3, respectively) that appear in this exact order after broadly descriptive titles. Notebook 1 is published not in the original three-column format but in three successive chapters (entitled "Wages of Labor," "Profit of Capital," and "Rent of Land," respectively). The edition is careful enough to show a facsimile page of the original, on which the original three-column structure is visible.[16] But as each column is converted into a running text, the overall impression is that of a more finished work rather than notes for a process of self-clarification. The separate folio sheet with only one column, originally sewn into the third notebook, appears now as a separate notebook (4), which forms an appendix, including some of Marx's "exzerpte" from that time. All this implies rearrangement rather than the editor acting as the mere recipient of a fixed form. But the rearrangement is restrained, and the reader is offered a rare glimpse into the original, against which some changes can be measured.

If we turn to the Landshut-Mayer edition, we find a rather different text. This is not only because what we have are only selections from the second and third manuscripts rather than the full text. It is also because the layout changes radically. The "preface" has been similarly lifted from notebook 3 to the front of the text, producing a book effect similar to the MEGA I's. But notebook 3 has itself been lifted, now coming first, thus conferring centrality on Marx's philosophical reflections. In turn, notebook 1, which contains Marx's core engagement with key categories of classical political economy, directly or indirectly extracted from Smith's *The Wealth of Nations*, does not figure at all. With some omissions and some selective insertions here and there (of Marx's discussions of Hegel in particular), the text is presented in an entirely different order (i.e., 3, 2, 4) from the order in which the parts are assumed to have been written. What emerges from this new layout is not only *a* work; it is a work endowed with distinctive intentionality. If there was sense to be made of it, it was rather different from the critique of political economy suggested by the MEGA I edition. As Keith Tribe rightly puts it, "the general effect" of the Landshut-Mayer edition is "that Marx's comments on political economy are secondary, and his philosophical ruminations placed centrally" (2015, 49) and at the origin of his theory of alienation.[17] Marx is a philosopher and his philosophy is one of man and society.

This effect is accentuated through a series of editorial interventions at various thresholds of interpretation between reader and text. The starting point is the title. And there is an irony in it. While the manuscripts came to be known by the MEGA I title, Landshut and Mayer's title was the one that framed how their content was to be read for decades to come. In the Landshut-Mayer edition, the manuscripts appear under the title "Nationalökonomie und Philosophie" ("Political Economy and Philosophy"), followed by the long subtitle "On the Connection of Political Economy with the State, Law, Ethics and Civic Life." This long-winded title stands in contrast to the pared-down title under which they appeared in MEGA I/3: "The Economic-Philosophic Manuscripts of 1844." But restraint is not the only issue here. More is at stake. The emphasis was clearly being shifted toward the ethical grounding of Marx's economic analysis. Whereas the title stresses the "connection," Marx himself, in the preface, maintains that questions about "the state, law, ethics, civil life, etc.," will be addressed, if they are addressed at all, only to the extent that "political economy itself expressly touches upon these subjects." Marx's order of priority is clear, but the title of the Landshut-Mayer edition subtly confounds it, preparing the way for a vague claim of "connection" to evolve into the subversive claim to a "grounding."

What the title starts to voice, the editors' introductory note fleshes out fully. Again, the comparison with the MEGA I edition is enlightening, as it emphasizes how the manuscripts were to become a central piece in the schism between "Soviet Marxism" and "Western Marxism." Viktor Adoratskii, the bureaucrat who replaced Riazanov as director of the Marx-Engels Institute in 1931, presents the manuscripts as a "general characterisation of capitalism" comprising a series of aspects that he lists drily—that is, an "analysis of money, wages, the interest of capital, and ground rent" (quoted in Musto 2015, 241). Betraying a lack of enthusiasm for the import of the work, this laconic presentation contrasts vividly with Landshut and Mayer's effusiveness. If any doubt remained as to the privileged place of the *1844 Manuscripts* in Marx's intellectual development, the editors take it away: "This work is in a certain sense the most central work of Marx" (1932, xxx) and the one after which later work is to be read, including *Capital*. In a clear instance of the myth of prolepsis (Skinner 1969, 22), the editors speak of the manuscripts as a work that "in essence already anticipated *Capital*," a work whose retrospective significance, therefore, was far more important than what it could have signified for the author and the public at the time. Landshut and Mayer have no doubt that the manuscripts are the "nodal point of the entire development of his [Marx's] thinking" insofar as they show that his "principles of economic analysis" do not stand on their own but rather "derive directly from a philosophical anthropology," or his "idea of the genuine reality of man" (1932, xxx). To understand this much was also to realize how misread Marx had been. If there was a grounding to Marx's theory, it was not economics but ethics. If there was a core to it, it was not class conflict but the alienation of human essence. If there was a purpose to it, it was not the abolition of private property but emancipation. The discovery of the *1844 Manuscripts* warranted the rewriting of the first sentence of the *Communist Manifesto*, revealing the truth of history: "All the history until now is a history of the alienation of human beings." Prior to 1932, "alienation" hardly figured in Marxist vocabulary. The Landshut-Mayer edition made it unavoidable. Alienation, not exploitation, it claimed, was the driving force in Marx's thinking.

## THE RECEPTION OF THE TWO 1932 EDITIONS

This framing had a profound impact on the interpretation and critical reception of the manuscripts. As soon as they made their way to print in the competing MEGA I and Landshut-Mayer editions, the manuscripts became the primary focus of contention between "Soviet Marxism" and "Western Marxism." In the absence of an English translation of the manuscripts, Germany and France were the first battlegrounds in which the collision took place. Following the terms set by the Landshut-Mayer edition, "Western" Marxists found in the manuscripts the long-lost key to Marx's work and ammunition against Soviet orthodoxy. They believed its so-called scientific Marxism, governed by the "laws" of historical materialism and a rigid model of economic determinism, was discredited by the emergence of a young humanist Marx, whose thinking trumped or, at least continued to underpin, that of his later self. A note of praise for those in the heterodox camp, the term *young* was used as one of derision by their orthodox opponents. As a work produced in Marx's twenties, they claimed, the manuscripts bore all the signs of youth. They adopted the humanist or idealistic stance that accompanies the naïveté of that age. A fundamental contrast, perhaps even a sharp discontinuity, was therefore to be drawn between Marx's juvenilia and his accomplished mature writings culminating in his thesis of historical materialism. If Marx's juvenilia were of any worth, it was only because they documented a transitional stage in his thought that needed to be abandoned and overcome before it could reach fruition.

The first two reviews of the *1844 Manuscripts* appeared shortly after their release. Their authors—Henri De Man, leader of the Belgian Labor Party and a prominent socialist theoretician, and Herbert Marcuse, then a postdoctoral student of Heidegger who would later become a prominent figure of the Frankfurt school and the New Left—firmly aligned themselves with the Marx of the Landshut-Mayer edition.

De Man wrote his review for *Der Kampf*, the weekly newspaper of the Communist Party in Luxembourg, and his chosen title enticed readers by offering them a preview of "The Newly Discovered Marx." This new primary source material, De Man claimed, lay bare the ethical-humanist foundations of Marx's socialism. In the *1844 Manuscripts*, one could witness Marx's major theoretical breakthroughs at work and find all the major concepts out of which his later work would be developed, with an emphasis on alienation as a universal feature of any class-based society. These concepts and advancements were also to be found there in their best formulation, for Marx's later work suffered from "a decline in his creative capacities" (quoted in Musto 2015, 242). The significance of the *1844 Manuscripts* could not, therefore, be overestimated. There was a Marx before and a far more valuable Marx after their discovery.

Like De Man, Marcuse believed the publication of the *1844 Manuscripts* was "a crucial event in this history of Marxist studies" and of Marxism itself. The *1844 Manuscripts* did much more than simply reexamine the vexed question of the relationship between Marx and Hegel. As the title of Marcuse's review, "New Sources on the Foundation of Historical Materialism," made clear, they also promised to shake the whole "discussion about the origins and original meaning of historical materialism, and the entire theory of 'scientific socialism.'" The *1844 Manuscripts* offered an invaluable glimpse into the "origins" of Marx's system of thought, where its "basic categories" appeared in a clearer and more forcible light than ever. As one of the first to descend into these "origins," Marcuse hoped to resurface as the first iconoclast. His review boldly disproved the interpretations of Marx developed by the Second International and in Soviet Marxism. Since the manuscripts surfaced, these had become untenable. It was a grave mistake to consider Marxism as an essentially economic doctrine eschewing "philosophical speculation." Marx's always and still was "a *philosophical* critique of political economy" (Marcuse 2007, 73) whose basic categories were *philosophical* and effectively drawn from a lifelong confrontation with Hegel (and to a lesser extent with Kant and Feuerbach). Unlike what its detractors suggested, it was Marx's philosophical humanism—his idea of the essence of man and its realization—that laid the groundwork for a properly understood historical materialism. Moreover, this was a foundation that was not self-referential and sterile. Rather, it was practically consequential, since it already contained a "revolutionary praxis." In other words, Marx's theory of revolution was dependent on a philosophical critique of political economy that established the superseding of alienation as its goal. Marx's theory was revolutionary, therefore, not because it advocated the socialization of the means of production but because it aimed at disalienation that, because it was not merely an economic condition, did not enable a mere economic solution either. Marcuse's challenge to the "scientific" Marx was laid out in a long review essay published in the Social Democrat journal *Die Gesellschaft*. Being the first to give the challenge in print helped Marcuse establish himself as a rising figure of Western Marxism and one of the most promising social theorists of his generation.

Marcuse's reinterpretation of the problem of alienation in Marx was central to his argument. In addition, this rereading prefigured many of the themes and theses to be explored in his future work. In articulating it, Marcuse felt it necessary to engage with the form of the original manuscripts, primarily because, on a first analysis, it might seem to contradict his reading and suggest that alienation was, after all, yet another purely economic category, for as Marx describes the "circumstances of alienation and estrangement," Marcuse explains, he seems "to proceed completely on the ground of traditional political economy and its theorems." This much, Marcuse admits, seems to be indicated by the familiar headings of the three-column-per-page division of the first manuscript: "The Wages of Labor," "The Profit of Capital," and "The Rent of Land," Adam Smith's central economic categories. However, from page xxii onward, where others identify a logical sequence from premises to conclusion, Marcuse sees a radical departure being openly performed through a change to the manuscripts' physical form. The threefold division and its headings, Marcuse suggestively explains, are suddenly "exploded and abandoned," with Marx now writing across and disregarding them, in a clear "sign" that he is moving "in a completely new direction" (2007, 77).

The change of direction and the concomitant presentation of an independent theory of alienation, Margaret Fay argues, were produced by editorial interventions in the next chapter. But where Fay sees an instance of problematic rearrangement, Marcuse sees an intervention enabling the reader to see the text's true aim. That Marx was deliberately effecting a departure or changing subject, Marcuse insists, is further, and rightly, signaled by the editors of the MEGA I, where the six pages (xxii–xxvii) that follow stand out as an inserted fourth chapter under the heading "Estranged Labor."[18] A "remarkable discovery," Marcuse announces, is gained from their reading. Estranged or alienated labor is no mere "economic matter"; it is rather "a matter of man as man." Hence understanding Marx's philosophical anthropology—that is, his understanding of the historical and sensuous character of human essence—is a necessary prerequisite for understanding his concept of alienated labor and the "whole foundation of revolutionary theory" (Marcuse 2007, 83). In other words, as Marcuse will reiterate decades later (1972b, 3), with the publication of the *1844 Manuscripts* in 1932, the understanding of Marxism as strictly an economic doctrine becomes increasingly untenable.

MARX REBORN: THE FIRST TWENTY YEARS

Once published, the *1844 Manuscripts* served as a springboard from which to reexamine the relationship between the young Marx and Hegel. This was the case, of course, only if one was ready to question orthodox Marxist hermeneutics. In the United States, Sidney Hook's option to read Marx as a naturalist in order to defend the validity of historical materialism as a philosophical system led him to ignore the *1844 Manuscripts* and the very category of alienation (which does not occur once in the text) in his 1936 study of Marx's early intellectual development, *From Hegel to Marx*, whereas in Europe, the Hungarian philosopher Georg Lukács was keen to pursue a much less orthodox line of inquiry.

Lukács rediscovered the idea of alienation as a central philosophical concept in Marx's thinking. Crucially, this "rediscovery" occurred in the absence of the *1844 Manuscripts*. Their physical absence, however, did not prevent the brilliant young Lukács from deducing their content—and the central importance of alienation—from a close and creative reading of Marx's other writings in the context of Marx's relationship with Hegel. In an essay published in the collection *History and Class Consciousness* (1971), Lukács, a former student of Georg Simmel, who articulates a theory of alienation in the final chapter of *The Philosophy of Money* (Simmel 1978, 455ff.; see also Coser 1977, 189–93), traces Marx's idea of the alienation of labor back to Hegel's notion of the self-alienation of man from the Absolute Idea. In 1930, Lukács took refuge in the Soviet Union. Once in Moscow, he was assigned to work alongside Riazanov at the Marx-Engels Institute. There he enjoyed privileged access to the manuscripts of the early Marx, including a collaboration on the editing of the MEGA I edition of the *1844 Manuscripts*. As Lukács later recalled,

> You can imagine my excitement: reading these manuscripts changed my whole relation to Marxism and transformed my philosophical outlook. A German scholar from the Soviet Union was working on the manuscripts, preparing them for publication. The mice had got at them, and there were many places where letters or even words were missing. Because of my philosophical knowledge, I worked with him, determining what the letters or the words that disappeared were: one often had words beginning with, say, "g" and ending with, say, "s" and one had to guess what came between. I think that the edition that eventually came out was a very good one—I know because of collaborating in the editing of it. (1983, 179–80)

Lukács's little-known, never acknowledged collaboration on the MEGA I edition, alongside the recently published manuscripts from Hegel's period in Jena (Hegel 1923, 1931), enabled Lukács, in *History and Class*

*Consciousness*, to revisit the earlier, more speculative engagement with Marx. In *The Young Hegel*, published in 1938, Lukács was now able to locate the encounter between Marx and Hegel in the pages of the *1844 Manuscripts*. "The link between economics and philosophy . . . in these manuscripts of Marx is a profound methodological necessity, the precondition for actually transcending Hegel's idealist dialectic," Lukács observes (1975, 548). But Lukács goes beyond the textual evidence provided by the *1844 Manuscripts* to suggest that rather than limited to the passages in which Marx directly refers to Hegel, the influence of Hegel is in fact much broader and more fundamental. He writes, "For this reason, it would be superficial to imagine that Marx's concern with Hegel begins in the last portion of the manuscript which contains the critique of the *Phenomenology*. The four preceding sections, which do not expressly concern themselves with Hegel at all, are nevertheless the foundation on which that criticism is built: they provide the economic clarification of the real nature of alienation" (1975, 548). The philosophical discussion of the extent to which the early Marx was indebted to Hegel and, as a consequence, his political economy began as a philosophical critique of Hegel would continue in subsequent years. During the Second World War, the main work on this problematic was published not in Europe but in the United States. In 1941 Marcuse published *Reason and Revolution* in New York. In this work, Marcuse set out to discuss the implications of Hegel's social theory for Marx's analysis of the alienation of labor as presented in the *1844 Manuscripts* (1941, 278ff.). After the war, as the Iron Curtain descended on Eastern Europe, the *1844 Manuscripts* found a hospitable intellectual climate in Western Europe. This first occurred in the German Federal Republic in the early 1950s, where Erich Thier's *Anthropology of the Young Marx in the Paris Economic-Philosophical Manuscripts*, Heinrich Popitz's *Alienated Man*, and Jacob Hommes's *The Eros of Technology* helped establish the *1844 Manuscripts* as the centerpiece around which Marx's entire work revolved. But it was in postwar France that the young Marx attracted the greatest following. From the mid-1940s until well into the 1960s, a bold yet unstable combination of phenomenology[19] and Marxism gave rise to the "existentialist Marx," a philosophical-political-aesthetic program built on the *1844 Manuscripts* by thinkers such as Jean-Paul Sartre (1958, 237), Maurice Merleau-Ponty (1964, 125–36), and Jean Hyppolite (1969, 148–50), as well as one of the century's greatest Marx editors, Maximilien Rubel (1957, 121–23). Suddenly *tout le Paris*, especially on the Left Bank, was drawn to the young Marx, with the heretic *1844 Manuscripts* eclipsing, even if only for a brief moment, *Capital* and the Marxist-Leninist orthodoxy.[20]

## THE DEBATE ON ALIENATION: THE *1844 MANUSCRIPTS* IN THE 1960S

The reception of the *1844 Manuscripts* in the English-speaking world drew on these developments (e.g., Maidan 1990). In continental Europe, the *1844 Manuscripts*—in their various editions and translations, their paratexts offering opposing thresholds of interpretation sometimes of the same edition—constituted the focal point of the struggle between the guardians of orthodoxy, who downplayed the significance of the early writings, and the revisionists, often independent thinkers whose heretic attempts to rethink the Marxian doctrine independently of its official guardians depended on them. To emphasize continuity was to stress the relevance of the early humanist, more philosophical Marx. To emphasize discontinuity, epistemological or not, was to emphasize the distinctive character of Marx's political economy and its ultimate expression—*Capital*. In the long shadow of *Capital*, however, lurked a dialectic of dissent. In the 1950s and 1960s, an eclectic group of thinkers set out to think of alternatives to Marxist orthodoxy by editing, translating, introducing, and commenting on the *1844 Manuscripts*. The cultural work of these agents *in* and *on* the book eventually contributed to Marx's inclusion in the sociological canon as the analyst of alienation.[21]

The first English translation of the manuscripts was by Martin Milligan, who was to become a professor of philosophy at the University of Leeds. It was first published in 1956 by the Foreign Languages Publishing House in Moscow and then in London by Lawrence and Wishart three years later.[22] Its circulation and impact were limited, however. The first translation to gain wider currency appeared in the United States in 1961. This time the translator was Tom Bottomore, secretary of the International Sociological Association between 1953 and 1959 and by 1961 a reader in sociology at the University of London. Bottomore was to play an important role as editor and translator of Marx's works into English.

This much is evidenced by the two collections Bottomore published—that is, *Karl Marx: Early Writings* (1963) and (with Maximilien Rubel) *Karl Marx: Selected Writings in Sociology and Social Philosophy* (1956). The former included the first three manuscripts of the "Economic and Philosophic Manuscripts," whereas the latter had only excerpts from that work, alongside excerpts from a wide range of other works cutting across more than forty years of Marx's intellectual production, including *The German Ideology, A Contribution to the Critique of Political Economy*, Marx and Engels's *The Communist Manifesto, The Eighteenth Brumaire of Louis Bonaparte*, the first three volumes of *Capital*, and others. A significant difference between these volumes is that *Selected Writings* is specifically directed at a sociological audience. This is clear from what Bottomore says in the introduction, where the sociological significance of Marx is examined, sometimes with some excessive interpretative license.[23] It also becomes clear from his selection of excerpts from the *1844 Manuscripts* and their inclusion in *Selected Writings*. It figures prominently in the methodological foundations of Marx's thinking (Bottomore and Rubel 1956, 67–79), is used to document the importance of alienation as the "fundamental evil of capitalist society" (27, 167–77), and helps Bottomore establish the textual basis for the future-oriented, utopian character of Marx's work (243ff.). By the time of his death in 1992, this particular volume was considered Bottomore's most popular book for generations of English-speaking sociologists: "After several rounds of reprints under the Penguin paperback banner," it remained "the most useful source-book for thousands of young beginners, and hence the best short collection to this day" (Dhanagare 1993, 2582).

The release of these volumes was a significant achievement given that some of the works, notably the *Grundrisse*, were hardly known outside Europe and even there remained, for the most part, the preserve of a small circle of Marx scholars. Furthermore, the publication of the two collections in the late 1950s and early 1960s in America, a country still grappling with McCarthyism and already confronting the darkest days of the Cold War, was a somewhat perilous act. Perhaps to make it more palatable, the 1963 edition of *Karl Marx: Early Writings* included a new foreword by Erich Fromm, by then a relatively well-known public intellectual whose accessible writing style and public success cost him academic preferment but secured generous sales. In effect, Fromm played a key role in popularizing the *1844 Manuscripts* in the English-speaking world prior to the Bottomore edition.

Fromm's *Marx's Concept of Man* (1961) included a 110-page translation from the *1844 Manuscripts* by Bottomore and 23 pages from assorted works by Marx (notably *The German Ideology* and *The Critique of Political Economy*) and was preceded by Fromm's own extensive, 90-page introductory essay advancing Marxist socialist humanism, of which Marcuse and Fromm were two main founders. Fromm's was to become one of the most widely read collections of Marx's writings. Critically, the collection was highly selective. In Fromm's edition of the manuscripts, as in the Landshut-Mayer edition before it, only the section on "alienation" was reproduced, while the economic sections leading to it were surreptitiously omitted.[24] In this manner, Fromm saved himself the trouble Marcuse faced in addressing the relationship between the two parts.

Both in *Marx's Concept of Man* and in his brief foreword to *Karl Marx: Early Writings*, Fromm directly challenged the two-Marx thesis first put forth by Daniel Bell in 1959 in his well-known essay "The Debate on Alienation" (D. Bell 1962).[25] There was no need to split Marx into two, Fromm argued. From the "young Marx" to the "mature Marx," any changes observed ran only on the surface. They were terminological at best and never touched the core of his philosophy—namely, the understanding of human nature and the related concept of "alienation and de-alienation" (the "key concept" in the *1844 Manuscripts*) that tied it all together and confirmed the unity of his work. Fromm's conclusion was as bold as it was controversial: "Marx was a humanist, from whom man's freedom, dignity, and activity were the basic premises of the 'good society.'" This was not to be a capitalist society in which "man is made to be a person who *has* much, who *uses* much, but who *is* little" (Fromm 1964, iii). But neither was it to be socialism "Soviet style," limited to the sphere of economics and the satisfaction of material needs, which was no socialism at all. To avoid the errors of both, he proposed a new Messianism: Marxist humanist socialism, with its focus on freedom, or the emancipation of man as an individual. This, Louis Althusser would come to claim in *For Marx*, first published in France in 1965, was an ideological slogan deprived of any theoretical value. The attempt to ground it in Marx suffered from the incapacity to see the radical epistemological break between "two long essential periods: the 'ideological' period before, and the scientific period after, the break in 1845" (Althusser 1969, 34). The Marxist humanists' heavy reliance on the manuscripts to bolster their thesis that Marx could not be understood apart from the philosophical foundations they disclosed was the product of a process of reification, whereby an object—namely, the printed book—was rendered the active, determining factor: "We do not publish our own drafts, that is, our own mistakes, but we do sometimes publish other people's" (Althusser 1995, 385). The *1844 Manuscripts* were not only a mistake; they were a mistake taken to its ultimate consequences so that it allowed for its absolute and irreversible defeat (Althusser 1969, 159). Whereas for Fromm, the young Marx was Marxism, for Althusser, one "could not say absolutely that '*Marx's youth is part of Marxism*'" (83). If it had led to Marxism, it was only insofar as it was radically abandoned and its illusions dispelled. Althusser was Fromm's nemesis, and Fromm made sure to keep this insight relatively obscure. In 1965, one year after the publication of Althusser's combative "Marx and Humanism," Fromm edited an influential collection of essays titled *Socialist Humanism* with what was at the time a significantly large American publishing house, Doubleday. Althusser's contribution of an essay on the young Marx was rejected, and with this rejection, his antihumanist stance was denied easy entry into and wide circulation in America.

However strong the imprint of Marxist humanism in *Karl Marx: Early Writings*, it remains a book of two minds, as it were. The progression from the foreword to the introduction makes for a schizophrenic reading experience, as Fromm and Bottomore offer visibly conflicting readings of the manuscripts and their significance. Fromm's celebratory tone contrasts with Bottomore's more restrained assessment, which seeks to temper the excesses of humanist and religious readings of Marx. For Bottomore, "the cast of Marx's mind was fundamentally scientific" (Bottomore 1964, xiii), not philosophical. This scientific bent manifested itself in "a passion for empirical inquiry and factual knowledge" that was accompanied by a "distaste for speculative philosophy" (xiii). Whereas Fromm claimed that Marx had no primary interest in economics, Bottomore saw the young Marx primarily "grappling with contemporary economic problems" (xiv) and therefore "proceeding from a critical examination of Hegelian philosophy to a direct study of the economic and political problems of modern society as they are represented in the works of the economists" (xiii). This much, he argued, was shown by the long analysis of the three sources of revenue (which Fromm had excised in 1961 from Bottomore's translation) and the living conditions of industrial workers. The manuscripts, together with other early writings by Marx, were best conceived "as a stage in the development of his ideas" rather than, as Fromm and others saw them, "the expression of a distinctive doctrine which has to be brought in to correct our judgment of his later theories" (xiv). They evidenced a reorientation of Marx's theory after 1843 (not Althusser's 1845) from "philosophical disputation about the nature of man, or human social development as a whole," to "the empirical study of modern economic and political problems" (xiv). Bottomore's Marx is, first and foremost, an empirically grounded social theorist seeking to understand one particular type of society (capitalist society) and one process of social change. As such, he takes issue with Marcuse's attempt to emphasize "the historical and philosophical character" of Marx's theory against "positivistic sociology" (Marcuse 1941, 343–44). For his part, Bottomore saw "little evidence in Marx's own writings (including his early writings)" that Marx wanted to draw "a radical distinction between the sciences of nature and of man" or that he saw an incompatibility between "a positive science of man and society," on the one hand, and "the practical activity of changing society" on the other. Bottomore's Marx believes, on the contrary, in a close interdependence between "humanism (socialism) and positivism (a science of society)" (1964, xiv).

These tensions in the body of the book, between an orthodox and a heterodox reading of Marx and Marxism, reflect and enhance wider sociopolitical, economic, and intellectual changes occurring at the time.

CONCLUSION

"In contemporary America the situation of sociology has been likened to that of Marxism in Mao's China in the thousand flowers period. After a long period of a prevailing orthodoxy ... suddenly ... everyone seemed licensed to say what he liked about anything and call it sociology" (Rex 1974, 1). This was how, in the early 1970s, John Rex described the sudden demise of the two dominant paradigms of postwar American sociology: Parsons's structural functionalism and empiricism. Also at this time, Marx was finally included in the sociological canon. Marx's relatively late canonization, of course, is but a chapter of a much more complex and diverse history of the relation between Marxism and sociology (Bottomore 1984).[26] In the remainder of this chapter, we offer a brief account of the reception of Marx's *1844 Manuscripts* in American sociology.[27]

This process of disciplinary reception occurred through two intellectual movements, each with its distinctive figures, themes, and favored publication outlets. Yet while one movement shifted away from the *1844 Manuscripts* and Hegel's philosophy of history toward a scientific theory of society whose main tenets are its theory of class, account of ideology, and theory of revolution, the other found in them the interpretative key to Marx's entire oeuvre in the form of the problematic of alienation. Uniting both movements was an appreciation of Marx's immense sociological contributions, either already implicit in the *1844 Manuscripts* or as a more positive theory of society of which the *1844 Manuscripts* were an early, still metaphysical stage. The combined efforts of these otherwise very distinct movements proved crucial for sociologists—not only Marxist but *all* sociologists—in coming to regard Marx as one of their founding fathers.[28]

**Conflict Theory**
The first of these movements was conflict theory. From the 1950s through the 1960s, a loosely defined "conflict sociology" emerged as a theoretical alternative to Parsons's structural functionalism, which politically connoted the defense of the status quo in American society. Although it is the case that the work of conflict sociologists such as Lewis A. Coser, Reinhard Bendix, or Randall Collins in the United States and Ralf Dahrendorf, David Lockwood, and Tom Bottomore in the UK helped replace functionalist theory's emphasis on

consensus and equilibrium with an emphasis on conflict and contradiction (Burawoy 1982, S4), it would be a mistake to infer from this the central role of the *1844 Manuscripts* or the concept of alienation. As a rule, conflict theorists did not draw exclusively, nor even primarily, on Marx to develop their alternative to Parsons. To many, Weber and Simmel were as important as Marx. For instance, in *The Functions of Social Conflict* (1956), Coser presents Weber's emphasis on the importance of struggle in social life as a corrective to Durkheim's excessive emphasis on social integration through shared values (21–23) and subscribes to Simmel's positive attitude toward social conflict, which he sees performing important and positive social functions: "Groups require disharmony as well as harmony, dissociation as well as association; and conflicts within them are by no means altogether disruptive factors. Group formation is the result of both types of processes" (31). More important to our argument, when conflict theorists did resort to Marx, their "Marx" is not the Marx of the *1844 Manuscripts* but the one who moved away from them as he adopted a more scientific, and more prophetic, outlook. Commenting on Marx's sociological theory of social change, Bendix writes, "I believe that Marx forfeited his genuine insight into the indeterminacy of the relationship between class situation and class action by his prophetic fervor, which prompted him to forecast the capitalist development with a certainty often belied by his own historical sense" (1952, 362). Similarly, in *Class and Class Conflict in Industrial Society* (1957), Dahrendorf proposes to complement Parsons's analysis of social integration with a Marxist theory of change adequately distilled from its early metaphysical underpinnings and reduced to its chief sociological insight—the explanation of social conflict (1959, 136).

This attempt to rescue Marx from Marxism, as it were, while avoiding an altogether heterodox reading could also be seen at play in a plenary session of the American Sociological Association (ASA) in 1965. Entitled "Re-evaluating Karl Marx," this memorable session brought together Parsons and two of the most prominent conflict sociologists of the day, Coser and Bottomore.[29] Parsons's object of critique is the Marx whose "predictions about the course of the socioeconomic system have been deeply invalidated by the course of events in most advanced industrial societies" (1967, 109). Parsons's verdict, delivered in the presence of a representative of the Soviet Academy of Sciences, was harsh—Marxian theory was "obsolete" (132). Bottomore, whose work as translator, editor, and commentator did more to establish the continuing relevance of Marx than anyone in the English-speaking world, replied with "Karl Marx: Sociologist or Marxist?" Bottomore's Marx, however, was not the orthodox Marx the representative of the Soviet Academy of Sciences had in mind. Marx "was not a Marxist" either in the sense of possessing a complete and finished theory of society or in the still more important sense of the political history of the twentieth century: "He did not regard himself as the originator of a political creed which must be adopted as the unique doctrine of the working class movement" (Bottomore 2012, 79). Having rescued Marx from orthodox Marxism, Bottomore specifies what he believes is the validity or usefulness of his theories for contemporary sociology. He begins by positioning himself vis-à-vis the young Marx versus mature Marx controversy. "It is my contention," he writes, "that the general inclination of Marx's work, when it is traced from his earlier to his later writings, is clearly away from the philosophy of history and towards a scientific theory of society" (76). From this, Bottomore defends Marx's sociological contribution as an alternative to Parsons's consensus functionalism: "Marx's 'conflict model,' and especially the theory of classes, his account of ideologies, his theory of revolution, must find a place in sociological theory" (84). As this episode vividly illustrates, understandings of the relative position of the *1844 Manuscripts* in Marx's oeuvre framed the conflict-theoretical opposition to Parsons's "consensus" structural functionalism. Soon Bottomore's judgment would become common currency for a new "disobedient generation" of radical students.[30] The days of Parsons as one of the "three great figures of the Capitoline triad of the American sociological Pantheon" (Bourdieu 1991, 378)[31] were numbered.

Following an article published in the *New York Times* covering Bottomore's and Coser's interventions, the ASA's activities became a target of FBI interest. Records released in the late 1980s reveal that the special agent in charge of the FBI Chicago office wrote a memo to Director J. Edgar Hoover recommending that "Chicago should submit to the Bureau any reports on this convention which appeared in Chicago newspapers." The memo concluded with a further recommendation for details of the discussion of Marxism at the ASA meeting to be discreetly obtained, as "it is felt that we should make an effort to obtain details of any effort to make Marxism respectable" (Keen 1999, 5).

Hoover's FBI had reason to be concerned. "Dangerous" ideas were indeed being circulated not only in specialized papers delivered at academic congresses but also in best-selling books read by thousands of university students and members of the general public. From the mid-1960s onward, New Left literature acted as a catalyst for political protest, fueling radical, antiracist, and antiwar student movements on American campuses. While short lived, the sudden revival of Marxist-inspired radicalism at the heart of Western developed democracies was striking and significant. Certainly hostile to capitalism, it was also critical of the political repression and dogmatic thinking associated with the Soviet Union. The radicals of 1968, from Paris to Berkeley, pushed for sexual freedom, egalitarianism, and democratic antiauthoritarianism against the determinism of orthodox classical Marxist-Leninism, with its focus on class politics and material considerations. As Argentinian revolutionary Ernesto "Che" Guevara wrote, "We are fighting against misery, but we are also fighting against alienation.... Marx was preoccupied both with economic factors and with their repercussions on the spirit" (quoted in N. Hamilton 1992, 38). Che and the radicals of 1968 emphasized the humanist Marx, not the positivist Marx. They sought spiritual guidance and intellectual clarification not in *Capital* but in the works of both Marxist thinkers such as Lukács and Gramsci and certain members of the Frankfurt school of critical theory, namely, the libertarian socialism of Fromm and Marcuse, two key agents in the publication history and reception of the *1844 Manuscripts*.

**The New Left**
In the New Left's social critique of advanced capitalist societies, however, American sociologists found not merely an alternative to Parsons's structural functionalism but also a philosophically sophisticated criticism of positivistic empiricism, the other dominant feature of postwar mainstream sociology in America. This critique was based on the humanist lessons of the early Marx. Yet one did not have to be a pious Marxist to explore the sociological implications of the *1844 Manuscripts* and other early writings. A case in point is C. Wright Mills, whose radical "public sociology" (similar in intent, if not in content, to Walter Lippmann's "public philosophy") recuperates Marxist themes such as alienation and domination time and again (Mattson 2002, 43ff.). This is first seen in *White Collar*, published in 1951, in which Mills drew on these themes to criticize the moral malaise he saw afflicting white-collar workers in 1950s America. He writes, "Estranged from community and society in a context of distrust and manipulation; alienated from work and, on the personality market, from self; expropriated of individual rationality, and politically apathetic—these are the new little people, the unwilling vanguard of modern society" (2002, xviii). Mills's criticism of empiricism, which went hand in hand with his contempt for abstract grand narratives, would eventually coalesce in his humanist manifesto *The Sociological Imagination*—one of the most popular sociology books of the 1950s. There, Mills recuperates once again the humanism of the early Marx to argue that given the fundamental entanglement between agency and structure, the sociologist's task is to "always keep your eyes open to the image of man—the generic notion of his human nature—which

by your work you are assuming and implying" (2000, 225). This humanist understanding enables Mills to position himself critically vis-à-vis Marxism and liberalism, seeing them as "determinist" sociological approaches whose "images of man" betray the same antihumanist tendency to reduce history to causality and biography to social atoms (see Mills 1960a, 101ff.; 1962). Mills's alternative, built on a combination of pragmatism (itself a form of naturalized Hegelianism) and humanist socialism, pointed to a New Left understood as a radically egalitarian, libertarian political program. As he put it in an essay first published in 1960 in the *New Left Review*, a crucial outlet of the New Left, "Isn't all this, isn't it something of what we are trying to mean by the phrase, 'The New Left?' Let the old men ask sourly, 'Out of Apathy—into what?' The Age of Complacency is ending. Let the old women complain wisely about 'the end of ideology.' We are beginning to move again" (Mills 1960b, 23). Mills's dissent from mainstream empirical sociology was to inspire a generation of radical sociologists whose disillusionment with arid grand theory and survey-based research would be overcome by a sociology with a human face, as it were.

Mills's thesis that there was continuity in Marx's thought from the *1844 Manuscripts* to *Capital* while the theme of alienation was central throughout was shared by most other Anglo-American interpreters in the 1960s and 1970s (R. Tucker 2000, 238; Ollman 1971, xiv). As noted, however, this understanding first originates in Europe. As interest on the manuscripts increased in Western Europe, they became a tool of dissent in Eastern Europe. It was as a reaction to Stalinism in countries such as Hungary (with the "Lukács school"), Czechoslovakia, Yugoslavia (the *Praxis* group), and Poland that the critical use of Marxist thought as a basis for a rejection of official ideology first emerged in the 1950s. Uniting these otherwise diverse Eastern European intellectual groupings was the project of a Marxist humanism, a revisionist approach based as much on the young Marx of the *1844 Manuscripts* as on non-Marxist sources such as existentialism and phenomenology.

It is here that the expression "dialectic of dissent" was first coined to refer to the "subtle interplay between content and form, thought and structure" (Satterwhite 1992, 7) that dissident intellectuals needed to navigate given the all-encompassing nature of Marxist ideology in that part of the world. Thus the work of Polish sociologist Zygmunt Bauman—with the philosopher Leszek Kołakowski, one of the main figures of Polish humanist Marxism—in thinking how sociology would contribute to the revisionist humanist critique of Stalinism from 1956 onward can be seen as an expression of such a dialectic, a project that continues today in Bauman's profoundly humanist critique of liquid modernity. Here we use it in a slightly more focused sense. We likewise refer to an interplay between form and content, but now in the more specific process of engagement by English-speaking left-wing intellectuals with the *1844 Manuscripts*, as a means of establishing the early Marx as either the real Marx or at least the first stage of a continuous process of intellectual development that would in time prove decisive for Marx's sociological canonization. In this more specific sense, a dialectic of dissent is also apparent in the writings of the *other* intellectual hero of the New Left—Herbert Marcuse.

From his 1932 review of the *1844 Manuscripts* until the end of his career, Marcuse never abandoned the belief that rediscovery of the humanist message of the early Marx entailed a profound reexamination of not only the whole corpus of Marx's work in the light of those early writings but Marxism as well insofar as it calls into question its reliance on the later, largely economic, and more "scientific" writings. This can be seen in his most influential works of the 1960s—*Eros and Civilization*, published in 1956, and *One-Dimensional Man* (2002), which Marcuse worked on from the late 1950s and published in 1964. Before publishing these works, Marcuse was known as a neo-Marxist philosopher writing for a mainly academic audience. After their publication, he came to be known as a spiritual leader to radical students in America and abroad and one of the most recognizable public intellectuals of the age.

References to Marx's early writings, or indeed to Marx himself, are nowhere to be found in *Eros and Civilization*. Given the constraints of the McCarthy era, Marcuse chose not to make any explicit reference to the author of the *1844 Manuscripts*. The young Marx's influence, however, is everywhere to be seen. Thinly veiled references to alienated labor and commodity fetishism permeate Marcuse's theory of technology: "The alienation of labor is almost complete. The mechanics of the assembly line, the routine of the office, the ritual of buying and selling are freed from any connection with human potentialities. Work relations have become to a great extent relations between persons as exchangeable objects of scientific management and efficiency experts" (1956, 102). Marcuse's attempt to reconcile Freud with Marx aims to show how the problem of work, in the sense of a socially useful activity, can be restated without (repressive) sublimation (214). He concedes that there can be "pleasure" in alienated labor: "The typist who hands in a perfect transcript, the tailor who delivers a perfectly fitting suit . . . all may feel a pleasure in a 'job well done.'" However, Marcuse insists, this is a false pleasure because it is

> either extraneous (anticipation of reward), or it is the satisfaction (itself a token of repression) of being well occupied, in the right place,

of contributing one's part to the functioning of the apparatus. In either case, such pleasure has nothing to do with primary instinctual gratification. . . . To say that the job must be done because it is a "job" is truly the apex of alienation, the total loss of instinctual and intellectual freedom—repression has become, not the second, but the first nature of man. (1956, 221)

Crucially, as Marcuse explains in *Soviet Marxism*, published in 1958, this is not an exclusive feature of capitalism. On the contrary, Soviet-style planned economies are equally to blame for alienating workers and repressing their true nature: "The Soviet state exercises throughout political and governmental functions against the proletariat itself; domination remains a specialized function in the division of labor and is as such the monopoly of a political, economic, and military bureaucracy" (Marcuse 1985, 104). For Marcuse, this de facto negation of the emancipatory promises of the October Revolution under Stalin had been made possible by the systematic erasure of the legacy of the humanist Marx and its replacement by the impoverished, positivistic Marx of orthodox dialectical materialism. By emphasizing the importance of the *1844 Manuscripts* and other early Marxian writings, Marcuse places himself in strategic equidistance between the two Cold War superpowers. His criticisms of the Soviet Union granted Marcuse the dissident status that enabled him to criticize America as well. This proved decisive for the success of his social criticism of advanced industrial societies, capitalist and communist alike.

Nowhere is this clearer than in *One-Dimensional Man*, in which Marcuse turns his attention to the advanced industrial societies of the West while holding on to the vision of liberation articulated in *Eros and Civilization*. However, if in *Eros and Civilization* Marcuse supplemented Marx with psychoanalysis, in *One-Dimensional Man* he supplements Marx with phenomenology. This is Marcuse's most well-known work aimed at a general readership, and no less important, it became the "official text" at the training sessions for antiwar activists of the Students for a Democratic Society (SDS). This immensely influential social critique of contemporary societies draws inspiration from the *1844 Manuscripts* in three key regards. First, it provides Marcuse with a critical, negative understanding of alienation (as opposed to Hegel's more neutral definition). Second, it enables him to revisit the early Marx's notion of the "abolition of labor" as the "pacification of existence" (Marcuse 2002, 18). Third, it enables Marcuse to make use of the concept of "necessity," not in the sense of a historical inevitability, as in the mature Marx, but as a categorical moral imperative, in the spirit of the humanist Marx.

These three elements, which form the basis of Marcuse's philosophy of liberation, can be seen at play in the central idea of *One-Dimensional Man*: the concept of the "great refusal." Marcuse's "great refusal" was rooted in Hegel's concept of negativity, wherein a positive is constructed even as the old is being negated. "Negativity," or absolute negativity, was of course what Marx in the *1844 Manuscripts* considered to be the "moving and creating principle" of Hegel's philosophy (Marx 1964, 202). Marcuse uses this Hegelian-Marxian category to explore the inherent contradictions of "one-dimensional man" and society during the postwar period. A one-dimensional society is a society without opposition, one in which there is no space for critique and where *Bildung*, that is, the cultivation of one's individuality, is absent. It is a fundamentally conformist society, in which individuals are alienated from their humanity and from each other (Marcuse 2002, 13) as they fall prey to "false" consumer needs whose goal is not the satisfaction of any fundamental human instinct but merely the integration of individuals into the system of production and consumption through mass media, advertising, and uncritical modes of thought. It is also a society that closes off the historical alternative of a "pacification of existence" in the sense of the "development of man's struggle with man and with nature, under conditions where the competing needs, desires, and aspirations are no longer organized by vested interests in domination and scarcity" (18). In *Counterrevolution and Revolt* (1972a, 65), Marcuse resorts again to the *1844 Manuscripts*—"The sun is the object of the plant... just as the plant is the object for the sun" (Marx 1964, 139)—to illustrate how "pacified" nature is no longer merely an object to be appropriated but a "subject-object" that inspires a human attitude of harmony and respect rather than dominance and exploitative destruction.

For Marcuse, hope resides in three fundamental domains where negativity still resists conformity and oppression and where real freedom can still be enjoyed and authentic individuality realized. These are the domain of man (the human faculties of analysis, critique, and creativeness), the domain of philosophy (where critical concepts enable one to explore the contradictions of real-world arrangements), and the domain of politics (where protest and revolution are pathways to social transformation and emancipation). All three domains, Marcuse argues, were being eroded at an alarming pace in contemporary "one-dimensional" societies. To halt this erosion, Marcuse places his hopes not on *insiders* (i.e., the working classes with stable employment and contributive careers) but on *outsiders* (i.e., all those who refused "the rules of the game," such as bohemians, the unemployed, and racial minorities):

> Underneath the conservative popular base is the substratum of the outcasts and outsiders, the exploited and persecuted of other races and other colors, the unemployed and the unemployable. They exist outside the democratic process; their life is the most immediate and the most real need for ending intolerable conditions and institutions. Their opposition is revolutionary even if their consciousness is not. Their opposition hits the system from without and is therefore not deflected by the system. . . . The critical theory of society possesses no concepts which could bridge the gap between the present and its future; holding no promise and showing no success, it remains negative. Thus it wants to remain loyal to those who, without hope, have given and give their life to the Great Refusal. (2007, 260–61)

Reminding his readers of Walter Benjamin's famous words "It is *only* for the sake of those without hope that hope is given to us" (2007, 261), Marcuse joins a long tradition of critical thinkers who find in outsiders and outcasts the beacons of social hope and political regeneration, of which Jacques Rancière's recent "anarchic" (2009, 46), or populist, theory of democracy[32] is but the latest instance.

If one is to continue the project of exploring the dialectic of dissent deployed by those who have used the *1844 Manuscripts* to imagine an alternative social order, one should start here.

CHAPTER 4

## WHEN SOULS CAME
## TO MATTER

### The Many Lives of Du Bois's
### *The Souls of Black Folk*

*The Souls of Black Folk*, W. E. B. Du Bois's most famous work, was first published in April 1903. Its publisher was A. C. McClurg, based in Chicago. The book's prose—both critical and lyrical, philosophical and personal, polemical and poetical—marked Du Bois's entry into the race for African American leadership. It immediately struck a chord with the public, with the book entering into its third printing only two months after its initial release. The book was reprinted no fewer than twenty-four times from the first set of plates. By the time it was last issued, in 1940, it had sold between eighteen thousand and twenty thousand copies. With the Great Depression and the war, sales slowed down considerably. Du Bois's plans to issue a cheaper edition did not get off the ground. McClurg was struggling, and the book was falling out of view. This fate was only marginally avoided by having it published by Blue Heron Press in 1953. Established by Howard Fast, Blue Heron published two thousand copies of the fiftieth-anniversary edition of *Souls*, which included a new foreword by Du Bois. Despite the book's earlier acclaim, there was little commercial activity surrounding the book's new release, a testament to the social and political climate and publishing pressures during the McCarthy years. Shirley

Graham Du Bois engaged in a grassroots effort to seek advance orders from Du Bois's friends and colleagues, and the book risked becoming a tome to be owned and displayed by the converted. But its public extended and diversified in the 1960s. The book then played an important role in the African American studies movement and emerged as a primer for the civil rights movement. As the 1960s drew to a close, however, *Souls* became a point of major contention between its mainstream and more radical wings, explaining its evanescence in the 1970s. Through the 1980s and 1990s, the field of African American studies reopened due to the adoption of a transnational perspective, and *Souls* traversed into other disciplines, most notably literary studies. It came to be read as a statement of multiculturalism that is race conscious but instigates the blending of races and cultural identities, as well as an early exemplar of race and black identity understood as social and cultural constructs. As the book and its meaning moved from the parochial to the global, the internationalism of a distinctive tradition of black writing woven out of the trope of double consciousness was brought to the fore. In the process, double consciousness broadened as a concept integral to the theory of modernity and as an experience inseparable from that of modern subjectivity. As a result, *Souls* spread its influence outward from African American literature and history to cultural studies and sociology.[1]

INTRODUCTION

Long before sociology was a science he was pioneering in the field of social study of Negro life and completed works on health, education, employment, urban conditions, and religion. This was at a time when scientific inquiry of Negro life was so unbelievably neglected that only a single university in the entire nation had such a program, and it was funded with $5,000 for a year's work.

DR. MARTIN LUTHER KING JR., "HONORING DR. DU BOIS"

W. E. B. Du Bois was a sociologist before sociology existed as a scientific discipline in America. He identified himself as such and produced work attesting to it. He published in the *American Journal of Sociology*, the oldest and most revered journal of the discipline. He was responsible for some of the earliest research studies of rural and urban Negro life. Years before the famous studies of the Chicago school, he published *The Philadelphia Negro* (1899), a pathbreaking study based on rigorous fieldwork submitted to sharp sociological analysis. He organized the annual Atlanta conferences (1897–1914), setting the ground for serious empirical research on blacks in America that sought to "put science into sociology" (Du Bois 2011, 51). He followed very consciously in the footsteps of Henry Mayhew's and Charles Booth's pioneering work of social reportage. Even though there is no direct line of descent, Du Bois's work foreshadows what we now call "intersectionality." Yet until very recently, Du Bois was kept out of the sociological canon.[2] Mainstream accounts of the origins of American sociology rarely acknowledged him or his sociological school. Contemporary sociologists hardly ever acknowledged his work, let alone claimed his influence. And when, much later, sociologists began to take him as a valuable interlocutor, it was to *The Souls of Black Folk* (1903; henceforth *Souls*) and not *The Philadelphia Negro* that they turned.

The version of *Souls* recuperated and reconstructed in sociology—in domains such as critical race research as it spread from the confines of legal studies into sociology at the turn of the millennium—is a late production and one of the many *Souls* that have existed in the twentieth century. In this chapter, we revisit how *Souls* has been viewed by and presented to the public from its release in 1903 to the centennial editions celebrating it as one of the most iconic texts of the twentieth century. As with any other book of note, *Souls* has been received against shifting horizons of expectation, and it has been a different book for different communities of readers confronting its pages over time. Living through many incarnations, *Souls* experienced periods of notoriety and relative oblivion. We capture these by following the editorial activity surrounding the book, zooming into the presentational features of especially relevant editions intended to support and guide certain "readings" of the text. Our primary focus is on introductions or prefatory texts and how they are used to establish relevant background and context while priming the readers to interpret the text, its meaning, and its intended effects in certain ways. As the book is made to stand for considerably different projects, its meaning is construed retroactively as a meditation on history and the political. Interventions through and on the book are deeply ingrained in intellectual and political-ideological contexts, which we seek to bring out. As we do so, it will become apparent how political and disciplinary struggles sometimes conflate and how disciplinary boundaries come to redefine the nature and extent of the political problems at hand. Bridging scholarship, experience, and activism, *Souls* has faced the question of how to articulate the two discourses, political and intellectual, activist and literary, from its birth. But in the readings provided by editors and prefacers, *Souls* has been made to sit quite rigidly in different genres—from political manifesto to literary work—even if the relative depoliticization involved in the transformation of genre serves the very political project of creating a new national culture, perhaps a new polity, by means of a university curriculum. As Henry Louis Gates Jr., the leading figure of this attempt, has put it, "teaching literature" is tantamount to "the teaching of an aesthetic and political order" (1992, 35). The one proposed by Gates is one in which "African-American culture," as epitomized by writers like Du Bois, provides a "model of multiculturalism and plurality" in whose footsteps America is to follow (xvii).

Through our analysis of *Souls'* life cycles, we have been able to establish four distinct stages in its publication history:[3] an initial phase between 1903 and 1953, which broadly coincides with A. C. McClurg's rights of publication (1903–49); the first wave of reissues of the 1960s; the second wave of reissues of the 1980s/1990s; and finally, the current phase marked by the critical and digital centenary editions. In what follows, we take you through these distinct phases and the distinctive framings of the book they offer. But before we assess the multiple ways in which the book's presentational features have been used to redirect the meaning, we must look into how the book originated.

### THE SOULS OF BLACK FOLK: A BOOK OF MANY PARTS

All life cycles begin with birth. Books are commonly thought to descend from one progenitor: the author. It is often the case, however, that paternity is more shared. In the case of *Souls*, the book was the brainchild of its editors. One of them in particular, Francis Fisher Browne, remained, to the end, the driving force behind the project.[4] In the Jubilee edition of *Souls*, Du Bois relates how "the Brownes" at A. C. McClurg first approached him with the idea for a book. The invitation, he explains, was part of a wider cultural initiative: "to build a literary and publishing center in the Midwest" (Du Bois 1953, ix).[5]

It is easy to see how Du Bois's book might have been an attractive choice for a publisher's portfolio. Literary launches require young and promising authors. Du Bois, by then a rising African American star with a growing public profile, fit the category perfectly. He was the author of two monographs published by reputed university presses—*Suppression of the African Slave Trade to America* with Harvard and *The Philadelphia Negro* with the University of Pennsylvania Press—and multiple essays published in large circulation and specialized periodicals. These included *The Dial*, the politics and literary magazine owned by A. C. McClurg.

A. C. McClurg sent out its invitation around 1900, when Du Bois had embarked on his Atlanta project in hopes of producing "a broad and exhaustive study of the Negro Problem in the United States"; such was the book he outlined to the editors. But an expansive scholarly monograph aimed at a select readership some years down the line was not what they had in mind—"they naturally wanted something more limited," Du Bois recollects, "aimed at a popular audience" (Du Bois 1953, ix).

Time was a key issue. The idea of assembling a collection of previously published and unpublished essays, and perhaps adding a few new ones to the mix, seemed more effective given the time pressures. The editors were pleased with it, but Du Bois was unenthusiastic. He questioned the cohesiveness of anthologies. Assemblages of methodologically diverse essays, written at different times, for radically different purposes, he confided, "always fall so flat" (1940, 80). At the end of the project, he was no less emphatic in his skepticism and professed how underwhelmed he was with the final result: "This was incomplete and unsatisfactory" (1953, ix). But three years after the original invitation, the manuscript was nonetheless sent off.

While *Souls* was to be by far his most successful book, Du Bois's reservations about the anthology would never quite go away. They seemed serious enough to have stood in the way of the project and may explain its long period of completion, given how much was prepublished and prewritten material. The interesting question, however, is not why Du Bois struggled; it is why he persevered.

One intervening event likely gave the project a new sense of purpose. In 1901, Booker T. Washington released his autobiography, *Up from Slavery*.[6] It was an immediate best seller, reinforcing Washington's celebrity status and his influence on decision-makers. As Du Bois notes in his July 1901 review for *The Dial*, the book, drawing on the slave narrative format, described Washington's rise to prominence in heroic terms. It used this compelling narrative to promote the Tuskegee argument that the amelioration of the black condition depended on a twofold strategy—an ethics of self-improvement and industriousness and accommodation with the South based on trading the black right to vote and social equality for the better economic opportunities that only vocational training could afford (Du Bois 1901). If Du Bois was to have the chance to hold back Washington's political machine, he had to act quickly. He did not have Washington's organizational power and neither was he his match as a public speaker. But what he did have was the power of the pen and a potential book in which to exercise it.

Du Bois was a far better writer than Washington. But not just any writing would do to write his way into leadership. Written a few years earlier, in 1899, Du Bois's *The Philadelphia Negro* harbored his hopes of social reform. It contained quite a few novelistic vignettes and a fair amount of moral commentary, just as *Souls* contains some distinctively descriptive-analytical sociological sections.[7] Yet overall, *The Philadelphia Negro* fell into the genre of the scholarly monograph. It was a "social study" (the book's subtitle) relying on the collection and systematic examination of empirical data. As such, it showed without necessarily moving, and it proved without necessarily persuading. To stand any chance in the battle of ideas against Washington, *Souls* had to be a different kind of work. As the editors hoped, it needed to reach out to a far larger and less specialized audience. Its truths needed to be felt rather than simply understood. Knowledge had to be used as power. This implied a radical change of approach, in form as well as in content.

The rhetorical posture of speaking to its readers in an "intimate tone of self-revelation" (Aptheker 1977, 9) runs through *Souls* and is integral to its attempt to turn words into actions and demands into reality (see also Rogers 2012). When compared to *Philadelphia Negro*, *Souls* distinguishes itself by moving from detachment to sympathy, from observation to identification, and from data to lived experience, suitably expanded through metaphor. If *Philadelphia Negro* provided the data and the analytic-scientific discourse, *Souls* invested it with new poetic meaning and a new poietic power. Early readers confessed to being moved by it; later reviewers and activists remember it as instigating desire and making an irresistible call to political action.

The book's intimate style fits its adoption of an internalist perspective whereby the author identifies with the subject and simultaneously positions himself as one *of* them and one *with* them. This offers a riposte to Washington's slave narrative. His self-construction as the hero arises from the notion of exceptionality and produces a distancing whereby Washington, the charismatic leader, becomes the nemesis of other ex-slaves. This otherness is exactly what Du Bois sublates in *Souls* so that he may become a representative and legitimately "speak from within—to depict a world as we see it who dwell therein" (Du Bois quoted in Aptheker 1977, 1152). From this "insider" position (Merton 1972), Du Bois promises to tap into the deep structures of meaning that animate racial prejudice and the institution of slavery itself. This is done not in the abstract but from an understanding of how racism works itself into his own life and the everyday lives of fellow African Americans.

But the internalist perspective was not without its challenges. When speaking to the *Independent* of the book's style, Du Bois admitted that the fact that he was a Negro and embraced the cause of racial emancipation predestined him "to a certain narrowness of view, and at the same time to some clearness of vision." As an insider, he could disclose to the reader how different the world looked from his side of the color line. But because his judgment was so manifestly located, he expected them to contest him and set their judgment against his. This, Du Bois observed, violated the discursive norms of the scholarly authorial voice. Authors typically speak from an authoritative viewpoint—distanced, rational, avoiding empathetic identification. Hence there is a cost for abandoning "the usual impersonal and judicial attitude of the traditional author." But what is lost in authoritativeness is "gained in vividness" and that intensity of feeling "which both wins and repels sympathy" (Du Bois quoted in Aptheker 1977, 1152).

There is, of course, much self-fashioning in the way Du Bois presents his giving up of the author position and its prerogatives, for, in effect, he continues to write at times with analytical detachment, putting that which is too close at some distance so that he may see it more distinctively. His grasping of the "strange meaning of being black" depends as much on introspection and his direct experience of the South as it does on study and on his capacity to imaginatively occupy the standpoints of others, black and white, as if they are his own (Du Bois 1903, "The Forethought"). His theoretical vision ultimately depends on his capacity to move into, about, and out of such positions (Gooding-Williams 2009). This and the elaborate style and workmanship of the writing speak not of an author giving up his authorial position but of one actively using his authorial prerogatives to direct meaning and control reception.

*Souls* is a work in search of perlocutionary effects, and it makes sure to obtain them. Unlike Washington's, Du Bois's strategy for black advancement is contingent on black mobilization and white moral evolution. Accordingly, Du Bois's purpose in *Souls* is twofold. The first is to inspire his black readers with a political vision for the future direction of their struggle: Du Bois, after all, was quite moralistic toward "loafers" and other wasters in his own "race."[8] The second is to harness his white readers' support for his vision by cultivating their sympathy for black suffering and their shame for their role in its perpetuation (Rogers 2012). "All art is propaganda and ever must be," writes Du Bois (1986, 1000). His book too was to be propaganda, deploying the transformative power of rhetoric to bring about a new American polity.

Du Bois makes this purpose clear in two of the most important paratexts of the book: "The Forethought" and "The After-Thought." The notion of the paratext as performative is integral to these pieces. Although *Souls* is a book written for both audiences, black and white, these two paratexts primarily address white readers. In "The Forethought," Du Bois speaks to his "Gentle Reader" with deference and humility. He invites readers to see beyond his excesses and shortcomings and into "the grain of truth" hidden in the book. He warns them of the foreignness of what they will find as he lifts the veil separating their two worlds and discloses "the strange meaning of being black here in the dawning of the Twentieth Century." He anticipates their resistance to go visiting and alerts them to their vested interest in looking therein, "for the problem of the Twentieth Century," which is also necessarily theirs, "is the problem of the color-line" (Du Bois 1903, "The Forethought"). In "The After-Thought," Du Bois addresses his readers' guilt more directly to explore the opportunities it creates for their moral restoration and the establishment of that "human brotherhood," which remains only "mockery and a snare." He urges them to let his book act on them, reigniting their reflective judgment (their "vigor of thought") and their willingness to act on it (through "thoughtful deed"). Such energy should fuel the book's call to arms.

To speak to white readers in these terms and enlist black readers in his political project, Du Bois had to address them not only as himself but as a representative black man capable of mediating between their worlds. In "The Forethought," he acknowledges that this might not be as easy as it would first appear. Making his the words of Adam upon the creation of Eve, he concludes with an open question: "Need I add that I who speak here am bone of the bone and flesh of the flesh of them that live within the Veil?" The question is rhetorical but not trivial.

*Souls* is Du Bois's battleground in the cause of black leadership. In writing his autobiography, Washington emulated Frederick Douglass (whose biography he would rewrite) and claimed for himself the title of his rightful heir. Born a slave on a small farm in the Virginia backcountry, Washington claimed to speak for poor Southern blacks who lacked Du Bois's opportunities. He was their natural leader. A mulatto born into a relatively tolerant and integrated community in Massachusetts, Du Bois, the cold intellectual, seemed to share little with such folk. *Souls* was a space in which to construct his belonging.

THE MAKING OF *SOULS*

Building sites are often chaotic, with their mix of used and unused materials scattered here and there. *Souls* might have resembled such a space, being a work drawn from fourteen essays—published, unpublished, and newly written—whose untamed, almost wild diversity Du Bois highlights: "There are bits of history and biography, some description of scenes and persons, something of controversy and criticism, some statistics and a bit of storytelling" (quoted in Aptheker 1977, 1152). If this was to be a book, how were its disparate parts to be woven together into one piece? Du Bois's answer to the challenge of such unity was threefold—tone, form, and metaphor. Together they made *one* book.

First is tone. Reflecting on what gives "a unity to the book," Du Bois maintains it is "not simply the general unity of the larger topic, but a unity of purpose in the distinctively subjective note that runs in each essay" (quoted in Griffin 2003, 32). By "subjective note," Du Bois means, primarily, his use of his own biographical experience to illuminate the question of race in America. This reaches its peak in "Of the Passing of the First-Born," an autobiographical essay in which Du Bois discloses his pathos for the untimely and possibly avoidable death of his infant son. But the chapter is in many ways unrepresentative. It is an outburst of emotion against a sea of measured exposure. The subjective note Du Bois imparts to *Souls* works, for the most part, in far more subtle ways. With the exception of a few life-changing episodes both large and small, Du Bois kept his personal life out of the book while using the particularized experience of racial segregation of other characters, both real and fictional, to put the general racial situation in striking relief. As Shamoon Zamir rightly observes, personal experience "is always woven along the edges of the cultural and political commentaries of the book." It therefore "reinforces and counterpoints, but is never the primary or sole site of exploration" (1995, 189–90). The power of restraint, Du Bois knew all too well, can be experienced with great intensity.

The subjective note is not Du Bois's only way of plotting meaning. Much more is done through multiple layers of framing. It all starts with the choice of the title. Early reviewers noticed how "significant" the title is (Kelsey 1903), with its wide resonance, both secular and religious. In its denotative and connotative meanings—that black folks have souls and are hence human and that their souls are plural and hence fragmented—the title conveys the fundamental messages of the book. It also announces that this is a book about the spiritual life of the black community, which relies on "soul" feelings and related cultural practices to bring itself together as such.

That *Souls* is a prophetic book about a spiritual community is a message conveyed, again, by the titles of individual chapters. The preposition "of" at the beginning of each chapter reminds one of *The Book of Common Prayer* or other similar religious texts, such as the thirty-nine articles of religion adopted by the Protestant Episcopal Church in the United States in 1801.[9] The heading of the table of contents, written in a solemn passive voice—"Herein is Written"— adds to the suggestion that *Souls* is destined to be revered as a sacred text. A book of revelation (of the African American experience), as well as a book seeking to found a hybridized American polity, *Souls* establishes Du Bois as a prophetic leader conducting his people through their own exodus. It would not take long for readers to recognize this. As early as 1913, William Ferris referred to *Souls* as "the political Bible of the Negro race" (quoted in Blight and Gooding-Williams 1997, 21). His assessment would be shared by generations of Negro intellectuals to come.[10]

Another dominant frame constructing textual unity is plotted into the text's formal organization. For Du Bois, form is substance, and *Souls* has its own distinctive form—that is, a dual structure pointing toward the book's unresolved dialectics of antagonism and interdependence. This manifests itself most clearly in the pair of quotations that frames each of the chapters. Each pair comprises one piece of verse by a renowned Western poet and one musical bar from an African American spiritual.[11] Although the chosen sorrow songs are well known, they are unidentified. No title or text accompanies them. For those who can "read" them alongside the Western epigraph, they function as a metatext, a kind of preface or extra layer of interpretation, adding to the hermeneutic thickness of the essay that follows. "Of the Passing of the First-Born" has for its epigraph the consoling words of the Negro spiritual "I Hope My Mother Will Be There." "Of Mr. Booker T. Washington and Others," arguably the epicenter of Du Bois's dispute with Washington's leadership, is prefaced by "A Great Camp Meeting in the Promised Land," an exhortative prophetic chant fit for a new leader offering guidance to his people from pursuit to bondage and from bondage to escape in a dialectical movement that hopefully finds earthly resolution. But there is meaning in the sorrow song's muteness too. It speaks of a parting of worlds—that is, of a cultural world that had remained alien to most whites and had been alienated by many middle-class blacks seeking new postslavery identities for themselves. As such, the typographical juxtaposing of each pair of quotations begs two different readings. On the one hand, it presents two soulful communities and the as-yet-unrealized possibility of a community of soul between them grounded on mutual cultural fertilization. On the other hand, it speaks of incommunicability—mostly asymmetrical, even though the erudite Western epigraphs too would have been undecipherable for common black folk—in a society radically divided against itself. The moment of cultural synthesis may be Du Bois's distant hope, but it is one the future may well deny.

Alongside tone and form, there is a third unifying element in the book: conceptual imagery. Two metaphors reign supreme in the text, casting a wide web that holds the essays together—that of the veil separating the worlds of black and white America and that of the doubling that characterizes the social, psychological, and spiritual condition of African Americans. Let us start with the veil. At its simplest, the veil stands for the color line, or the racial barrier dividing black Americans from white Americans. But the meaning of the veil is more complex and its workings more dynamic than this might suggest. Taken strictly as a barrier, the veil is something that separates "the world within" from "the world without" and therefore works as an obstacle to mutual recognition. But while trapping one within, the veil can also work as a soft protective casing sheltering the veiled from the full impact of the world outside, a world dominated by racial prejudice. Veils are, moreover, not perfectly opaque but transparent. They allow some seeing, however limited or distorted. This means that veils can be as much a barrier as a connective channel or a mediatory surface. In its multiple functionalities and incidences, both micro and macro, individual and collective, subjective and intersubjective, the veil offers an imagistic expression to the pervasive dialectics of alienation and interdependence conveyed by the typographical juxtaposition of verse and sorrow song.[12]

But while the veil refers primarily to societal estrangement, it also encompasses an individual estrangement within the racialized self. It therefore cuts across the fabric of American society, from every institution and community to its members' personal identities. This takes us to the second image unifying Du Bois's book—double consciousness. Nowadays, double consciousness is the synecdoche of the book. Interestingly, however, although Du Bois deploys the concept at multiple junctures, he never mentions it explicitly as a key part of the book's legacy, notably in its paratexts, either in the original or in subsequent editions. In his words, "One ever feels his two-ness,— an American, a Negro; two souls, two thoughts, two irreconcilable strivings; two warring ideals in one dark body, whose dogged strength alone keeps it from being torn asunder" (1903, 2). Doubling becomes depicted as a violent inner fight between one's Negro-ness and one's American-ness, mobilizing their competing callings and their competing claims on oneself.[13] This is also presented as an embodied fight, taking the body apart but met with a tenacious resistance fed by the instinct to stay—or indeed become—whole. The racialization of the self stands in the way of this, however, rendering the reconnection between two halves impossible. It also impedes self-consciousness, or blacks becoming aware of themselves.

Thus the veil is not only something *between* but also something *within*. Identity is always interpersonal, shaped through our relations to others, and in a racist society, a black person's image as reflected by others will almost inevitably be demeaning, actively undermining feelings of self-worth, putting one at war with oneself. The lived experience of racial oppression therefore comes with the affliction of double consciousness, which Du Bois describes as both a curse and a gift—a second sight enabling one to see beyond the ordinary and disclose to America the disquieting truth it must know about itself. In "The Forethought," Du Bois presents himself as well placed to affect this revelation, being someone who can travel and "sketch in swift outline" both worlds, "within and without the Veil" (Du Bois 1903, "The Forethought").

Acting simultaneously at three levels—form, tone, and conceptual imagery, with the latter unfolding in three distinct but closely related images (the veil, second sight, and double consciousness)—Du Bois's structure is a scaffolding that proves sturdy enough to bind the internal diversity of his book. The final essay, on the songs of slavery, speaks in eschatological terms of "that sometime, somewhere, [when] men will judge men by their souls and not their skins."[14] It offers the keystone for the text and makes it ready for production as *one* book presenting a powerful distinct voice in the debate on race and racism in America. It is a debate in which, according to advocates of public sociology such as Michael Burawoy, Du Bois personified the "traditional public sociologist," who brings his sociological expertise to foster dialogue within and between publics on issues of public concern, his book acting as "a *catalyst* of public debate and discussion" (2005b, 72). As showcased in *Souls*, Du Bois's contribution to sociology was as deep as it was wide, ranging from subfields such as the sociology of race, to the sociology of culture, to the sociology of religion. In all of these, Du Bois wrote as the polymath effectively defying the "enclosure" of sociology as an academic discipline. For most of the twentieth century, academic sociology ignored Du Bois's contributions to the discipline, and *Souls*—his most widely read and most boundary-transgressive work, whose primary goal was emancipatory rather than scholarly—was no exception. The reading public that was to engage primarily with the work was nonexpert and sat behind the veil. Hence if Du Bois was ever a public sociologist, he was so before sociology was ready to hear the sociological significance of his work and before the public who read him was ready to recognize him (also) as a sociologist. Disillusioned with the lack of opportunity and funding for the Atlanta conferences, Du Bois eventually abandoned academic sociology to become a professional activist. As Matthew Dawson observes, after 1920, Du Bois continued to make use of the tools of sociological analysis but would do so from "*outside* the academy, as an activist" (2016, 69; our emphasis). As someone who combined progressive political struggle for racial justice with a sociology that doubled as a critique of sociology and the system of education as part of the problem, Du Bois was condemned to such a pilgrimage.

THE EARLY LIFE: 1903 AND 1953

On April 18, 1903, *Souls* went on sale. However, as with any other publication, the fate of the book was not sealed. Much depended on its finding a readership. It is to the reader that the power of life and death over a book ultimately falls, hence Du Bois's dramatic appeal in "The After-Thought": "Hear my cry, O God the Reader, vouchsafe that this my book fall not still-born."

If Du Bois's fears were ever real, they were soon to be appeased. Sales spoke of a healthy birth. By October 1903, the book was already in its second edition and selling about 200 copies a week. Five years later, sales amounted to an impressive 9,595 copies. Interest at home was followed by growing interest abroad. As early as 1905, *Souls* was into its first British reprint by Archibald Constable & Co. in London, and its translation into German was under way under the auspices of Max Weber, who first met Du Bois in Germany in the 1890s.[15]

This early success was not without obstacles, however. Vicissitudes in the life cycle of a book are to be expected. Many will be accidental, but they can also track with power relations. This was the case with Du Bois's book. Its success depended on that elusive book publicity, which only reviews in the press might achieve. The "Tuskegee Machine"[16] knew this. As one early reviewer put it, the Tuskegee Machine saw the book's critique of its racial program "as only a less malignant form of lèse-majesté than criticism of the war program of a President" (*Nation* 1903, 481–82). In entering the struggle for the symbolic representation of African Americans and the power to order American society, *Souls* constituted high treason. It needed silencing. With its powerful control over the press, especially the black press, the Tuskegee Machine was reasonably successful in keeping the book out of its pages. So was the Southern press, which ignored it as much as possible.

Despite this, however, reviews did emerge in various outlets targeting multiple audiences: the black middle-class elite, Northern white liberals, Southern conservatives, and even foreign observers curious about how the problem of the color line expressed itself both within and beyond U.S. borders.[17] As expected, the tenor of the reviews was mixed. While some treated the book as a "must read" for blacks and whites alike, others deemed it riotous and too "dangerous for the negro to read, for it will only excite discontent and fill his imagination with things that do not exist, or things that should not bear upon his mind."[18] If some praised its literary qualities—namely, its polished and affecting prose—others criticized it for its extravagance, elitism, and opacity. And if some sought to deauthorize the book by questioning Du Bois's black credentials and his proximity to his subject matter, others asserted the book's authority on the grounds of its author's knowledge of the Negro condition and his personal representativeness.

The nature of the book itself was contested. The polemical treatise was contrasted with the literary masterpiece. No one made this clearer than John Daniels, the reviewer for *Alexander's Magazine*, a Boston-based black periodical. *Souls*, Daniels forecasted, was a classic, to be taken not as "a polemic, a transient thing" but as "a poem, a thing permanent." Daniels was in the minority, however. For most of its early readers and critics, the book was the sum total of the polemics against Booker T. Washington. It established the terms of the feud between Du Bois, the radical pushing for full racial equality, and Washington, the conservative content with economic betterment. These same polemics drew some of the book's staunchest opposition and the Northern liberal press's wary handling of it. With North/South relations hanging on a fragile racial status quo, the Northern press would not take sides, or when it did, it would take Washington's. The liberal *Collier's Weekly*, one of the largest-selling magazines in the United States, urged the black population to follow Washington, the sensible leader, rather than Du Bois, the attractive yet dangerous dreamer. The *New York Times* handled the book tactfully, handing over its review to a skeptical anonymous Southern reader. The reviewer recognized its value but doubted its author's blackness and his knowledge of the subject matter. The *New York Evening Post* followed suit but tried to adopt a more balanced position. In a review later anonymously reprinted in *The Nation* (June 11, 1903) but that betrayed the authorship of Oswald Garrison Villard, a Bookerite, the book was deemed "remarkable as a piece of literature" (reprinted in Griffin 2003, 18–20). Villard agreed that *Souls* was the product of a man "not so black as he has painted himself" but insisted that Du Bois's mind was nevertheless "characteristic of his people" (18). Du Bois's critique of Washington, he noted, could have been more evenhanded, but it was insightful and informed enough to "deserve the carefullest consideration" (20). A similar view appeared in the *Independent*, another bastion of white liberal opinion, but now through the pen of William Hayes Ward. "As an index of the negro's inner life and feeling" and as a diagnosis of the Negro's "unique situation in American social life," Ward stressed, *Souls* was unmatched (quoted in Aptheker 1989, 60). It could have been fairer to Washington, for sure, but the reviewer confessed his own skepticism about some of Washington's proposals. To acknowledge this much was not to endorse Du Bois's uncompromising defense of the black ballot, civil rights, and liberal education as the only means to emancipate the African American from his current half slavery. But it showed that a crack had formed in the Tuskegee Machine that would not easily mend.

Reviews in academic journals were equally mixed. Theophilus Bolden Stuart reviewed the book favorably for the *American Journal of Sociology*. Broadly sympathetic with the terms of Du Bois's opposition to Washington, Stuart admired, in particular, his understanding of "the negro's emotional nature" and the new type of "industrial bondage" that had trapped the black population in a lasting master-slave dialectic (reprinted in Griffin 2003, 31). Carl Kelsey, professor of sociology at the University of Pennsylvania, wrote the review for the *Annals of the American Academy of Political and Social Sciences* (1903). Considered an authority on the Negro question in Philadelphia's reform circles, Kelsey was the author of *The Negro Farmer*, a study indebted to the notion of the black population's inherent incompetence. Kelsey was clearly taken aback by the book. "A more interesting book," he claimed, "seldom comes into one's hands." He was also especially sensitive to matters of form. He noticed the book's "significant title of 'The Souls of Black Folk'" and reflected on how its material form befitted its meaning and its literary form its subject matter. He drew attention to the craftsmanship involved in the book's assemblage: "The simple black cover with its gilt letters, the chapters headed with a few bars of some of the old negro melodies, the sorrow songs, seem in keeping with them. The interest in the subject is increased by the literary form in which it is couched." The religious, even biblical, imagery in the book also came through in its design. Kelsey seems to be inspecting a Bible, ascetically bound in black, only the gilt letters on the cover announcing that we are in the presence of not just any book but the "book of books," both in itself and in what it stands for. But if *Souls* was a Bible, it was a *political* Bible that collided with Kelsey's conservative sympathies. The South, Kelsey concurred with Du Bois, "is a most fruitful field of social study," but Du Bois was too enraged to see it. He saw darkness where Kelsey saw light: "There is more of good in the relationship of the two races than Mr. Dubois would have us believe." As was the case with many other early reviewers, Kelsey also thought the *entente cordiale* signed by the Wizard of Tuskegee in Alabama did not need much fixing, and certainly no fixing of the magnitude urged by Du Bois.

Despite the Tuskegee Machine's attempts to halt it, the book picked up sales. *Life Magazine* hailed it "the most thought-arresting challenge in the whole race problem campaign." Catapulted into the spotlight by this and similar reviews, it left a trail of admiration and controversy in its wake. Between 1903 and 1938, A. C. McClurg reprinted the book no fewer than twenty-two times, and although each print run was relatively small, by 1935 it had sold approximately fifteen thousand copies, a considerable achievement for a book written by an African American, and made uncomfortable reading for a sizeable part of its limited white readership.

The Great Depression and the Second World War slowed sales down. In 1940, the book went out of print. Six years later, it was out of stock and became practically unobtainable. The beginning of the Cold War, especially the "Great Fear" of McCarthyism in the early 1950s, represented a low point in the book's publication history. Along with other works by Du Bois, it was the object of censorship, often being "removed from libraries as examples of Communist-inspired propaganda" (Marable 2006, 8). McCarthyite harassment—which in Du Bois's case included his indictment and trial as a foreign agent—left Du Bois worrying that his book would go out of print (Winant 2007, 564). His fears proved warranted. On January 11, 1946, the president of A. C. McClurg, whose publishing department was by that time practically inactive owing to the death of their publishing manager, approached Du Bois with its wish to discontinue printing and relinquish its publication rights. The death of the book was imminent. Du Bois reacted promptly, demonstrating an interest in acquiring the printing plates, provided a "reasonable price" was offered. A. C. McClurg established a price of $100[19] but received no reply from Du Bois. In December 1948, the editor insisted, asking Du Bois whether he remained interested in the plates. A week later, Du Bois replied positively and asked that the transaction be delayed for about a month. In January 1949, Du Bois received the plates of a book that was almost lost to readers.

The survival of the book was far from secure, however. If the book were to have a second life, Du Bois still needed to have it produced, reprinted, and circulated. Yet he struggled to find a publisher among the established publishing houses. With the fiftieth anniversary of the book approaching, its fate seemed unpromising. But fate has a capricious nature, and writer Shirley Graham, who married Du Bois in 1951, was pivotal in its turn. Graham contacted Howard Fast, a member of the Communist Party and a close friend. Fast was the mastermind behind the Blue Heron Press, established in New York in 1952 to assist left-wing intellectuals forced underground by McCarthyite repression. Chief among them was Fast himself, whose novel *Spartacus*, a fictionalization of a slave revolt in ancient Rome, was rejected outright by publishers only to become a best seller when self-published by Fast through Blue Heron. Fast agreed enthusiastically to assist in the publication of Du Bois's book, which he ultimately described as "a no-profit-net-loss project, but a very beautiful book that made me quite proud" (1990, 298–99). With Fast's help, Du Bois was finally in a position to see his book reprinted for its jubilee. But what seemed straightforward proved to be far more complicated.

Problems did not come from external resistance this time but from authorial angst about its reception in a post-Holocaust world. For several months in early 1952, Du Bois battled with concerns about passages in the work that could be read as anti-Semitic. He eventually altered the original text by introducing changes to the relevant passages. However, he would not explain to his readers what he had changed, nor why, beyond a vague prefatory statement about trying "to avoid any possible misunderstanding today of what I meant to say yesterday" (Du Bois 1953, "Foreword"). Although evasive about the changes, Du Bois's newly written "Foreword" was defiant in other respects. Du Bois stressed how his intervening engagement with Freud, and especially Marx, enabled him to grasp more fully the problematic of race in ways that moved beyond the analysis originally provided in *Souls*. Freud, he claimed, helped him gain a better understanding of the role of unconscious thought and custom in the perpetuation of racial prejudice. But it was Marx who expanded his understanding the most (see, e.g., Stanfield 2010, 178–83) by disclosing "a greater problem which both obscures and implements" the problem of race. This now came to be conceived of as an effect of economic exploitation worldwide and "the fact that so many civilized persons are willing to live in comfort even if the price of this is poverty, ignorance, and disease of the majority of their fellowmen; [and] that to maintain this privilege men have waged war until today war tends to become universal and continuous, and the excuse for this war continues to be color and race" (Du Bois 1953, "Foreword"). Marxism, Du Bois claimed, was essential to unlock the true reach and meaning of the problem of race. More radical political thinking was necessary to confront it in its full dimensions: Pan-Africanism. "Today the whole world is being called to account to its dark peoples," announced Graham in her introduction to the 1953 edition (Graham 1953, xv). Their anticolonial efforts (the Mau Mau uprising in British Kenya began in 1952), she submitted, bore similarities to the struggle for civil and economic rights in the United States. Hence it was only proper that he who first called white America to account and played a key role in the Pan-African political movement now should be republished. In October 1953, the hardcover 8vo, two-thousand-copy print run of the Blue Heron Fiftieth-Anniversary Jubilee edition of *Souls* appeared. No commercial activity surrounded the book's release. In its absence, Shirley

Graham personally mobilized Du Bois's friends and colleagues to make advance orders. Limited, numbered, autographed, and sold at $5.00 a copy,[20] each containing a certification of authenticity, the Blue Heron *Souls* circulated as a collectible item aimed at a select few.[21] McCarthyism had made *Souls* into a cult object for the converted.[22]

### *SOULS*, THE POLITICAL MANIFESTO: THE 1960S

During the 1960s, circulation rose from a select few to reach a mass readership. In 1961, the first affordable pocket-sized edition was issued. The Premier Americana paperback, published by Fawcett, marked the beginning of the third stage in the life of the book. This was a period anchored by two major events—Du Bois's death in Accra, Ghana, on August 27, 1963, at age ninety-five on the one hand and the 1960s civil rights movement on the other. In the last two years of his life, Du Bois cut all ties and embarked on the life of an outsider. He joined the Communist Party, moved to Ghana, and renounced his American citizenship. As a result, he became an outcast among the establishment and an uncomfortable figure even among civil rights leaders. While the latter were gathering for the triumphant 1963 March on Washington, Du Bois's long and eventful life was coming to an end on the other side of the ocean. That same day, more than two hundred thousand demonstrators—most of them black—took to the streets of Washington demanding their civil and economic rights. The evening before the march, they were greeted by a telegram of support addressed by Du Bois to Martin Luther King Jr. The next day, gathered on the Mall in Washington, they received the news of Du Bois's death with grief and consternation. The radicalism of Du Bois's later years waned in the face of his disappearance. The path was now open for the remarkable rehabilitation of *Souls*, the most prominent of his early works.

With the rise of the civil rights movement, Du Bois's ideas gained new relevance. The revival of interest is reflected in the wave of reissues of *Souls* in the 1960s. Besides the Premier Americana paperback, edited and introduced by Saunders Redding, new mass-market paperback editions included the 1965 *Three Negro Classics* collection, edited and introduced by John Hope Franklin; the 1965 Longmans edition, introduced by C. L. R. James; and the 1969 Signet / New American Library edition, edited and introduced by Nathan Hare and Alvin Poussaint. All these introductions played a crucial role in reframing Du Bois's book and priming its readers. However, they have little in common. No sooner was Du Bois beatified than the feud over his political legacy started.

Let us take the commonalities first. They all construct *Souls* primarily as a political manifesto. Gone were the days of the book as a poem. If there is poetry in *Souls*, it is the poetry of political change, possibly even revolution. The book emerges from the paperback introductions as a text committed to doing things with words, to changing the world beyond its covers. As Redding encapsulates it, "The *Souls of Black Folk* is more history-making than historical" (1961, ix). *Souls* is not just a past reference but a new resource for the advancement of emancipation (Rabaka 2010a, 349). This is therefore no longer simply the text of the historical debate between self-help and integration. Neither is this the text of Du Bois the social scientist. It is rather the text of a Du Bois who had inaugurated the present struggle for white equality and who had grown disenchanted with the power of science to propel social reform and right the wrongs of a deeply racialized society (Poussaint 1969). If only science were introduced into sociology in the study of race, if only objective quantitative truth were disclosed and allowed to dispel prejudice, then social reform would eventually follow—as the pre-*Souls* Du Bois might have believed (Hare 1969, xii). But the Du Bois of *Souls* had come to see differently. "Detached inquiry is not enough"; we, standing here and now, must act (Redding 1961). In *Souls*, the pen had been the first means, or instrument, of acting toward America's self-foundation. Now someone else's agency was required to enact it further.

But this is where the common framing finishes and the introductions part ways. A complex political game is played hereafter, with various strands within the civil rights movement seeking legitimacy by positioning themselves in respect to the text in its peritexts. The chief contrast here is between Du Bois as the architect of the mainstream civil rights movement and Du Bois as the forebear of black power activism.

Redding's Du Bois is the former. A pioneering critic and historian of African American literature and a member of the Joint Centre for Political Studies in Washington, Redding is unequivocal about the significance of Du Bois's book. This is a book offering a "new approach to social reform: patriotic, non-violent activism" (1961, ix). If any doubt persisted about the book's allegiance, the 1965 reissue of the Premier Americana paperback dispelled it. Whereas the 1961 edition featured on its cover a plaudit from *Life Magazine*, the 1965 edition replaced it with an endorsement by Roy Wilkins, executive secretary of the National Association for the Advancement of Colored People (NAACP). By association, *Souls* comes into view as the brainchild of Du Bois, the cofounder of the NAACP, the editor of *The Crisis*, and the advocate of moderate activism and racial integration. Redding's words in the introduction reassure readers of this. The Montgomery bus boycott in

Alabama had many roots, Redding contends, but none more important than *Souls*. A closer relationship between its ideas and the practices and tactics of the civil rights movement could hardly be imagined.

In the 1969 Signet / New American Library edition, Hare too repeatedly praises Du Bois for his capacity to anticipate future political developments. But what Du Bois proposes now is strikingly different. He predicts "the strife and conflicts of today" while setting up the particular "model of black struggle and black innovation" proposed by "black power advocates" (Hare 1969, xiii). It all starts with Du Bois's polemics against Booker T. Washington. Hare, who had become involved with the black power movement while teaching at Howard University, distinguishes Du Bois for "his black power prescience" (xxiii). He is the activist advocating "a tough, uncompromising stand" (xxvi), which includes the advocacy of self-determination, black economic self-sufficiency, cultural and artistic pride in race, self-help and armed self-defense, and importantly, separate black civic, political, cultural, and educational institutions. Even more so than the Signet edition, with its colorfully designed cover showing the torso of a young black man with the Confederate flag juxtaposed alongside it, the Longmans 1965 edition visually encapsulates Hare's framing of Du Bois's works by choosing for its cover the symbol of the "black power" movement, conjuring an image of black left-wing militancy—a clenched black fist against a reddish background.

Education policy is of special concern to Hare. While Du Bois's writings on education are hardly confined to *Souls* (or, for that matter, to "The Talented Tenth"), through the 1960s and 1970s, *Souls* played a key role in the African American studies movement. *Souls* contains one of the most vocal pronouncements against the mis(education) of African Americans. Five of its fourteen chapters were devoted to this or to how the education offered to blacks is used to perpetuate their condition as menials and dependents. This is an education meant to prevent not only individual social mobility but, more importantly, the critical raising of black consciousness and their ability to conceive alternative futures. It severs blacks from their history and their culture. It deprives them of access to their own thought and practice traditions. It limits their ambitions. And in so doing, it despoils them of the very resources on which any such alternative futures might be built. A black presence on campus—in the student body and in a radically reformed curriculum (perhaps modeled after Du Bois's *Encyclopedia Africana*) and pedagogy—can do something to change this. But this will amount to small change if the black community is taken as a passive object of study rather than a partner *in* and *of* its own critical remaking. For pragmatic reasons, Du Bois, otherwise an advocate of full integration, sees himself defaulting to the power of cooperative enterprises within the black community when he comes out in support of voluntary all-black schooling. "Other things being equal," he maintains, "the mixed school is the broader, more natural basis for education of all youth" (Du Bois 1935, 335). Under conditions of deeply embedded white supremacy, in which the burden of desegregation would fall almost exclusively on blacks, things may be different. Adequately funded black education institutions might be the black population's only hope of receiving proper education, the education that best suits their emancipatory needs. Necessity, Du Bois claimed, can be turned into fortune and eventually do away with itself.

Whereas for Du Bois separation was a necessity, for Hare, it is a desire. Six years after being hired by Howard University as an assistant sociology professor in 1961, Hare held a press conference with a group of students identified as "The Black Power Committee," at which he read "The Black University Manifesto." It called for "the overthrow of the Negro College with white innards and to raise in its place a black university, relevant to the black community and its needs." That same year, Hare was dismissed from Howard after having Muhammad Ali deliver his famous "Black Is Best" speech on campus. He was soon to be hired by San Francisco University to coordinate a black studies program at the university level. There he quickly joined the Black Student Union in a strike pushing for the creation of an autonomous department of black studies. Tumultuous almost from the beginning, Hare's stay at San Francisco was short lived. On February 28, 1969, he was dismissed as chairman of the newly formed black studies department, the first in the United States, effective June 1, 1969.

But Hare's fight would continue. *Souls*, which was to become a focal point of the black studies curriculum on American campuses (Andrews 1985, 3), offered a propitious battleground. In his introduction, Hare presents himself as walking in Du Bois's footsteps in his quest for the autonomy of black studies departments and the radical reformulation of their curricula. *Souls*, Hare argues, is the type of work that should be integral to such curricula, for it presents a clear case for scholarly reparation. A sociologist himself, Hare does not hesitate to call Du Bois "the father of the empirical approach to sociology in America" or to denounce his marginalization in the discipline, despite his having introduced "mankind to the scientific study of racial conflict" (1969, xxii). In Hare's words, Du Bois is not only a "must read" for black studies curricula. He is the forerunner of "the present college cry for black studies," redirecting their "curricula toward greater relevancy"—namely, to "the black community and its struggles"—as "part of his general program of black self-sufficiency" (xxiii). All this—Hare contends—Du Bois endeavored to put into actual operation. However, he had the will but lacked the means. Only black power could heighten the will to power of black people to realize it.

Alvin Poussaint agrees with Hare's conclusion but rejects its premises. Asked to supply the second "interpretative essay" to the Signet edition, Poussaint, who had grown disillusioned with the politics of the Student Nonviolent Coordinating Committee (SNCC) after 1966, is far less hortatory than Hare. Where Hare saw foresight, Poussaint sees hindsight. Regarded by many as "a minor classic," Poussaint writes, *Souls* is a dated book, "no longer relevant to the post-1954 struggles of the black man in America" (1969, xxviii). Its shortcomings are varied. The book addresses itself primarily to a white audience, not Du Bois's black brothers. It wrongly assumes the goodwill of its readership, whom it seeks to engage through reasoned argument and in whom it seeks to trigger emotional states of sympathy, guilt, and shame. It expects its readership to accept responsibility for racial oppression. But it does all this in vain, as time has shown. Because Du Bois trusted an educated elite, black and white, to create channels of communication beyond the racial divide and lead reformist action, Poussaint claims, he designed *Souls* "for the ears of the aristocrat." Its prose is riddled with "flowery, overly abstruse imagery." Its contents redound in an overly optimistic "integrationist vision," which was to ensnarl the mind and heart of generations up to the sit-in movement of the 1960s (xxxv, xxxvii). Caught up in his elitism and naïf belief in gradual moral reformation, Du Bois could not envisage the "massive rise of his people to the streets" (xxxiii–xxxiv). Only in his later years, Poussaint contended, would Du Bois come to see what the black power movement so clearly understood from the beginning—that the black man waited in vain for a white response. "Now the black man no longer simply expects, he demands," Poussaint declares. And since his demands find no echo, he must simply do it for himself (xxxviii). The time was for action, not for the deferent words of *Souls*.

FADING *SOULS*: THE 1970S

Whereas Hare portrayed *Souls* as sowing the seeds of black power, Poussaint believed it to have spread the false belief that delayed its ripening and harvesting. Poussaint's critical assessment of the book's legacy foresees the waning of the book's influence in the next decade. With the rise to prominence of the black power movement and the hardening of positions, *Souls*'s characterization of the dual nature of African American consciousness seemed to many to be an invitation to numb complacency. Double consciousness, it was claimed, was not fate. It was rather the condition befalling those blacks who insisted on wanting to live between, and be accepted by, two clashing worlds—black and white—and remained exiles, locked (at least partly) beyond both as a consequence. Where Du Bois saw a complex dialectic of antagonism and interdependence whose resolution depended on the merging of the two selves into a truer self in which none of the older selves would be lost, new black leaders such as Malcolm X saw a stark choice offering an opportunity for a full, one-sided resolution. Malcolm X rejected attempts to resolve contradictions through synthesis—the black-white contradiction lent itself to no resolution except through black self-love, black self-determination, and black separatism (West 1994, 98). The likes of *Souls*, by contrast, articulated an alienated black identity in terms of double consciousness. New militant intellectuals, including prominent figures of the Black Arts movement of the 1960s and 1970s, trusted that this doubleness would be overcome through self-identification at both the individual and group levels. "We must," urged Larry Neal, "liberate ourselves, destroy the double-consciousness. We must integrate with ourselves" (2000, 78). *Souls* was still present, lurking in the background, but as a nemesis. This was conducive to editorial neglect. Throughout the 1970s, only one edition—the Fisk Diamond Jubilee edition—was printed. Edited at Du Bois's alma mater in Nashville, it carried all the marks of ceremonial honor. But it also seemed to bear with it a burial rite.

The political resonance of the mass-marketed paperback editions of *Souls* of the 1960s was lost in the 1970s. In 1973, the Marxist historian Herbert Aptheker began the gargantuan task of collating, editing, and publishing Du Bois's complete works, the centerpiece of any canonization process.[23] In mainstream American sociology, however, the book's invisibility continued. Du Bois's historical role in the discipline and his specific contribution to the sociology of race, which developed "almost exclusively as a conversation among whites" (Winant 2007, 538), went on virtually unacknowledged (A. Morris 2007, 510; E. Wright 2002, 336).[24]

This marginalization by the "sociological establishment" (Rabaka 2010b, xvi) persisted into the heyday of structural functionalism. Its leading figures, Talcott Parsons and Robert K. Merton, wrote on questions of race, prejudice, and discrimination, but in terms that jarred with Du Bois's. Parsons's understanding of racial prejudice as a value problem and his structural functionalist stress on the integrative qualities of American society (Parsons 1965) contrasted radically with Du Bois's understanding of racial injustice as foundational to American society and his embracing of Marxism as the framework within which to understand and explain race dynamics. Merton, for his part, approached race relations from the perspective of the sociology of knowledge. He praised Du Bois's "pioneering revisionist efforts" in the institutionalization of scholarship dedicated to the interchange of knowledge between "Insiders and Outsiders, between black historians and white" (1972, 42), an effort pursued in the 1960s by the likes of John Hope Franklin. But he was highly critical of Hare's claims of "insider" epistemological superiority. Hare's suggestion that programs of black studies could only be pursued by black scholars was readily dismissed by Merton, who sneered at the suggestion that "any white professors involved in the program would have to be black in spirit in order to last" (Hare quoted in Merton 1972, 13). He believed any such claims to privileged sight to be conducive to epistemic apartheid, leading to the "balkanization of social science, with separate baronies kept exclusively in the hands of Insiders bearing their credentials in the shape of one or another ascribed status" (Merton 1972, 13). Parsons and Merton are, of course, not just any figures of sociology but the two main agents of the postwar professionalization of the discipline. Unlike the critical and public sociology Du Bois envisaged, intent on identifying and advancing paths for emancipation through the history- and culture-centered theorizing of pressing sociopolitical problems, this professionalized discipline effected a separation of sociology from general publics and, in its search for conceptual unification, effected a narrowing of the canon (Burawoy 2005a). As the influence of structural functionalism declined in the 1970s, a new phase in the institutional development of American sociology ensued. Two reinforcing movements marked this new phase. On the one hand, professional sociology strove to accommodate critical perspectives, moving subfield after subfield to the left: stratification and education became the study of social inequality, the sociology of culture incorporated ideology, and industrial sociology became the study of domination in the labor process. At the same time, gender and race became ever more prominent (Burawoy 2005b, 70). On the other hand, growing attention was paid to theoretical approaches hitherto sidelined by mainstream sociology, such as symbolic interactionism, conflict theory, ethnomethodology, and figurational sociology. Accompanying this paradigmatic fragmentation, efforts were made to either deconstruct the "Weber-Durkheim-Marx" canon of the 1960s (Seidman 2008; Connell 1997) or at least expand it to include representative figures of alternative theoretical approaches, such as G. H. Mead, Norbert Elias, or indeed, Du Bois.

But the time of *Souls* was yet to arrive. Its radical political resonance faded in the liberal hangover of the 1970s. The few isolated attempts made to inscribe Du Bois in the sociological canon turned not to *Souls* but to *The Philadelphia Negro* and Du Bois's early efforts at institutionalizing sociology through the

Atlanta school. Two in particular are worth mentioning. In 1974, Elliott M. Rudwick published "W. E. B. Du Bois as Sociologist," a wide-ranging survey of Du Bois's contribution to sociology and the ways in which it prefigured future developments in the discipline.[25] More importantly, the second of these attempts hinged on a publication initiative. In 1978, sociologists Dan S. Green and Edwin D. Driver, who had written an earlier article denouncing Du Bois's neglect in sociology (Green and Driver 1976),[26] edited *W. E. B. Du Bois on Sociology and the Black Community*, an anthology of Du Bois's "most important sociological writings from 1898 to 1910" for University of Chicago Press. Symptomatically, none of the seventeen texts that made it into the anthology was drawn from *Souls*.

TRANSATLANTIC *SOULS*

If American social scientists mainly turned a blind eye to Du Bois's *Souls*, its fate in Europe proved somewhat different. Important in this regard was the 1965 Longmans edition, edited by historian and critical theorist, Trotskyist Marxist, and Pan-Africanist essayist C. L. R. James. James was the author of *Black Jacobins* (1938), an influential study of the Haitian revolution. Centering on the figure of Toussaint L'Ouverture, the revolution's best-known leader, James's study looked at revolutions past to incentivize revolutions future—namely, nascent anticolonial movements in Africa. A critique of imperialist and colonialist historiography, it sought to deprovincialize Eurocentric accounts of modernity by showing how the story of the French Revolution could not be told apart from the history of racial capitalism or the complex web of interactions and fluxes within the French Empire between center and periphery. Not surprisingly, therefore, James's focus is the French colonies in the Caribbean, whose slaveholding economies, he submits, not only sustained the development of capitalism in France but offered the economic basis for the French Revolution.

*Black Jacobins* and *Souls* were books born before their age. Well received by a selected black readership upon publication, they came into their prime in the 1960s. They were then both republished just two years apart—in 1963 and 1965, respectively. As this happened, they were *seen* as speaking, while they were also actively *made* to speak, to the movement for black rights in the United States and the anticolonial movements in Africa. The authors themselves promoted such a retrospective reading through their newly added prefaces. The 1938 edition of *Black Jacobins* closed with a letter taken from the original report of the Copperbelt disturbances of 1935, from "an obscure

Rhodesian black in who burns the fire that burnt in Toussaint l'Ouverture." In the new preface to the 1963 Vintage edition of *Black Jacobins*, James confessed that this call to arms was meant to "stimulate the coming emancipation of Africa" (1963, viii).

In pursuing the Pan-Africanist liberation project, James followed in the footsteps of Du Bois, the recently deceased veteran of early Pan-Africanism. The 1965 edition of *Souls*, introduced by James, provided a new generation of social and human scientists based in Britain with easy access to Du Bois's work, while it also invited a reading of the work from a more global and more radical perspective. This is no mere coincidence. Through the 1960s, *Black Jacobins* was becoming one of the foundational texts in the growing study of the African diaspora. In his introduction to *Souls*, James rendered Du Bois, as a biographical subject, and *Souls*, as the work delivering the sentence that had become almost a cliché of Pan-Africanism ("The problem of the twentieth century is the color-line"), as agents behind the early advancement of the world-historical significance of American slavery in the age of capitalism and a diasporan understanding of African history, culture, and struggles. With the black power fist, symbolizing solidarity and resistance, on its cover, the Longmans edition called for the color line to be seen as a global issue rather than a peculiarly American problem. Radical black politics, bridging back to the Atlantic and the African diaspora, was the only way to confront it and chart the way forward.

This much was clear from James's introductory essay, which read as a biographical account of Du Bois, but one with distinctive emphases. James begins his introduction with a refusal to reduce Du Bois to marginalizing labels, such as that of "a great leader of Negroes" or a "spiritual African expatriate" (1963, viii). If Du Bois's "Americanism" needs stressing, it is because without it, one cannot understand his becoming "one of the great citizens of the modern world" who revived "the impulses of 1776 to the world of the 20th century" in and beyond America. Du Bois's contributions are said to be threefold and closely connected: as a pioneer of the social rights movement, as an early generation Pan-Africanist and staunch opponent of Marcus Garvey's Back-to-Africa movement, and as a fine historian who deftly placed the history of American race relations within the context of the world forces that accounted for them. These were forces that only Marxism could explain and that only the dialectical method laid down by Marx could hope to overcome. Fittingly, James closes the introduction by citing Du Bois's "Retrospect" to the 1953 Blue Heron edition, with its socialist critique of capitalism as the root cause of race wars. A Pan-Africanist angle compounded with socialism reappeared fleetingly in the introductory essays to the 1969 Signet edition. But it was James who firmly placed Du Bois's thought on race in a wider, diasporic context. This shift was pregnant with consequences.

A mere two years after the publication of *Souls* in Britain, Stuart Hall wrote *Young Englanders* (1967). This marked the beginning of a lifelong engagement of "the Du Bois of Britain" with *Souls* (Gates quoted in Edwards 2014). It would take Hall from a focus on the "struggle over the relations of representation" to the "politics of representation itself" (Hall 1996, 442). *Young Englanders* is a short study of raced or nonwhite emigrant youngsters torn between two cultures, trying to reclaim their agency and visibility from hegemonic conceptions of whiteness. "Suffused with a hint of Dubois' 'double consciousness'" (C. Alexander 2009, 470), Hall argues that "there is the identity which belongs to the part of [the young man] that is West Indian, or Pakistani or Indian. . . . There is also the identity of 'the young Englander' toward which every new experience beckons. . . . Somehow he must learn to reconcile his two identities and make them one. But many of the avenues into wider society are closed to him. . . . The route back is closed. But so too is the route forward" (1967, 12). These racialized selves found themselves trapped within and between two essentialisms. Hall perceived, however, the grounds for the development of a new politics of presentation that embraced a new understanding of ethnicity separating itself from both essentialisms—the essentialism of alienation (or of being inevitably an-Other) and the essentialism of assimilation (or of being integrally English).

In the late 1980s, Hall's thinking on race moved accordingly from "what Gramsci called the 'war of manoeuvre' to the 'war of position'—the struggle around positionalities" (1996, 444). But Hall's positionalities differ significantly from Gramsci's positions. While the former are occupied by historically located political actors and social classes, the latter are enunciative modes emerging from the linguistic turn in cultural studies. No longer the essence of a black subject and black experience stabilized by nature, Hall's new concept of ethnicity acknowledges "the place of history, language and culture in the construction of subjectivity and identity, as well as the fact that all discourse is placed, positioned, situated, and all knowledge is contextual" (446). Two implications follow. First, representation is possible only because enunciation is always produced within codes that have a history. While Hall acknowledges that this grounding of ethnicity in difference as a site of utterance and identification in the domains of cultural and political representation helped disavow the realities of racism, he is keen to stress that the same contestation needs to take place regarding "its position in the discourse of 'multi-culturalism' and [be] transcoded, just as we previously had to recuperate the term 'black' from its place in a system of negative equivalences" (446). Second, this new politics of representation entails an awareness of the black experience as a diaspora experience, one fed and nourished by, for instance, the consumption of cultural products from Asia, Africa, and the Caribbean and leading to contestation over what it means to be "British." Hall pursues both of these themes in "Race, the Floating Signifier."

First delivered as a lecture at Goldsmiths College in London in 1997, "Race, the Floating Signifier" presents race as a discursive construct, working more in the manner of language than biology (Hall 1997). It positions Du Bois as a forerunner of the turn from a scientific or biological understanding of race to a sociohistorical or cultural understanding of it. Du Bois, Hall stresses, was right to start with "the grosser physical differences of color, hair, and bone" (13) and emphasize their inevitable visibility. But he was equally right to suspect that such differences are "the signs of a code" (14) that has a history that most cannot see but nevertheless act according to. The "very obviousness of the visibility of race," Hall explains, functions precisely because race "is a text, which we can read" (15). In other words, it is only when such differences come to be "organized within language, within discourse, within systems of meaning," that they become a major "factor in human culture and regulate conduct" (10). Therefore, race is, for Hall, one of "those major concepts, which organize the great classificatory systems of difference, which operate in human society" (alongside gender, class, etc.). Neither "fixed in its inner nature" nor "secure in its meaning" (9), race is a signifier floating in a sea of relational difference that is never static nor the same. Hall's distinctively culturalist understanding of race claimed Du Bois—including, controversially, the Du Bois of "The Conservation of Races"—as one of its progenitors and primed him for appropriation by sociology.[27]

This is most noticeable in the work of Hall's former collaborator Paul Gilroy (Centre for Contemporary Cultural Studies, 1982)—namely, in his "black Atlantic" thesis (Gilroy 1993). This is given in the work of the same name, whose subtitle, *Modernity and Double Consciousness*, signals the book's indebtedness to Du Bois's *Souls*. Gilroy recognizes that Du Bois construed the concept as a means of "conveying the special difficulties arising from black internalization of an American identity," but he claims that Du Bois also conferred on it a more expansive meaning, which he used "to illuminate the experience of post-slave populations in general" (126). Building on Du Bois's theories of race and double consciousness (58) and on "the rich transnational textures of his [Du Bois's] long and nomadic life" (19), Gilroy rewrites the history of modernity by placing black people and the cultural hybridization produced by slavery—the history of the black Atlantic and the African diaspora—at its center. Alongside the rejection of "absolutist conceptions of cultural difference" (15), central to Gilroy's endeavor is the rejection of methodological nationalism, which loses track of key economic, political, and cultural structures of domination not coextensive with national units. Gilroy expects his "outernational, transcultural reconceptualization" to have a profound impact on the understanding of modern black political culture, either by making sense of Du Bois's Bismarckian nationalist sympathies[28] or by reinterpreting its most important movements—from the Haitian revolution to Garveyism—"as hemispheric if not global phenomena" (17). Du Bois's concept of double consciousness is, again, believed to be key to understanding the latter. As the concept that best captures "the core dynamic of racial oppression" and "the fundamental antinomy of diaspora blacks," we must ask ourselves how doubleness affected "the conduct of political movements against racial oppression and towards black autonomy" (30). Ironically, Gilroy notes, Du Bois—himself a product of the black Atlantic—given his engagement with the European canon of the time (namely, Hegel), was taken in by the double consciousness effect, as his thought came to be inscribed by the likes of Cornel West "in the all-American landscape provided by a genealogy of pragmatism" (137).[29] But such intellectual ethnocentrism must be resisted, as it curtails "the novelty and power of his [Du Bois's] critique of modernity" (137), on which *Black Atlantic* seeks to expand. The Du Bois–inspired *Black Atlantic* became the cornerstone of a new and hugely successful interdisciplinary framework for the study of diasporic identities as constituted through the Atlantic as a space of domination, re-creation, and creolization enacted through multiple continuities and discontinuities, connections and disconnections. With it, the political geography of race changed, and *Souls* was back on the map.

## *SOULS*, THE LITERARY ACT: THE 1980S/1990S

In the 1980s, America witnessed a pronounced right-wing turn in national politics, with mounting attacks on public welfare and state regulation calling the very idea of the social into question. As the market panacea gained credence, sociology was pushed onto the defensive and the field moved rightward. Critical sociology, for its part, turned for inspiration to the Nietzschean postmodernist critique of modernity (Stauth and Turner 1988) and postcolonial studies (Spivak 1988). This, in turn, paved the way for a critical reexamination of prevailing understandings of race, both by abandoning essentialist notions of blackness (hooks 1990) and by exploring the ways in which race intersects with other forms of stratification (Crenshaw 1989, 1993). This coincided with a resurgence of editorial activity around Du Bois's book: the 1989 Penguin edition, introduced by Donald B. Gibson; the 1989 Bantam edition, introduced by Henry Louis Gates Jr.; the 1990 Library of America edition, introduced by John Edgar Wideman; the 1993 Knopf edition, introduced by Arnold Rampersad; and the 1999 Norton Critical Edition, edited and introduced by Gates. Judging from the figures chosen to introduce these editions, it seems fair to say that the book was now in the hands of literary critics. The observation may seem trivial, but it warrants reflection, for it designates less a fact than a project—that of establishing Du Bois as a man of letters and *Souls* as "a classic text in American Literature" (Gibson 1989, xxxv).

The 1989 Bantam edition articulates this design most clearly.[30] Gates's introduction does not hide its intent to constitute a black canon alongside the hegemonic Western canon, with *Souls* at its center. Keenly aware of the "politics and ironies of canon formation" (1992, 32), Gates comes to question the ways in which the inclusions and exclusions of "*the* canon" affect one's self-understanding as "American" (34) as well as the development of African American literature as a proper subject of instruction in the American academy (22). If this state of affairs is to be challenged, publishing politics will be critical, and Gates has established himself as *the* key player in it.[31] He has come to insist on the importance of foundational research, enabling the work of scholars in the black cultural tradition, such as bibliographies, concordances, dictionaries, bibliographies, and encyclopedias. Integral to this research is the editing of "the *Encyclopedia Africana*, a project first defined by W. E. B. Du Bois" but whose curricular implications for the education of Americans (beyond the confinements of "black studies" departments) are to be drawn by Gates (122).

Gates's most direct intervention in the redefinition of the literary canon, however, is in his role as general editor (alongside Valerie Smith) of the prestigious *Norton Anthology of African American Literature* (1996). Gates admits the constitutive effect of such editorial interventions, since writing "a well-marked anthology functions in the academy to *create* a tradition, as well as to define and preserve it" (1992, 31). Such a tradition, Gates adds, should be conceived of not as something "defined by a pseudoscience of racial biology, or a mystically shared essence called blackness, but by the repetition and revision of shared themes" (39). That *Souls* is one of the pivotal texts of the black literary tradition is something Gates already makes unequivocally clear in the 1989 Bantam edition. Speaking of the reception of Du Bois's book among black writers and critics, Gates writes, "No other text, save possibly the King James Bible, has had a more fundamental impact on the shaping of the African-American literary tradition" (1989, xxx). As "an urtext of the African-American experience" and the "silent second text" in most subsequent African American texts, Gates claims that *Souls* deserves canonization, dissemination, and wide use in the classroom (xxx). In pushing for this, he confesses his indebtedness to 1960s struggles for African American studies. But he criticizes the overpoliticization of such programs in the 1970s (1992, 92). He sides with those, such as Saunders Redding, who turned their attention to the "literariness" of black texts and their rightful place in the curriculum of traditional English departments (whose "other" texts, Gibson and Gates suggest, are part of the complex ancestry of black texts). This alignment explains much about the way Du Bois's book is now framed. In the 1960s editions, *Souls* was presented as a political manifesto. Neither Gibson nor Gates deny the text's political intention or its implications. But in a poststructuralist context in which attention shifted from the structural properties of language to the open-ended playfulness of speech, they make any such implications subordinate to, and dependent of, the book's aesthetic and rhetorical qualities. *Souls* is the site of struggle for black leadership, but the political authority Du Bois gains through it is "generated in large part by the rhetorical authority revealed in it" (Gates 1989, xxx). Du Bois's book is now to be conceived primarily as a "literary act" of momentous consequence and must be approached as such (xxx). This means that if form trumps historical content in *making* the book, then there is even more reason for form to trump content in its *analysis*. As Gates explains, *Souls* is a classic "not because of the phase of Du Bois's ideological development that it expresses but because of the manner in which he expressed his ideology" (xxx). Saunders Redding was therefore correct in deeming the work "history-making" (Gates 1989, xxx). But by this Redding meant the book's contribution to the cause of civil rights; Gates offers a different reason for the work's world-historical significance. *Souls* has made history by presenting itself as "an object to be experienced, analyzed, and enjoyed *aesthetically*" (Gates 1989, xxx; our emphasis). A cultural artifact central to a black tradition enacted by black writers who, across time and space, read and responded to each other's texts, *Souls* remains critical for one's understanding of race, for "race is a text (an array of discursive practices), not an essence," and as such, it requires close reading (Gates 1992, 79).

Derided by turn-of-the-century sociologists for its literary excesses and historicalness, *Souls* is for Gates worthy of canonization precisely for the time-transcending literary qualities that forged an entire literary tradition, from James Weldon Johnson to Toni Morrison. For many readers today, *Souls* is such a literary work, the key to which is the concept of double consciousness. Understood as a sociocultural construct whose instability and political contestability have been elaborated by the likes of Hall, double consciousness has become integral to our understanding of the racialized self and any attempts to question rigidly fixed racial identities. It is mostly through the reworkings of this concept that *Souls* has reached its present resonance in the sociology of race.

But as our analysis has shown, double consciousness was not always the dominant synecdoche for *Souls*. What *Souls* stands for has changed over time. It would be easy to construe this change in terms of a radical shift from a political reading of Du Bois centering on the polemics with Washington to a literary reading of it centering on the culturally specific metaphor of double consciousness (Reed 1997, 12–13, 45–46, 91, 127–30). There is some truth to this reading, of course, but it does not paint the whole picture. In Gates's framing of the book, double consciousness does undergo a process of abstraction that results in a relative depoliticization. It ceases to be "just a black thing" and becomes the metaphor for the "condition of modernity itself," as characterized by the "fragmentation of culture and consciousness," the "vigorous intermixing of black culture and white, high culture and low," and multiple intersecting identities taking the place of two warring ones (Gates 2007, xiv–xv). Through the lens of Gates's celebratory multiculturalism, such "cultural multiplicity" ceases to be "the problem" and becomes "the solution," ceases to be "a disorder" and becomes "the cure" (xv). But there is a sting in the tail of this pluralism that doubles as a washed-out multiculturalism. To borrow Adorno's words, as the particular is subsumed under the universal category, or—to apply—as Gates transforms "the Negro" and his double consciousness into "a metaphor, a universal aspect of the human condition" (Gates 1999, x), Du Bois's concept runs the risk of becoming "part of the mechanism of domination" that "forbid[s] recognition of the suffering it produces" (Adorno 2005, 63).

CONCLUSION

In *Dissemination*, Derrida mentions that Hegel disqualified introductory materials, from the prefaces to the "forewords, introductions, preludes, preliminaries, preambles, prologues and prolegomena" (1981, 7). Such materials typically open a window into the text. They are part of the *pre-* "which presents and precedes, or rather forestalls, the presentative production" and that "in order to put before the reader's eyes what is not yet visible, is obliged to speak, predict, and predicate" (8). Hegel's objection to these materials, Derrida explains, rests on the distinction between the main body of a philosophical work, which should be self-foundational, and pretexts, which are never so. These texts are not, however, of a kind, Derrida stresses. Introductions are unique. They are also higher in the scale of value because they have "a more systematic, less historical, less circumstantial link with the logic of the book" (14). Prefaces, by contrast, "are multiplied from edition to edition and take into account a more empirical historicity" (14). They exhibit contextualized assumptions and make prophetic projections. What disqualified them for Hegel is exactly what makes pretexts interesting for us. Their historical locatedness gives us a privileged glimpse into changing receptions and the resulting many lives of books.

Although rules of good scholarly editorial practice dictate a considerable difference in content and style between introductions and prefaces, the lines of separation are actually far more blurred. This is, if anything, the more so when both types of intervention in the book are posthumously allocated to third parties. It is also more clearly the case in nonscholarly editions. As we have seen with Du Bois, the author uses the original preface to make a declaration of intent, to secure the "proper" reading of the text, to provide unity where different texts are clubbed together, and to identify the reader his book wishes to address and tell him what is expected of him. In subsequent editions, he addresses new readers by adding a new preface that reflects on, and sometimes corrects, the approach, argument, and purpose of the original text while seeking to accommodate his newly evolved ideas. As pretexts are posthumously handed over to "third persons," they are expected to provide relevant information and recommend reading. But just as "information" (contextualization, biography, etc.) can strongly shape reading, so can a preface or an introduction verge on a critical essay or become a quasi-autonomous piece. The performativity of pretexts must not be underestimated. Pretexts are thresholds or window frames onto the text. They are also marks—boundary marks or signs of territory. As windows, they draw readers *in* and offer them a promise of access. As signs, they indicate that access is never unmediated but provided through particular frames. Frames are normally construed in relation *to*, while not necessarily *against*, previous frames. As such, they are tales in themselves. They are tales about what the book is *about* and about what the book *stands for* and *is for* and about how the answer to these related questions has evolved over time. Pretexts guide reading while they also prime the book for certain modes of enunciation and appropriation. Their ability to invite and displace interpretations, to credit projects and delegitimize alternatives, can be such that they might question our understanding of some texts as central and others as peripheral.

In our analysis of *Souls*, we have treated its "Forethought" and "After-Thought" as two of the most important apparatuses of the book. We have argued that they are an integral part of that which makes the book exist as *one* book, and not as just any one book, but one intent on *doing* things—namely, on expanding and radically reconstituting America along racial lines. In the 1953 preface, Du Bois made it clear that America's predicament could not be understood or indeed overcome without a better understanding of capitalism, which got at the causes of plunders such as slavery, racism, and colonialism and offered potential ways out. For all the praise it received upon its publication among its mostly black readership and for its more underground survival during McCarthyism, *Souls* was a book that had to wait until the 1960s to reach a larger mass audience. This was the age of the paperback, with the resulting changes in edition, format, price, commercial practices, and distribution outlets having considerable implications on who was introducing, prefacing, and reading *Souls*, with what expectations, and for what purposes. This was also the age of the rise of new social movements, which, together with the new paperback print culture, helped generate broader reading publics eager to read themselves into claimed "foundational" texts and construct these texts in ways that reflected, legitimized, and furthered their current political experience. The civil rights movement, in particular, offered *the* horizon of expectation in which *Souls* was to be constructed, received, and reworked (Holub 1984; Jauss 1970).

Du Bois's death in 1963 helped ease this reconstruction. It toned down some of the controversy surrounding his later years and enabled the mainstream civil rights movement to claim the earlier Du Bois unreservedly as a founding father of their fight for black equality. The détente did not last long, however. The civil rights battle had its own internal struggles, and *Souls* became immersed in them: did it offer a conciliatory model for integration, or was it a separatist manifesto, encouraging the black community to proudly embrace blackness, articulate its own goals, and run its own affairs? If some hailed *Souls* for its moderate, nonviolent stance, others despaired of its utopian idealism and excessively conciliatory tone. If some saw it as slowing down progress toward black emancipation at home and abroad, others saw it as inspiring Third World independence struggles on which both emancipations depended.

A token in the fight for control over the soul—the meaning and the purpose—of the civil rights movement, *Souls* was also pivotal in the African American studies movement born out of it. Here, *Souls* acted at two different levels. It offered a window onto Du Bois's views on the link between education and social power and was deployed to reopen the discussion of what the black presence in higher education should be like, and aim at, to affect a radical redistribution of power. As Du Bois's masterpiece, it also raised questions about the politics of canon (mis)formation and how it affected the self-understanding of some academic disciplines, traditions, and a whole society. This is nowhere clearer than in the strikingly contrasting ways in which Hare and Gates use *Souls* to found and refound black studies, respectively. While both Hare and Gates claim Du Bois as their intellectual hero, from Hare's conception of black studies as having a legitimacy drawn from activism to Gates's search for an intellectual legitimacy construed apart from it, we see Du Bois going full circle from the later Du Bois, who abjured the idea of the Talented Tenth, back to the earlier Du Bois, who fully embraced it. Hare and Gates also represent very different positions in respect to processes of canonization. Hare approaches the canon as an instrument of white supremacy. He sees Du Bois as having founded the modern scientific study of the black condition and deems Du Bois's exclusion from the sociological canon a matter of disciplinary apartheid—nay, usurpation. In response, he seeks to reinstate Du Bois in the black studies curriculum. Black studies should not be mere "carbon copies of conventional education" (Hare 1969, 736). Their curriculum should thus include Duboisian subjects such as the sociology of blackness and black consciousness intent on acting on and substantially transforming society. This implied, in Hare's view, instilling "in black youth a sense of pride or self, of collective destiny"; fostering in it the practical skills sniffed at in "liberal arts" programs; and incentivizing continuous "community involvement" (727). Gates is fully aware of the racial politics behind the canon and the black studies curriculum. Unlike the heirs of Hare in the cultural left, however, who have come to reject the idea of a canon altogether, he wants to keep it. He shifts the epicenter of black studies curriculum from practical knowledge and the social sciences into the arts and humanities while rejecting Hare's submission of scholarship to criteria of "immediate political utility" (Gates 2006, 97). He wants African American studies to become, if anything, more like the academic establishment: not a pariah that is tolerated but not respected but an intellectual equal. This involves some "carbon copying"—namely, in the form of a black literary canon set alongside the Western one. Gates's literary orientation is indebted to the cultural studies turn that, drawing on Du Bois, led to the creation of African Diaspora studies *in* or *alongside* African American studies. Gates does not reject such a diasporic perspective. He acknowledges that African American texts are hybrid—both black and white; simultaneously African, American, and European. But to deliver an autonomous black canon (one that affirms a coherent black literary tradition woven out of *Souls*) through a whole series of high-profile scholarly and editorial undertakings, he claims, best serves the project of institutionalizing the teaching of African American literature, which doubles as a process of preserving, reproducing, and disseminating the canon as created. Indeed, cultural capital can be made to circulate and accumulate in restricted channels.

Gates's effort to rehabilitate Du Bois through the affirmation of *Souls*'s classicity in literary studies finds an echo in the many recent attempts to bring Du Bois back into the sociological canon (Bulmer 1991; Winant 2000; Edwards 2006; Hunter 2013; Bhambra 2014; Loughran 2015; Itzigsohn and Brown 2015). This effort has reached its apex in two monographs: Reiland Rabaka's *Against Epistemic Apartheid* (2010) and Aldon Morris's prize-winning *The Scholar Denied* (2015). As the titles suggest, both books emphasize the neglect and marginalization to which Du Bois's ideas have been subjected in the discipline. Whereas the term *epistemic apartheid* in Rabaka's title is a direct reference to the power-knowledge mechanism through which ideas are filtered by race, gender, and class, Morris's title alludes to the institutional racism that he claims denied American sociology access to Du Bois's seminal contributions by keeping him out of professional sociology. While their shared mission is to rescue Du Bois from disciplinary oblivion, Rabaka and Morris pursue this goal in markedly different ways.

In *Against Epistemic Apartheid*, the concluding volume of a trio of studies that Rabaka recently dedicated to Du Bois (2007, 2008), the author of *Souls* emerges as a "transdisciplinary critical social theorist" (2010a, 6). Even though Rabaka is keen on emphasizing that many of his writings transcend sociology, Du Bois's specifically sociological contributions encompass such different fields as urban and rural areas, race, gender, religion, education, and crime. *Souls* occupies a place of pride in Rabaka's all-encompassing reading. It is through a close reading of *Souls* alongside "The Conservation of Races," *Dusk of Dawn*, "The Souls of White Folk," and *The Gift of Black Folk* that Rabaka reconstructs Du Bois's social constructionist conception of race. Rabaka is as much invested in divulging Du Bois's multiple contributions to sociology as he is in exploring the inherent tensions in Du Bois's thought, however. Instead of an imposing theoretical colossus whose consistency overshadows his ability to develop and learn, Rabaka stresses how Du Bois's love for Europe did nothing to diminish his Pan-Africanism, how Du Bois's politics of black nationalism could go hand in hand with his radical humanist agenda, how hands-on policy making could benefit from abstract social-scientific theorizing, and how as a "race man" he was nonetheless a precursor in the fight for women's rights.

*The Scholar Denied*, by contrast, can be best understood as an exercise in canonization. "There is an intriguing, well-kept secret regarding the founding of scientific sociology in America," Morris whispers in his readers' ears in the opening paragraph. "The first school of scientific sociology in the United States was founded by a black professor located in a historically black university in the South" (2015, 1). The focus is on the beginning of Du Bois's career, roughly the first two decades of the twentieth century. As a result, other dimensions of Du Bois's thinking—such as his engagement with Marxism, his comparative-historical studies or his Pan-Africanism—are left out of Morris's analysis. No less important is Morris's attempt to assert Du Bois's "scientific" credentials as a professional sociologist who not only undertook extensive empirical research but also trained a substantial number of black sociologists. Du Bois introduced sociology to his students as "a weapon of liberation" (59) whose effectiveness depended on its scientific exactness and rigor. This focus on data-driven, "scientific" sociology leads Morris to take *The Philadelphia Negro*, not *Souls*, as Du Bois's quintessential sociological work.

Still, Morris does not ignore the importance of *Souls* for Du Bois's theorization of race and identity. For Morris, more than a theorist of race, Du Bois should be viewed as a theorist of social organization and stratification who found in race a constitutive element of the modern social order. This enables him to place Du Bois on a par with Marx and Weber: "While Marx had argued that the basic dynamic of modern society was the class struggle, Weber insisted it was the process of bureaucratic rationalization that was sweeping the world in tandem with modern capitalism. As Du Bois surveyed the globe, he focused on a specific phenomenon that enabled European societies to build capitalist empires: the colonization, exploitation, and domination of peoples of color" (A. Morris 2015, 155). With the stroke of a pen, Morris transforms *Souls* into a pivotal element of his origins story.

Despite the obvious scholarly qualities of these two works, the fact remains that neither *The Scholar Denied*'s subscription of the idea of a canon, however reshuffled, nor *Against Epistemic Apartheid*'s sweeping theoretical interpretation are representative of the current reception of Du Bois in sociology. While the latter operates with an explicitly transdisciplinary framework that makes Du Bois's specifically sociological contributions more difficult to ascertain (unless one embraces, as Rabaka does, the necessarily polymathic nature of the discipline), the problem with Morris's origins story is that, like all origins stories, it tends to blur the fine line separating history from mythology. This leaves one wondering, with Monica Bell, whether Morris might be "fastening Du Bois into a trophy case" (2016).

Judging from the examples provided by prominent sociologists such as Patricia Hill Collins or Charles Lemert, Du Bois and *Souls* in particular have value less as symbols than as resources. They are interested less in using Du Bois to rewrite the *history* of sociology (Morris) or to propose an altogether different way of *doing* sociology (Rabaka) than in isolating Du Boisian approaches and ideas that can help them better think about current social issues. Collins's review of *The Scholar Denied* is exemplary in this respect (2016). In her view, there is a tendency in Morris to fall back into the mythological tale of the exceptional man, the self-created genius able to think alone against the grain of received opinion. "Because Morris seemingly assumes that those who founded sociology held the reins so tightly that one had to wait until now for sociology's grudging acceptance of Du Bois's ideas," Collins remarks, he "may overestimate the influence of the solitary scholar on the collective process of knowledge production" (2016, 1400). Collins uses the example of intersectionality to illustrate her claims. Her notion of "outsider within" (1986) locates itself in a wider African American sociological tradition in which Du Bois's idea of double consciousness plays a pivotal role. But to take Du Bois for the tradition and operate a "double erasure" of, for example, black women intellectuals in the process is to leave intersectionality orphan of some of its most relevant precursors (2016, 1405). While it is through the lenses of intersectionality that Collins approaches the Du Bois of *Souls*, Lemert finds in its culturalist approach a crucial resource for his sociology of global cultural differences (1995, 2004, 2007). It is not by coincidence, therefore, that one of the most recent but also more significant encounters of Lemert with Du Bois occurs in none other than a pretext to the 2004 centennial edition of *Souls*. In what is one of the most sociologically minded forewords to *Souls* ever written, Lemert emphasizes, alongside the text's literary qualities, "the *sociological* importance of the book," by which he means the "deep underlying engagement of its author with the effects of global economics on the local social realities of men and women the world over" (2004, i). "You must read what must be read," Lemert tells today's Gentle Reader, "in order to reconsider your history of exclusions in light of future prospects for currency in the global marketplace" (ii). Lemert's *Souls* speaks of two worlds, material and cultural, and of their irreconcilable present strivings. In so doing, it might well be the *Souls* that makes Du Bois whole.

CHAPTER 5

## A WORK IN TRANSLATION

## Weber's *The Protestant Ethic*

*The Protestant Ethic*, for many the consummate sociological classic, had a convoluted origin. In 1904, Max Weber published a two-part essay entitled "Die protestantische Ethik und der 'Geist' des Kapitalismus" in the *Archiv für Sozialwissenschaft und Sozialpolitik*, of which he was principal coeditor. In 1906, Weber published an additional essay on organized religion in North America in two different German periodicals. In 1920, Weber published a three-volume collection of studies on the world's religions, which includes the 1904–5 and 1906 essays. The publisher was Mohr Siebeck, then directed by Oskar Siebeck. It was Siebeck who, in 1928, coordinated the translation of the work into English by Talcott Parsons for the London-based publisher Allen and Unwin. Nine different publishers have reissued Parsons's translation in at least sixteen different reprints. In 2002, Stephen Kalberg (Roxbury) and Peter Baehr and Gordon Wells (Oxford University Press) published the first new translations of *The Protestant Ethic* since Parsons's.

INTRODUCTION

That American sociology is difficult to imagine without Talcott Parsons's translation of Max Weber's *The Protestant Ethic and the Spirit of Capitalism* is undisputable. But if Parsons's rendering of Weber's text into American English created the "world images" of Weber and his sociological significance that were to act "like switchmen" on a railroad, changing irrevocably the course of history by becoming it (Weber 1946, 280), what exactly did he do to make such a difference? Hence this chapter is as much about Weber and his ideas as it is about Parsons and how his mediation of those ideas through his translation of the "sacred text" (Scaff 2005) of Weberian scholarship set the direction for future generations of scholars.

Parsons (1902–1979) was one of the most influential sociologists of the twentieth century. His ideas and organizational skills helped define American sociology after 1945 as a behavioral science, an understanding that would rapidly be exported to other parts of the world (S. Turner 2014, 35ff.). The general theory of action, structural functionalism, systems theory, and modernization theory that issued from his pen were aspects and manifestations of a single highly abstract and supremely ambitious theoretical project that Parsons developed and pursued in the course of his forty-two-year-long career at Harvard, a period that coincided with the maturation and institutionalization of sociology in American academia (Trevino 2001). And yet when the *New York Times*, interviewing him on his retirement, asked what his greatest contribution to sociology had been, Parsons singled out neither his immense theoretical achievements nor his personal contribution to institutionalizing sociology as an academic discipline. He pointed instead to the translation of Weber's *The Protestant Ethic and the Spirit of Capitalism* he had published in 1930. Parsons went on to explain that by translating Weber's seminal essay, he had acted "as an importer" of Weber's ideas about religion and capitalism into the Anglo-Saxon world.[1] This remark provides the starting point for our argument in this chapter. As we will show, Parsons's "importation" of Weber's ideas via his translation-interpretation of Weber's book turned out to be a pivotal moment not only in Parsons's career but for the very path sociology would take in the twentieth century.

## THE TRANSLATOR-INTERPRETER

Parsons was only twenty-three when he read Weber for the first time. He embarked on the translation of *The Protestant Ethic* a little over a year later. The immediate cue seems to have been a suggestion by a senior colleague interested in promoting Weber's ideas in America, but the deeper reason was intellectual. The young Parsons was convinced he had found in Weber the theoretical and methodological answer to the origins and implications of capitalism, the problem that engrossed him at the time. This explains both his interest in pursuing a doctorate in Germany on Sombart's and Weber's theories of capitalism and his translation of Weber's essay.

Contrary to what is widely assumed (e.g., Camic 1991, xxvii), Parsons's doctoral dissertation did not postdate his translation. Archival research shows that Parsons wrote his dissertation while he was translating Weber's essay (Gerhardt 2011). In fact, the translation stands between two strikingly different versions of the doctoral dissertation. The first, written in German, has been almost universally ignored until now. The second, in English, was published in 1928–29 in the form of two articles in the *Journal of Political Economy*. Hence the need to approach Parsons as a translator-interpreter. His early encounter with Weber's theories and methodology was an organic and cumulative process in which Weber's book was a foil, not merely a springboard. Erasing Parsons's German dissertation from the story removes a crucial early step in the development of his sociological thinking. From this mistake, much misunderstanding results.

One result is that Parsons's early work is read as the anticipation of his later writings, overflowing with "implicit" (e.g., Wearne 1989, 57) signs of positions Parsons was to adopt years later. This fails to do justice to a discrete and highly consequential phase in his intellectual development. Another result has been to reduce Parsons's theoretical efforts to strategic and materialistic career-oriented choices (Camic 1987; Alexander and Sciortino 1996, 167). While the latter certainly helped frame some of Parsons's decisions at the time, the fact remains that this crudely misrepresents the intellectual labors involved in the interpretation of texts. (It may be that misrepresentation comes easier when the interpretation produced is uncongenial.)[2] Our focus here is on the translator[3] behind the author—that is, the work of translation comprising not only interpretation but also the material composition of a new work, which is especially appropriate when, as in this case, the translator also happens to be the editor. Here, hermeneutics meets material culture studies halfway. Parsons's translation involves not just words but also sentences and even the whole text, shaped by and reflecting Weber's thinking as a whole. But the truth is that no translator ever provides a full description of the whole (but see Ghosh 1994, 2001). The most that any translator, Parsons included, can offer is "points of view, perspectives, partial visions of the world" (Ricoeur 2006, 27). This is one reason Parsons never ceased to clarify what Weber meant and what Weber's contribution to sociology was. That clarity was an emergent property of Parsons's editorial and translation work and his material composition of the partial text that gave expression to his vision of Weber.

Focusing on the figure of the translator-interpreter, this chapter is also about the circulation and transmission of ideas. Weber's ideas about the religious origins of capitalism originated in turn-of-the-century Germany, traveled across the Atlantic (via Parsons's translation and interpretation), returned to postwar Germany as a sociological classic, and were eventually disseminated across the globe as they became part and parcel of sociology's self-understanding (e.g., Gerhardt 2011; Lidz 2010; Scaff 2014, 17ff.). As we shall see, the politics of the book play a significant role in this process, for the struggle over the control of the material format that sustains those ideas is a key component of their reception by any community of readers. Whether writing a new preface to a reprint of *The Protestant Ethic* in the late 1950s, a time when German historiography was actively attempting to associate Weber's work with monarchist and plebiscitary political tendencies (Mommsen 1959, 1963); highlighting the theoretical relevance of Weber's 1920 "Author's Introduction" in his work in the late 1960s and early 1970s; or resolutely holding his ground as the editorial gatekeeper of the English-language version of *The Protestant Ethic* in a heated epistolary exchange with Anthony Giddens shortly before passing away, Parsons never wavered in his belief that to control the Weberian legacy was to control the most widely read book in twentieth-century sociology and the material embodiment of that legacy—*The Protestant Ethic*. In order to better understand Parsons's reasons for this belief, as well as the circumstances that framed his choices, we must return to the moment and place at which Parsons's lifelong engagement with the work began—autumn 1925 in Heidelberg, Germany.

## THE FORGOTTEN TEXT: PARSONS'S GERMAN DOCTORAL DISSERTATION

A central problem drove Parsons's sojourn at Heidelberg in the 1925–26 academic year, a transformative experience that turned the young Parsons into a lifelong Weberian (pace Camic 2005, 249). That problem is capitalism: What is it, where does it come from, and how should one account for its implications for civilization? Parsons approached this problem as a sociologist, drawing Weber away from the realm of economic history and into the annals of sociological theory.

Parsons's approach to this problem involved two interrelated intellectual tasks, which in turn paved the way for his subsequent theorizing and canon-making endeavor in *The Structure of Social Action* (1937). The first task was to write a doctoral dissertation on capitalism in the works of Werner Sombart and Max Weber. Contrary to what is widely believed, this first task was divided into two separate phases in which Parsons wrote two different versions of the doctoral dissertation. Standing between and separating these two versions was the second task: the edition and translation of Weber's essay on the religious origins of capitalism. Parsons's decision to pursue doctoral studies abroad was far from unusual for the time. Having graduated from Amherst magna cum laude in 1924, Parsons, who was unimpressed by the graduate programs offered in the United States, turned to the obvious and traditional context of higher learning—Europe. His first port of call was not Germany but England. Parsons spent the 1924–25 academic year as a nondegree student at the London School of Economics (LSE). There L. T. Hobhouse introduced Parsons to the field of sociology, a broadly construed inquiry into the "social" encompassing both social philosophy and economic and political institutions (Parsons 1977, 18). This, his undergraduate studies on institutional economics (with Walton Hamilton and Clarence Ayres at Amherst), and Richard Tawney and Edwin Cannan's lectures on economic history at the LSE provided Parsons with the basic tools for understanding the problem of the age—the nature and origins of capitalism.

Germany was not his idea. As Parsons would later recall (1980, 38), he was awarded a fellowship in a postwar exchange program for the 1925–26 academic year. Without any say in the matter, he was assigned to the University of Heidelberg. Parsons was enthused by the prospect of joining the oldest university in Germany. He visited in June 1925, when he heard about Weber for the first time (38). But there was a problem. His command of German, which had been good enough to study German philosophy at Amherst, was inadequate to the rigors of a German higher education program. The solution involved moving to Vienna and attending an intensive summer course in German. Finally, his German much improved and eager to learn what sociology had to say about the problem of capitalism, a youthful Parsons arrived in Heidelberg in the early autumn of 1925.

His time in Heidelberg was marked by his encounter with two figures who would change his intellectual life forever. One was Max Weber, who, despite having died five years earlier, remained the dominant intellectual presence in Heidelberg through the famous "Weber circle" that included such personalities as Alfred Weber, Marianne Weber, Karl Jaspers, Karl Mannheim, and Alexander von Schelting. The first of Weber's writings that Parsons read was none other than "Die protestantische Ethik und der 'Geist' des Kapitalismus," which gripped him immediately. He later recalled having read the essay "as if it were a detective story" (Parsons 1980, 39).

The second figure was Edgar Salin, who agreed to supervise his DPhil on capitalism. Based at Basel and temporarily at Heidelberg at the time of Parsons's visit (Gerhardt 2011, 71), Salin was an economist conversant with the German historical school of economics and its critics. Unsurprisingly, it was Salin who suggested that the dissertation focus on Marx's, Sombart's, and Weber's theories of capitalism. Parsons duly began working on his doctoral dissertation—entitled *Der Kapitalismus bei Sombart und Max Weber*[4]—at the start of his second semester in Heidelberg in early 1926.

The first noteworthy aspect of Parsons's doctoral project is the role of Marx. Parsons liked to give the impression that his role was vital, but in fact, there was no chapter on Marx in either version of the dissertation. This is not to say that Marx was irrelevant to Parsons's argument. On the contrary, his views provided the theoretical benchmark against which Sombart and Weber's theories of capitalism were evaluated. Marx took his place with Hegel as one of the two main exponents of a distinctively German philosophical approach to history and, by extension, to capitalism. This German tradition constituted, in the eyes of the young Parsons, the main alternative to the utilitarian, individualistic, and rationalistic approach dominant in orthodox economics.

Parsons's research question was, To what extent were Sombart and Weber viable alternatives to both orthodox economics and the German historical school? Answering this question meant identifying the right theoretical-methodological approach to the problem of capitalism. The structure of the dissertation embodied this ambition.

The work, which is 140 pages long, falls into six chapters. After a brief general introduction, there is a substantive chapter on three contemporary German theories of capitalism (Richard Passow's, Georg von Below's, and Lujo Brentano's, respectively). This is followed by two longer chapters that constitute the bulk of the dissertation. The first is on Sombart's analysis of modern capitalism (17–64); the other is on Max Weber (65–106). The fifth chapter, entitled "The Facts of Capitalism," offers a synthetic analysis of key aspects of the capitalist system, such as market relations and the role of technology. The dissertation concludes with a general critical assessment of Sombart's and Weber's theories of capitalism. The few scattered comments on Marx in the text are there exclusively to help Parsons frame his argument and help him evaluate Sombart's and Weber's achievements.

One difficulty with this enterprise was that while Sombart had articulated a comprehensive theory of capitalism, Weber had left only fragments and individual investigations. An "element of construction is therefore unavoidable, to a greater extent than in the case of Sombart," observes Parsons in the chapter devoted to Weber's analysis of capitalism (1927, 66). Such "construction" involved a critical inquiry into what Parsons identified as a fundamental ambiguity in Weber's definition of capitalism, for there were, he suggested, "two different meanings of capitalism present in the works of Max Weber, which have relatively little to do with each other" (66). One was "capitalism in general," which was supposed to encompass all historical instances of the phenomenon. The other was "modern capitalism," which referred to the historically specific experience of capitalist development in the West. The thrust of Parsons's argument in this chapter—indeed, in the German version of the dissertation as a whole—was to explain the origins of this conceptual ambiguity, document its implications for Weber's capacity to explain capitalism, and hence suggest an alternative approach.

The first instance of this ambiguity is found in Weber's discussion of "objectivity," the methodical, rational, and continual pursuit of profit that Weber claims characterizes both capitalism in general and modern capitalism. For Sombart and Marx, Parsons notes, this is a trait peculiar to modern capitalism. Parsons finds a possible explanation for this apparent contradiction in Weber's talk of the "capitalist ordering of the entire society." "Capitalist businesses, and therefore capitalism, exist everywhere," Parsons writes, "but a 'capitalist ordering of the entire society' exists only in the West" (1927, 68). Objectivity, in other words, is a matter of degree. If traces of it can be found in all human societies, the fact remains that only in Western societies has it become a dominant feature. Of course, analysis of the societal process of rationalization is a key element of Weber's sociological diagnosis of our epoch, one marked by an irreversible pessimism. It is also, as we shall see, one of the key issues around which Parsons's interpretation turns.

"It can hardly be this capitalism of which Max Weber writes: 'the most fateful power of our modern life,'" Parsons observes (1927, 80). He must be referring to modern capitalism. After examining the noneconomic preconditions of modern capitalism, which include science, bureaucracy, the judicial system, and urbanization, Parsons discusses its main features. These include the separation of the household from the business environment, double-entry bookkeeping, and the rational organization of work. In its pure form, the rational organization of work amounts to bureaucratization. Its main characteristics include competencies, official hierarchy, monetary economy, rigid discipline (which Parsons connects to the spirit of capitalism), and education—namely, the training of experts and specialists. In Weber's view, bureaucratization is the end result of rationalization and therefore can be found in both capitalist and socialist systems. More important than its general character, however, are its ethical implications. Parsons notes that here "we are confronted with Weber's pessimistic fatalism" (84). Indeed, Weber is haunted by the prospect of an increasingly bureaucratized world, leading inexorably toward the fossilization and petrification of the human spirit.

For Weber, however, the tendency toward rationalization is far from homogeneous, as there is no single, universal type of rationality. Rather, Weber stresses the relativity of all processes of rationalization in different societal domains. For instance, what is seen as rational in the domain of economics can be regarded as irrational in the domain of technology. The Weberian understanding of a "value-free science" asserting the full relativism of all rationality emerges most plainly in *The Protestant Ethic*, to which Parsons devotes a fifteen-page discussion. This discussion did not survive in the English version of the dissertation. This is partly due to its descriptive character but also because it reflected assumptions about Weber's overall theory of capitalism that Parsons would either abandon altogether or refine.

The first assumption concerned the utilitarian implications of the spirit of capitalism and the subsequent materialism it helped generate. In the German dissertation, Weber's analysis of modern capitalism is said to portray the capitalist system as primarily defined by its totalizing rationality and mechanistic quality but also by its overriding materialism: "Things govern men, not the other way around." Despite Weber's criticism of Marx's materialist conception of history, "even presenting his theory of Protestantism as a counter-thesis," the truth is that "there is undeniably a tendency in capitalism itself to realize this idea. It will even happen if the development continues, that the mind actually plays no role in history and more will be reduced to mere servants." Parsons concludes, "Here the materialist conception of history is put into perspective and made the characteristic of the capitalist age" (1927, 102). This conclusion derives, in Parsons's view, from the way in which Weber conceived of the character and historical role of the spirit of capitalism. While the social ethics illustrated by Benjamin Franklin is not concerned with the maximization of happiness (far from it: it is entirely irrational and the source of profound anxiety), it ultimately leads "into a utilitarianism" (89)

The second assumption refers back to the conceptual ambiguity between the two meanings of capitalism. *The Protestant Ethic* is a historical case, not a study of capitalism in general. Yet Weber ends up confusing the two "under the concept of the ideal type" (Parsons 1927, 105). This is due to his "comparative method." As Parsons explains, Weber "selects societal atoms and uses them to construct historical epochs and cultures. But the fact is that these atoms have a different meaning in different times and cultures. Here a 'change of meaning' takes place, in the sense of Karl Mannheim. That he neglects this makes it impossible for him to elaborate a capitalist culture as a whole. Therefore, we think, he overexaggerates the importance of the rational organization of work and everything connected with it." Parsons believes the source of this theoretical difficulty is conceptual: "The spirit of capitalism is, of course, a specific modern-occidental thing. It is certainly not the spirit of capitalism in general. The result of such use of the term is a bad conceptual ambiguity" (104). Parsons's verdict is clear. "The main reason for this confusion," he concludes, "is that Weber is trying to accommodate two different things under the concept of the ideal type." "One has to make a choice," Parsons argues; either "capitalism is a general ideal type" or "capitalism must be a 'historical individual.'" Given this conceptual confusion on Weber's part, "the attempt failed" (105). While Parsons would maintain this verdict in the English version of the DPhil,[5] the grounds shifted, evolving from a relatively minor issue of conceptual ambiguity in need of purgation to a more sophisticated argument over Weber's employment of ideal types as a concept formation strategy.

Parsons finished the German version of the dissertation by the end of the summer semester of 1926 and submitted it to Salin. He returned to the United States, where he had a one-year post as an instructor in economics waiting for him at Amherst College. A few months later, in December, Parsons requested that his doctoral dissertation be sent back to him by mail, arguing that he wished to add a third substantive chapter to the ones on Sombart and Weber. As it turned out, he never returned the original manuscript in German. Claiming it was lost in the mail, Parsons would in fact resubmit a revised version of his dissertation in English in July 1927, and it was accepted by Heidelberg's philosophy department. This version was eventually published in two parts in 1928 and 1929 in the *Journal of Political Economy*.[6] As presented, the story is pretty unlikely—not quite "the dog ate it," but not far off. Could this really be all there was to it?

COMPOSING *THE PROTESTANT ETHIC*

The outlines of a likelier explanation appear in a letter Parsons sent to Marianne Weber in April 1927. He begins, "Some months ago, I was asked to translate something from Max Weber into English. The proposal seemed exceedingly attractive, and I have started negotiations on it with several people." Parsons then asks Marianne Weber's opinion, letting her know his own thoughts: "Would you like to see this work of Max Weber appear in English? I do not know whether I am sufficiently familiar with the work of Max Weber and with the German language, such that I would be qualified to the task. Nevertheless, I shall do my best, because I believe that especially this essay will be exceedingly important for us in America and would deserve to be much better known."[7]

As the letter suggests, Parsons's contribution is a complex work of translation and editorial composition undertaken with an eye to the future. His translation choices, editorial decisions as to what text and selections to use, and the paratext he penned offer precious insights into the dialectic between form and content through which his early sociological thinking unfolded. It was by editing, translating, and writing for the English version of Weber's book that Parsons gradually reached his mature understanding of Weber's ideas. Quite literally, Parsons became a Weberian by immersing himself in the materiality of Weber's ideas on the religious nature of capitalism, an intensive intellectual and manual labor conducted between early 1927 and 1930, when the book was eventually published in London and New York. But how did a twenty-three-year-old exchange student like Parsons end up translating Weber's essay? What did his editorial and translation work entail exactly? And how did it shape Parsons's later views and choices? These are the three main questions we will try to answer in what follows.

The suggestion that Parsons should translate Weber's essay seems to have been argued first of all by a senior colleague of his, Professor Harry Elmer Barnes. A historically minded sociologist then based at Smith College, Barnes suggested that his language skills and academic training made Parsons an ideal person for the job (Scaff 2005, 210). Parsons replied enthusiastically for two reasons. On the one hand, his reply seems to have been motivated by genuine intellectual interest. As Parsons would later recall, Weber's linking of Puritanism and capitalism fascinated him (1980, 39). The second reason was more pragmatic. Upon taking his role at Amherst, Parsons taught both an introductory economics course and his own senior course, "Recent European Social Developments and Social Theories." Parsons's receipt of Barnes's suggestion coincides with his preparation of materials for his students who did not read German—materials that included *The Protestant Ethic*.[8]

If Barnes provided the cue, once Parsons decided to move this project forward, none other than Marianne Weber, Max Weber's widow and a fierce gatekeeper of her late husband's intellectual legacy, acted as its crucial facilitator. This unlikely alliance between a young American exchange student and Weber's widow, an alliance that would deepen in affection over the years, proved invaluable in light of the exceedingly difficult negotiations with the German editor, Oskar Siebeck, and the English-language publishers in London and New York (see Scaff 2005, 212–18). It was Marianne Weber who mediated Parsons's proposal for a translation, first by contacting Siebeck herself and then by arranging a meeting between Parsons and Siebeck.[9] This led Parsons to a follow-up conversation with Siebeck, who reportedly "had a very good impression of him" (quoted in Scaff 2005, 212). As Lawrence Scaff summarizes, without "Parsons' stubborn persistence and Marianne Weber's unwavering support, accepted by Siebeck, it is highly improbable the translation would have appeared at all, and certainly not when it did" (2005, 213).

Parsons's activities as editor and translator of Weber's book were part of a larger collective effort over the course of three years involving more than a dozen academic and nonacademic figures based in Germany, England, and the United States who were united by a common wish to see Weber's text in English. The translation was an international affair, with the German side keen on protecting both Weber's intellectual legacy and the financial interests of his widow and the Anglo-American front divided into editors interested in the commercial side of the venture and academic figures with different conceptions of Weber's achievements. In the middle of it all, there was Parsons, still young, with no experience as a translator and very few academic credentials.

As a result, Parsons played a rather limited role in the decision-making process over what to publish. He was kept informed of decisions and consulted on occasion, but the main editorial decisions were made elsewhere. The editors—Oskar Siebeck on the German side and at first Kegan Paul and Alfred Knopf and then Stanley Unwin on the English side—decided the essential features of this translation. To speak of decisions belies a process of strenuous negotiation that went on for several months, involving editorial, typographic, and commercial preferences often clashing with academic and intellectual considerations. Then there was the nature of the work.

Originally published as a two-part article and later published in revised form as a book,[10] translating *Die protestantische Ethik* was always going to be a difficult enterprise. At first, Parsons was of the opinion that the essay should have been translated not as a freestanding volume but as part of Weber's three-volume work on world religions, *Gesammelte Aufsätze zur Religionssoziologie*.[11] From a scholarly perspective, this would have been the most appropriate choice. Oskar Siebeck was of the same opinion. The difficulty was to convince the English and American editors of the commercial viability and editorial interest of this option. Kegan Paul in London and Alfred A. Knopf in New

York doubted that a massive three-volume work by a relatively unknown German scholar would sell and insisted on publishing only a segment. At first, there was an agreement to publish at least two out of the three volumes, but this eventually foundered, putting the whole project at risk.

At this point, Parsons intervened. He put scholarly compunctions to one side and, believing it was preferable to compromise rather than have the translation run into the sands, he urged Siebeck to consider translating only the first of the three volumes with another publisher. It worked. Siebeck reached out to Stanley Unwin in London, with whom he had already worked, proposing that the first volume of Weber's *Religionssoziologie* should be translated into English. Despite his reservations about working with an American translator, in July 1927 Unwin accepted Siebeck's proposal to edit a one-volume work comprising pages 1 to 275 of the first Weber volume. Worried about the commercial viability of even this project, Unwin backtracked and suggested the translation be scaled back still further. The final round of negotiations between Unwin, Siebeck, Marianne Weber, and Parsons ended with an agreement reflected in the book as we know it. The essay on the Protestant sects and the "Eileitung" to the subsequent series of essays on world religions were dropped, but Weber's 1920 "Author's Introduction" survived. This eleventh-hour decision, for which Parsons was coresponsible, would have momentous consequences. Combined with his own "Translator's Preface," this particular paratext proved invaluable for Parsons's interpretation and appropriation of Weber.

But before we consider these paratexts, let us examine more closely Parsons's involvement with the text, a sensuous dialectic of material-formal considerations and intellectual decisions. Modern commentators often overlook the degree to which Parsons's work was subject to constant editorial oversight by Allen and Unwin.[12] For one thing, the typography of Parsons's draft translation was profoundly changed as a result of the interventions of these higher powers. Against the common criticism that Parsons's translation was unfaithful to Weber's frequent use of italics and inverted commas (e.g., Ghosh 1994, 114), thus doing violence to the author's nuanced lines of reasoning, must be set the fact that this was the result of an explicit suggestion by R. H. Tawney (Scaff 2005, 219). The same applies to Parsons's original decision to keep Weber's paragraphs intact and include marginal pagination references to the German original: paragraphs and sentences were altered and the marginal pagination dropped at Tawney's recommendation. Parsons does not seem to have been consulted about the decision to replace Weber's copious footnotes with endnotes, a decision that profoundly affected the interpretation of the text by relocating much of Weber's more qualified and nuanced reasoning to the back of the book.

Parsons's translation choices do, however, seem to have been left alone. His stated aim of trying "to be faithful to the text rather than to present a work of art as far as English style is concerned"[13] is a masterpiece of understatement. Despite its obvious conceptual inconsistencies (Ghosh 1994; Tribe 2007; Scaff 2014, 25) when treating central Weberian concepts such as *Begriff* (concept), *Beruf* (calling, vocation, profession), *bürgerlich* (bourgeois), or *Lebensführung* (spirit, way of life), Parsons's translation of Weber remains second to none in its pathos, with memorable passages that eventually became an integral part of the Anglo-American sociological vocabulary. Parsons laid out his aims qua translator in his "Translator's Preface."

The preface, having established the relevant facts about the text under translation, developed four arguments. The first argument concerned Weber's voluminous footnotes. Distancing himself from the editorial decision to publish them at the end of the volume, Parsons advises his readers to undertake a "careful perusal of the notes," since "a great deal of important material is contained in them." He then reinforces this point and makes clear that his interpretation of Weber's text and the material form imposed by Unwin were anything but a coincidence: "The fact that they are printed separately from the main text should not be allowed to hinder their use" (Parsons 1930, ix). The second argument concerns the philosophy of translation. Parsons reiterates his earlier position regarding the priority of accuracy over style: "The translation is, as far as is possible, faithful to the text, rather than attempting to achieve any more than ordinary, clear English style" (ix).

The final arguments were more important, however. The first concerned the "Introduction." It is vital to understand that by this term Parsons does not mean Tawney's fifteen-page foreword, written as an introductory text to Weber's book, printed immediately after Parsons's preface. Indeed, he does not even mention Tawney's text at all, a telling sign of his opinion of it. Rather, Parsons uses the designation "Introduction"—the main paratextual threshold of interpretation of any text—to refer to Weber's 1920 "*Vorbemerkung*" (preface, introduction) to *Religionssoziologie*. This brings us to one of the most controversial aspects of Parsons's edition. The editorial decision to set the work in this order—first, Parsons's preface; followed by Tawney's foreword; Weber's introduction to *Religionssoziologie*; the text; and finally, the endnotes—and Parsons's justification that it "has been included in this translation because it gives some of the general background ideas and problems into which Weber himself meant this particular study of it" meant that Weber's eighteen-page

"Author's Introduction" would be read by generations of English-speaking readers as the introduction to *The Protestant Ethic*.

For some, the result of this dialectic between form and content was serious confusion, for the introduction outlines a broad question that *The Protestant Ethic* at best answers only tangentially (Riesebrodt 2005, 25). Yet, for Parsons, this was to miss the point entirely. In his view, and this was the view Parsons held throughout his life (e.g., 1970, 1971a, 1971b), Weber's "Author's Introduction" was key to the deep meaning and broader sociological relevance of *The Protestant Ethic*.

The fourth argument concerns the relative worth of the text in the context of Weber's sociological corpus. Parsons begins by recalling the omitted texts from the first volume of *Religionssoziologie*, which can only be read as yet another attempt to distance himself from the Unwin's editorial decisions. As a result, Parsons laments, what "is here presented to English-speaking readers is only a fragment." But, he tells his readers, "it is a fragment which is in many ways of central significance for Weber's philosophy of history, as well as being of very great and very general interest for the thesis it advances to explain some of the most important aspects of modern culture" (1930, xi). With the stroke of a pen and a limited yet crucial editorial influence on the material form of the work,[14] Parsons positions this work at the very heart of not only Weber's oeuvre but sociology itself. Crucial to this positioning was the typographic location of Weber's "Author's Introduction" as the introduction to the translation into English and Parsons's insistence on its relevance and importance, first in his "Translator's Preface" and then, subsequently, in his doctoral dissertation, published around the same time.

Parts of Parsons's dissertation can be read as a close, almost line-by-line commentary on Weber's "Author's Introduction" and, to a lesser extent, on *The Protestant Ethic*. In the "Author's Introduction" Weber begins with the research problem of why it is only in the West that cultural phenomena have appeared that have universal significance and value (Weber 1930, 13). Weber then enumerates the preconditions for this development: science, law, arts, education, bureaucracy, and the state. He next turns to the origins of modern Western capitalism, whose most distinctive feature is the rational organization of labor (21), although the separation of business from the household and rational bookkeeping were important too. Weber's conclusion points toward the explanatory role of the societal process of rationalization (26) and justifies the inclusion of *The Protestant Ethic* as a historical case that illuminates the unintended consequences of the long-forgotten religious origins of this process (27).

For Benjamin Nelson, this "Introduction," the last writing to have been penned by Weber, "offers us insights afforded only obliquely and intermittently elsewhere" and is the clearest example of Weber's "mature awareness that the realization of his master purposes as a sociologist was not possible without a definite commitment to a perspective he himself called 'universal historical'" (1974, 271). For Parsons, the "Author's Introduction" had an even more personal meaning. It was the key to his coming to terms with Weber's sociology. This was the text through which he realized the methodological-historical significance of *The Protestant Ethic* and that was to provide him with a stepping-stone for a nonmaterialistic yet nonutilitarian sociological theory of action. In short, this is the text that made Parsons a Weberian.

Composed over three strenuous years, under severe commercial constraints and involving an international team of collaborators centered around the unlikely figure of the young Talcott Parsons, the first English rendition of *The Protestant Ethic and the Spirit of Capitalism* was published by George Allen and Unwin in London in June 1930 and by Scribner's in New York a few months later.

## FROM TRANSLATOR TO INTERPRETER: *THE PROTESTANT ETHIC* AND THE SECOND DPHIL DISSERTATION

This work of composition and translation had an immediate and lasting impact on Parsons. It made him rethink his interpretation of Weber, an intellectual development that is clearest when one compares the two versions of his doctoral dissertation. The German version, composed *before* Parsons embarked on the translation of Weber's book, concluded with critical notes regarding Weber's supposed utilitarianism and the conceptual ambiguity of his definition of capitalism. The English version—written *after* he began his translation and submitted on July 12, 1927, at Heidelberg—is noticeably different. As noted, this means that the English dissertation was not the starting point of Parsons's interpretation of Weber. Rather, it was the end point of an attempt to understand Weber with the help of Weber's own methodological tools. But how did Parsons arrive at this understanding?

The English version of the dissertation is about half the length of the German one. Parsons's audacious move meant that he eventually submitted only a revised version of the two main chapters of his first dissertation, dropping the preface; the introductory chapter on Passow, von Below, and Brentano; and the last two chapters. The imaginary "lost" chapter on Marx remained just that—a myth Parsons fed over the years. More important, however, were the changes Parsons made to his argument in the chapters on Sombart and, in particular, Weber. One can almost picture Parsons at his desk at Amherst typing these two new chapters, with the German dissertation open before him on one side and his "translation sample" of *The Protestant Ethic*, including Weber's "Author's Introduction," on the other.

The outcome was a new, more sophisticated understanding of Weber's thinking. In the remainder of this section, we will follow Parsons's interventions in his dissertation—sometimes deletions, sometimes additions, and sometimes the movement of whole passages from one place in the argument to another. Thus Parsons's "construction" of Weber emerges as a dialectic process triggered by the German dissertation, mediated by the translation and editorial composition of *The Protestant Ethic*, and concluded by the English version of his DPhil. It is in the differences between the two versions of the dissertation, which can be traced back to Parsons's work as translator-interpreter in the first half of 1927, that the evolution of his appropriation of Weber becomes clear.

The first difference concerns the framing of the discussion. Whereas in the German dissertation, Parsons began by addressing what he designated as a problem of "conceptual ambiguity" between notions of capitalism in general and modern capitalism in Weber's writings—a theoretical dead end—now in the English version, his angle is thoroughly theoretical-methodological. This is a crucial shift. It enables Parsons to build on Weber and to start to formulate his own approach. He maintains a critical attitude toward Weber (that Weber had confused modern capitalism with capitalism in general), but now this is expressed through a detailed discussion of ideal types as a theoretical-methodological strategy to gain an "understanding" of historical phenomena, both in their uniqueness and in what they share with all other historical cases.

The uniqueness of "historical individuals"—that is, historical cases composed of a number of interlinked social agents—is expressed in the "infinite variety of facts from which a selection for purposes of analysis must be made" (Parsons 1927, 20). Given the historically contingent character of such historical cases, "the discovery of uniform relations and their formulation in terms of 'laws' cannot be the objective of such a science." For that, one needs to overcome the particular nature of historical "understanding" and reach the level of a general explanatory theory. This second type of "'understanding' Weber attempts to attain by means of the ideal type" (20).

An ideal type, Parsons explains, is "a special *construction* in the mind of the investigator of what social action would be if it were directed with perfect rationality toward a given end.... It is a picture of what things would be under 'ideal,' not actual, conditions" (1927, 20–21). Equipped with this instrument of analysis, the investigator ceases to be a "'mere' historian" (5) and becomes able to produce (sociological) theory—that is "a consistent and unified system of concepts to be used in the analysis of social phenomena" (5). That is to say, in Parsons's eyes, Weber ceases to be a mere economic historian and becomes a sociological theorist whose ideal-type methodology enables him to compare the "actual record of events in many different instances and thus attempt to 'understand' them, each in its individual uniqueness, by seeing how far they conform to action rationally directed toward the given ends, and to distinguish such elements as are not 'understandable' in these terms" (21).

Bruce C. Wearne rightly called our attention long ago to the fact that the young Parsons "used this instrument himself in his investigation of Weber's thought" (1989, 47) and that Weber's "Author's Introduction" acted as a "kind of ideal-typical representation of Weber's sociology as a whole" (48). But what Wearne failed to appreciate, we think, is the degree to which Parsons's hermeneutical moves were the result of a laborious rewriting of his German dissertation through closer contact with Weber's writings—namely, *The Protestant Ethic*, and the 1920 "Author's Introduction" but also sections of *Economy and Society* regarding charisma and routine—that he was translating into English and teaching his students at Amherst.

All other differences to a certain extent flowed from this first, crucial difference. The second difference concerns Weber's concept of capitalism in general. In the German dissertation, Parsons used Weber's paper "Agrarian Relations" and the 1920 "Author's Introduction" to illustrate Weber's concept of capitalism in general. In the English dissertation, he replaces this with a thoroughly methodological analysis of this concept. The references to Weber's writings are relegated to the endnotes (Parsons 1927, 22). Second, and more importantly, this leads Parsons to a different conclusion regarding this aspect of Weber's theory. In the German dissertation, Parsons concluded that the difference between modern capitalism and capitalism in general is a question of degree. In the English dissertation, Parsons maintains this idea but adds, "That is not the whole story, as will be shown presently" (24). Parsons then offers a new conclusion to his discussion of capitalism in general. Whereas before it included a description of two characteristics (its peaceful and calculable character), which Parsons now reserves for the discussion of *modern* capitalism, the new conclusion states that Weber uses a characteristic feature of modern society—namely, "a thoroughgoing systematization and adaptation of practical life to a particular set of ideals" (24)—to define capitalism in general, which "indicates that [Weber] did not clearly distinguish in his own mind the two separate concepts of capitalism to be found in his work" (24).

A third difference has to do with Parsons's examination of Weber's notion of modern capitalism. The first thing that changes is Parsons's depiction of modern capitalism as a "historical individual," following his new theoretical-methodological understanding of Weber's work. This paves the way for a whole new structure of argument regarding modern capitalism.

Showing the influence of a closer reading of Weber's "Author's Introduction," which Parsons analyzes step by step in this segment of his dissertation, he begins by inserting the theme of rationalization right at the outset of the discussion of modern capitalism. This was absent from the German dissertation; there, Parsons discussed bookkeeping, socialism, and bureaucracy, concluding with a lengthy description of the argument of *The Protestant Ethic*. The result of this sequence of argument was a (misguided) criticism of Weber's materialism and a methodological criticism that failed to do justice to Weber's actual use of the concept of the ideal type. The structure of the English dissertation is very different, discussing bookkeeping, bureaucracy, socialism, and the spirit of capitalism. This discussion of the spirit of capitalism replaces the description of *The Protestant Ethic* found in the German dissertation. Parsons now offers his readers a methodological discussion of the relative place of that historical case within Weber's general theory. In particular, Parsons now credits Weber for having developed a theory of modern capitalism, in the sense of a "historical individual," involving two key contributions: the exclusion of capitalist adventurers, because their irrationality directly contradicts the fundamental trait of modern society (rationality), and the concept of the spirit of capitalism, "which takes its departure from the dominant fact of rational bureaucratic organization" (1927, 27).

As in the German dissertation, Parsons then questions the "significance" of "this theory of the spirit of capitalism for Weber's view of capitalism as a whole" (1927, 30). But, while in the German dissertation, the answer involved criticizing Weber for having made materialism the distinctive feature of the capitalist age and construing the spirit of capitalism as a social ethics that led to utilitarianism, in the English version, all references to the alleged materialism and utilitarianism of Weber's thesis are dropped. All that Parsons's revision left was the much milder conclusion that Weber "does accept economic determinism as a characteristic of capitalism, and thus gives it a relative validity" (32). Parsons's new answer to the question of the significance of the (historically contingent) spirit of capitalism is that it enables us to see the main features of capitalism in general. The economic system as a whole, once refracted through the historical lenses of the spirit of capitalism, emerges as objective, rational, ascetic, mechanistic, and structural (31).

The significance of this change should not be overlooked. Note what Parsons has to say in *The Structure of Social Action* about utilitarianism (Lidz 2010, 45). Attesting to the relevance of the German dissertation as a historical document, here we find material evidence of the development of Parsons's theorizing from this early interpretation of Weber and *The Protestant Ethic* as protomaterialist and utilitarian to the mature view (Parsons 1968, 87–125) that a key element of the Weberian legacy is the distinction between utilitarianism (anomic, selfish behavior) and voluntarism, understood as normatively regulated community-oriented behavior.

The fourth difference lies in the way Parsons ends the dissertation. The German dissertation ended by pointing at Weber's tragic fatalism but offered no real alternative to it: all it asked of Weber was more conceptual clarity in the definition of capitalism. Parsons ends the English dissertation on a strikingly different note of optimism, both ethical and theoretical. Offering a more substantial analysis of Weber's treatment of the relation between charisma and routine, which had led Weber to the pessimistic view that "the really vital human forces appear only in charismatic forms" and that capitalism "presents a dead, mechanized condition of society in which there is no room left for these truly creative forces because all human activity is forced to follow the 'system'" (1927, 33), Parsons develops an alternative ethical-political scenario out of his new theoretical-methodological understanding of Weber's work.

A crucial addition to the English dissertation is the insight, delivered right at the beginning of the chapter on Weber, that ideal types refer to one aspect or side of a historical case and are a means to an end, while "historical individuals" cover the whole essence of the phenomena and constitute the end of the research itself (Parsons 1927, 21–22). Parsons criticizes Weber for not following through with this distinction between a historical and a methodological form of the concept of the ideal type. This novel understanding permits Parsons to point to a way out of the rationalization conundrum envisaged by Weber in a doleful Nietzschean mood: "Weber's ironbound process of rationalization lies in the isolation of one aspect of social development and the attribution of historical reality to an ideal type which was never meant to represent it." Parsons concludes, "If this error is corrected the absolute domination of the process of rationalization over the whole social process falls to the ground" (35). His ethical-political alternative is clear too. "But is it not possible," Parsons asks, referring to the "either-or" terms in which Weber conceives of the charisma-routine relationship, "that all manner of combinations between them are possible, and that the present-day power of the bureaucratic mechanism is due to a very special set of circumstances which do not involve the necessity for its continued dominance over life, *but leave the possibility open that it may again be made to serve 'spiritual' aims?*" (34; our emphasis).

Translating, editing, and teaching *The Protestant Ethic* in 1926–27 at Amherst gave Parsons the theoretical-methodological means to read Weber in a "progressive light" (Brick 1993, 372) and to realize that we are not condemned to Weber's pessimistic fatalism—instead, we can use the creative power of theoretical reflection to become optimistic again (Wearne 1989, 56). This is the real origin of Parsons's famous "Agenda of 1927" (Brick 1993, 369ff.), the social reformist and neo-Kantian epistemological agenda that Parsons pursued from the submission of the English dissertation until the publication of *The Structure of Social Action* in 1937.

The two basic premises of this agenda are Weberian. Both can be traced back to the crucial juncture when Parsons revised his German dissertation and for the first time articulated his mature vision. The first premise is that sociology should be founded on the study of social action in terms of the subjective motives that guide it. The second premise is the neo-Kantian emphasis on theory as a guide for scientific research, pushing Parsons to develop his own highly abstract and general sociological theory. The next step was for Parsons to compare Weber's contributions to those of other theorists. This eventually led him to consider the works of Alfred Marshall, Vilfredo Pareto, Émile Durkheim, and Max Weber in the quest for incipient traces of a common "voluntaristic theory of action." In time, this would coalesce around the "narrative of voluntarism" (Scaff 2014, 283), the image that captured the imagination of American readers in the 1950s and 1960s when applied to the idea of religious sects and their effects on individual and social action. It is by selectively appropriating Weber for his purposes that Parsons, along with contributions from other seminal thinkers, built the grand theoretical scheme that reigned supreme in postwar American sociology.

One should not forget, however, the starting point of this theoretical pilgrimage. Out of the dialectic between form and content emerges a sort of interaction effect—namely, between the work of translation and theory building and from theory building back to translation. Parsons's often remarked on but little understood choice to expurgate from his English rendition of *The Protestant Ethic* most of its references to Nietzsche, especially at the end of the text, must be understood in this context. To allow Nietzsche's shadow to fall over Weber's thesis would be to encourage fatalism.[15] Having found his own way out of Weber's self-imposed pessimism using a theoretically grounded optimism, Parsons was happy enough to sacrifice textual accuracy in order to light the way. If translation is indeed a form of interpretation and interpretation is to be evaluated in terms of its world-making capacity, then the liberties Parsons took in translating Weber are amply justified.

CONCLUSION

The enduring pride and affection Parsons felt for this little book may seem surprising. Set beside Parsons's voluminous intellectual productions, one may be tempted to discount it as a juvenile exercise of little consequence in comparison to the monuments he went on to erect. Nothing could be further from the truth. On the contrary, Parsons thought of his first editorial project as a Janus-faced icon, a material signifier that provided a link to one of the "immortals" (1980, 43) in sociology while acting as an exemplar for future sociological research, as he emphasized in his last public lectures delivered in the shadow of Weber's statue in Munich the day before his death. And he did not hesitate to act when he felt his bond with the work was either in need of renewal or somehow in danger. Two examples will suffice to illustrate Parsons's heartfelt attachment to this work.

The first example is the new preface Parsons wrote for the first paperback reissue of the work. In fact, *The Protestant Ethic* had a difficult reception in the period leading up to the Second World War[16] and only began to gain traction after 1945 (Roth 1999, 521). It would take another decade and a new material form to finally reach the mass market of undergraduate and graduate students of the postwar years.[17] Appearing as part of the Scribner Library, a series of best-selling classics in paperback established in 1958, *The Protestant Ethic* gained (another) new life.

Contributing to this rebirth was Parsons's "Preface to New Edition," in which he begins by expressing his "great satisfaction" with the new edition "given the kind of status as a modern classic which, for serious scholarly books, comes with issue to the paper cover trade" (1958, xii). Thirty years had passed since the first English translation, and the lessons to be gleaned from the work changed accordingly. In typical fashion, Parsons equates the progress made by the social sciences in this period with the development of his structural functionalist version of systems theory: "Weber's trend of interpretation of the modern industrial society was couched within the framework of a more general theoretical analysis of the structure and functioning of social systems" (xv). Reiterating the "convergence thesis" of *The Structure of Social Action*,

Parsons argues that "the important thing about Weber's work was not how he judged the relative importance of economic factors, but rather the way in which he analyzed the systems of social action within which ideas and values as well as 'economic forces' operate to influence action" (xvi). The convergence of Weber's contribution with those of Durkheim, Cooley, Mead, and Freud was obvious to Parsons.

The second example is the controversy[18] between Parsons and British sociologist Anthony Giddens over control of *The Protestant Ethic* and, by extension, the interpretation of Weber's legacy.[19] At the center of the controversy is the 1976 Allen and Unwin edition of *The Protestant Ethic*, the first new edition since 1930.[20] The controversy between Parsons and Giddens originated from the fact that neither the publisher nor Giddens sought Parsons's approval before moving ahead. To make matters worse, this new edition had been scheduled without Parsons's "Translator's Preface" of 1930 and left out his "Preface to New Edition" of 1958. Parsons's translation of Weber's "Author's Introduction" was retained, however. And, a trifle tactlessly, this new edition was to include a newly written introduction by Giddens. Giddens, then fellow of King's College, Cambridge, was a rising star in the sociological establishment partly due to his theoretical attempt to replace what he believed to be Parsons's idealist reading of Weber with an interpretation of Weber as a conflict theorist.[21] An exchange of angry and apologetic correspondence between Parsons, Giddens, and the publisher in London led to a compromise—Parsons's "Translator's Preface" of 1930 was reinstated.

The lesson to be drawn from these two examples is that crucial struggles over the control of meaning play out through the control of books as material objects. While the first case illustrates how Parsons used *The Protestant Ethic* as a vehicle for his ideas, the second shows his willingness to react to any perceived threat to his control over the work. Likewise, Giddens's career as a social theorist is virtually impossible to understand in its scope and consequences without reference to his parallel work as an editor and commentator. Translators, editors, and commentators are key agents in the politics of the book.

CHAPTER 6

## PROPHETS AND PRINCES

On the Editing and Translation of Tocqueville's *Democracy in America*

Alexis de Tocqueville's *De la démocratie en Amérique* was first published in two installments, in 1835 and 1840, respectively. The publisher was Charles Gosselin, a central figure in the Paris publishing industry at the time. The print run of the first edition of the first volume was five hundred copies. Immediately hailed a classic in its native France, the work was rapidly translated into English by Henry Reeve, a friend of Tocqueville: *Democracy in America* was born. A new edition with a revised translation by Francis Bowen appeared in 1862. Between 1898 and 1912, *Democracy in America* was reprinted several times: first in 1898 in an edition by Daniel C. Gilman, then in 1899 by Ingalls and Morgan, and finally in 1904 by John Bigelow. It was last reprinted in 1912 by Bigelow. After World War II, there was a renewed interest in the work. In 1945, Alfred Knopf published a new edition of *Democracy in America* with a revised version of the Reeve-Bowen translation by Phillips Bradley. That same year, Oxford University Press published an abridgment of the work under the direction of Henry Steele Commager, an American historian. These editions heralded a new episode in the history of the book, with a new translation in 1966 by George Lawrence. Dozens of reprints and abridgments have been published since. In the 2000s, several new translations made it to the bookstores, some wrapped in controversy. Claimed by the conservative right in the United States, *Democracy in America* remains bitterly contested terrain: it shaped, and has been shaped by, America's evolving self-conception as a democracy.

INTRODUCTION

The history of *Democracy in America* is the history of its becoming the book it is today. This is also a history that cannot be told in isolation from the multiple interventions—production, editing, translation, and textual commentary—whereby the book has been construed as a classic of social and political thought. Apart from a few exceptions, however, histories of *Democracy in America* continue to be one-dimensional: they start and stop with the author, understood as *the* agent behind the making of the book.[1]

This chapter challenges this view by considering the activities of a far less visible category of agents who worked painstakingly *on* and *through* the text. We refer to editors-cum-commentators and editors-cum-translators who have engaged in what we shall call "authorship *through* editorial labor." Although this is arguably always exercised, in this chapter we turn our attention to one type of editor in particular: the one whose editing and translating of *Democracy in America* was enmeshed in a broader interpretative engagement with the work. The people we will be writing about are therefore not *simply* editors and translators—although editing and translating *Democracy in America* was a fundamental part of what they did as Tocqueville scholars. They were also authors in their own right. Originating on both the left and the right of the political spectrum, they wrote important commentaries on Tocqueville and *Democracy in America* that set the stage for (or, indeed, confirmed it, in retrospect) their "authoring" of the work as editors and translators. In editing and translating *Democracy in America*, they found a way to extend their influence over the meaning of the work and its reception, first, within academia itself—most notably within those two disciplines between which *Democracy in America* has vacillated over time, sociology and political philosophy—and then to the wider public. Direct intervention in the body of the text's typographic material and its paratexts provided these agents with a privileged position from which to fight over its meaning (and how to make meaning of it). This was also a position from which the work's ideological identity and its disciplinary "belonging" could be shaped and exercised. In what follows, we examine the conflicts between purposes and between values behind their editorial choices. The editing and translating of *Democracy in*

*America* emerge from this less as technical processes leading from scholarly research to book production than as deeply contested terrains on which different visions of the book, its disciplinary identity, and the book's very subject—ourselves—are being enacted.

ORIGINS: THE PROPHET OF THE MASS AGE

The year 1935 marked the centenary of the publication of volume 1 of *Democracy in America*. Several articles were published in America around this time to celebrate the event. One was by the German-Jewish émigré and sociologist Albert Salomon, who lamented "the present lack of interest in . . . Tocqueville" (1935b, 405). This lack of interest was evident on various fronts. One was the difficulty of obtaining Tocqueville's books. As Salomon reported, "At that time, it was impossible to buy a single copy of the book in New York."[2] Not only was the book hard to get, but publishers were not particularly excited by the prospect of producing a new edition. Years later, when reflecting on the fortieth anniversary of his Tocquevillian book, *The Quest for Community* (1953), another sociologist and key Tocqueville popularizer, Robert A. Nisbet, recollected how representatives of publishing houses had shown little interest in producing a new edition of Tocqueville's major work when approached by him before he joined the army in 1943 (Nisbet 1993). Figuring low in publishers' priorities, Tocqueville had also virtually disappeared from the classroom. This was true even in top American universities responsible for the training of eventually prominent Tocqueville-inspired sociologists—Nisbet, certainly, but also others, such as Edward Digby Baltzell. There was no mention of Tocqueville in the courses Nisbet attended at Berkeley. Similarly, Baltzell heard Tocqueville named only once at Columbia. This mention occurred in the fall of 1947 and was made by none other than Salomon, a guest lecturer from the New School for Social Research who claimed Tocqueville's *The Old Regime* to be "the greatest book in the social sciences" (Baltzell quoted in Schneidermann 2001, xvii). Baltzell had to wait to satisfy his fresh curiosity about the work, however. He could not find a single copy in New York and spent a whole year trying to track one down, eventually buying his copy from Blackwell's in Oxford. It would have not been much different had he tried to find a copy of *Democracy in America* in a bookstore on either side of the Atlantic before 1945. This was the time before Tocqueville's books were made readily available in mass-market editions. The struggle to find copies of his books was the first rite of passage for any Tocquevillian in the making.

Everything changed in 1945. Not by chance, that year Baltzell found his first copy of *Democracy in America* as he browsed the Columbia bookstore. This was also the year in which, upon his return to campus after the war, Nisbet came across "a handsome, boxed, two volume edition, edited by Phillips Bradley, published by Knopf." It was now "to be found in every bookstore" (Nisbet 1993, 43). The ready availability of this new edition, Nisbet contends, paved the way for a major Tocquevillian revival in the 1950s, with Tocqueville emerging as the main challenger of Marx and his name mentioned just as frequently "over faculty club lunch tables" (43).

Nisbet's epic story of a Tocquevillian rebirth rising like a phoenix from the ashes would be retold, *in* and *for* a different intellectual context, by sociologist Raymond Aron in the late 1970s in the newly launched *The Tocqueville Review* (Aron 1979). Both versions of Nisbet's story are somewhat overstated. It is more likely that both in the United States and in France, the burnt coal had some combustible matter in it and that rather than being simply forgotten, Tocqueville was actually still being discussed in some circles in the decades leading up to his 1950s and 1960s revival. But the painstaking disclosure of episodic interest in Tocqueville or even broken lines of reception (Mancini 2006) does not necessarily disprove the larger thesis—that is, that rather than a more or less straight line with the occasional bump, Tocqueville's reception has indeed had its peaks and troughs. In particular, the 1950s and 1960s witnessed a remarkable surge of interest in Tocqueville and marked his zenith in sociology. This resurgence did not come by fiat, however. As Nisbet himself hints, in the 1930s and 1940s, a combination of watershed scholarship and strategic publishing set up the basic conditions for Tocqueville to once again take center stage.

Scholarship and editing were not mere parallel developments; they were eminently connected. The connection is easily traceable because it is personal. Two scholars in particular—one American, the other European—lay simultaneously behind some of the best scholarly work on Tocqueville to emerge in the 1930s and the two new editions of *Democracy in America* arriving in bookstores in the 1940s and the 1960s, respectively. The first is George Wilson Pierson, then a young professor of history at Yale. The second is Jacob-Peter Mayer, a Jewish émigré who edited Marx's *Economic-Philosophical Manuscripts* with Siegfried Landshut in 1932. Four years later, in 1936, Mayer was forced to flee Germany for England, where he would eventually settle at the University of Reading. There, in the early 1970s, he created the Alexis de Tocqueville Institute.

This chapter follows in Pierson's, Mayer's, and Harvey Mansfield Jr.'s (our third editor-cum-translator) footsteps in the hope of reconstituting some of the most important intellectual links among those who have written about, edited, and translated Tocqueville since the Second World War. In so doing, we will inevitably tap into the process of creation—or, more concretely, authorship through editorial labor—through which *Democracy in America* has been remade for new publics and even new disciplines over time.

Our genealogy begins in the 1930s. These were troubled times in which both Pierson and Mayer turned to Tocqueville to make sense of their own predicament. As the decade drew to a close, they saw the resulting work through to publication, and Oxford University Press released Pierson's *Tocqueville and Beaumont in America* in 1938. Following the resurgence of interest in Tocqueville, Doubleday, then one of the largest publishers in the United States, published an abridged version of the work in 1959. As happened often with abridgments of Tocqueville's own work, the abridged 1959 edition of Pierson's companion work was sanitized of its sections on Tocqueville's journeys to the South and the frontier West and accompanying observations on the fate of Native Americans, the institution of slavery, and American women. As for Mayer's *Alexis de Tocqueville: Prophet of the Mass Age*, it was, fittingly, published in 1939 by J. M. Dent and Sons in London just before the outbreak of the war. An American edition, by Viking Press, appeared the following year under a far less alluring title: *Alexis de Tocqueville: A Biographical Essay in Political Science*. This was revised later in 1960 for Harper and Row as a fresh edition with a new and important essay examining Tocqueville's reception—"Tocqueville After a Century."

For all their differences, Pierson's and Mayer's books belonged broadly to the same genre: the biographical essay. Both of these works also doubled as a political commentary on their times. But they made different types of contributions. While Pierson's book established and exhibited an as-yet-unmatched level of Tocqueville scholarship, Mayer's much shorter and somewhat sketchy study offered a thesis about the meaning of Tocqueville's work for the 1930s that would prove deeply resonant.

Pierson's *Tocqueville and Beaumont in America*—renamed *Tocqueville in America* by Johns Hopkins University Press for their reprint paperback edition of the work in 1996—is a painstakingly researched biographical study responsible for inaugurating modern Tocquevillian scholarship. As such, and despite the many biographies of Tocqueville that have emerged since, it remains a reference to this day. A personal biography of Tocqueville, Pierson's study is primarily about the making of *Democracy in America*. Pierson follows closely in the footsteps of Tocqueville and Beaumont during their intense but rather brief nine-month tour of the country. The physical journey is, however, only the vehicle for a far more exciting intellectual journey, which Pierson vividly reconstructs. Equipped with an extraordinary array of secondary and primary sources, some of which he acquired directly from the Tocqueville family, Pierson reenacts the circumstances and sets forth the influences under which the outline of *Democracy in America* developed and the book's main theses took shape. Letters, diaries, travel notes, sketches, and unpublished manuscripts profusely inhabit Pierson's account and allow for frequent switches to the first-person voice, making the account more intimate. These materials cohabit, however, with quotes from contemporary newspapers and Pierson's own running commentaries, which provide the reader with a more distanced third-person perspective. So impressive is Pierson's reconstruction of Tocqueville's journeys, both spatial and intellectual, that readers are literally made to "see" Tocqueville's thought process. Tocqueville's theorizing emerges as an instance of looking at things simultaneously with the eyes and the mind, which enables one to see the general in the particular: "more than America . . . the image of democracy itself" (Tocqueville 2000, 13). Thus we find Tocqueville, as the back cover of the 1996 reprint aptly summarizes it, "near Detroit, noting the scattered settlement patterns of the frontier and the affinity of Americans for solitude; in Boston, witnessing the jury system at work; in Philadelphia, observing the suffocating moral regimen at the new Eastern State Prison; and in New Orleans, disturbed by the racial caste system and the lassitude of the French-speaking population." More than any of these, however, it is the theme of administrative centralization that resonates with Pierson. In Tocqueville's grim warnings against the effects of centralization, Pierson sees an intimation of the dangers of direct action and intervention by the federal government under the New Deal. He bows to Tocqueville's insight that the splitting of society into atoms happily sacrificing individual distinction and liberty in return for generalized well-being generates a strong pull toward an increasingly intrusive central state. Democracy and centralization, Tocqueville intimated, work hand in hand. Combined, they pave the way for a new and especially insidious form of despotism. Pierson concurs. In his concluding remarks, he reminds his readers that Tocqueville trusted Americans' "political *dualism*," "their happy reconciliation of local self-rule with national government," to partly halt the process ([1938] 1996, 776; his emphasis). But Pierson is skeptical, and so too, he thinks, should be Americans. As the central state amasses power, Pierson sees it casting its shadow ever more menacingly and fears that effective "semi-independent localism" as a bastion and school of freedom has become a thing of the past (776–77). A substitute is desperately needed but not readily available.

Hence Pierson leaves his readers with the image of a democracy that remains uncertain and eminently vulnerable to its own destructive impulses.

While Pierson worried about New Deal interventionism, Mayer's concerns turned instead to the rise of totalitarianism in Europe. As Mayer explains in the preface of the abridged 1968 French edition of *Democracy in America*, he came to Tocqueville between 1933 and 1938 as he sought to understand "the sociological structure of plebiscitary democracy" (J.-P. Mayer 1968, 9). While Marxism proved to be of limited assistance, in Tocqueville, on the contrary, Mayer sees an explanation for why some democracies may be free while others are definitely not. Mayer's Tocqueville serves as a mirror of the anxieties of interwar Europe and a harbinger of greater horrors to come. "The manuscript of this book," Mayer writes in his foreword to *Tocqueville: The Prophet of the Masses*, "went to press a few days before Hitler began *his* war" (1939, xii). Only Tocqueville, Mayer insists, could illuminate how it had come to this, for he "originally demonstrated the structure of the modern mass state" and "the possible negative and degenerate form it might assume" as shown by the plebiscitary drift of regimes in Italy and Germany. Yet, Mayer stresses, few were aware of Tocqueville's unique insight. "The great prophet of the Mass Age," Mayer proclaims, "has still to be discovered" (xvi). It fell on Mayer's book to change this state of affairs.

Highlighting the timeliness of his book, Mayer refers to both contemporary political developments and the state of Tocqueville scholarship. Tocqueville, Mayer asserts, had been inexplicably forgotten. This, he observes, was evident from the dismal editorial state in which his writings were found. But it was also apparent from the scarcity of commentary on them: one had yet to find a worthy "analysis of de Tocqueville's works" in Germany; in England, "up to the present day," there was "no book on one who was probably the most important sociologist of the nineteenth century"; and in France, even Tocqueville's complete works were out of print, and Tocqueville remained on the whole either ignored or subject to the misunderstanding of commentators who took him for the political liberal he never was (J.-P. Mayer 1939, xv, 150).[3] The only exception, Mayer claims, was Antoine Rédier and his long-forgotten 1925 study *Comme disait Monsieur de Tocqueville*. Mayer's praise for Rédier is somewhat surprising given Rédier's association with the far-right political movement *Action Française* and the visceral distaste for democracy he showed in his analysis of Tocqueville. But in Rédier, Mayer finds an ally in his challenge to the mainstream treatment of Tocqueville as a liberal. Rédier highlighted Tocqueville's wariness of individualism, egoism, and liberty without religion—that is, liberty without that which prevented it from drifting perilously into license (an amoral "laissez faire, laissez passer") and without that which allowed a civic sensitivity to develop in communities. If Tocqueville was a liberal at all, Rédier had made it clear he was no ordinary liberal but a "liberal of a new kind" (J.-P. Mayer 1939). Mayer fully endorses Rédier's skepticism about the use of the liberal label. Like Mayer's own work, Rédier's *Comme disait Monsieur de Tocqueville* was a biographical study to which Mayer confesses his indebtedness, both for the thrust of its main thesis and because there was little else to draw on. As Mayer reminds us, in 1925 Rédier's book had been ironically dedicated to "all those who have hitherto [been] unaware of his [Tocqueville's] work." Fourteen years had passed, and, Mayer complains, little had changed.

Mayer's focus on Rédier's book has a clear polemical intent. It is directed at French academia, which Mayer seems intent to address. Unlike the reading of Tocqueville that would dominate the author's (incipient) reception in France, Mayer's Tocqueville is not a liberal. Tocqueville, Mayer defiantly insists, "detested the fat philistine who asked nothing of the State except to guarantee him a good night's rest" (1939, 137). Neither is his Tocqueville Marx's nemesis. This would come to be Aron's—not Mayer's—construction. Like Mayer, Aron would stress how Tocqueville had been forgotten in France prior to his rediscovery (Audier 2004). Partly true, this was primarily also a tactical move by Aron to create the empty space that Tocqueville could then inhabit more fully. But in so doing, Aron had to keep silent regarding figures like Rédier (with his questioning of Tocqueville's liberal credentials) and Mayer, who in 1948 published his own biographical study of Tocqueville in French. With Aron, Tocqueville would become a key liberal thinker, the posthumous founder of a "French school" of political sociology (coined by Aron himself) who set the terms of the choice between democracy and totalitarianism, and the only figure who might rival the dominant Marxist tradition of sociological thinking (Aron 1959).

Mayer's reading was far more nuanced. He praised Tocqueville for showing him how tendencies toward despotism inhered in democracy. He saw Tocqueville as having already "overstepped ... the boundaries of liberalism" (1939, 151). As such, he praised Harold Laski's analysis of Tocqueville in *The Rise of European Liberalism* (1936, 244) for bringing out a series of antinomies originally identified by Tocqueville—between "individualist economy" and "political democracy," between "the privileges of property" and "popular sovereignty"—that, in his view, sufficed to demonstrate the fallacy of calling Tocqueville a liberal in the common sense of the word. But he also chastised Laski for holding to the label "liberal" even in the face of the evidence presented and thereby failing to signal that Tocqueville's thought was in fact already evolving to "a new world." This was partly the world of Marx. Mayer, himself a Social Democrat, saw faults as well as virtues in both authors. Rather than asking for the substitution of one for the other, Mayer construed and called for their complementarity. He went so far as to suggest the influence of Tocqueville on Marx via Proudhon.[4] But more than this, he sought to show how one could beneficially come in where the other failed. "Marxian socialism," he wrote, lacked "that all-rounded penetration of political structures which Tocqueville ... took for granted," but however penetrating, Tocqueville's thought remained "admittedly bounded by the dying bourgeois world" beyond which only Marx would see. Only by combining and refining them[5] could one find "a systematic basis ... for the political philosophy of the future" (J.-P. Mayer 1939, 136).

Mayer's labeling of Tocqueville as "the prophet of the Mass Age" was a masterstroke of human ingenuity. Politically astute, the labeling would also prove to be immensely influential. It inaugurated a new line of interpretation of Tocqueville as a theorist of modern mass societies. For Mayer, Tocqueville's political philosophy spoke to the future—that is, Mayer's present—simultaneously as "a burden and a warning" (J.-P. Mayer 1939, 157). Mayer placed Tocqueville firmly in a classic line of prognosticators and critics of the pathologies of modernity—Goethe, Burckhardt, Nietzsche, Sorel, and especially Max Weber. Just as Mayer construed Tocqueville's relation to Marx as one of complementarity, so did he construe Weber as a disciple of Tocqueville. He spoke of Weber as someone who offered a mere "recapitulation of de Tocqueville's formulation of the problem" of modern societies (157) and even gained the assent of Weber's wife, Marianne, to this idea (Offe 2005). As seen by Mayer through the lenses provided by Tocqueville, modernity's problem was a complex one with its multiple, closely interrelated facets: leveling egalitarianism, crass materialism, growing individualism, loss of individuality, and privatizing of opinions with the resulting rise of stifling uniformity and conformism. All of these tendencies of democratic societies, Mayer concluded, conflated explosively in the contemporaneous observed soft despotism of the masses, not the least over themselves. Such ideas were, at the same time, likely to empower leaders seeking mass plebiscitary approval, along with the increasingly centralized, technicized, bureaucratic states lying behind them. The masses were being dramatically disempowered by "the monstrous tutelary power" of this new Leviathan, which was providing for their security, necessities, and pleasures. Tocqueville's tutelary state bore the specter of the totalitarian regime Mayer saw growing at home. Mayer saw in Tocqueville the first thinker to set forth the problem of modernity, but he also insisted that Tocqueville did not and could not, within his own premises, ever solve it (1939, 115). The way out, Mayer the Social Democrat suggested, depended on an almost impossible development neither foreseen nor encouraged by Tocqueville. Here, Mayer's reference is Sorel, whom he depicts as a Tocquevillian capable of "drawing the logical conclusion from de Tocqueville's premises" (116)—namely, the need for a new proletarian elite at the helm of the state refusing to model itself on the bourgeois one.[6] But any such hopes remained largely unfulfilled. Like Pierson's, Mayer's book ends on a somber note. His portrayal of Tocqueville as a prophet and a staunch critic of "the modern egalitarian mass society" (161), conjoined with his call for socialist redemption, must have sounded strangely foreign—if not heretic—to the ears of many.

## THE POSTWAR YEARS

Mayer's assessment of Tocqueville's "permanent contribution to political sociology" (1960, 117) survived into the American editions of *The Prophet of the Mass Age: A Study of Alexis de Tocqueville* of 1940 and 1960, respectively. These editions kept the body of the text and its historical references intact. But continuity coexisted with change. Some changes are immediately apparent: the prophetic title with its allusion to the overall tendency of Western democratic societies toward "mass society" disappeared. In its place, we find a much-softened, descriptive title—*Alexis de Tocqueville: A Biographical Essay in Political Science*—that inscribes Tocqueville in an academic discipline more dominant in the United States than the (political) sociology in which Mayer originally inscribed him. Although the body of the text remained unchanged, the American edition of 1960 includes a new commemorative essay, taking the centenary of Tocqueville's death as a pretext to reflect on his legacy. Here Mayer makes it clear that contrary to what many earlier readers of Tocqueville had believed, in the last two volumes of *Democracy in America*, Tocqueville "showed his real greatness" (117). However, the fact that they remained misunderstood for so long explains, in Mayer's view, why Tocqueville "could not form a school" (125). But it is not too late to do so, Mayer suggests, as there is still much to learn from Tocqueville in both substance and method. Tocqueville's powerful insights into the future of democratic societies, Mayer claims, were made possible by a fundamental methodological innovation. Tocqueville inaugurated "the sociological method, which Max Weber was to use with great success . . . the ideal type." This enabled Tocqueville to tap into tendencies of democratic societies well before they fully manifested themselves, and it lent the last two volumes their distinctive "contemporary character" (118). In his ongoing attempt to reserve Tocqueville a central place in the sociological canon, Mayer also revisits Tocqueville's relationship to Weber. As before, Mayer finds continuities and discontinuities between the two. But now Tocqueville emerges as a clear winner for his rejection of absolute systems, his intuition that a classless society that establishes equality or near equality is not necessarily the realm of the free and equal, and in particular, his denial of the "slow death of the state" (124). As Mayer had insisted since the first edition of his study, Tocqueville could achieve these conclusions because his sociological mode of inquiry differed radically from that of Mayer's contemporaries. It is therefore wrong to conclude, as Audier does (2004, 38), that Mayer, contrary to Aron, does not seek to transform Tocqueville into one of the forerunners of sociology but instead treats him as a political philosopher. It is rather the case that Mayer embraced a view of sociology that hinged on the close affinity between the two disciplines and rejected the contemporary dominance of Marxist sociology. As Mayer puts it,

> De Tocqueville's sociology of the eighteenth-century French intelligentsia as treated in the chapters under consideration did not confine itself, like our fashionable sociology today, to an exposition of special class relationships and the sociological significance of the contrasts they present in some given social situation, but rather comprised in its analysis the norm of a definite political and philosophical attitude of the kind that our contemporary sociology poor-spiritedly rejects under the plea of scientific objectivity. The fact, its interpretation, and a deliberate political standpoint are inseparable—such is the very meaning of the philosophical approach to history, and such is the lesson which may be learned again and again in reading *The Ancien Régime and the Revolution*. (1960, 73)

This passage was already there in 1939, but in the essay added to the 1960 edition, Mayer reminds readers that for the reasons noted above, *The Old Regime* is *Democracy in America*'s companion "sociological work" (1960, 126). Contrary to what would become the norm in America for many decades, he insists that one cannot be understood without the other and that reading *Democracy in America* separately, especially when one stops reading after the first two volumes, is likely to provide an overly rose-colored image of democracy. Together, however, the works show unequivocally that the category of "unfree democratic societies" (85) is a real one and indeed a risk furtively inhering in all existing democracies, as shown by the movements that led from the French Revolution to Napoleon III's plebiscitary dictatorship and from the Weimar Republic to the Third Reich. Whereas Marx, Mayer stresses, dreamt of the death of the state, Tocqueville's *The Old Regime* and *Democracy in America* show exactly the opposite—its ever-expanding powers. More concretely, these works show that democratization and centralization are bedfellows and that the dangers to the human condition presented by administrative centralization are too serious for us to dispense reflection on the political methods that may curtail them. Something as seemingly positive and innocuous as a welfare state recognizing and responding to a plethora of social rights can have an underside, Mayer insists, that Tocqueville would not have passed over. Written for an American public, Mayer's assessment of Tocqueville's relevance comes closer to that which Pierson—who endorses the book on the back cover—advanced twenty-two years earlier.

This marks a change of emphasis from the critique of mass society as the underside of democracy to the critique of administrative centralization and a welfare state establishing rights without corresponding duties (J.-P. Mayer 1960, 128–29). Both are, of course, closely related. The drive for equality strengthened and centralized governments, whose power had become more uniform, inquisitorial, and detailed (35). Administrative centralization is therefore one of the key worries in the original 1939 edition of Mayer's work and is often treated as synonymous with the new soft despotism that Mayer, following Tocqueville, disparages. Similarly, Mayer's critique of mass society, more strictly understood, does figure in the review essay appended to the 1960 edition. But it appears in a condensed form and now, more clearly, as cultural critique. Following a line of analysis common among critical theorists, Mayer invokes his own studies of mass media (J.-P. Mayer 1946)—namely, film and "how our emotions (indeed, our very instincts) are stultified and stereotyped by commercial movies" (J.-P. Mayer 1960, 120)—to highlight how the growth of the mass culture audience through cinema and television accelerated and magnified the process of massification envisaged by Tocqueville. The leitmotif of Mayer's interpretation of Tocqueville since the late 1930s—the critique of mass society—works here less as a critique of totalitarianism than as a critique of the culture industry flourishing in contemporary consumer societies. This is clearly shown by Mayer's reference to Frederic Wetham's much-vilified studies of the morally deleterious effects of comic books on children as part of the same intellectual project. But it would also manifest itself, a decade later, in Mayer's enthusiastic foreword to Jean Baudrillard's sociological study *The Consumer Society* (1970). In other words, in 1960 Mayer saw popular culture as being not much different from state propaganda in its complicity with the nurturing of herd-like uniformity.

By the time the 1960 edition of Mayer's *Alexis de Tocqueville* reached bookshelves, his refashioning of Tocqueville as a theorist of mass society had already proved enormously influential. Its influence stretched in various directions, both geographically and ideologically. Some of these impacts were somewhat surprising. Mayer's interpretation was, for instance, taken up in West German conservative circles from the early 1950s onward in a clear manifestation of how political right and left joined together in their cultural critique of mass consumerist society.[7] Figures such as Carl J. Burckhardt, Hans-Joachim Schoeps, Hans Zbinden, and Wilhelm Ropke deployed Tocqueville, in Mayer's construction, to advance their own critiques of massification and the accompanying loss of individuality and freedom. A sign of rising interest, Mayer's study was translated into German in 1954. But just as decisively, the book most indebted to Mayer's framing of Tocqueville as a theorist of mass society—David Riesman's *The Lonely Crowd*—appeared in West Germany in 1956, introduced by the eminent German sociologist Helmut Schelsky. Originally published in 1950, this was also the book that most contributed to the pique of interest in Tocqueville in America in the 1950s and 1960s.

## DEMOCRACY IN AMERICA IN THE AGE OF ANXIETY

It is hard to overestimate the impact of Riesman's *The Lonely Crowd* on its immediate readership, the American public. The book was a best seller. It molded the way Americans saw themselves and one another, with its conceptual categories quickly entering everyday conversation. Such success was not, however, expected at the beginning. For the launch of the book in 1950, Yale University Press had a print run of three thousand copies. Yet despite lukewarm reviews in professional journals, the three thousand copies proved insufficient; nonprofessional readers showed signs of assessing the book otherwise. Before an abridged edition appeared in bookstores in 1953, the book would go through thirteen additional printings (M. Mayer 2009, 639). The abridged version was a commercial response to growing interest, but both Riesman and Yale University Press doubted that the book would sell more than a few thousand more copies to the niche market of social science courses. However, its new format reached out to a mass public, especially among the middle classes, to whose anxieties the book spoke. *The Lonely Crowd* was also one of the very first pocket-sized "quality paperbacks" in the Anchor Books series. This secured wider access and circulation, with Riesman gaining popular notoriety and his image and the question he put to Americans, "What is the American character?" making the cover of *Time* magazine in 1954. Such was the book's reception that *The Lonely Crowd* has been found to be the best-selling book by an American sociologist ever, with well over a million copies sold, mostly in paperback editions (see Gans 1998). Even today, it is not unusual to see the book described as one of the most influential social science works of the twentieth century.

In 1960, Mayer would refer to *The Lonely Crowd* as a book "much influenced by Tocqueville" (1960, 120). This influence shows itself most strikingly in the many quotations from Tocqueville throughout the book. But as Mayer hinted, this was not just any Tocqueville. Riesman's Tocqueville echoed Mayer's—that is, Tocqueville as the theorist of democratic mass society—and his presence permeates the book. *The Lonely Crowd* is an analysis of social character in a postindustrial society, moving from an emphasis on production to a stress on consumption and services. As a study of character, culture, and personality, the book shows its indebtedness to the work of neo-Freudians, notably Erich Fromm, with whom Riesman had a close relationship. But Riesman saw "character" differently, as the socially and historically conditioned structuring of individual drives and behaviors. From this resulted his definition of three main character types corresponding to a progressive loosening of authority in societies: tradition-directed, inner-directed, and other-directed. The focus of Riesman's study was the shift from inner-directedness to other-directedness in American upper social strata—namely, its growing new middle class. Inner-directed people internalized parental standards, whereas other-directed people took their cues from peer groups and mass media. The more rigid vertical hierarchy of parental authority of the past had given way to a more diffuse horizontal authority of peers. In a powerful visual metaphor, Riesman portrayed the difference between inner-directed and other-directed as that between people guided by an internal gyroscope and people guided by radar. While the former looked inside to the internalization of voices of an older generation for guidance as to what to do, the latter looked outward for the guidance, opinions, and approbation of contemporaries. Each orientation was secured by an accompanying emotion: in the case of inner-directed people, guilt for not living up to the image of what elders would like them to do or be; in the case of other-directed people, widespread anxiety for failing to know who to trust, how to relate emotionally to others, and what to do to meet the expectations of a now much more diffuse and uncertain authority. Riesman was silent as to the value of each orientation. He saw each bearing different advantages and presenting different problems. In particular, he was wary of identifying inner-directedness with autonomy and other-directedness with conformism. Rather, conformism was a constant of all societies, and the very existence of something one could call "social structure" depended on it. The difference was, therefore, not one of quantity—societies with more or less conformism—but of quality, or the mechanisms whereby it was produced and reproduced, then and now.

This was not how Riesman was read, however. The book spoke to the anxieties of an ever more prosperous middle class desperately trying to keep at bay any forces, at home or abroad, that might upset their upward trajectory and disrupt their current status. Many Americans faced a society in which family hierarchies were being dismantled, with elders and fathers removed from their former positions of authority, and peer voices or their amplifying chambers—namely, mass media—were taking over their position and being followed in their stead, which presented Americans with a dystopian vision that they confronted with fear and a sense of aching loss. In light of this, it becomes apparent why so many readers took Riesman's analysis as a conservative call for a return to an idyllic past, away from a rapidly deteriorating present. Such times were commonly presented as offering a contrast between autonomy (or self-reliance) and the lack thereof (or other-reliance)—that is, folks relying on their own instincts and judgments when deciding how to act as opposed to folks depending on the judgments, opinions, and approval of others to take any step at all. The dichotomy persisted even in radical-left-leaning interpretations of the book emerging in the 1960s. Then the book came to be read as a demeaning portrait of 1950s America, where prosperity and the consumerist culture it thrived on translated into a stifling society that curtailed all autonomy, individuality, and conflict. For the left, this found architectonic expression in socially homogeneous, leafy, aspirational neighborhoods, their very uniformity and witlessness reflecting the conformist power of the crowd in an otherwise crumbling democratic society. According to this more radical reading, Riesman's book was an offensive against conformism. It explained the sense of alienation and legitimized a rebellious youth culture. Both interpretations looked for support in *The Lonely Crowd*. But both amounted to misreadings of Riesman's intentions construed by readers in search for the meaning of their own contrasting experiences of the changing times. This was an inevitable consequence of the book's success. It quickly took on a life of its own. Riesman searched in vain to regain authorial control. He redoubled his efforts, in the prefaces of new editions of his book (in 1961 and in 1969), to delegitimize such readings. Riesman reminded conservatives that he never claimed that his book tracked a change for the worst, nor did he argue that "Americans of an earlier day" were "freer and of more upstanding human quality" than his contemporaries ([1969] 2001, x). Rather than negatively measuring his other-oriented folk against a purportedly bygone ideal of self-reliance, he had always seen positive traits in other-directedness. Rather than conformism *simpliciter*, Riesman saw it bearing "a greater resonance with others, a heightened self-consciousness about relations to people, and a widening of the circle of people with whom one wants to feel in touch" (xxiv), generally accompanied by a softening of manners and an increase of consideration, sensitivity, and tolerance toward others. It was, therefore, wrong to take the book as an assault on a rampant American postwar conformity; the book reached no such conclusion. This also meant that it was wrongly taken by the radical left as a call for a rebellious break from existing society in search of a tie-free autonomy. But Riesman's efforts to return the book to its "proper" meaning proved futile. The simplistic reading of the book as a critique of a loss of freedom at the hands of rising conformism not only gained the minds of nonspecialist readers but impinged on specialists too. Even Mayer capitulated to it.[8] It also became the guiding assumption of publishers and informs the cues they give to new readers to this day. In 2001, shortly before Riesman's death, Yale University Press published a new version of the 1969 abridged edition of the book. Its cover featured a crowd of sheep.

## STRATEGIC PUBLISHING

In different ways, Pierson's and Mayer's scholarly works both contributed to a revival of interest in Tocqueville. But their contribution did not stop there. They were also key players in editorial efforts to make Tocqueville's work available to the reading public. In late 1944, in *The Condition of Man*, Lewis Mumford deplored how "relatively inaccessible and too often neglected" (1944, 445) Tocqueville's work had become. The following spring, Mumford's lament was no longer warranted. The Knopf edition of *Democracy in America*, to which Nisbet referred with warm approval, appeared on the bookstands. It was April 16, 1945, shortly before the Nazi surrender. This was the first, and the most successful, edition of *Democracy in America* in the twentieth century. The origins of the edition go back to 1938, however—the year Pierson's

*Tocqueville and Beaumont in America* appeared. That same year, Pierson counseled Alfred A. Knopf to republish the work, suggesting that Phillips Bradley, a Queens College professor of political science familiar with Tocqueville's work (Bradley 1937, 1939a, 1939b), be the editor. As the project started taking shape, Pierson persuaded Bradley not to produce a new translation but rather to revise the Reeve-Bowen translation. He feared "the very great risk that a new translation, however full of the contemporary vocabulary, might be genuinely inferior to the old."⁹ For the next six years, Pierson monitored Bradley's translation work, which amounted to the introduction of more than one thousand corrections to the Reeve-Bowen text, not to mention his lengthy, thirty-thousand-word introduction and the compilation of four appendices (Bradley 1945, ci). Tocqueville's original division of the work into two parts was respected in the final version. Pierson's name was nowhere to be seen in the book, but his intellectual imprint was there from conception to its final pages.

Mancini describes the 1945 Bradley edition as "flawed" (2006, 171) and its success as a myth. However, this conclusion is at odds with the available evidence. First is the assessment of contemporaries. A connoisseur of Tocqueville's work whom in 1938 had been entrusted by Gallimard with the editing of Tocqueville's complete works, Mayer did not hesitate to deem the primary sources of Pierson's seminal *Tocqueville and Beaumont in America* "partly faulty and incomplete" (J.-P. Mayer 1959, 352). By contrast, he described the Bradley edition as "very important" and commended it for having broken "new ground in many directions' (350). Some of this new ground related to content, but there was also an innovation in form. The modernized, more readable rendering of the Reeve-Bowen translation found its match in the Bradley edition's overhauled look. Together they proved successful in finding the book a new, wider generation of readers.

As Nisbet noticed, this was not just another edition. It was an edition not meant to sink into obscurity. An expensive-looking book produced with evident care for the Vintage Classic series, the original two-volume hardbound edition stood out from other books. The design of the jacket was by W. A. Dwiggins, Knopf's chief outside book designer at the time.¹⁰ Dwiggins had coined the term *graphic design* back in 1922, when he confidently asserted that "advertising design is the only form of graphic design that gets home to everybody" (1922, 13). His graphic design, which combined classical and American iconography, conveys the message that the book is a modern classic. The cover includes Harold Laski's quote—"It is, perhaps, the greatest work ever written on one country by the citizen of another"—whetting the reader's appetite. Finally, there are the sales.

In the first five years alone, the hardbound Bradley edition sold eleven thousand copies—more than all previous editions combined.[11] In late 1945, a Random House Vintage Books paperback version appeared that would prove even more commercially popular. Thanks to this edition, *Democracy in America* would be one of the first works in the social sciences to benefit from the "paperback revolution" (Escarpit 1966). Pocket sized, relatively low cost, and with a distinctively modern appearance, successive reprints of Tocqueville's book would sell in the hundreds of thousands well into the 1960s.[12]

At first glance, Phillips Bradley would not seem an obvious candidate to edit Tocqueville's masterpiece. His specialization was in public administration—namely, labor and industrial relations—and his somewhat erratic academic career played out in that field, moving from one American higher education institution to the next. But his intellectual curiosity ranged far wider, and his interest in Tocqueville was apparent from a number of articles published before the outbreak of World War II (e.g., 1937) and his two reviews of Pierson's study (Bradley 1939a, 1939b). Bradley used the paratexts of the Knopf edition to offer readers a distinctively progressive framing of *Democracy in America*.

This shows itself immediately in the choice of Harold Laski, Bradley's personal friend, to write the foreword. Laski was then chairman of the British Labour Party Executive Council and possibly the best-known socialist of the time. He was also the academic baron of British political theory and an important gatekeeper of arguments about the role of the state.[13] The two and a half pages of his foreword are brief but blazing. He hails *Democracy in America* as one of the "seminal sociological works of the nineteenth century," remarkable for its "prophetic quality." But the prophecy he has in mind would have surprised many American readers: "Few writers have seen so magisterially as Tocqueville the difficulties of capitalist society" (Laski 1945, 1). Justifying Tocqueville's longevity as a classic, Laski explains, is his ability to stand above those once-influential writers of the nineteenth century "who could not free themselves from the obsession that the propertied middle-class is the natural government of the human race" (ii). "Only half a Liberal," Laski polemically remarks, Tocqueville took to heart the problem of equality among men. He accepted the irresistible modern trend toward the equalization of conditions, but unlike others, he saw real equality and the abolition of material differences as its logical conclusion, achieved through a higher form of social organization capable of putting an end to exploitation. For reasons not difficult to discern, Laski's foreword disappeared from reprints after 1948. His framing of the book as a socialist plea for material equality was simply too unpalatable for the red-baiting, conformist America of the late 1940s and 1950s.

Laski's brief and striking foreword was followed by Bradley's expansive and somewhat meandering introduction, which combined biography, reception history, and analysis and included a critical examination of the successes and failures of Tocqueville's diagnoses and prognoses. Unlike Laski's foreword, Bradley's introductory essay would accompany the Knopf edition (and the Vintage paperback) throughout its life. It did not have the polemical force of Laski's opening remarks, but it did elaborate on their progressive theme. It construed Tocqueville as a pioneering social scientist of a philosophical nature who broke new ground in several aspects of his inquiry. Bradley's attention turned to Tocqueville's "sociological insights" and how they might touch "areas of contemporary concern" (1945, xcix). Where others have found crippling ambiguity in Tocqueville's broader definition of democracy as a social, political, economic, and philosophical phenomenon, Bradley finds a penetrating purposiveness. No one before Tocqueville, Bradley maintains, "had so clearly presented or so cogently demonstrated the interrelations of the political, the economic, and the social aspects of democracy" (lix). Bradley rightfully points out that Tocqueville's objective was to provide an "analysis of democracy as a working principle of society and government" (xii). This, he explains, required him to engage in a kind of "social philosophy" (xx) that he put to practice in the second volume of *Democracy in America*, which "is essentially a philosophical examination of social, and economic as well as political change" (xix). Tocqueville was, in Bradley's appreciation, a "pioneer social scientist" (lviii) responsible for a "great advance in sociological inquiry" (xcv)—namely, the use of "American experience as a backdrop for his general analytical and methodological portrayal of the general problem of change in society" (lviii).

In his appraisal of Tocqueville's methodological contributions, Bradley finds himself in agreement with Albert Salomon, a former colleague at the New School and a clear influence on Bradley as he prepared his edition of *Democracy in America*. Both shared not only an understanding of Tocqueville's contribution to sociological inquiry but also the progressive political convictions that drove Bradley's choice of "areas of contemporary concern" (Bradley 1945, xcix) in Tocqueville's study. Paramount among these, as Laski had stressed earlier, were "the problems posed by and resulting from social inequality and its effects on the practice of political democracy" (xcvi). A clear example was the "manipulative control of legislatures" by a particular form of association—that is, lobbies representing special interests (lxx). More than Tocqueville's "tyranny of the majority," these presented a real danger to American democracy, since they produced "the distortion of the majority concern—the promotion of the general welfare—by the organized and concentrated pressures of specific minorities pursuing special interests" (lxx). But while Bradley sees Tocqueville stating a clear case for economic equality, he notes his warning against the dangers of "an equalitarian materialism" (xcvii), which, in Tocqueville's view, only religion, "not sectarianism or dogmatism," could mitigate (xcviii). Like Mayer, or indeed Salomon, Bradley sees how these latter two—notably in the form of national history and race mythologies—are now used as foundations for totalitarian societies "founded on worship of the State and ritualistic obeisance to the Leaders," which thus erect "Leviathan as the Baal of the masses" (xcviii).

Though not mentioned explicitly at this juncture, the question of race and the lasting consequences of slavery and racism for society are nevertheless central to Bradley's analysis of Tocqueville's legacy. He stresses how Tocqueville saw race relations as part of the fabric of American democracy and regrets the silence to which Beaumont's novel *Marie*, the natural companion to Tocqueville's reflections, has been consigned: "Never translated into English, it has remained relatively unknown" (Bradley 1945, xv). He offers a summary of the plot in the hope that his readers will read it alongside *Democracy in America*. Bradley implies that American democracy is constitutively racial, and at its core, the problem of race remains an open wound. Part novel, part sociological study, *Marie* may hold the key to a discussion about the reconstitution of the polity: "As a novel of protest, *Marie* drives home the basic issues in race relations in our time as for Beaumont's readers a century ago, with an emotional force perhaps more inexorable than the more intellectual analysis of democracy" (xvii). Thirteen years would pass before an English translation of *Marie* would be made available to the American reader. That the civil rights movement was also taking shape at this time is probably more than mere coincidence (Garvin and Hess 2008, 165).

Bradley's progressive leanings did not go unnoticed. His edition was widely reviewed in contemporary academic journals. While some reviewers acknowledged Pierson's tutelary influence (Sydnor 1945, 458), others praised Dwiggins's graphic design as "a triumph of wartime bookmaking" (Rosenberger 1945, 367). Others still, such as Lancaster Greene, emphasized the edition's timely appearance: "Some years ago, on hearing that this work was the chief treatise on popular government after Machiavelli and Rousseau, this reviewer spent two years waiting for a copy on order with his book dealers before obtaining his set, printed in 1889" (1945, 556). But more importantly, Bradley's portrayal of Tocqueville as a progressive thinker found its echo in the reviews, with one reviewer insisting that Tocqueville should have gone even further in his appraisal of "popular government generally" (W. Anderson 1945, 183) and another suggesting that he believed "in the irresistible ultimate advent of classless society" (Frank 1945, 461; see also Binkley 1945; Kiniery 1945; B. Wright 1946). Reviews such as these played an important role in the mediation among author, editor, and specialized public and worked as amplifying chambers for a progressive reading of Tocqueville.

Isaac Kramnick, who wrote the introduction to the 2003 edition of *Democracy in America* by Penguin Books and is the author of a separate Tocqueville biography, has argued that the early postwar reception of Tocqueville was a left-wing affair, with progressive editors as its agents (2003, xliv). While Kramnick is right to point out that at the time there was a strong leftist strand of editorial initiative, as epitomized by the Bradley edition (and as we shall see, the Mayer-Lerner edition), his account leaves out another initiative that played a crucial role in the ideological struggle over Tocqueville in the 1940s and 1950s and took the work in a conservative direction.

The publication of Bradley's Knopf edition of *Democracy in America* almost coincided with the launch of the book by another major publisher, Oxford University Press. Published in 1945 and 1946, respectively, the two editions could not have been more different. Bradley's was a glossy, painstakingly revised version of the Reeve-Bowen translation of Tocqueville's text, which Bradley, with the help of Laski, framed in distinctively progressive terms. In contrast, Oxford released a radically abridged version of the text in its World's Classics series preceded by an introduction in which Tocqueville's work is presented as distinctively anti-Marxist. Tocqueville, we read, was one of "the first students of the political to discern the truth . . . that the great forces of history do not operate uniformly and automatically in every society" (Commager 1946, xiii). He is also said to have grasped the fact "that democracy makes for conservatism and that the surest guarantee of stability is the wide distribution of property" (xxi). The rest of the introduction reads like an exhortation on behalf of the exceptional nature of American politics, with Tocqueville figuring as the first to recognize and coin "American exceptionalism."

The scholar Oxford University Press chose to introduce and preside over its edition of *Democracy in America* was the American historian Henry Steele Commager. A rising figure in American historiography, Commager spent his long academic career at a number of prestigious universities in America and abroad, including Cambridge, where he was Pitt Professor of American History in 1941 and again in 1947 and 1948, soon after the Oxford edition was released. Commager was therefore a seemingly appropriate choice for the task at hand. However, his editorial judgment was questionable at best. The introduction to the Oxford abridged edition, with its many lapses and typographical errors, did nothing to hide the rush and lack of care with which the book was compiled. The explanatory note added to the 1952 reprint would only confirm these earlier warnings.

Commager's reasons to return to the Reeve-Bowen translation confuse more than clarify: "The translation by Henry Reeve has been used, and no attempt has been made to check it with the French" (1946, v). There is no attempt to explain why. Five years earlier, however, upon the launch of the Oxford edition in America, Commager had halfheartedly claimed that his choice not to consult the original French version was determined by the fact that the Reeve-Bowen translation seemed "to catch more the spirit and style of the original." But the explanation is unconvincing. It seems more plausible that the "choice" was forced—that is, "Bradley had taken the Reeve-Bowen text out of circulation" (Mancini 2006, 173). To keep the upper hand, in 1947, Commager confessed his hope that despite his decision not to embark on a new translation, "some day, perhaps, the long-needed new translation will be given [to] us." Nineteen years would elapse before George Lawrence answered the call.

The other decision Commager felt compelled to justify was the radical cuts of the text's abridgment, which reduced the original text "to approximately half of its original length" (1946, v). Abridgments were common at the time and a recurring feature of the history of *Democracy in America*. It was an especially lengthy book whose abridgment was seen as necessary to secure market penetration. As Bradley put it, commenting on the success of the work upon its release in the mid-nineteenth century, "In America the *Democracy* ran through many early editions and was soon issued in various abridgements for school use" (1945, xxii). Nowadays we tend to see abridgments as a crippling of the text, a violent, perhaps even arbitrary, disfigurement that leaves us missing something essential. But this has not always been the case. Attitudes toward abridgments have changed dramatically, and they were once seen as a key to widening reading audiences and an especially powerful and valuable tool in education. Commager's justification, "if not an apology" (1952, v), for his substantial abridgment of Tocqueville's work follows these lines. Bradley's complete text was for "the scholar"; Commager's "met the needs of the general reader," in particular students, who, it was felt, would struggle to get through "the eight hundred or more large pages of the complete edition" (v). Besides responding to the commercial pressures exerted by the commissioning editor at Oxford University Press for the production of a version cheaper than the Bradley edition (the resulting book is minuscule, printed on 8mo size paper with narrow margins and small print), his abridgment provided a shortcut for the otherwise potentially disengaged student audience.[14] It encouraged the nonprofessional public to read the work and effected "no tampering with the text" (v).

Commager's is an overly narrow understanding of what may count as tampering, however. While "tampering" carries a negative connotation of meddling, causing damage, or making unauthorized alterations that one wishes to avoid, Commager's description of his "excisions" as a mere question of getting rid of the dated, "useless," or "easily dispensed with" in order to present the "essential in more succinct and palatable form" (1952, v) neutralizes and downplays his role as abridger. Abridgments are not necessarily to be condemned, but they constitute a more or less dramatic remaking of a text, which inevitably affects how readers can, do, or should come to read them. They actively mediate between author and reader in ways that shape the text's reception. As is often the case, Commager's decisions as an abridger betray his attitudes toward readers and his interpretation of the text—toward what is essential and what is accessory. They speak of his ideological motivations, even in the face of their silencing. As he tailored the book for his student audience, Commager thought it needless to "preserve the rather tiresome account of the geography, native races, colonial history, local and state government of the United States," as well as "the numerous digressions on contemporary France and the speculations on the future of the three races in the United States" (5). That Commager considered Tocqueville's reflections on America's colonial legacy, the comparison with France, and race relations "excisable" says less about their relevance to 1950s America than about what might arouse its anxieties. Historians, especially "consensus historians" such as Commager, were all too willing to represent Jacksonian America as one of remarkable social harmony and normative cohesion (e.g., Commager 1950). This pushed them to ignore the "complex representations of difference, identity and national character and promote, instead, a sanitized version of Tocqueville's meditation of America's evolving democracy" (Fergerson 1999, xi). That Commager thought American democracy to be understandable apart from any reflections on social conflict and race was by no means a mere pragmatic judgment about where to cut down on words where needed.[15] It was a fundamental ideological intervention into what might shorten while maintaining sense, or indeed what might enhance a *certain* sense. In other words, Commager's abridgments constitute a text in its own right, which must be read as such. His intervention was partly repeated in many other abridged editions where the longest chapter of *Democracy in America*, "The Future Condition of the Three Races in the United States," succumbed to the weight of the abridger's hand (Heffner 1956; Hacker 1964; see also Kuehnelt-Leddihn 1966). In each and every one of these excisions, a particular sense was lost: that of American democracy as structurally founded on racial exclusion. In its place another sense—a myth—was created and successfully reproduced, that of American exceptionalism.

If doubts remain, Commager's introduction removes them. Many foreign travelers had a special curiosity about America. Tocqueville was therefore not alone in this, nor was his curiosity unwarranted. The country fashioned by the Founding Fathers had a uniquely healthy and perfect birth; America was "something new under the sun, a republic, a democracy, a federal union, the hope (as Turgot put it) of [the] human race" (1952, viii). In it, Enlightenment ideals were realized like in no other place. It showed the old troubled Continent how newly chiseled political institutions could outstrip the robustness of their now scarred classical monuments. Unlike many fellow travelers, Commager notes, Tocqueville arrived in America with an open, unprejudiced mind. He was able to see that the Old World had ceased to be the norm and that the New World was now the key to the future, a beacon of what was to come: "America was, it seemed, merely the laboratory; the findings were designed for application abroad" (xii). He added, "It held the answer to the questions which were abound to trouble the Old World" (xiv). While others had simply written about America, Tocqueville achieved something much more profound: he had managed "to relate America to world history, to fix the significance of America in history" (xviii).

Commager's abridgment eliminated most of what might upset this pristine significance. It also proved successful in securing the broadest possible access to the book. The edition sold more than twenty thousand copies between 1946 and 1960.[16] This was such an achievement for the series that Oxford University Press would never publish it in paperback.[17] A number of other abridged versions followed. Particularly notorious for its conservative disposition is Richard D. Heffner's 1956 abridgment (Republican congressman Newt Gingrich's personal favorite) (Mancini 2006, 218). Like Commager, Heffner keeps the Reeve-Bowen translation and eliminates much that might interfere with a belief in American exceptionalism or point to the limits of American democracy. Heffner's introduction is a tripartite manual for a conservative reading of the book. First, there is the opposition to Marx (1956, 17). Then Tocqueville's ability to go beyond Marx is traced back to his antiegalitarianism and discomfort with the equation of democracy with freedom: "*Democracy in America* is no paean to the virtues of equalitarianism and majority rule. Quite on the contrary—and this is precisely what makes it so provocative and valuable for us today—this classic study thoroughly rejects Americans' now more than century-old, magical equation of equality and freedom, of democracy with liberty" (11). Finally, there is a diagnosis of the present, in which the conservative critique meets the progressive critique of massification: "Today, of course, Tocqueville's concern for the growing tyranny of the majority strikes home with particular force. . . . Modern, frontierless, industrial America—with its factory-made, standardized food, clothing, housing, communications and even amusements—has surely placed a premium upon sameness, undermined individualism" (21). The ideological slant enabled by selective abridgment did not pass unnoticed by reviewers. In "Tocqueville on Race in America," an exhaustive survey article published in 1967, James L. Colwell provides a broadly negative review of these editorial projects, which he sees primarily as exercises in political propaganda.[18]

## A SOCIOLOGICAL CLASSIC: THE MAYER-LAWRENCE EDITION OF *DEMOCRACY IN AMERICA*

Without a doubt, in the postwar years, *Democracy in America* became the battleground between politically opposed camps. The contrast between Commager's introduction and that offered by Bradley a year earlier is striking. Where one is celebratory, focusing on the achievements of American democracy, the other highlights its failure in advancing the egalitarian ideal that marked, however contradictorily, its birth. A similarly cautious tone permeates the introduction to the new edition of *Democracy in America* that appeared in 1966 to replace Bradley's. Its introduction is by Max Lerner, an American Jewish sociologist and journalist-turned-American-studies-scholar and friend of Laski's. As J.-P. Mayer had done twenty-seven years earlier, Lerner presents Tocqueville as "one of the early prophets, if something less than a champion, of the modern mass democracy" (1966, xxvi). This is no coincidence. Mayer was the editor with Lerner of the 1966 Harper and Row edition, which offered the first new translation of the text in more than a century. The translator was George Lawrence, Mayer's personal friend. As the collaboration between Mayer and Lerner shows, from the mid-1930s onward, the history of Tocqueville in America intersects closely with Albert Salomon—another German sociologist and another socialist émigré repeatedly cited by Bradley—who exercised a major influence on Tocqueville scholarship as both a commentator and an editor.[19] But their trajectories were the inverse, from editing to commentary in the case of Salomon and from commentary to editing in the case of Mayer.

In 1935, shortly before he left for the United States, where he would become a teacher and researcher at the New School, Salomon edited a selection of Tocqueville's writings in German, which appeared in neighboring Switzerland (Salomon 1935a). These writings would serve as the basis for some of Salomon's first scholarly articles in English (1935b, 1939). We find a similar interlacing of roles in Mayer, who dedicated much of his life to the study and editing of Tocqueville's works. In effect, when scrutinized closely, his 1939 study *The Prophet of the Mass Age* reads as the work of someone carving out an editorial space for himself in a foreign country, before a potentially unwelcoming academia. In 1939, this was primarily French academia. Mayer's construction of Tocqueville as a theorist of modern mass society sets itself against the way he was read in French scholarship—that is, as a liberal theorist. This critique is, in turn, set against the editorial landscape Mayer describes as a wasteland, either populated by "unreliable, and indeed in part mutilated" editions (1939, xiii) or simply unpopulated by any edition at all. This wasteland, as it were, is the space Mayer proposed to occupy with his own editorial initiatives. In *Prophet of the Mass Age*, he announces in passing a new edition of Tocqueville's writings and letters that he is preparing with Antoine Rédier, including unknown treasures from the family archives of the Counts de Tocqueville. This, he hopes, will come to replace Beaumont's faulty nineteenth-century edition. French academia, Mayer writes in a defiant tone, has turned its back on Tocqueville—so much so that "the *Oeuvres Complètes* are out of print, and not one French man has come forward to dedicate a new and more worthy edition of his works to one of the greatest sons of France" (J.-P. Mayer 1939, 150). A foreigner must come forth to take on the role. In a footnote, Mayer announces that the situation is about to change. Since the completion of his book, Mayer declares, Gallimard has decided to publish a new edition of Tocqueville's main works and letters (J.-P. Mayer 1939, 150). He silently passes over the fact that he may have been the person commissioned to direct it. Yet Gaston Gallimard and Bernard Groethuysen had invited Mayer to direct the edition of Tocqueville's complete works in 1938 (J.-P. Mayer 1951, 7). This would be the start of a lifelong relationship with Gallimard.

In 1948, Gallimard published Mayer's study of Tocqueville in French under the title *Alexis de Tocqueville*. After a long interruption dictated by the war, in 1947 Mayer resumed his work on the editing of the complete works, which was launched in 1951. He had worked on the Gallimard edition for years, and the quality of the resulting work did not go unnoticed. Pierson uses the back cover of the 1960 edition of Mayer's biographical study on Tocqueville to praise the work as a study "by the editor of the new definitive edition of his [Tocqueville's] works" (1960). Prominent as it was, this would not be Mayer's only contribution to the editing of Tocqueville's writings.[20] In 1949, Mayer was responsible for an edition of Tocqueville's *Recollections* that remained the key reference work for years to come. He went on to produce several other editions, both in French and in English, of Tocqueville's works (see J.-P. Mayer 1957, 1958), but none as significant as the one he produced for Harper and Row in 1966.

This edition reaped the benefits of the mass-market editions of *Democracy in America* of the 1940s and 1950s, which reached a significant portion of the reading public of the time. But it also moved the scholarly benchmark higher. Impeccably produced and offering a new translation of the work, the 785-page volume was received avidly. Laudatory reviews appeared in major academic journals. In his review for the *William and Mary Quarterly*, Durand Echeverria, an expert in French history and culture, expressed his gratitude to the editors for having produced "for the first time in 126 years an English version of what Max Lerner justly calls the 'greatest book ever written on America' that in both form and content reproduces the original" (1967, 638). In her review for the *Journal of American History*, Lynn L. Marshall applauded the sound scholarly fashion in which the book was edited (1967, 378). Excitement about the new edition spilled over to *Book Week*. Its 1966 Christmas issue reserved space on two of its pages for the new editorial sensation (Ward 1966).

The new translation contributed decisively to the general interest. As Mayer stresses in the foreword, Reeve's translation, more than one hundred years old, was an inevitably "*dated* text," which neither Bowen's nor Bradley's revisions could salvage. Deemed "faulty" and "inadequate for the needs of the contemporary reader" (1966, vii), it was in need of replacement. Bradley himself, Mayer observed, recognized this much in his introduction to the Vintage edition. But more importantly, the new translation served "the author's wish" (viii). Tocqueville had expressed serious doubts about Reeve letting his distaste for democracy imprint itself on his text, thereby corrupting the book's character, "which is a veritable impartiality in the theoretical judgment of the two societies, the old and the new, and even the sincere wish to see the new one establish itself" (Tocqueville 1951, 47). With funding provided by Harper and Row in 1960, Mayer could bring his friend George Lawrence on board to translate the work anew, respecting the author's intention. Lawrence had already been the translator of Mayer's edition of Tocqueville's *Journey to America*. In his quest for fidelity to the original, Mayer closely supervised Lawrence's translation, reading his text, comparing it with the original, and revising Lawrence's renditions whenever necessary, as well as consulting nearly all the books and documents to which Tocqueville refers in the process.

Mayer would also contribute an introductory essay on Tocqueville's reception and reputation. For the most part, the essay reads like a hurried assemblage of quotations. But the attempt to place Tocqueville at the center of the sociological canon initiated by his 1939 study persists. Mayer returns to his early critique of Tocqueville's eclipse in France. "Durkheim, Tarde, or Bouglé" had read him, but then he disappeared. One had to wait for Mayer's own edition of Tocqueville's complete works and for Raymond Aron's writings, which had, in turn, eclipsed Mayer's, for a "fundamental shift in French contemporary appreciation of Tocqueville" (J.-P. Mayer 1966, xvii).[21] Mayer finds in postwar America an "accentuated revival in Tocqueville studies" (xxiii) and stresses Tocqueville's impact on a long line of historians and social and political theorists, including Charles H. Cooley, Francis Liber, Robert Dahl, Henry Adams, Charles A. Beard, and David Riesman. In Riesman, Mayer sees the deepest "affinities with Tocqueville's thought," and it was also he who extended "Tocqueville's influence on the contemporary European mind" (xxiii), not the least, as we have seen, in his native Germany.

Alongside Aron, Commager, and Pierson, Riesman also appeared in the list of those who offered comments to Max Lerner on his long introduction to the edition. Lerner was the author of *America as a Civilization* (1957), a 1,036-page sweeping study advocating, as the title indicates, the idea of America as a distinct civilization. Along with Riesman's *The Lonely Crowd*, Lerner's book was one of the great popularizers of Tocqueville in the 1950s. Lerner's publisher, Simon and Schuster, had no hesitation in placing the book in "the great tradition of De Tocqueville and Bryce," and neither did many contemporary reviewers (e.g., Ziegler 1958). But not everyone agreed. The Harvard-based sociologist Daniel Bell was a dissenting voice. In his famous collection of essays, *The End of Ideology* (1960), Bell argued that Lerner's work was best understood by reference to Laski's *The American Democracy* (1948). He noted that both Laski's and Lerner's books covered similar ground. But he also drew attention to the fact that Lerner's included chapters on parent-child relations and American character. These, he maintained, showed a "deference to newer concerns" (D. Bell 1960, 96) that were integral to a burgeoning genre—studies of national character such as Riesman's.

In effect, Bell claimed, the decade between Laski's and Lerner's studies represented a dramatic shift, one whose echoes we can appreciate if we compare Laski's foreword and Lerner's introduction to Bradley's and Mayer's *Democracy in America*, respectively: "Laski was trying to write a Marxist analysis of America" (D. Bell 1960, 96). For Laski, America was a political democracy increasingly undermined by an economic foundation growing oligarchical in character. For all its distinctive characteristics, America would remain unexceptional, an offshoot of Europe: "The history of the United States would, despite everything, follow the general pattern of capitalist democracy in Europe" (Laski quoted in D. Bell 1960, 97). "Americanism" was therefore, for Laski, nothing but an ideological cover-up, a chauvinistic doctrine propagated by the oligarchical elite to conceal "the failure [in America] of the historic drive towards the egalitarian society" (98) that Tocqueville had identified. Laski's dismay contrasted with Lerner's optimism. He put America on par with ancient Greece and Rome as one of the great civilizations of history. He deemed its revolution more significant than the Russian Revolution, and despite all the problems that remained to be resolved, its legacy was that of a pluralistic liberal democracy capable of sustaining a thriving open society. America was therefore the "epitome of all societies," and the American the "archetypal modern man." As Bell powerfully summarizes it, the American was "restless, mobile, a man of energy, mastery and power" (98).

Reverberations of this appear in Bell's introduction to the 1966 edition of Tocqueville's masterpiece. That Lerner's conclusions ran counter to Laski's is beyond doubt. But the contrast was also one of idiom and form. As Bell insightfully observes, Lerner's "language is no longer Marx, but cultural anthropology *cum* a Jungian and nervous sociological idiom. Where for Laski the U.S. comes into perspective only through *socio-economic forces, vested interests*, and *power*, in Lerner there are *myth, norms, character, culture* and *personality*" (1960, 97). This is not by chance. The study of national character had originally grown out of the work of anthropologists and neo-Freudian psychoanalysts interested in the relationship between culture and personality who turned their attention to the question of what made an American an American (Gilkeson 2010). Some postwar studies of national character, however, became embroiled in such controversy that their culture and personality research would fall out of favor with social scientists. This forced the redefinition of the notion of "national character" and its migration into departments of American history, where it was often used to construct a "consensus" view of the postwar United States, and departments of American studies in the 1950s and 1960s. Tocqueville was a central figure in this movement. Those emphasizing American uniqueness on multiple levels—from identity and class politics even to, as Lerner controversially argued, civilization—regarded Tocqueville as their patron saint and contributed decisively through their authorial and editorial labor to the explosion of interest in Tocqueville throughout the 1960s.

The question of Tocqueville's place in the sociological canon is central to Lerner's introduction: "Tocqueville almost single-handedly shaped a political sociology, a military sociology, a sociology of intellectual life, a theory of alienation, a theory of mass culture and mass tyranny in a democracy" (1966, xl). Lerner agrees, again, with Mayer's earlier assessment that next to Marx, Tocqueville was the "greatest historian and political sociologist of the last century" (lxxxiii). Like Mayer, he believes that in his rejection of determinism in history (xliii) and his assessment of the meaning of the progression to a classless society and its compatibility with unfreedom, Tocqueville effectively surpassed Marx: "Of the two, it was Tocqueville who was the realist, and it was Marx who—for all his talk about 'scientific' socialism—was following an abstraction" (lxviii). Lerner's Tocqueville is Mayer's "great analyst and prophet of mass society" (l) who foresaw a "not impossible future society, in which the few will govern with a paternalistic efficiency, sustained by the 'general apathy,' have an Orwellian nightmare quality of the placid society of sheep and the Big Brother shepherd" (lxxx). This Tocqueville echoes Mayer's unmatched prognosticator and similarly anticipates the emergence of "the Leviathan state," a "paternalistic state that would come in Europe to govern an inert people" (l).

Unlike Mayer, however, Lerner criticizes Tocqueville for not having foreseen "a dictatorship elite, like the Communist or Nazi, armed with the gospel of dynamism" (1966, lxxx). In America, Lerner explains, Tocqueville saw another (milder) "Leviathan sprawling over a huge power network, subsidizing, protecting, controlling, coercing, cajoling, but always . . . unmistakably *there*" (l). More than anyone before or since, Tocqueville offered a "biting portrait of a mass society in action" (lxv) coming to grips with rising individualism, loneliness, and atomization, giving in to a compulsion toward conformity, which operated as a "internal sensor," inhibiting individuality and stifling "dissent from within" (lxiv). Lerner agreed with the broad brushstrokes of the portrait Tocqueville offered, but he doubted it ever applied to America in its entirety: "Only where the mass society has had built in inequalities and injustices of its own to replace the inequalities of its predecessor societies, as under modern totalitarianism, has it produced a cultural wasteland" of the kind Tocqueville announced (xliii). In America, however, "mass society" has developed "a great measure of diversity and creativeness of its own, along with the conformity" (lxiii). Lerner stresses how Tocqueville's somewhat overdrawn critique of the "tyranny of narrow minds" (lxiv) plaguing democracies had been inspirational, indeed instrumental, to "American liberals during the struggles of the McCarthy period in the early 1950s, giving a fillip to the study of political repression and to the political sociology of the 'Radical Right'" (lxiv). Lerner rightly observes that Tocqueville's fears of a new incarnation of despotism in the wake of the mediocrity of public opinion "gave the prevailing tone to the studies of American culture in the 1950s and 1960s" on both the left and the right. With the help of Commager, he also notes mordantly that unlike intellectuals on both sides, Tocqueville saw that pressures toward conformism came as much from the majority as from the minority—namely, elites (not the least, intellectual elites) who did not hesitate to make members "lose their in-group status if they cut against the grain of their opinions" (lxvi). The comment has a polemical bite. Many on the liberal side, upon the publication of *America as a Civilization*, ostracized Lerner—a combative liberal writer who in the 1930s and 1940s denounced many aspects of American life—for his excessive optimism (see, e.g., Redlich 1958).

In Lerner's expansive introduction to the 1966 edition of *Democracy in America*, we see multiple and often prolonged flashes of Tocqueville as the author of choice of progressive democratic forces inside and outside academia. Lerner's is the Tocqueville whom Mayer enlisted almost thirty years earlier as a critic of mass society and mass culture. This is also the Tocqueville who feared the creation of a new moneyed elite, an industrial aristocracy; insisted on "popular sovereignty in action" understood as "constant participation" in politics (Lerner 1966, xlvii); and saw the problem of race insidiously linger even after the abolition of slavery in an America now "caught in a protracted civil rights struggle in South and North alike, which Tocqueville foresaw, missing only its timing" (lxix). But there was also much in the analysis that was distinctively Lerner's: the stress on the singularity of America's own "social revolution—creating the 'first new nation,' as Lipset has put it—but not in the European fashion" (liii); the division of a civilization, and Tocqueville's own reflection on it, "into three clusters of concern, which are coined in the language of system theory as 'power system,' 'society,' and 'culture'"; and a complaint about the excessive conformism and flatness of character that Tocqueville (and others after him, including Riesman) saw in America, which, in Lerner's view, overlooked the internal pluralism, creativity, and dynamism of American society (lxvii). Democracy in America had its problems, for sure. But it also had what it took to do better than the left ever anticipated.

The 1950s and 1960s witnessed a steep rise in interest in Tocqueville, and the 1966 Mayer-Lerner edition of *Democracy in America* crowned it. The new translation, framed by paratexts presenting Tocqueville as a political sociologist and the forerunner of many specialized subfields within the discipline, reads as a canonization of Tocqueville's work as a sociological classic. By the time it was published, Tocqueville's name had become common currency in a wide variety of disciplinary subfields, from national character studies, abounding in American history and American studies departments, to the American pluralist literature that poured from political science departments. In the postwar period, pluralist social and political thought turned to ideas of civil society (Lichtenstein 2005). The study of voluntary associations, pressure groups, and political culture occupied political scientists (e.g., Almond and Verba 1963; Elazar 1966). Tocqueville's views on democracy's dependence on a robust associational life and a thriving civic culture capable of counteracting the perils of excessive centralization and federal bureaucracy were a cornerstone of much American pluralist thought of the time. This was also the Tocqueville most commonly highlighted in American social science during the Cold War, as it erected its own wall between, on the one hand, American liberal democracy and, on the other, totalitarianism. *Totalitarianism* was the term Mayer used to conceptually link dictatorships on the right and left in the mid-1930s. But it came to be employed mainly as a synonym for communism during the 1950s and 1960s. Any suggestion of a contiguity between mass democracies and totalitarian states, or of capitalist societies (through their culture industries) harboring totalitarian tendencies, was now too sensitive.

Evidence abounds in the 1950s and 1960s that Tocqueville came to be seen as the author that best captured the character of America and American social life. Renowned Tocqueville scholar Seymour Drescher quantified this burst of interest in *Tocqueville and Beaumont on Social Reform* (1968) by showing that almost half (44 percent) of all existing Tocqueville scholarship appeared between 1950 and 1968 (200). This was certainly true in sociology. Besides Salomon, Nisbet, and Riesman, other prominent figures in the discipline claimed Tocqueville as their intellectual mentor. Examples include Seymour Lipset, Martin A. Trow, and James S. Coleman, who saw their examination of the basis of democracy in *Union Democracy* (1956) as close to Tocqueville's. Reinhard Bendix, a dominant (indeed founding) figure in the Berkeley department of sociology, undertook an analysis of political modernization, or of how state and civil societies interact in the formation of new political communities, in *Nation-Building and Citizenship* (1964), which he himself confessed was inspired by Tocqueville (and Weber). Edward Digby

Baltzell sought the model for his analysis of the rise and fall of the Protestant establishment in America (1964; see also 1962) in Tocqueville's *The Old Regime*.

Tocqueville's influence is further attested by his incorporation in textbooks and readers of the time. Don Martindale, in *The Nature and Types of Sociological Theory*, a treatise written in the pluralist genre inaugurated by Sorokin in the 1920s, describes Tocqueville's *Democracy in America* as one of the studies responsible for turning political science into an empirical discipline in the context of the birth of the social sciences in the nineteenth century (1960, 39). In the famous "The Calling of Sociology," the epilogue to *Theories of Society* (Parsons, Shils, Naegele, and Pitts 1961), where he discusses the nature and functions of the sociological canon, Edward Shils positions *Democracy in America* not as one of those great works that are the antecedents of modern sociology, such as Aristotle's *Politics* or Adam Smith's *Theory of Moral Sentiments*, nor as a modern sociological classic, such as the writings of Weber or Durkheim, but as one of those "works of analytical scholarship and reflective observation" that "retain[s] a freshness and pertinence to contemporary sociological analysis—despite the corrections and improvements that later scholars can bring to them—for the same reasons that the great classics of social and political philosophy retain their power" (1447).

Yet as progressivists started doubting the value of Tocqueville's insights, their most enthusiastic endorsement came from sociological works with a more conservative bent locating themselves within the humanist tradition. Raymond Aron's *Les Étapes de la Pensée Sociologique*, the book that did the most to elevate Tocqueville to the status of founding father of sociology, is a case in point. It was first published in France by Gallimard in 1965 and 1967 (first and second volumes, respectively) and was quickly translated into English by Anchor Books, the oldest trade paperback publisher in America, as *Main Currents in Sociological Thought* in 1968 and 1969. In *The Sociological Tradition* ([1966] 2004), Nisbet concurs with Aron's assessment of Tocqueville's place in the discipline. His recounting of the sociological tradition revolves around what he designates "unit-ideas," which provide "fundamental, constitutive substance to sociology" (5). Sociology's unit-ideas—community, authority, status (identity, role, function), the sacred (religion, the church, morality), and alienation—were, in Nisbet's view, all derived from one philosophical tradition: conservatism. This meant that sociology was about not only the empirical analysis of capitalist modernity but also, and fundamentally, moral critique. Unit-ideas were preconditions for civilizations to prosper. Yet capitalist modernity was rendering every one of them problematic. Problems of order, loss of meaning, and loss of community afflicting the modern world, Nisbet stresses, point to the importance of values, shared assumptions, and associational life in guaranteeing some form of social stability and progress. They also suggest the need to return to the classic texts of the sociological tradition, where such resources can be found. Tocqueville is reserved pride of place. For Nisbet, Tocqueville ranks alongside "Marx, Weber, and Durkheim" as one of those men who laid "the foundations of modern sociological thought" (2004, 5). *Democracy in America* is a timeless and fundamental contribution to the discussion of the unit-idea of "authority" (107ff.), the "first systematic and empirical study of the effects of political power on modern society" (120). It prefigures Tocqueville's seminal analysis of centralization and bureaucratization in *The Old Regime*. His concerns were as relevant then as today.

TOCQUEVILLE'S DEMISE

Toward the late 1960s, disagreements about the status of Tocqueville among the "classics" spoke of a more fundamental disagreement about the *point* of sociology itself. Such disagreement foreshadowed what was to become of "Tocqueville, the sociological classic" in the next decade. Randall Collins's "law of small numbers"[22] seems to explain why Giddens's (1971) masterstroke of reducing the canon to a holy trinity of Durkheim, Marx, and Weber was so successful and how it threw Tocqueville out of a canon that would admit no peripheral works. But it fails to explain why Gianfranco Poggi's similar attempt to position Tocqueville next to Marx and Durkheim as one of the "few sociological greats" (1972, xi) floundered. The explanation is to be found in the discipline. As sociology moved away from grand sociological theorizing and abstract schemes toward concrete social and political issues—notably, gender and race—interpretations of *Democracy in America* like Poggi's, accepting the extirpation of the latter categories from Tocqueville and hinging on the typological difference between aristocracy and democracy (3–61), sounded desperately out of touch. As Michael Burawoy explains, sociology in the 1970s "moved to accommodate critical perspectives, absorbing the blows directed its way by becoming more open to political pressures. Subfield after subfield thus moved to the Left" (2005b, 70). This represented a break away from the liberal consensus of the postwar period toward greater theoretical diversity and epistemological eclecticism. Works like *Democracy in America*, which had been used to consolidate that consensus, were now relics of an almost bygone past. As a result, *Democracy in America* gradually withered from view in sociology (J. Abbott 2007). The era of the likes of Mayer, Aron, and Nisbet, for whom sociology could still be considered an "art form" and *Democracy in America* one of its masterpieces—a "landscape" as "distinctive and compelling as any to be found among the greater novels or paintings" (Nisbet 2002, 7)—was coming to an end.

In the next decade, there were a few ignitions of interest, but they were quickly suppressed. They corresponded with the ascendency of the communitarian Tocqueville, or Tocqueville as a critic of individualism and the resulting atomization and privatization of societies. Robert Bellah's *Habits of the Heart* (1985) drew its title and some of its inspiration from Tocqueville.[23] It diagnosed the malaise of modern American society and in a Tocquevillian vein urged it to draw on its diverse civic and religious traditions to rebuild itself as a democratic community capable of resisting the dehumanizing effects of the market and the administrative state. The book became embroiled in vigorous popular and scholarly debate—namely, among political theorists. But sociologists remained resistant to a Tocqueville revival. Likewise, the only deliberate attempt to reestablish Tocqueville's work as a classic in the discipline (Pope 1986) fell on deaf ears in the sociological community. Even the burgeoning literature on "social capital" in the 1990s and 2000s following the revival of Tocqueville instigated by Robert D. Putnam's work (1993) was mainly a political science affair, with some spilling into political sociology. It was also greeted with early skepticism by sociologists on the democratic left, who saw the danger in Putnam's "Tocqueville romanticism," or the idea that "social capital" arises somewhat ex nihilo, apart from politics and government (Skocpol 1996).

More recent attempts to rehabilitate Tocqueville for sociologists—notably by Jon Elster (2009), Raymond Boudon (2006), and Richard Swedberg (2009)—have failed to gain traction.[24] Textbooks provide a good illustration of Tocqueville's near-complete demise among sociologists. Macionis's *Sociology* (2016), the most influential introductory sociology textbook in America today, does not list *Democracy in America* in its references, and virtually all eight mentions of Tocqueville in the text (or in the notes) are superficial. A similar pattern emerges in other textbooks. Henslin (2014, 177) makes one reference to Tocqueville (on voluntary associations), while Schaefer (2011) and Kendall (2011) make no reference at all. In seventeen textbooks published between 1997 and 2000, Tocqueville is mentioned in only seven (R. Hamilton 2003, 292). Textbooks of sociological theory paint a similar picture. Turner (2002), Ashley and Orenstein (2005), Goodwin and Scimecca (2005), and Appelrouth and Edles (2008) make no reference to the author of *Democracy in America*. The same is true in social theory textbooks. The exceptions are very few: Baert and Silva (2010, 118) present Tocqueville as a classic and discuss contemporary appropriations of his thought, and Seidman's *Contested Knowledge* (2008) makes only one reference to Tocqueville. Elliott and Lemert's sweeping *Introduction to Contemporary Social Theory* (2014) does not list *Democracy in America* among the "classics" of contemporary relevance. It is "simply not regarded today as crucial to the training of professional sociologists . . . as opposed to well-read undergraduates or scholars of other kindred disciplines," laments John Torpey (2006, 696; see also Kasinitz 2006), editor, with Stephen Mennell, of one of the last selections of Tocqueville's writings specifically aimed at a sociological audience (Tocqueville 1980). The assessment rings true with the sociological community. In 1998 members of the International Sociological Association (ISA) found no place for *Democracy in America* among the books that were most influential on their work as sociologists.[25] They were more likely to trace their research agendas back to the work of W. E. B. Du Bois, Harriet Martineau, or Jane Addams than to Tocqueville. "Dead by suicide or at the hands of person or persons unknown": the fate of Tocqueville in sociology seems to agree with the coroner's verdict.

TRANSLATION WARS

The early revival of Tocqueville in the 1950s and 1960s was not a singularly leftist affair, but it was dominated by progressive readings and editorial initiatives closely imbricated with them. The Tocqueville emerging from them had a double nature: at the same time a historically minded social scientist and a political thinker, he belonged in the company of Weber and Marx. Since the 1980s, however, a conservative Tocqueville has been on the rise, and his nature has undergone a substantial change: from social scientist, or even historically grounded political thinker, to political philosopher in quest of universally valid moral laws. This conservative turn has not gone unnoticed. While Pulitzer Prize–winning historian Michael Kammen observes that "conservatives have appropriated *Democracy in America* as their favorite source of cerebral ammunition" (Kammen 1998, 38), Isaac Kramnick identifies exactly when this appropriation began. In Kramnick's view, "since the sesquicentennial celebration of *Democracy in America* in the 1980s and 1990s the intellectual right has virtually owned Tocqueville" (2003, xliv). Under conservative ownership, a new cultural icon formed: "the aristocratic liberal, who accepts the inevitability of democracy, but insists in spelling out its shortcomings" and fears "big government" most of all (xliv). This portrayal befits the conservative litany of loss, a narrative about a lowering of standards that transforms the goals of a nonvirtuous, gratification-seeking multitude into the end of society itself.

In its earlier, progressive readings, *Democracy in America* was a seminal inquiry into the modern problematic of equality. In the conservative reading, it is transformed into a classic defense of civilized values, individual freedoms, and civic virtues against the corrosive workings of egalitarianism and moral relativism. The moral critique of egalitarianism doubles as a defense of elitism. Tocqueville is recalled less as the author who recognized and embraced the inevitable advance of equality than as he who remained faithful to the elitist belief in inequality as an ineradicable aspect of the human condition. In the words of Harvey C. Mansfield Jr., perhaps America's most notorious living neoconservative political philosopher, Tocqueville was uniquely insightful in seeing how egalitarianism and "rugged individualism" (2010, 68) shaped a liberal-democratic order that failed to nurture human excellence and gladly embraced complacency, philistinism, and mass conformism. The new liberalism Tocqueville envisaged, however, was to be "infused with pride as well as impelled by self-interest" (3). The "desire for greatness," Mansfield explains, "is the motive that justifies and ennobles democratic patriotism, even democratic imperialism and colonialism." Tocqueville viewed the latter "as the expression of a desire for greatness necessary to dignify democracy above the assertion of a mediocre universal equality" (111). Where Mansfield sees consistency, others might find the kind of tension that makes Tocqueville worth revisiting: notably, a disclosure of democracy's structural entanglement in inegalitarian relations with non-Europeans (within the empire but also at home). It is not hard to see why Mansfield's Tocqueville should be of little interest to contemporary sociologists. But the Tocqueville of democratic paradox is not as easily dismissible and has been recently revived as a critical race theorist (Tillery 2009).

Such revivals are rare, however. Political philosophy has kept Tocqueville among its founding fathers, but his re-creation through editing and translation has of late been a distinctively conservative enterprise. Just as the ascendance of the progressive Tocqueville was facilitated by the Bradley edition and had its editorial coronation in the Mayer-Lerner edition, so the ascendance of the conservative Tocqueville reached its climax in the 2000 University of Chicago Press edition of *Democracy in America*. Its editors and translators are none other than Mansfield and Delba Winthrop, herself a respected Straussian political philosopher. This translation project resulted from Mansfield's long-standing engagement with Tocqueville. Ironically, however, Mansfield first encountered Tocqueville not through Leo Strauss, as one might expect, but through J.-P. Mayer, whom he befriended during Mayer's stay at Harvard (Mancini 2006, 210). It was Mayer's 1966 edition of *Democracy in America*—more precisely, George Lawrence's translation—that Mansfield sought to displace decades later in a confrontation between "originalist" and "progressivist" approaches to translation.

Knowledge production and circulation have their costs. The sponsorship of private foundations has been key in the construction and diffusion of the conservative Tocqueville in America. Two conservative institutions, the Bradley and the John M. Olin foundations, funded work on the 2000 Chicago edition. And there was a serious amount of work involved in it. Mansfield and Winthrop's was the first English translation of *Democracy in America* for many years following Lawrence's almost forty years before and Henry Reeve's more than a century earlier.[26] As soon as it appeared, it became embroiled in controversy. Praised in conservative circles and their professional outlets, it became an object of contempt among liberal intellectuals: Caleb Crain famously referred to it as "Tocqueville for neocons" in a piece for the *New York Times* (2001). What is interesting, however, is that the controversy did not concentrate on the paratexts—despite the long, sixty-nine-page introductory essay—but on the translation itself.[27] Whether Tocqueville had been lost—or ideologically refashioned—in translation became the question preoccupying its defenders and its detractors. All translation is to some extent an act of betrayal to the original. But for some, the Mansfield-Winthrop translation was a step too far.

Much of the discussion was informed by the belief that translation can dramatically affect a book's interpretation and reception by readers. As we have seen, Tocqueville was painfully aware of this. Upon the original English publication of the first volume of *Democracy in America*, Tocqueville felt obliged to admonish his friend and original translator Reeve for his interpretative license: "Your translation must maintain my attitude; this I demand not only from the translator, but from the man." Tocqueville concluded, "It has seemed to me that in the translation of the last book you have, without wanting it, following the instinct of your opinions, very lively colored what was contrary to democracy and rather appeased what could do wrong to aristocracy" (quoted in Mayer 1966, vii). Similarly, the professed aim of Mansfield and Winthrop's translation is to rein in the license of previous translations and revisions. However, unlike Tocqueville, they stop short of accusing these renditions of introducing a political bias.

If not ideological prejudice, what was wrong with previous translations? After all, the 1966 Harper and Row edition,[28] with George Lawrence's translation, seemed to have achieved what it set out to do. This edition prided itself, as the blurb on the front cover made clear, on making "Tocqueville, whose brilliance has always been granted by academics . . . now accessible to readers who don't mind brilliance *as long as it is readable*" (Tocqueville 1966). Modernization for the sake of accessibility was Mayer's goal, and accessibility to many readers—then and now—was achieved. But for Mansfield and Winthrop, therein lies the problem. Accessibility bore too great a cost in compromised authenticity.

Mansfield and Winthrop claim that in translating *Democracy in America* anew, they tried not so much to modernize the text and make it more readable for the turn-of-the-millennium reading public as "to be modest, cautious, and faithful." They had to make their choices, for sure—every translator does—but they guided themselves "by the principle, admittedly an ideal, that our business is to convey Tocqueville's thought as he held it rather than to restate it in comparable terms today" (2000, 91). But there is more to their choice than this suggests. By offering a more literal translation, one closer to the original word order and phrase structure, they believe that they are acting as political philosophers, or "students of texts," should—that is, by doing justice to Tocqueville as a philosopher of the first rank ("a deep thinker"; 2000, 154) and leaving Tocqueville's thinking open to other serious "students of texts" to interpret, even if this makes it more difficult for virtually everyone else to access.

As translators, they believe themselves to be at odds with earlier translators of *Democracy in America*, who were "literary persons" presuming "to know the meaning of the author," mindless of "the need to study the book." Yet Tocqueville's seeming accessibility, his being "a wonderful pleasure to read" (Mansfield and Winthrop 2000, 154), is deceptive at best, for he is an exceptional man writing for a "democratic age whose preference for ready and recognizable pleasure he describes, but the truths he conveys do not obediently follow the trends he sets forth" (154). In other words, there are two levels to the text for two levels of readers. The ability to pass from one to the other and to mine the genuine teachings depends on leaving any cues left by Tocqueville intact. However, this is exactly what "literary" translators do not do: "When the disharmonies—nay contradictions—in the text are too obvious to be missed, they harmonize them, which is to say they cover them over." This amounts to an exercise of sovereignty over the author that Mansfield and Winthrop characterize as "passing from saying what he means to saying what he must have meant or ought to have meant" (155). As loyal followers of Leo Strauss's "art of reading," Mansfield and Winthrop argue that exactly the opposite is required: a philosopher-translator knows not to resolve contradictions but to comprehend them as part of the truth. Contradictions and ambiguities of the interpreted text, they claim, encode deeper meanings, which must be left untouched by the translator. They are secret handshakes or passageways to the true intentions of the author and what he or she sought to convey. Excavating this hidden meaning is arduous work best left to the philosopher's expertise, hence the necessity of leaving "the difficulty to be seen by the reader," for otherwise "one deprives him of a discovery that might force him to think" (156).

Unsurprisingly, Mansfield and Winthrop also draw their model of the ideal translator from Strauss. "The perfect translator," Strauss claimed, "is either one who understands nothing of what he translates and never presumes that he does, or one who understands everything in the text and knows what he is doing" (quoted in Mansfield and Winthrop 2000, 155). In an attempt to control the reception of their translation, Mansfield and Winthrop profess modesty and align themselves with the former. Their literalism—or fidelity to individual words and sentence structures rather than meaning—seems to confirm this. But their status as "students of the text" and their presumption of access to "Tocqueville's thought as he held it" tell otherwise.

Arthur Goldhammer, the renowned translator responsible for the Library of America edition of *Democracy in America* (2004), takes the Straussian distinction up a notch so as to identify the assumptions that underpin it. He claims that for Mansfield and Winthrop, "translation either must be rote transcription—the cryptographic clerk, Strauss's know-nothing translator—or else must proceed *in tandem* with decipherment, which is work for the scholar" (Goldhammer 2003, 117). That they effectively aim at the latter is shown by their insistence on "the study of the book" (116). No doubt such study is required, Goldhammer agrees, but what is really at stake is what counts as "the study of the book" and how the relationship between the book's message and its material embodiment in language is ultimately conceived. By "the study of the book," Goldhammer suggests, Mansfield and Winthrop mean the study of the text as a self-sufficient object of inquiry, the text being here conceived as a "cipher" encoding the message that requires excavation through attention to oblique ways of conveying truth that only literalism can preserve for the reader's perusal. But as Goldhammer rightly stresses, once the text is perceived as the cultural artifact that it is, it becomes at least equally as important "to study the language, and the culture of which that language is an expression" (117). The only faithful translation then involves a shift between cultures to give the text a similar function in the target cultural system. To be able to do this, Goldhammer claims, one needs to develop "a good ear" for it. The material embodiment of the message has, in his view, "more in common with a musical performance than with a cipher" (118), and the translator's work is akin to that of a musical interpreter who must preserve a sense of the original's qualities as they play on both the original and the sensibilities of the target cultures. In other words, language is not simply an algorithm for performing encryption or decryption. It is rather the case that an author's thinking cannot exist or express itself apart from the language in which the text is construed, its particular rhythm and tonal cadence. To this one might add the necessity of knowing the linguistic context—the historically given language in which the author worked, the modes of speech available to him, the structural constraints they imposed, and the resources they made available. This is why when translating, a practical knowledge (Goldhammer's "good ear") of history, culture, and convention regarding the target language is necessary to produce meaningful rather than mere formal equivalence between translated text and its translation.

The turn of the millennium saw a race to translate Tocqueville's *Democracy in America*, leaving the camps divided in a translation war. For some liberal critics, the Mansfield-Winthrop translation was politically charged. Interpreting Tocqueville as an "arch-neoconservative" was no longer enough. His thought had to be reworked from the inside out to disallow any other interpretation. Most critics, however, stopped short of claiming ideological manipulation. Rather, they stressed the pitfalls of the translators' literalist approach and questioned the equation of literalness with fidelity (e.g., Drescher 2001; Goldhammer 2003). They showed how the word-for-word, phrase-by-phrase translation resulted in distortions in which sense was either confused or lost. This created a curtain that made it impossible to make sense of Tocqueville's analysis, let alone confront it on its own terms. Subtler differences in word choice, word order, rhythm, and tone were required to render Tocqueville's thinking and style into English. Other critics reacted more sharply to the philosophical elitism underpinning the translators' choices. This is also possibly where the Mansfield-Winthrop translation departed most dramatically from that produced by Lawrence in 1966. Mansfield-Winthrop's choices are dictated by the needs of the philosopher-interpreter. Lawrence's choices, by contrast, were dictated as much by commercial demands as by a progressive ideal of accessibility. Lawrence sought to leave behind the "aristocratic style" of French writing to embrace fully the "democratic style" of its American counterpart. As the blurb on the front cover of the Harper and Row edition made clear, the duty of the translator was to make "brilliance . . . readable" to contemporary lay readers. To this purpose, various actions were allowed, even demanded: to clarify and make plain, to seek elegance where elegance could be achieved, and to rewrite to fit contemporary standards of language and taste. Pleasurable accessibility was the goal. Writers want to be read. Abstruse wording and phrasing only get in the way of their reaching an ever-expanding middle-class reading public. With the Mansfield-Winthrop translation, these democratizing ideals came full circle.

CONCLUSION

As it happens with most disciplines, in the mid-twentieth century sociology defined itself through the retrospective creation of a "classical" canon. Toward the end of that century, the discipline was lending its tools to the deconstruction of the very notion of "canonicity" (e.g., Guillory 1994). Many had come to believe sociology had told itself (and others) an "untenable foundation story of men theorizing European modernity" (Connell 1997, 1511). It was time to question it and refound the discipline.

Canons have life cycles, cores, and peripheries, and works typically move among them over time. The theorists who sought to shape the sociological canon most actively—Parsons, Merton, Mills, Bourdieu, Collins, Giddens, Alexander, Habermas—saw some works in the history of the discipline as exceeding their immediate contexts and being worthy of engagement and appropriation for present use. All of them gave, at best, cursory treatment to Tocqueville. He was always kept at the outermost fringes of the sociological canon, except for in the 1950s and 1960s, in which commentary, editing, translation, and original research of Tocqueville-inspired work combined in bringing Tocqueville the sociologist to the fore.

Unlike Tocqueville, Marx, Durkheim, and Weber, whom we addressed in previous chapters, have occupied the inner core of the sociological canon and remained there for a while. But not even they have resisted fluctuations. In the mid-1980s, for instance, Durkheim was persona non grata for his alleged positivism, indifference to agency, and succumbing to the conservative pull of "collective conscience." Similar stories could be told of Marx and Weber. Auguste Comte, Herbert Spencer, and Georg Simmel have formed a volatile second team. Ferdinand Tönnies, Vilfredo Pareto, Graham Sumner, Charles H. Cooley, G. H. Mead, and Norbert Elias have held even more unstable positions. Of late, figures like Du Bois, Harriet Martineau, and Jane Addams have been conscripted. Tocqueville, for his part, has slipped almost into oblivion.

When speaking of "classic" authors and "classic" texts today, hardly anyone is referring simply to an "intrinsic" ability to speak meaningfully to other times. Their "classicality," we know, is not built on thin air. Ideas matter, for sure, but so do the cultural, economic, political, institutional, and academic conditions and interests that secure their visibility and affect their material and intellectual sustenance over time. This awareness has turned the study of the canon into a kind of sociology. Yet to date, this has also been a sociology that has systematically overlooked "book matters," or what can be made *with* and *through* the book form. This is where this book started; it is also where this chapter finishes.

In the case of Tocqueville's *Democracy in America*, the Mayer-Lerner edition, together with Lawrence's new translation, democratized the work. It brought the book *into* the present *for* the present. The high-level flow of the translation spoke to readers' ears. It made Tocqueville's aristocratic prose and bent of mind accessible and meaningful to a larger public. It also befitted Mayer's progressivist interpretation of the text less as political theory than as cultural criticism and his coronation of Tocqueville as the politically minded sociologist who immersed himself in and grasped most clearly the sociological structure of the mass age. It also marks the peak and the fall of sociology's short-lived affair with Tocqueville.

The Mansfield-Winthrop edition, by contrast, revives Tocqueville's unease with the fate of distinctions—reinstated, this time, as between the student of philosophy and the layman—in democratic times. It retranslates the book for a double-layered reading in which such distinctions can make themselves, once again, manifest. It reinstates Tocqueville firmly within political philosophy and its canon or, perhaps more narrowly, within its Straussian canon. Not once does it refer to Tocqueville's concerns or his insights as sociological. It follows Tocqueville in equating his "new political science" with the art of writing but specifies that this is the art of philosophical writing, serving "the logic of ideas" (Mansfield and Winthrop 2000, xxii) and cultivating an aristocratic taste for the fine and the original. It paraphrases Strauss in contrasting this art to "political science," which confers "the authority of science" to something as philistine as public opinion (xlv). In substance and style, the Winthrop-Mansfield edition is the *clef de voûte* of the conservative identification with Tocqueville.

This much emanates from Mansfield and Winthrop's long introduction. The introduction is a short book in itself, as Mansfield's subsequent contribution to Oxford's very short introductions series confirms (Mansfield 2010). The introduction presents Tocqueville as a philosopher whose thinking bears "many points of similarity with that of the ancients" (2000, xxx) but is in close dialogue with Pascal, Montesquieu, and Rousseau. It places him firmly in the canon of political philosophy, not social theory, even if Mansfield and Winthrop agree with Mayer that Tocqueville "anticipates the 'ideal type' invented by Max Weber which is a commonplace of social science today" (xxxv). They are far less hesitant than Mayer in classifying Tocqueville as a liberal belonging in the center of the canon of liberalism. But they make sure to stress that his is a peculiar liberalism appealing first and foremost to the right of the political spectrum.

The sweeping overview of Tocqueville's thinking offered in the introduction bears the marks of the Straussian hermeneutic, with its characteristic ambivalence toward liberal democracy and the project of modernity. Tocqueville is believed to stand out from naïve nineteenth-century liberalism "by refusing to accept either a safe distancing of freedom from democracy or an easy convergence of the two" (2000, xxix). He views "the liberal doctrines of progress, property, and the right to self-preservation" (xxxii) with critical distance and "has none of the enthusiasm of modernity in the heyday of its founding ambition" (xxx).

Mansfield and Winthrop commend Tocqueville for his skepticism and sobriety. But they unmoor themselves from them as they stress Tocqueville's visceral rejection of "big government" (2000, lxxii)—a strangely anachronistic and ideologically loaded term in a text searching for fidelity to the original. This ideological cast is confirmed by the veiled critique of the welfare state and the morally charged opposition between, on the one hand, socioeconomic rights, the rights of dependence, and on the other hand, political rights, the rights of freedom. The former, Mansfield and Winthrop insinuate, aim not at responsibility but at "freedom from risk," even if this implies embracing an "immense being—replacing God" (lxx), an omnipresent state increasing its reach and penetration with every new "governmental program and often governmental expenditure" (lxxxii). Mansfield's and Winthrop's concerns with the purported fascistic tendencies embedded in progressivism bring them strangely near to Mayer, the progressivist who worried about the welfare state's power to regulate as it empowered.

Extremes can touch in curious ways, but not so much as to make us lose sight of the broader picture. Mayer's and Mansfield's secondary authoring of Tocqueville's work through commentary, editing, and translation results in two very different books and two very different Tocquevilles. They both see and construe Tocqueville as a canonic sage. But while Mayer's Tocqueville is a perceptive sociologist engaged in cultural criticism, Mansfield's is a political philosopher serving the logic of ideas. Like Tocqueville's characters negotiating the transition between aristocratic and democratic social and political structures, these two editions are worlds together and yet worlds apart. They are an integral part of the travels of Alexis de Tocqueville—the appropriation of his ideas and their journey into and out of academic disciplines—so painstakingly re-created originally by Pierson.

## CONCLUSION

As so often happens, this book started as a manuscript and was then pushed through all the hoops of traditional publishing. The resulting printed book is before you. If you are reading these words, you have made the decision to pick it up. Perhaps intrigued by its title, you might have turned some of its pages, wanting to know more. Your experience of this will have been different if you read it as a traditional book or an e-book, as the work will be formatted and read differently in each case. Either way, however, this will still be, to a large extent, an experience unique to you and one bearing the outward traits of a one-to-one experience: between you and us—reader and authors, respectively—albeit mediated by a vast array of more or less anonymous agents involved in the (e-)book's conception and production. The copy you hold or scroll through at the end of this process bears some resemblance to the original manuscript. If you went through the trouble of comparing both, you would see similarities but also differences. You would probably be tempted to compare both on a word-by-word basis, taking the word as the key to the production of meaning and any shifts introduced to that meaning. But this literal comparison would miss important ways in which the literary form and the bibliographical form combine, blend, and affect one another. This dynamic and complex process makes the printed book. When compared to the manuscript, it also makes the printed book, or indeed the e-book, an altogether different thing to engage with. We are not just speaking of the same thing in a different format, as if just any form could be applied to any contents, with no transposition or transformation of meaning. Your own experience of this and other books will probably be different based on the reasons you came to it and the cues in the book's internal and external makeup that helped you make sense of it. What brought you to this book? What sense did you make of its form and structure? To what extent did the type of book you encountered add or detract from its meaning? To what extent did it make you read the book in this or that manner? Put simply, form affects meaning, and it is difficult to ascertain which comes first in the order of creation for both author and interpreter.

This has been the point of departure of this book. As such, this has been a book of books. It has looked into the makeup of books as a key site for the struggle over their meaning. These were not just any books, however. These were a set of books that have circulated between core and periphery of the canon of a particular discipline—sociology—and cognate disciplines. In analyzing them, we have therefore addressed a range of disciplines and a range of perspectives on the books themselves, from genealogy and book history to pragmatism. Notwithstanding the diversity of disciplines and perspectives, however, the book has focused on a central message of ideas as products of an embodied mind and their physical embodiments, notably in the printed book, as integral to their meaning and legacy. Each chapter was therefore a case study in how books can be made and unmade, produced and reworked, in their many physical and literary permutations. To say this much is to imply that matter has agency—that the life of ideas cannot be lived apart from our experience of them through our physical senses and that our cognitive functions cannot be separated from our sensory powers as exercised over sense objects. Ours were manuscripts and printed books—things manmade. Hence our attention turned to a vast array of agents who work on readers by working on texts and all those things in a published work that accompany them. These can be internal or external to the book, and hence we have started this book with the figure of the commentator and closed it with a discussion of the politics of translation. A commentator can redefine a book and reinscribe it in a new paradigm of interpretation. As we have seen, his or her priming of the work for further appropriation can itself be inspired by, or indeed inspire, a new edition of the work that paves the way for a paradigmatic shift and its dissemination. Similarly, given the centrality of language to the process of meaning construction, the politics of translation can take on a life of its own by either giving a whole new sense to a work (e.g., by reworking its fundamental concepts through translation) or adopting a politics of translation that doubles as a politics of interpretation. After all, the question of what a work is cannot be answered apart from the question of how the work is to be read.

Ideas, texts, and books are different entities whose lives are nonetheless profoundly entwined. That they are different is clear from the example of "books" with no discernible meaningful text, the most famous example of which is perhaps the Voynich manuscript, an early fifteenth-century document written in what is (so far) an indecipherable script. That the manuscript has no discernable meaning did not prevent Yale University Press from publishing a full-size colored facsimile in 2017 with an extensive paratextual apparatus, including essays on its history and cryptological puzzles. The manuscript had been digitized in 2004 and has been available on Yale's library website in high-resolution images ever since. But the press wanted to give an avid public of lay and specialist readers something more: a sense of the book as a physical object, the closest thing to the experience of sitting before it in the library. In the case of the Voynich, its inscrutable meaning has resulted in wild meaning making by a number of followers whose imaginations continue to feed on the manuscript's many unknowns. The contextualization offered in the Yale edition seeks to spark the interest of historians, who might be best equipped to treat the manuscript not as an alien object to be admired in awe or simply cast aside but rather as a product of the medieval period and its manuscript conventions. The Voynich is a peculiar object and is constructed as such. The books we examine here are more common objects, often the product of mass production techniques that are as desacralizing as they are integral to their canonization. In tapping into particular episodes in their history, we have demonstrated the extent to which the formation and meaning of certain key ideas and texts are not ethereal affairs or products of a disembodied mind. Quite the opposite, their epoch-making meaning is an embodied realization, often in the shape of a book.

Books are everywhere. Ours is a book-reading culture. Yet in many ways, we have barely begun to study books as the battlegrounds where wars over the meaning of ideas are waged. Our chosen title—*The Politics of the Book: A Study on the Materiality of Ideas*—refers to this fundamental insight. If we are to understand and explain how ideas originate, develop, and shape our lives, then we need to pay more attention to the interplay between form and meaning production that takes place *in* and *through* those little parallelepipeds that populate our shelves and gain life through our manipulation.

In the cases of the six books discussed here, we have examined how their physical embodiments have changed dramatically over the years and, with these changes, have altered our relationships to the works themselves. We have looked at how paratexts were introduced or removed as a result of the agendas of their authors, editors, and those writing the introductions. These changes had varying impacts on the sense that could be—and indeed was—made of these works. We have also explored how translation choices sometimes produced effects well beyond the original intentions of the books' authors—and often the translators themselves. Their histories have crossed centuries, continents, natural languages, and academic disciplines. Disciplinary boundaries and the canons that help legitimize them emerge from our study less as natural divisions of intellectual labor than as highly permeable and historically contingent frontiers separating epistemic communities whose identities are partly formed through the making and reading of books—namely, of certain books as classics of the discipline that makes them.

This book is also about the agents behind the creation and re-creation of these books. Although authors figure prominently in every conventional intellectual history and have not been ignored here, our focus has been on the much less studied collective of agents responsible for securing the survival and creation of these books. These agents include those seeing the works into production and, once printed, into the commercial world of bookshops and the academic world of libraries, where they gain a life of their own. Theirs is far from a homogenous collective, however. As we have shown, it includes not only commentators, professional translators, and (commercial and academic) editors but also hybrid categories such as commentators-cum-editors or commentators-cum-translators whose impact on the book's reception has been paramount. It also includes authors in their own right who use paratexts such as prefaces, introductions, and endorsements in other authors' books to frame those works in certain ways and advance their own political and disciplinary agendas. They sometimes double as book reviewers who, especially when writing in scientific journals, also play a significant role in shaping the meaning and therefore the future uses of these works. The appropriation of these books—their redirection by new and hitherto unimaginable framings and readings that become part of the body of the books themselves and therefore also part of many readers' engagement with them—is still a much-neglected dimension of the life of books, including the lives of those books whose social disciplines deemed them critical for us to think productively (or indeed to think at all). To ignore the book "makers'" work on and in the book—which is not only the physical embodiment of its author's ideas but the very iconic representation of those ideas—would come at the cost of ignoring a crucial aspect of the vagaries of intellectual life.

Our attention to human agents and books, however, should not be misread as indicative of a relative lack of interest in ideas per se. On the contrary, it is because we are deeply invested in studying ideas that this book has focused on the materiality of ideas—namely, of highly abstract and complex ones. Our conclusion is a modest one. The task of understanding and explaining the origins, development, and consequences of social and political thought would benefit, we believe, from a more rigorous knowledge of the history of its material embodiments. This history is permeated by passionate struggles over the import of those ideas—struggles that are more often than not as much ideological and aesthetic as they are academic. It is also a history punctuated by accidents, errors, silences, injustices, and misunderstandings, not the least about which authors' works should continue to be read and why. But if one is to really move beyond self-referential mythologies, it is a history that must be told.

# NOTES

INTRODUCTION

1. See Darnton (1982) for an apt description of the field of "history of the book" (known in France as "*histoire du livre*" and in Germany as "*Geschichte des Buchwesens*"), as well as for a fascinating illustration of its contributions to intellectual history more generally through the example of Voltaire's *Questions sur l'Encyclopédie*. A recent important institutional development in this area was the creation of the Center for the Study of Books and Media at Princeton University in 2002. In the UK, the HoBo website (formerly known as "History of Book at Oxford") has been an important source of information on book history since 1996 (see http://www.english.ox.ac.uk/hobo/).
2. See Genette's discussion of the meaning of form (1997, 16–22).
3. Locke (1707). See Locke's example discussed in McKenzie (1985, 46–47).
4. For a critique of this view, see Gardiner (2000, 258).
5. Genette includes translations, especially those in which the author collaborates in some form, in his list of paratexts in the epilogue of his book.
6. In this sense, our approach differs from Bruno Latour's object-oriented politics (Latour and Weibel 2005) in that we reject the assumption that (political) agency is equally distributed between human and nonhuman agents. On the notion of distributed agency, see also Callon (1998).
7. We thank one of our reviewers for having raised this point.

CHAPTER 1

1. Donald N. Levine's seminal description and analysis of the various narratives of the sociological tradition suffers from at least one difficulty. The status of Levine's "dialogical" narrative is problematic. Although pluralistic in its character, it does not present itself in such terms. The label *pluralist* is left for the likes of Pitirim Sorokin or Don Martindale. Yet what distinguishes Levine's pluralism from, say, Sorokin's is a question not of nature but of degree—his pluralism emphasizes dialogue and mutual accommodation as opposed to silence or conflict. Thus "dialogical pluralism" seems to be the most rigorous way to describe Levine's

approach to the sociological tradition. For an assessment, see Camic and Joas (2003).
2. Social realism is one of the earlier sociological schools that "scientific" sociology was meant to replace.
3. See also Sorokin (1966, 280), in which *Elementary Forms* is presented as an exemplar of cultural systems theory.
4. But see Silva (2007).
5. The main exception was Robert Bellah (1967), who supervised Alexander's PhD dissertation.
6. For the first claim, see the opinion survey on the most influential books for sociologists presented at ISA World Congress of Sociology in Montreal in 1998: https://www.isa-sociology.org/en/about-isa/history-of-isa/books-of-the-xx-century. As to the second claim, see the six-part op-ed in the *Guardian* by Gordon Lynch in 2012–13: "Emile Durkheim: Religion—the Very Idea, Part 1: The Analysis of Moral Life," *Guardian*, December 10, 2012, https://www.theguardian.com/commentisfree/belief/2012/dec/10/emile-durkheim-analysis-of-moral-life.
7. For a critical examination of the different narrative modes of the sociological tradition, including the "synthetic narrative" exemplified by Parsons and Alexander, see Levine (2015; 1995, 35–58).
8. This task was made possible by the historically minded scholarship of the "new Durkheim studies" of the 1970s.
9. It would be a mistake to consider Alexander's strong program in cultural sociology as a solitary intellectual endeavor prosecuted through academic publications alone. There is a pronounced institutional dimension to the program in cultural sociology, as evidenced first by the creation of the Center for Cultural Sociology at Yale in 2004, several academic book series, and more recently, the founding of the *American Journal of Cultural Sociology*.
10. The idea of effervescence has a long yet checkered history in Durkheim's writings. On the metaphoric role of other chemical ideas, such as aggregation, association, affinity, and combination, in Durkheim's thinking, see Fernandes (2008). On the role of metaphors in shaping Durkheim's argument in *Elementary Forms* in general, see McKinnon (2014).
11. On July 24, 1908, Durkheim wrote to his friend and editor of the *Revue de métaphysique et de morale*, Xavier Léon, "Vous savez peut-être que j'ai commencé la rédaction de mon livre sur les *Formes élémentaires de la pensée et de la pratique religieuse*" (Durkheim 1975, 2:467). The draft was published in the second volume of Victor Karady's 1975 anthology of Durkheim's texts as "La religion: Les origins."
12. Letter from Durkheim to Hubert, July 12, 1912 (quoted in Borlandi 2012).
13. Karen Fields translates this crucial statement as follows: "The power of the rite over minds, which is real, made them believe in its power over things, which is imaginary" (1995, 364). She adds a footnote explaining, "Here the term 'moral' refers to mind as opposed to matter" (364).
14. The influence of Kant on Durkheim through the work of the French neo-Kantians Charles Renouvier, Émile Boutroux, and Octave Hamelin is well documented. See, for example, Pickering (1984, 2002).
15. This cowritten essay on the evolution from "primitive" to "modern" styles of thought is where Durkheim first extends French neo-Kantianism in the direction of a groundbreaking sociology of knowledge.
16. The book is the fourth volume of the series Travaux de L'Année sociologique/"Bibliothèque de philosophie contemporaine," edited by Durkheim himself. The first three volumes are all by other

Durkheimians: *Fonctions mentales dans les sociétés inférieures* by Lucien Lévi-Bruhl (1910), *Mélanges d'histoire des religions* by Hubert and Marcel Mauss (1909), and *Essais sur le régime des castes* by Célestin Bouglé (1908). The travels of the 1,650 copies of the first edition (a second would follow in 1925 and a third in 1937) were about to begin. See the global reception map at Digital Durkheim (http://digitaldurkheim.hypotheses.org/1151, last accessed December 1, 2015) for a comprehensive database of all translations and covers of Durkheim's *Formes élémentaires*.

17. Swain finished his translation in 1915 and, a year later, defended his doctoral dissertation at Columbia University on Hellenistic influences on Christian asceticism. Unsurprisingly, despite its many merits, Swain's translation bears many marks of haste (Fields 2005, 164).
18. George Allen and Unwin Archive, University of Reading, United Kingdom (hereafter GAUA).
19. Letter from Swain to Allen and Unwin, October 14, 1914, GAUA.
20. Swain to Allen and Unwin.
21. Swain to Allen and Unwin.
22. According to Swain, Durkheim's first suggestion was "Totemism: A Study of the Elementary Religious Life." Durkheim then suggested a second title, which he told Swain he preferred: "Totemism: A Study in Religious Sociology." This is the title Swain used in the manuscript he sent to the publisher.
23. In a letter dated May 21, Swain wrote, "I must say that I am greatly mortified that my translation should be open to the criticisms which Professor Muirhead has made of it. In regard to the 'solecisms of syntax,' I presume that they are largely 'Americanisms' which sound strange to British people. Though I carefully went over my entire MS for the purpose of removing all such expressions, but it seems that I was not completely successful. The others cause of my greater shame for they seem to be simple blunders. However, I hope that they are not as numerous as Professor Muirhead's remarks would lead one to suppose. Will it be too late to change these if I carefully go over the entire proof again as soon as possible? I shall be only too glad to do so, if it will do any good" (GAUA). As it happens, no changes were made, and Swain's poor translation choices plagued this edition throughout its existence.
24. It would cost $354.66 in 2015.
25. In fact, Durkheim's canonization in sociology owes little to *Elementary Forms*. Anthony Giddens's (1972) *Émile Durkheim: Selected Writings* illustrates this well. It relegates *Elementary Forms* to a secondary position—only a few passages in the chapter on religion and ritual, itself one of thirteen chapters, appear. The bulk of the book is devoted to methodology and the division of labor in modern societies. By and large, it is only around the middle-period works *Suicide*, *Division of Labor*, and *Rules* that Durkheim, the master analyst of capitalist society, was canonized alongside Marx and Weber in the late 1960s and early 1970s. Pickering commented on Giddens's efforts at canonization: "Repeatedly one hears it said that the three men who contributed more than any others to sociology in the nineteenth century were Durkheim, Weber and Marx. If some may doubt the presence of Marx within the trinity and would prefer to see Simmel, Pareto or Spencer as the substitute, the fact remains that no one can dethrone Durkheim from being one of its members." He continues, pointing to an aspect that would prove central to Durkheim's reception in decades to come: "However, there is one point that ought to be

emphasised . . . : the prominence that Durkheim gave to religion" (1975, 3).
26. These include the proponents of the strong program of cultural sociology, according to whom this new intellectual climate "opened up a new breathing space for the later Durkheim" (Smith and Alexander 1996, 587).
27. However, see Ricoeur (2006, 5) on the "fantasy of the perfect translation."
28. Unlike Swain's, which had very few by the translator himself and expands Durkheim's often highly abbreviated references in the footnotes.
29. More recently, however, Alexander reexamined Mead's notion of "feeling consciousness" (2008, 782) in order to discuss the materiality of icons in terms that avoid the twin pitfalls of idealism and materialism.
30. This is not to say, of course, that the physical efficacy of the rite takes precedence over its moral or social efficacy. As Durkheim stresses in his discussion of the Wollunka, this is "a totem of a very special kind." This special status comes from the fact that the Wollunka, which natives imagine as a colossal snake whose "head is lost in the clouds when it stands on its tail," is not a plant or an animal, but a unique being—"a purely mythical being" (1995, 450). It is, in other words, a purely representative totem.
31. Bachiocchi and Fabiani's (2012) exploration of the pragmatic dimension of the late Durkheim is a case in point.

CHAPTER 2

This chapter uses material originally published by the authors in 2011 as "Books and Canon Building in Sociology: The Case of *Mind, Self, and Society*," *Journal of Classical Sociology* 11(3): 356–77.
1. Here we follow Alexander's analysis of iconic consciousness (2008). For a discussion of the role of icons based on the work of Thomas Hobbes, see Vieira (2009).
2. The editor of *Essays in Psychology*, Mary Jo Deegan, mistakenly titles this article "The Social Character of Instinct" (Mead 2001, 3). The original, however, reads "The Social Character of Instincts" and can be found in *Essays on Psychology*, University of Chicago Archival Biographical Files, Special Collections Research Center, Joseph P. Regenstein Library, University of Chicago, "Mead, George Herbert, I–II" Files (hereafter ABF), Addenda, box 1, folders 9–14 (fol. 9). There were good reasons behind Mead's decision not to go ahead with the publication of *Essays in Social Psychology* in 1910. Mead was then undergoing a major revision in his social psychological ideas, and he no longer subscribed to the positions he had argued for in those earlier writings. See Silva (2008, 140ff.).
3. See, for example, Orbach (1983). Orbach's paper, however, focused on the early history of the book and did not address the history of its reception, nor did he explore the implications of the history of *Mind, Self, and Society* for the history of sociology itself. See also Huebner's *Becoming Mead*, which we discuss below.
4. Morris was a former student of Mead, under whom he did his PhD. Between 1925 and 1931, Morris taught at Rice University in Houston, Texas. In 1931, he returned to Chicago as an associate professor in the philosophy department of the University of Chicago and assumed the task of editing and publishing *Mind, Self, and Society*. Morris pursued a career as a philosopher, having published numerous books, including *The Pragmatic Movement in American Philosophy*, which includes a mistaken account of Mead's intellectual affiliation as independent of Dewey's (1970, 33).

5. For instance, in his 1936 review of *Mind, Self, and Society*, Ellsworth Faris asserts, "Mead never wrote his book on social psychology. The present volume was assembled from the notebooks of students who heard him in the latter part of his career" (1936, 809).
6. An exception is Silva (2008). Even Gary Alan Cook's historically minded study asserts that *Mind, Self, and Society* "is based upon student notes taken in several different offerings of Mead's course on advanced social psychology" (1993, xvii).
7. These notes can be found in ABF, box 2, folders 10–17.
8. Advanced Social Psychology (Philosophy 321), winter quarter of 1928. Mead taught this course between 1918 and 1930. See Lewis and Smith (1980, 267–71).
9. ABF, box 2, folder 1.
10. We thank Harold Orbach, who kindly provided us with this particular information in an exchange of emails in 2003.
11. A good illustration of this is Lewis's "A Social Behaviorist Interpretation of the Meadian 'I,'" in which the author, relying primarily on *Mind, Self, and Society*, tries to suggest a reexamination of Mead's social psychology. It never occurred to Lewis that his starting point, "social behaviorism," is an apocryphal depiction of Mead's social psychology. See Lewis (1979).
12. We borrow the notion of "radical instability" from Stephen Orgel's essay "What Is a Text?" (1981), which provides a reflection on the authorship of Renaissance dramas. However, our sense of the freely "collaborative" nature of *Mind, Self, and Society* is rather different from Orgel's.
13. To a certain extent, the lectures from which *Mind, Self, and Society* is constructed document Mead's cognitive processes and become justifiable sources of new scholarly interest for revisionists, especially when the study of these lectures is combined with that of Mead's manuscripts and texts written and published by Mead himself.
14. In his course on social psychology, however, Blumer was more interested in contrasting Mead's ideas with instinctual determinism (per Freud) and Watsonian behaviorism and cultural determinism (per anthropology). We thank Donald N. Levine, a pupil of Blumer in that course, for this information.
15. A good analysis of the current situation of this sociological approach is given in Fine (1993).
16. After retiring from teaching in 1967, Blumer remained as professor emeritus in Berkeley, California, until 1986.
17. Starting with W. I. Thomas's classic notion of the "definition of the situation" and continuing through to Becker's labeling theory (1963) and Goffman's frame analysis (1974), there are innumerable examples of how a symbolic interactionist approach to social reality perceives it as constructed, at least partly, by both social scientists and social actors themselves.
18. For a sophisticated social constructionist analysis of the past, see, for example, Zerubavel (1981).
19. Joseph Woelfel, for instance, criticizes Blumer's role as Mead's "official interpreter" by pointing out that "it makes no sense at all to try to discover what Mead 'really said' or 'really meant.' Blumer's article itself, then," Woelfel concluded, "is logically absurd according to Blumer's own reasoning" (1967, 409).
20. For a history of the development of symbolic interactionism and its link with the Chicago school of sociology, see, for example, Fisher and Strauss (1978).
21. See, for example, Fisher and Strauss (1978), Lewis and Smith (1980), Camic (1995), and A. Abbott (1999).

22. *Mind, Self, and Society* was translated as *Geist, Identität und Gesellschaft aus der Sicht des Sozialbehaviorismus* and published by Suhrkamp at Habermas's suggestion. This is not a reliable translation, though. As Ernst Tugendhat observes, the translator's choice of numerous terms (e.g., "self" was translated as identity [*Identität*], even though there is a German word for self [*Selbst*]) is highly questionable (1991, 170–71). Nevertheless, this translation has been widely used by the German-speaking readership as it has been reprinted several times (1973, 1975, 1978, 1983, 2000, and 2008).
23. We say "part" because the ideas of other pragmatists—including James, Peirce, and Dewey—had already been subject to scrutiny by German thinkers since the 1920s.
24. See Honneth and Joas (1988) for a critical analysis of Gehlen's interpretation of Mead's ideas.
25. A good bird's-eye-view analysis of this tradition is provided in Joas (1987).
26. We refer to Harvard, where Parsons worked all his life, and to Columbia University, where Merton and Lazarsfeld worked (beginning in 1941 and 1940, respectively).
27. Parsons's 1937 *The Structure of Social Action* makes no reference at all to Mead or the Chicago school; Merton's *Social Theory and Social Structure* (1949) makes only cursory remarks on Mead's work.

CHAPTER 3

1. There was a prior English version by Ria Stone, a mimeographed pamphlet going by the name "Selected from the Economic Philosophical Manuscripts." However, this is very hard to find and was only ever circulated in mimeographed form. The first French translation of the *Manuskripte* dates from 1962 and belongs to Émile Bottigelli. This too was preceded by an earlier manifestation, Jules Molitor's translation of Marx's writings (1927–37), which was not based on the MEGA I organization of the text and omitted the "first manuscript" altogether.
2. In this sense, this chapter does for Marx's *1844 Manuscripts* what Terrell Carver and Daniel Blank have done for the manuscripts written between 1845 and 1846, while Marx and Engels were in exile in Brussels, that came to be known as *The German Ideology*, in terms of both the political history through which these manuscripts were editorially fabricated so that they could represent a legitimate presentation of Marx's "theory of history" (2014b) and the analysis of the ways in which Marx's and Engels's thinking developed in duologue as they composed the so-called Feuerbach manuscripts (2014a). We thank one of the reviewers for having made this suggestion.
3. The original MEGA edition of Marx's works excluded his books of quotations (*Exzerpthefte*). In a report of 1923, their editor, David Riazanov questioned their significance: "Sometimes in reconsidering these Notebooks, the question arises: Why did he waste so much time on this systematic, fundamental summary, or expend so much labour as he spent as late as the year of 1881 on one basic book on geology, summarizing it chapter by chapter" (Riazanov quoted in Anderson 2010, 248). Riazanov would change his mind, however. In 1929 he recognized that the notebooks were worthy of publication. Given Marx's work method, they functioned very often as preparatory work and were therefore essential to tracing the genealogy of his critique of political economy. See Hecker (2002, 50–51).
4. Although notebooks may enable access to a creative process, their analysis is

fraught with ambiguity, and allowing for any conclusions, these will always be case specific. For a discussion of work of this type, see Biasi (1998).

5. As Margaret Fay puts it, with its three-column division, Notebook 1 represents "a consistent attempt to reorganize his source material and to draw conclusions implicit in Smith's work which Smith himself did not draw and which point beyond and contradict the analysis which Smith himself explicitly developed" (1983, 134).

6. This tactile quality lies behind Fay's suggestion that, to appreciate the design of the manuscripts, there is nothing better than a "Do It Yourself" approach (Fay 1983). Whether this is simply what Marx thought he was doing or what he effectively achieved is contested though (see Tribe 2014, 51–52).

7. Our reference to the figure of the artisan, rather than the artist, marks a departure from Gary Tedman's treatment of the manuscripts as "a work of art," in the manner of the "avant-garde visual artists." Although Tedman finds part of Marx's reading insightful, we believe his conclusion that "Marx must have been attempting to restructure his own material method of textual production in line with the results of his research" (2004, 440) to read too much into the form the manuscripts eventually took and to assume intentionality where we see experimentation.

8. For a sympathetic but in some aspects alternative reading of the meaning of this relationship between core and outer parts, see Tedman (2004).

9. The distinction is extracted from *Capital*, vol. 1 (Marx 1967, 19).

10. The selection was reissued two years later. The text appeared in German the same year.

11. In 1929 Riazanov's text was translated into French in two parts for *La Revue Marxiste*. The text reappeared the same year in a second Russian edition of the works of Marx and Engels, and in 1931, the German journal *Unter dem Banner des Marxismus* published the "Critique of the Hegelian Dialectic and Philosophy in General" for the first time in German.

12. Mayer was a leading figure in the Anti-Nazi movement in Germany in the mid-1930s, having been involved in the planning of an abortive SPD coup d'état in 1934. The classification of Landshut and Mayer as "political sociologists" may be somewhat reductive given its current meaning. Disciplinary areas were then less defined, and both had strong philosophical training and a keen interest in the history of political ideas, as their published work shows.

13. The editorial guidelines for the MEGA I are laid out in Hecker (1997).

14. Besides a failed attempt to date them: "probably written by Marx between the end of February 1844 and the end of August," whereas the current consensus is that Marx's work on the manuscripts did not begin until late May and was concluded by the end of August of 1844 (Musto 2009, 399–400).

15. "Forty-nine sideways folios, mostly written on both sides, which were not very professionally put together into one document—and in which a further 23 pages are left blank."

16. In the 1982 *Gesamtausgabe* edition, the three-column structure is maintained (189ff.). However, given the differences in the medium, the result is mixed and makes for a difficult reading. The original was written landscape on something similar to A4, where the 1982 edition is printed portrait and with a typeface larger than normal.

17. Whether Marx's concept of alienation has its source in a critique of philosophy (Hegel) or political economy (Smith) is a question we believe now settled in favor of the first

hypothesis. However, Gary Tedman is certainly right to point out that the inserted section heading "Estranged Labour" created the sense of the beginning of a "fresh subject, one now likely to be interpreted from a Hegelian or Feuerbachian position, rather than developing the concept of alienation directly from the more down-to-earth discussion of the three major economic categories of Adam Smith" (Tedman 2004, 436).

18. Tom Bottomore—in the introduction to *Karl Marx: Early Writings* (1964), which includes a translation of the first three manuscripts—reiterated Marcuse's "different subject" thesis in describing the form of notebook 1. Bottomore writes, "On page XII of the manuscript, however, Marx began to write on a different subject, ignoring the division of the pages into three columns; this portion of the manuscript was given the title 'Alienated Labor' by the editors of the MEGA" (1964, xvii). Whereas Marcuse and Bottomore see the inserted section heading as an apt editorial choice, which only comes to make Marx's intention clearer, Gary Tedman, following Fay, believes it muddles its inner logic: "The inserted section heading 'Estranged Labor' of the first notebooks is text that, in fact, flows from a logical progression of economic concepts developed in the core, but which is here separated" (Tedman 2004, 436).

19. Alexandre Kojève's 1933–39 lectures on Hegel's *Phenomenology of Spirit* at the École pratique des hautes études proved decisive in this regard.

20. In 1959 Daniel Bell commented on the renewed interest in Marx's early writings in France: "The French post-Stalinists, such as Lucien Goldmann or Edgar Morin, see in the idea of alienation a more sophisticated radical critique of contemporary society than the simplified and stilted Marxist analysis of class" (1962, 197). For an overview, see Poster (1975).

21. An early example is Boskoff (1972, 101–111).

22. The Milligan translation formed the basis of the 1964 International Publishers edition of the *1844 Manuscripts*, edited and generously introduced by the mathematician Dirk J. Struik. Struik would, however, intervene in the translation to improve its readability.

23. For instance, Max Weber is said to accept "the sociological conception of history as Marx had formulated it" (1956, 43), while G. H. Mead is portrayed as "one of the greatest American sociologists" in whose work "the influence of Marx is most apparent" (1956, 44) on the basis of an odd lecture he gave on the topic.

24. Struik draws the parallel between the two editions in terms of this omission and how class struggle is downplayed as a result (1964, 52–53).

25. For an analysis of the intellectual context of Bell's thinking at the time, see Brick (1986, 132–34).

26. In 1948 the Social Science Department of UNESCO sponsored the creation of professional associations in the social sciences—namely, economics, law, political science, and sociology. In the latter case, this led to the creation of the International Sociological Association (ISA). As the *1844 Manuscripts* began to circulate more widely in the Western world, Eastern bloc scholars took advantage of the death of Stalin and began to attend international conferences abroad. In the case of sociology, they accounted for 9 percent and 13 percent of those who attended ISA's World Congresses in 1956 and 1959, respectively (Platt 1998, 28). Although several Eastern and Western sociologists active at the time mentioned the first opportunity to meet colleagues from the other side

as a key part of their ISA experience, the fact remains that the theoretical-methodological orientations of their sociologies were distinctly opposed, with little or no real intellectual collaboration between the two groups.
27. This is not to say that sociology was the only academic discipline challenged by this renewed interest in Marx's ideas, by any means. But it does emphasize the singular character of Marx's sociological canonization as one of three founding fathers of the discipline. On the spread of Marxism in the American academy more generally, see Ollman and Vernoff (1982).
28. One explanation of Marx's sociological canonization in the late 1960s and early 1970s emphasizes contextual, societal-level factors such as the collapse of class-based politics and the emergence of new social movements—namely, in civil rights, the antiwar movement, and the student movements (Rex 1974, 2). The "radical sociology" proposed by the student movement in particular is said to have centered around Marx and Marxists (Horowitz 1971), thus contributing decisively to Marx's inclusion in the sociological canon (Connell 1997, 1522; Manza and McCarthy 2011, 157). Another explanation focuses on the intellectual opposition to mainstream sociology as embodied by Parsons's structural functionalism and its emphasis on consensus. One subtype of this kind of explanation emphasizes opposition to the empiricism of "mainstream sociology," as exemplified by Lazarsfeld and his associates in Columbia. This opposition gravitated around the critical theory of the Frankfurt school, whose attacks on positivist empirical sociology were inspired in the early Marx. The focus on the genealogy of the *1844 Manuscripts* cuts across both explanation.
29. See http://www.asanet.org/sites/default/files/1965_annual_meeting_program.pdf. An evening session on the first day offered a reevaluation of Karl Marx with observations advanced by X. N. Momdjian, a representative of the Soviet Academy of Sciences; T. B. Bottomore, Simon Fraser University, Vancouver, BC; Talcott Parsons of Harvard; and Lewis A. Coser of Brandeis University. The 60th Annual Meeting of the American Sociological Association was held in the Edgewater Beach Hotel from August 30 to September 2, 1965
30. This cohort of graduate students has come to be known as the "disobedient generation" (Sica and Turner 2005). Their engagement with Marx illustrated the cleavage between the "hard left" and the "soft left" (McAdam 2007, 416)—that is, orthodox Marxism and "Western Marxism." Michael Burawoy became an "instant convert" of the structuralist Marx while studying with Adam Przeworski, a member of the Analytical Marxism movement, in Chicago in 1973 (Burawoy 2005a, 57). By contrast, Jeffrey C. Alexander presented New Left Marxism's insights that the objective only seems so, while the political and the economic are infused with subjectivity, as lifelong lessons (2005, 42).
31. The other two were Robert K. Merton and Paul Lazarsfeld.
32. In which resistance comes not from the *populus*, as a subordinate social class, but from the *plebes*, a political category of those who remain outside the community while holding the ultimate political prerogative: the power to constitute a community anew (see also Vatter 2012).

CHAPTER 4

1. Charles Lemert has observed that Du Bois is now considered to be a founder of cultural studies (namely,

a pioneer in the sense that culture is always necessarily *cultures*, an unsettled plurality), and *Souls* is "a kind of manifesto before the fact of a general theory of culture as cultures" (2006, 73) "is at heart a work of social theory, if not sociology outright—a politics of difference in the form of a cultural deception" (83).

2. On the absence of *Souls* in sociology textbooks on race, see, for example, Feagin (1978 [repr. 1996, 1999]) and Healey (1995)—hence Elijah Anderson's complaint about it being "possible to advance through a graduate program in sociology in this country without ever hearing about Du Bois'" (1995, xiv). This, of course, changed markedly in the 2000s. See, for example, Bush (2007).

3. The Open Library website offers a near comprehensive listing, with some available online in digital form (https://openlibrary.org/works/OL28577W/The_Souls_of_Black_folk#editions, last accessed December 1, 2016). See also the "selected publication history" compiled by M. Elaine Hughes (2003).

4. It was Francis Fisher Browne who insisted that Du Bois keep to his original plan for *Souls* and included as its final chapter, "The Sorrow Songs," now understood as one of its most powerful chapters and its *clef de voûte*, or that which brings the whole work together.

5. Du Bois reports having been approached by the Brownes, father and son.

6. Both Booker T. Washington and Du Bois understood "biography" to be a means to make a claim to black leadership. Their fight over Frederick Douglass's legacy resulted in competitive bids to write his biography for publisher George W. Jacobs and Company for their series *The American Crisis Biographies*. Washington eventually won the bid, and Du Bois was left to write the biography of John Brown.

7. Notably on life and labor in Dougherty County in chapter 8, "Of the Quest of the Golden Fleece." We thank one of the reviewers for having made this suggestion.

8. We thank one of our reviewers for this suggestion.

9. This was Du Bois's original church affiliation.

10. For the black intelligentsia affording the status of sacred book to *Souls*, see Rampersad (1985, 67).

11. In *Lines of Descent*, Kwame Anthony Appiah perceptively detects the influence of the romantic nationalism of Johann Gottfried Herder behind Du Bois's quotations in *Souls*—not only of German high culture but also of its folk culture, as a German folk song is cited at the end of the book (2004, 46–47). See also Zamir (1995, 172).

12. On different aspects of this dialectic, see Howard Winant (2004). See also Cornel West on the "dialectic of black self-recognition" (1982).

13. In his posthumously published *Autobiography*, Du Bois expands on the sense of "two-ness," which he now treats as a conflict of affections and loyalties: "I began to feel that dichotomy which all my life has characterized my thought: how far can love for my oppressed race accord with love for the oppressing country? And when these loyalties diverge, where shall my soul find refuge?" (1968, 169). This was not Du Bois's only autobiographical work. An earlier work using autobiographical information was *Darkwater*, first published in 1920. *Dusk of Dawn*, which came out in 1940, is also partly based on personal experience.

14. "Of the Sorrow Songs" made it into the final text on the insistence of Francis Fisher Browne, Du Bois's editor at A. C. McClurg. The essay was part of Du Bois's original plan for the book, but Du Bois seems to have toyed

with the idea of dropping it from the collection.

15. This German translation would not succeed owing to the poor health of Else von Richthofen, the translator Weber had arranged (see letter from Weber to Du Bois of March 30, 1905, in Aptheker 1973; see also Weber, Ploetz, and Du Bois 1973). The first translation of *Souls* into German appeared only in 2003, a hundred years after its original publication (see Du Bois 2003). This translation seems to have positively contributed to, or at least reinforced, current interest around Du Bois's work in Germany. See, for example, Bös (2015).

16. This term was coined by Du Bois in *Dusk of Dawn* (2011, 73–76) as a critique of the financial control Booker T. Washington exerted over black newspapers and periodicals, which discouraged criticism of Washington's views and policy preferences. We thank one of our reviewers for having made this suggestion.

17. See the review by C. F. G. Masterman in the *London Daily News* (Aptheker 1977).

18. Cincinnati, the black *Ohio Enterprise*, edited by Wendell Phillips Dabney, versus the *Nashville American*.

19. This would cost $1,293.06 in 2018 dollars.

20. This would cost $47.22 in 2018 dollars.

21. See "Howard Fast," accessed December 1, 2016, Trussel.com, http://www.trussel.com/hf/blueheron.htm.

22. There was another 1953 edition of *Souls* published by Fawcett.

23. Comprising a total of thirty-five volumes, this editorial project took twelve years to complete. A facsimile reproduction of the 1953 Blue Heron Press edition of Du Bois's book appears in the second volume of the *Collected Published Works* (1973) with a new introduction by Aptheker.

24. For patterns of citation of Du Bois up to the late 1960s, see Green and Driver (1976, 320–25).

25. In 1978, Aptheker published the three-volume *Correspondence of W. E. B. Du Bois*, the first collection of the correspondence of any black American.

26. See also Rudwick (1957) for a largely negative assessment of the methodological achievements of the Atlanta school. See Wright (2006) for a rebuttal.

27. As for Stuart Hall and British sociology, William Outhwaite has no doubts about placing him in "the cluster of immigrants who fundamentally shaped British sociology and social theory in the second half of the 20th century" (2009, 1035).

28. Similarly, Appiah suggests that Du Bois's effort to make sense of the particular and universal meanings of blackness can be traced back to German sources—namely, Herder (Appiah 2004, 46–51).

29. The origin of the concept of double consciousness is widely debated. Gilroy's critique is directed specifically at Cornel West. Besides William James's social psychology, Goethe, Emerson, Herder, Sojourner Truth, and Schopenhauer have all been deemed possible sources (see West 1989, 147; Rampersad 1990, 74–75; D. Lewis 1993, 282–83. Dickson 1992; Early 1993, xvii–xxii; Gates 1989, xviii–xxii; Appiah 2004). A recuperation of Du Bois for sociology was attempted in the 1990s through an exploration of this pragmatist lineage and Du Bois's critical contribution in his "theory of the self." See, for example, Lemert (1994), Sullivan (2003, 206), King (2008, 135), and Kahn (2009). For a skeptical view, see Moses (2004).

30. Although Gibson does stress the expressiveness and rhetorical qualities of *Souls*, offering an insightful analysis of its chief metaphors (the veil, double

consciousness, second sight) and their role in eliciting cognitive-affective judgment, he is far more reserved about centering exclusively on the text's "literariness": "*Souls* is not a *literary* text per se, though it has literary qualities" (Gibson 1989, xxxv; his emphasis).

31. On writing as a political act, see Gates (1984, 5).

## CHAPTER 5

1. "The importing," Parsons explained, "consisted of focusing the attention of American sociology in the nineteen-thirties on two great European social theorists, Max Weber and Émile Durkheim, who, though very different, tended to think in grand theoretical terms. Until then, American sociologists, with one or two important exceptions, had been concerned mainly with empirical studies of rather localized phenomena" (Reinhold 1973, 80).
2. Our claim here stands closer to the more hermeneutical strand of the so-called new Weber studies, which use detailed historical reconstructions to address questions pertaining to the sociology of translation, the sociology of knowledge, and the sociology of academic disciplines (e.g., Ghosh 2014; Chalcraft 2008).
3. In their study of the process of publication and reception of Weber's *The Protestant Ethic*, Swatos and Kivisto (2005) show that translators, reviewers, and commentators acted as gatekeepers to Weberian sociology in the United States. Likewise, Connell argues that "the process of translation is an important index of the formation of a canon" (1997, 1543) but says nothing about the intricacies of the translation process itself. Ricoeur, on the contrary, has a lot to say about translation as an interpretative act. This is why we follow Ricoeur in this regard.
4. The dissertation survives today in the Harvard University Archives, Papers of Talcott Parsons, 1921–79 (hereafter HUGFP), 42.8.2, box 1.
5. This is contrary to what Uta Gerhardt suggests. See Gerhardt (2011, 69).
6. This was a requirement for obtaining the doctorate in philosophy, which Parsons would eventually be awarded in April 1929. The best description of these events is in Gerhardt (2011, 71–72).
7. HUGFP 42.8.2, box 2.
8. Parsons was asked "to give the students [of his introductory course on principles of economics] some acquaintance with the doctrines of German sociologists and some knowledge of the developments of social institutions in Europe since the industrial revolution" in "Memorandum re. work of Parsons, from Professor Meriam to President Olds," HUGFP 42.8.2, box 2 (p. 71).
9. Parsons returned to Heidelberg and met Marianne Weber. On June 26, 1927, this crucial facilitator wrote, "Dear Mr. Parsons! I would like to invite you to come to my house for tea at 5 o'clock this coming Sunday, 26th. We shall then also talk about your proposal for translation, which I have passed on to the publisher some time ago." HUGFP 42.8.2, box 2.
10. There is a single essay, what we might call the "original" *Protestant Ethic*, which was published in German in two parts in 1904–5 in the *Archiv für Sozialwissenschaft und Sozialpolitik*, of which Max Weber was principal coeditor. Unfortunately, to complicate matters, the 1904 volume bore the date 1905. In 1906, Weber published an additional essay on organized religion in North America in two different German periodicals. During the years 1907–10, two critiques of the essays

appeared in Germany, to which Weber also responded in the *Archiv*. These have become known as his "anticritical remarks." In 1919, Weber reedited the 1904–5 and 1906 essays as a whole, and in 1920, they were published in the first part of a three-volume collection of studies on the world's religions (Swatos and Kivisto 2005, xiii). Contrary to Weber's claim in the first footnote to the second edition that he had not altered any sentence that contained any essential point, there are actually numerous and enough substantial changes to alter the meaning of the text. Lichtblau and Weiss (1993) have identified no fewer than 448 differences between the two versions, including both inserts in the main text and additional footnotes.

11. The second edition of *The Protestant Ethic* is included in Weber's *Collected Essays in the Sociology of Religion*. Besides *The Protestant Ethic* and the essay on Protestant sects, this collection contains the studies of the *Economic Ethics of the World Religions*. These texts were taken apart and published separately when translated into English, severing them from the theoretical essays in which they were originally embedded. The introduction to the *Economic Ethics of the World Religions* and the theoretical chapter explaining the transition from Chinese to Indian religions were published separately. The major substantive studies have been published as *The Religion of China*, *The Religion of India*, and *Ancient Judaism* as if they were independent monographs. Readers were barely aware that they originally belonged to a series of studies entitled the *Economic Ethics of the World Religions*. Moreover, in order to fit *The Protestant Ethic* into this new context, Weber wrote an introduction, translated as the "Author's Introduction," which attempted to explain how these different studies fit together (Riesebrodt 2005, 24–25).

12. Scaff suggests a total of nine people read and commented on Parsons's "sample translation": Stanley Unwin himself, three anonymous in-house reviewers, two professional translators, R. H. Tawney, Oskar Siebeck, and Marianne Weber (Scaff 2006, 75–77).

13. Letter of September 24, 1928, to Stanley Unwin, HUGFP 42.8.2 box 2.

14. Bruce Wearne, who tends to focus on the ideational dimension of this process, overlooks this crucial aspect. Wearne writes, "Parsons' interpretative involvement in the writings qua translator, secondary analyst and critical theorist led him to conclude that '*The Protestant Ethic*' is in many ways of central significance for Weber's philosophy of history" (1989, 53).

15. Unsurprisingly, the "postmodern Weber" of the 1980s, a product of the revival of interest in Nietzsche (e.g., Stauth and Turner 1988), is fundamentally pessimistic.

16. In the first three years, it sold only 1,009 copies. The governing director of Allen and Unwin wrote to J. C. B. Mohr (Paul Siebeck) in Tübingen on July 30, 1934, "The total sales up to the end of last year were 409 copies, apart from 600 sold at a reduced price in sheets to an American publisher [Scribner's], thus making the total sales up to 31st December last 1,009. There is now very little demand for the book, and it is unlikely that we shall ever sell as many as 2,500 copies." Collection Max Weber-Schaefer, Bavarian State Library, Munich.

17. Uta Gerhardt writes, "After World War II, the book became a bestseller, with a second printing in 1948, a third in 1950, and a fourth in 1952" (2011, 62). Gerhardt's mistake was to confuse reprints with sales. Archival research undertaken at the George Allen and Unwin Archive (hereafter GAUA),

University of Reading, United Kingdom, however, shows that such reprints often did not exceed 750 copies each. Scribner's editor ordered 750 copies of *The Protestant Ethic* from Stanley Unwin (letter, May 26, 1950, GAUA). As proof of their appreciation of the continuing collaboration in publishing this title, Unwin suggested having the book published as a "joint imprint" with both publishing houses named on the title page and the jackets (letter, June 27, 1950, GAUA). On March 17, 1952, Scribner's ordered another one thousand copies (letter, April 2, 1952, GAUA). Far from being a best seller, by the late 1950s, the book was selling so poorly that it was on the verge of going out of print—this *despite* the wave of new translations of Weber's works of the 1950s (Gerhardt 2011, 63n29). The steady decline of sales of Weber's book reported by Allen and Unwin in 1958 suggests these new translations had little or no immediate effect in increasing market interest in Weber.

18. See HUGFP 42.8.8, box 11.
19. The theoretical attack on Parsons's Weber, of course, cannot be fully (or even primarily) attributed to Giddens. Crucial in this regard was, for instance, the highly influential essay "De-Parsonizing Weber: A Critique of Parsons' Interpretation of Weber's Sociology" (Cohen, Hazelrigg, and Pope 1975), in which the authors mount a devastating attack on Parsons's choices as translator and his work as theorist. To this, characteristically, Parsons replied in kind (Parsons 1975).
20. The 1958 edition and the paperback editions from the 1960s were technically reprints of the original 1930 edition with the exception of the new preface by Parsons and some new graphic features.
21. Decisive in this regard were two books in which Giddens framed Weber's contributions in a radically different way from Parsons. The first is Giddens's *Capitalism and Social Theory* (1971), which "officially" identified Marx, Weber, and Durkheim as thinkers who established foundational frameworks for contemporary sociology despite the seemingly arbitrary nature of this choice. The second was Giddens's 1972 *Politics and Sociology in the Thought of Max Weber*. Giddens would eventually be accompanied in his interpretation by figures such as Michael Mann and Randall Collins, the eminent Weberian expert and editor of the second Roxbury edition of *The Protestant Ethic* (1998).

CHAPTER 6

1. For a reconstruction of this process, see Schleifer (2012).
2. Letter from Salomon to Knopf, March 26, 1945, University of Texas, Harry Ransom Humanities Research Center, Alfred A. Knopf, Inc. Papers (hereafter KA).
3. Meanwhile, the list extends to include the United States and Italy. See Mayer (1939, 149–54).
4. He also explores a stronger and more direct influence of Tocqueville on Georges Sorel (J.-P. Mayer 1939, 147).
5. After all, both left the problem of the political elite unsolved (J.-P. Mayer 1939, 158–61).
6. On Sorel's reading of Tocqueville as a fellow critic of Jacobinism and modernity, see Audier (2004, 26–30).
7. For a full account of the overlooked resurgence of interest in Tocqueville in West Germany from the late 1940s onward, see Steber (2015).
8. See Mayer's preface to the French abridged version of *Democracy in America* (1968, 41).
9. Letter to Knopf, January 24, 1946, KA.
10. The correspondence between Dwiggins and Knopf concerning this edition is in KA, box 732, folder 5.

11. Letter from Knopf to Bradley, January 16, 1951, KA.
12. One such reprint is from 1954. The book sold at 95 cents per volume (i.e., $8.90 in 2018) with a 5 percent royalty for Knopf on copies sold in the United States (KA).
13. On Laski's conception of the state, see Silva (2009, 367). We thank one of our reviewers for raising this point.
14. Letter to Hatcher, New York branch of OUP, September 7, 1944, Oxford University Press Archives, Oxford University Press, Oxford (hereafter OUPA).
15. As Jean-Claude Lamberti rightly puts it, "Severed from knowledge of the suffering and failure of revolution in Europe, reflection upon American democracy is likely to degenerate into utopian mythmaking, singing the praises of the 'blessed republic'... encourag[ing] belief in American exceptionalism while discouraging the use of comparative methods in political science" (1989, 2).
16. The balance on April 1, 1960, was 20,829 (OUPA).
17. Letter to OUP, New York, February 21, 1961 (OUPA).
18. Colwell comments on the excision of the three races chapter as follows: "This chapter is either omitted from most of the popular one-volume editions of *Democracy in America* or is abridged to leave out all mention of the Negro" (1967, 95). See also Salomon (1959), Resh (1963), Clignet (2001), and Janara (2004).
19. For more details on Salomon, see C. Mayer (2008).
20. A complete list of Mayer's works is available at "Mayer, Jacob Peter (1903–1992)," IdRef (Identifants et Référentiels pour l'Enseignement supérieur et la Recherche), accessed December 1, 2016, http://www.idref.fr/027019918.
21. Aron is one of the scholars Lerner thanks for offering critical comments on his introduction to the Mayer-Lerner edition (1966, lxxxiii).
22. According to Collins's law of small numbers, "the number of active schools of thought which reproduce themselves for more than one or two generations in an argumentative community is on the order of three to six" (1998, 81).
23. For the view that in terms of its analysis, the book does not owe much to Tocqueville, see Baltzell (1986, 803).
24. Elster, in particular, polemically dismisses Tocqueville's relevance as a "major political thinker" while he mines his work for "exportable causal mechanisms" that may enhance our social-scientific toolkit. With this appropriative project, he moves Tocqueville away from political philosophy and firmly into the territory of contemporary explanatory political science (2009, 1, 9).
25. Although ISA members were asked to list "five books published in the twentieth century which were most influential in their work as sociologists," several books published in the nineteenth century were listed (e.g., Marx's 1867 *Capital*). *Democracy in America* was not one of them. See "Books of the XX Century," International Sociological Association, https://www.isa-sociology.org/en/about-isa/history-of-isa/books-of-the-xx-century.
26. Mansfield and Winthrop's was not the only new translation to appear in 2000. Historian James T. Schleifer produced his own translation of *Democracy in America*, edited by Eduardo Nolla and published by the Liberty Fund, in an authoritative four-volume bilingual set, which used as its template Nolla's French critical edition of Tocqueville's text (Nolla 1990). Still in 2000, Stephen D. Grant translated *Democracy in America* for Hackett Classics in a heavily abridged edition introduced by Sanford Kessler. Since then, two more English translations

have appeared, clearly demonstrating that the Tocqueville industry is in full swing—Gerald Bevan's translation for the Penguin Classics edition of 2003 (introduced by Isaac Kramnick) and Arthur Goldhammer's translation for the Library of America edition of 2004.

27. Even Crain concedes that "Mansfield and Winthrop do not make the case for a neocon Tocqueville to their readers" (2001).

28. A somewhat revised paperback Anchor Books edition of this translation soon followed in 1969.

# REFERENCES

For additional bibliographical information on *The Elementary Forms of Religious Life*, the *1844 Economic and Philosophic Manuscripts*, *The Souls of Black Folk*, *The Protestant Ethic*, and *Democracy in America*, please see the List of Editions Consulted given below.

PUBLISHED MATERIALS

Abbott, Andrew. 1999. *Department and Discipline: Chicago Sociology at One Hundred*. Chicago: University of Chicago Press.

Abbott, James R. 2007. "Whither Tocqueville in American Sociology?" *American Sociologist* 38:60–77.

Adorno, Theodor. 2005. *Minima Moralia: Reflections from Damaged Life*. Translated by E. F. N. Jephcott. London: Verso.

Alexander, Claire. 2009. "Stuart Hall and 'Race.'" *Cultural Studies* 23:457–82

Alexander, Jeffrey C. 1982–83. *Theoretical Logic in Sociology*. 4 vols. Berkeley: University of California Press.

——. 1987. *Twenty Lectures: Sociological Theory Since World War II*. New York: Columbia University Press.

——. 1988. *Durkheimian Sociology: Cultural Studies*. Edited by Jeffrey C. Alexander. Cambridge: Cambridge University Press.

——. 1989. "Sociology and Discourse: On the Centrality of the Classics." In *Structure and Meaning*, edited by Jeffrey C. Alexander, 8–67. New York: Columbia University Press.

——. 1996. "On Choosing One's Intellectual Predecessors: The Reductionism of Camic's Treatment of Parsons and the Institutionalists." *Sociological Theory* 14:154–71.

——. 2001. "Editor's Introduction: Canons, Discourses, and Research Programs; Plurality, Progress and Competition in Classical, Modern, and Contemporary Sociology." In *Mainstream and Critical Social Theory: Classical, Modern and Contemporary*, edited by Jeffrey C. Alexander, i–xlvii. London: Sage.

——. 2005. "The Sixties and Me: From Cultural Revolution to Cultural Theory." In *The Disobedient Generation*, edited by Alan Sica and Stephen Turner, 37–47. Chicago: University of Chicago Press.

——. 2008. "Iconic Consciousness: The Material of Meaning." *Environment and Planning D: Society and Space* 26:782–94.

———. 2010. *The Performance of Politics: Obama's Victory and the Democratic Struggle for Power*. New York: Oxford University Press.

Alexander, Jeffrey C., and Giuseppe Sciortino. 1996. "On Choosing One's Intellectual Predecessors: The Reductionism of Camic's Treatment of Parsons and the Institutionalists." *Sociological Theory* 14:154–71.

Alexander, Jeffrey C., and Philip Smith. 2001. "The Strong Program in Cultural Theory: Elements of a Structural Hermeneutics." In *Handbook of Sociological Theory*, edited by Jonathan H. Turner, 135–50. New York: Kluwer Academic.

———, eds. 2005. *The Cambridge Companion to Durkheim*. Cambridge: Cambridge University Press.

Almond, G., and S. Verba. 1963. *The Civic Culture: Political Attitudes and Democracy in Five Nations*. Princeton: Princeton University Press.

Alpert, Harry. 1939. *Emile Durkheim and His Sociology*. New York: Columbia University Press.

Althusser, Louis. 1964. "Marxism and Humanism." *Cahiers de l'I.S.E.A.*, June 1964.

———. 1969. *For Marx*. Harmondsworth: Penguin. First published 1965.

———. 1995. Appendix to "Réponse à une critique." In *Écrits philosophiques et politiques* book 2, edited and introduced by François Matheron. Paris: Éditions Stock/IMEC. First published 1963.

Anderson, Elijah. 1995. Introduction to *The Philadelphia Negro: A Social Study*, by W. E. B. Du Bois, i–xx. Philadelphia: University of Pennsylvania Press. First published 1899.

Anderson, Kevin B. 2010. *Marx at the Margins: On Nationalism, Ethnicity, and Non-Western Societies*. Chicago: University of Chicago Press.

Anderson, William. 1945. "Tocqueville, Alexis de. *Democracy in America*." *Annals of the American Academy of Political and Social Science* 242:182–83.

Andrews, William, ed. 1985. Introduction to *Critical Essays on W. E. B. Du Bois*, 1–20. Boston: G. K. Hall.

Appelrouth, Scott, and Laura Edles. 2008. *Classical and Contemporary Sociological Theory: Text and Readings*. Los Angeles: Pine Forge.

Appiah, Kwame Anthony. 2004. *Lines of Descent*. Princeton: Princeton University Press.

Aptheker, Herbert, ed. 1973. *Collected Published Works of W. E. B. Du Bois*. Millwood, NY: Kraus-Thomson.

———. 1973–78. *The Correspondence of W. E. B. Du Bois*. Edited by Herbert Aptheker. 3 vols. Amherst: University of Massachusetts Press.

———. 1977. *Book Reviews of W. E. B. Du Bois*. Edited by Herbert Aptheker. Millwood, NY: Kraus-Thomson.

———. 1989. *The Literary Legacy of W. E. B. Du Bois*. White Plains, NY: Kraus International.

Aron, Raymond. 1959. "Relativism in History." In *The Philosophy of History in Our Time: An Anthology*, edited by Hans Meyerhoff, 153–61. Garden City: Doubleday.

———. 1967. *The Main Currents of Sociological Thought*. Vol. 2, *Durkheim, Pareto, Weber*. New York: Basic Books.

———. 1979. "Tocqueville Retrouvé." *The Tocqueville Review / La Revue Tocqueville* 1:8–23.

Ashley, David, and David Orenstein. 2005. *Sociological Theory: Classical Statements*. 6th ed. Boston: Pearson Books.

Audier, Serge. 2004. *Tocqueville retrouvé: Genèse et enjeux du renouveau tocquevillien français*. Paris: Vrin.

Bachiocchi, Stéphane, and Jean-Louis Fabiani. 2012. "Durkheim's Lost Argument (1895–1955): Critical Moves on Method and Truth." *Durkheimian Studies* 18:19–40.

Baehr, Peter. 2002. *Founders, Classics, Canons: Modern Disputes over the Origins and Appraisal of Sociology's Heritage*. New Brunswick: Transaction.

Baert, Patrick. 2012. "Positioning Theory and Intellectual Interventions." *Journal for the Theory of Social Behavior* 42:304–24.

Baert, Patrick, and Filipe Carreira da Silva. 2010. *Social Theory in the Twentieth Century and Beyond*. Cambridge: Polity.

Baltzell, Edward Digby. 1962. *American Business Aristocracy*. New York: Collier Books.

———. 1964. *The Protestant Establishment: Aristocracy and Caste in America*. New York: Random House.

———. 1986. "Review of *Habits of the Heart*, by Robert Bellah et al." *Social Forces* 64:802–4.

Barad, Karen. 2003. "Posthumanist Performativity: Toward an Understanding of How Matter Comes to Matter." *Signs* 28:801–31.

Baudrillard, Jean. 1970. *La Société de Consommation: Ses mythes, ses structures*. Foreword by J.-P. Mayer. Paris: Gallimard.

Becker, Howard S. 1963. *Outsiders*. New York: Free Press.

Bell, Daniel. 1960. *The End of Ideology*. Glencoe: Free Press.

———. 1962. "The Debate on Alienation." In *Revisionism: Essays on the History of Marxist Ideas*, edited by Leopold Labedz, 195–211. London: George Allen and Unwin.

Bell, Monica. 2016. "Sociology's Truth? W. E. B. Du Bois and the Origins of Sociology." *Los Angeles Review of Books*, September 2, 2016.

Bellah, Robert N. 1967. "Civil Religion in America." *Daedalus* 96:1–21.

Bendix, Reinhard. 1952. "Social Stratification and Political Power." *American Political Science Review* 46:357–75.

———. 1964. *Nation-Building and Citizenship: Studies of Our Changing Social Order*. New York: John Wiley and Sons.

Berman, Marshall. 1999. *Adventures in Marxism*. London: Verso.

Besnard, Philippe. 1979. "La formation de l'équipe de L'Année sociologique." *Revue française de sociologie* 20:7–31.

———. 1982. "Review of *Durkheim et le politique*." *Revue française de sociologie* 23:127–30.

———. 1983. *The Sociological Domain: The Durkheimians and the Founding of French Sociology*. Edited by Philippe Besnard. Cambridge: Cambridge University Press.

Bhambra, Gurminder K. 2014. "A Sociological Dilemma: Race, Segregation and US Sociology." *Current Sociology* 62:472–92.

Biasi, Pierre-Marc de. 1998. "Qu'est-ce qu'un brouillon? Le cas Flaubert: Essai de typologie fonctionnelle des documents de genèse." In *Pourquoi la critique génétique? Méthodes, theories*, edited by Michel Contât and Daniel Ferrer, 31–60. Paris: CNRS Éditions.

Binkley, W. E. 1945. "Review: America Through French Eyes." *Scientific Monthly* 61:494–95.

Birnbaum, Pierre. 1976. "La Conception Durkheimienne de l'Etat: L'Apolitisme des Fonctionnaires." *Revue française de sociologie* 17:247–58.

Blau, Peter M. 1960. "Structural Effects." *American Sociological Review* 25:178–93.

Blight, David W., and Robert Gooding-Williams, eds. 1997. *The Souls of Black Folk*. Reprint of 1903 ed. Bedford Cultural Editions. Boston: Bedford/St. Martin's.

Blumer, Herbert. 1937. "Social Psychology." In *Man and Society: A Substantial Introduction to the Social Sciences*, edited by E. Schmidt, 144–98. New York: Prentice Hall.

———. 1966. "Sociological Implications of the Thought of G. H. Mead."

*American Journal of Sociology* 71:535–44.
———. 1969. *Symbolic Interactionism: Perspective and Method*. Berkeley: University of California Press.
———. 1980. "Mead and Blumer: The Convergent Methodological Perspectives of Social Behaviorism and Symbolic Interactionism." *American Sociological Review* 45:409–19.
Borlandi, Massimo. 2012. "Présentation. Émile Durkheim: *Les Formes élémentaires de la vie religieuse*, un siècle après." *L'Année sociologique* 62:283–88.
Bös, Mathias. 2015. *Rasse und Ethnizität: Zur Problemgeschichte zweier Begriffe in der amerikanischen Soziologie*. Wiesbaden: Springer Verlag.
Boskoff, Alvin. 1972. *The Mosaic of Sociological Theory*. New York: Thomas Y. Crowell.
Bottomore, Tom B. 1963. *Karl Marx: Early Writings*. London: London: Watts & Co.
———, ed. 1964. *Karl Marx: Early Writings*. New York: McGraw-Hill Paperbacks.
———. 1984. *Sociology and Socialism*. New York: St. Martin's.
———. 2012. "Karl Marx: Sociologist or Marxist?" In *Sociology as Social Criticism*, 72–84. London: Routledge. First published 1966.
Bottomore, Tom, and M. Rubel. 1956. *Karl Marx: Selected Writings in Sociology and Social Philosophy*. London: London: Watts & Co.
Boudon, Raymond. 2006. *Tocqueville for Today*. Oxford: Bardwell.
Bourdieu, Pierre. 1991. "Epilogue: On the Possibility of a Field of World Sociology." In *Social Theory for a Changing World*, edited by Pierre Bourdieu and James S. Coleman, 373–87. Boulder: Westview.
Bradley, Phillips. 1937. "A Century of Democracy in America." *Journal of Adult Education* 9:14–22.
———. 1939a. "Review of *Tocqueville and Beaumont in America*, by George Wilson Pierson." *Annals of the American Academy of Political and Social Science* 201:271–72.
———. 1939b. "Review of *Tocqueville and Beaumont in America*, by George Wilson Pierson." *American Political Science Review* 33:107–8.
———, ed. 1945. Introduction to *Democracy in America*, by Alexis de Tocqueville. Based on the Henry Reeve translation as revised by Francis Bowen. 2 vols. New York: Vintage Books.
Brick, Howard. 1986. *Daniel Bell and the Decline of Intellectual Radicalism: Social Theory and Political Reconciliation in the 1940s*. Madison: University of Wisconsin Press.
———. 1993. "The Reformist Dimension of Talcott Parsons's Early Social Theory." In *The Culture of the Market*, edited by Thomas Haskell and Richard Teichgraeber III, 357–96. Cambridge: Cambridge University Press.
Bulmer, Martin. 1991. "W. E. B. Du Bois as a Social Investigator: *The Philadelphia Negro*, 1899." In *The Social Survey in Historical Perspective, 1880–1940*, edited by Martin Bulmer, Kevin Bales, and Kathryn Kish Sklar, 170–87. New York: Cambridge University Press.
Burawoy, Michael. 1982. "Introduction: The Resurgence of Marxism in American Sociology." *American Journal of Sociology* 88:S1–S30.
———. 2005a. "Antinomian Marxist." In *The Disobedient Generation*, edited by Alan Sica and Stephen Turner, 48–71. Chicago: University of Chicago Press.
———. 2005b. "The Return of the Repressed: Recovering the Public Face of U.S. Sociology, One Hundred Years On." *Annals of the American Academy of Political and Social Science* 600:68–85.
Bush, Melanie. 2007. "United Statesians: The Nationalism of Empire." In *Handbook of the Sociology of Racial and Ethnic Relations*, edited by Joe Feagin and Hernan Vera, 285–18. New York: Springer.

Callon, Michel. 1998. *The Laws of the Markets*. Edited by Michel Callon. New York: Blackwell.

Camic, Charles. 1987. "The Making of a Method: A Historical Reinterpretation of the Early Parsons." *American Sociological Review* 52:421–39.

———. 1991. "Introduction: Talcott Parsons Before *The Structure of Social Action*." In *Talcott Parsons: The Early Essays*, edited by Charles Camic, ix–lxix. Chicago: University of Chicago Press.

———. 1995. "Three Departments in Search of a Discipline: Localism and Interdisciplinary Interaction in American Sociology, 1890–1940." *Social Research* 62:1003–33.

———. 1997. *Reclaiming the Sociological Classics: The State of the Scholarship*. Oxford: Blackwell.

———. 2005. "From Amherst to Heidelberg." In *After Parsons*, edited by Renée Fox, Victor Lidz, and Harold Bershady, 240–63. New York: Russell Sage.

———. 2008. "Classics in What Sense?" *Social Psychology Quarterly* 71:324–30.

Camic, Charles, and Hans Joas, eds. 2003. *The Dialogical Turn: New Roles for Sociology in the Postdisciplinary Age*. Lanham: Rowman and Littlefield.

Carver, Terrell, and Daniel Blank. 2014a. *Marx and Engels's "German Ideology" Manuscripts*. Basingstoke: Palgrave Macmillan.

———. 2014b. *A Political History of the Editions of Marx and Engels's "German Ideology Manuscripts."* Basingstoke: Palgrave Macmillan.

Centre for Contemporary Cultural Studies. 1982. *The Empire Strikes Back: Race and Racism in 70s Britain*. London: Hutchinson.

Chalcraft, David. 2008. "Why Hermeneutics, the Text(s) and the Biography of the Work Matter in Max Weber Studies." In *Max Weber Matters*, edited by David Chalcraft, Fanon Howell, Marisol Menendez, and Hector Vera, 17–40. Farnham: Ashgate.

Chartier, Roger. 1994. *The Order of Books*. Cambridge: Polity. First published 1992.

Cladis, Mark S. 1992. *A Communitarian Defense of Liberalism: Émile Durkheim and Contemporary Social Theory*. Stanford: Stanford University Press.

———. 1999. *Durkheim and Foucault: Perspectives on Education and Punishment*. Oxford: Berghahn.

———. 2001. Introduction to *Elementary Forms of Religious Life*, by Émile Durkheim, vii–xxxv. Translated by Carol Cosman. Oxford: Oxford University Press.

Clark, Terry N. 1968. "Émile Durkheim and the Institutionalization of Sociology in the French University System." *European Journal of Sociology* 9:37–71.

———. 1973. *Prophets and Patrons: The French University and the Emergence of the Social Sciences*. Cambridge: Harvard University Press.

Clignet, Remi. 2001. "The Contributions of Beaumont to Democracy in America: His Analysis of Race Relations and Slavery." *American Studies International* 39:34–52.

Cohen, Jere, Lawrence E. Hazelrigg, and Whitney Pope. 1975. "De-Parsonizing Weber: A Critique of Parsons' Interpretation of Weber's Sociology." *American Sociological Review* 40, no. 2 (April): 229–41.

Collins, Patricia Hill. 1986. "Learning from the Outsider Within: The Sociological Significance of Black Feminist Thought." *Social Problems* 33:14–32.

———. 2016. "Du Bois's Contested Legacy." *Ethnic and Racial Studies* 39:1398–1406.

Collins, Randall. 1998. *The Sociology of Philosophies: A Global Theory of Intellectual Change*. Cambridge: Harvard University Press.

———. 2005. "The Durkheimian Movement in France and in World Sociology." In *The*

*Cambridge Companion to Durkheim*, edited by Jeffrey C. Alexander and Philip Smith, 101–35. Cambridge: Cambridge University Press.

Colwell, James L. 1967. "'The Calamities Which They Apprehend': Tocqueville on Race in America." *Western Humanities Review* 21:93–100.

Commager, Henry Steele, ed. 1946. Introduction to *Democracy in America*, by Alexis de Tocqueville. Translated by Henry Reeve. Abr. ed. London: Oxford University Press.

———. 1950. *The American Mind*. New Haven: Yale University Press.

Connell, R. W. 1997. "Why Is Classical Theory Classical?" *American Journal of Sociology* 102:1511–57.

Cook, Gary Alan. 1993. *George Herbert Mead: The Making of a Social Pragmatist*. Urbana: University of Illinois Press.

Coser, Lewis. 1956. *The Functions of Social Conflict*. New York: Free Press.

———. 1971. *Masters of Sociological Thought: Ideas in Historical and Social Context*. New York: Harcourt Brace Jovanovich.

———. 1977. *Masters of Sociological Thought: Ideas in Historical and Social Context*. 2nd rev. ed. New York: Harcourt Brace Jovanovich.

———. 1981. "The Uses of Classical Sociological Theory." In *The Future of Sociological Classics*, edited by Buford Rhea, 170–94. London: George Allen and Unwin.

Cosman, Carol. 2001. "Note on the Text." In *Elementary Forms of Religious Life*, by Émile Durkheim. Translated by Carol Cosman. Introduction and notes by Mark S. Cladis, xxxvi. Oxford: Oxford University Press.

Côté, Jean-François. 2015. *George Herbert Mead's Concept of Society: A Critical Reconstruction*. London: Routledge.

Crain, Caleb. 2001. "Tocqueville for the Neocons?" *New York Times*, January 14, 2001.

Crenshaw, Kimberlé. 1989. "Demarginalizing the Intersection of Race and Sex: A Black Feminist Critique of Antidiscrimination Doctrine, Feminist Theory, and Antiracist Politics." *University of Chicago Legal Forum* 140:139–67.

———. 1993. "Mapping the Margins: Intersectionality, Identity Politics and Violence Against Women of Color." *Stanford Law Review* 43:1241–99.

Dahrendorf, Ralf. 1959. *Class and Class Conflict in Industrial Society*. Stanford: Stanford University Press. First published 1957.

Darnton, Robert. 1982. "What Is the History of the Books?" *Daedalus* 111:65–83.

Dawson, Matthew. 2016. *Social Theory for Alternative Societies*. Basingstoke: Palgrave Macmillan.

Derrida, Jacques. 1981. *Dissemination*. Translated by Barbara Johnson. London: Continuum.

Dhanagare, Dinesh N. 1993. "Remembering Tom Bottomore." *Economic and Political Weekly* 28:2581–83.

Dickson, Bruce D., Jr. 1992. "W. E. B. Du Bois and the Idea of Double Consciousness." *American Literature* 64:229–309.

Drescher, Seymour. 1968. *Tocqueville and Beaumont on Social Reform*. Translated and edited by Seymour Drescher. New York: Harper and Row.

———. 2001. "Book Review of *Democracy in America*." *Journal of American History* 88:612–14.

Du Bois, W. E. B. 1901. "Review of *Up from Slavery: An Autobiography*, by Booker T. Washington (New York: Doubleday, Page and Company, 1901)." *The Dial* 16:53–55.

———. 1903. *The Souls of Black Folk: Essays and Sketches*. Chicago: A. C. McClurg.

———. 1935. "Does the Negro Need Separate Schools?" *Journal of Negro Education* 4:328–35.

———. 1953. *The Souls of Black Folk*. Reprint of 1903 ed. Greenwich, CT: Fawcett.

———. 1968. *The Autobiography of W. E. B. Du Bois: A Soliloquy on Viewing My Life from the Last Decade of Its First Century.* New York: International Publishers.

———. 1986. "Criteria of Negro Art." *The Crisis* (October 1926), 290–97. In *W. E. B. Du Bois: Writings*, edited by Nathan Huggins. New York: Library of America.

———. 1996. "By Professor W E. Burghardt Du Bois, Atlanta, Georgia. *Independent* 57 (November 17, 1904): 1152." In Erica L. Griffin, "Reviews of *The Souls of Black Folk*." In *The Souls of Black Folk: One Hundred Years Later*, edited by Dolan Hubbard, 32–33. Columbia: University of Missouri Press.

———. 2003. *Darkwater: Voices from Within the Veil.* Mineola, NY: Dover. First published 1920.

———. 2007. *The Philadelphia Negro: A Social Study.* Oxford: Oxford University Press. First published 1899.

———. 2011. *Dusk of Dawn.* Boulder: Transaction. First published 1940.

Durkheim, Émile. 1902. "Sur le totemism." *L'Année sociologique* 5:82–121.

———. 1905. "Review of Pellisson, Maurice. *La Sécularisation de la moral au XVIIe siècle.*" *L'Année sociologique* 8:381–82.

———. 1909. "Sociologie religieuse et théorie de la connaissance." *Revue de métaphysique et de morale* 17:733–58.

———. 1958. *Socialism and Saint-Simon.* Edited with an introduction by Alvin Gouldner. Yellow Springs, OH: Antioch. Originally published in 1928.

———. 1966. *The Rules of Sociological Method.* New York: Free Press. First published 1895.

———. 1975a. *Durkheim on Religion.* Translated by Jacqueline Redding. Edited by W. S. F. Pickering. London: Routledge. Abr. ed. Reprint, Atlanta: Scholars, 1994.

———. 1975b. "La religion: Les origins." In *Textes.* Vol. 2, edited by Victor Karady, 65–122. Paris: Les Editions de Minuit. First published 1907.

———. 1976. *The Elementary Forms of the Religious Life: A Study in Religious Sociology.* Translated by Joseph Ward Swain. London: George Allen and Unwin; 2nd ed., New York: Macmillan; reprint, New York: Dover, 2008.

———. 1994. "Concerning the Definition of Religious Phenomena." In *Durkheim on Religion*, edited by W. S. F. Pickering, 74–99 Atlanta: Scholars. First published 1899.

———. 1995. *The Elementary Forms of Religious Life.* Translated by Karen Fields. Glencoe: Free Press.

———. 2005. *Suicide.* London: Routledge. First published 1897.

———. 2014. *Division of Labor in Society.* Edited with a new introduction by Steven Lukes. Translated by W. D. Halls. New York: Free Press. First published 1893.

Durkheim, Émile and Marcel Mauss. 1903. "De quelques formes primitives de classification: Contribution à l'étude des représentations collectives." *L'Année sociologique* 6:1–72.

Dwiggins, William Addison. 1922. "New Kind of Printing Calls for New Kind of Design." *Boston Evening Transcript*, August 29, 2011, Graphic Arts Section, 3–6.

Early, Gerard, ed. 1993. *Lure and Loathing: Essays on Race, Identity, and the Ambivalence of Assimilation.* New York: Penguin.

Echeverria, Durand. 1967. "Review of *Democracy in America*, by Alexis de Tocqueville." *William and Mary Quarterly* 24:637–40.

Edwards, Barrington S. 2006. "W. E. B. Du Bois: Berlin, Empirical Social Research, and the Race Question." *Du Bois Review: Social Science Research on Race* 3:395–424.

Edwards, Breanna. 2014. "Jamaican Cultural Theorist Stuart Hall Dies at 82." *The Root*, February 10, 2014.

Elazar, Daniel J. 1966. *American Federalism: A View from the States*. New York: Thomas Y. Crowell.

Elliott, Anthony, and Charles Lemert. 2014. Introduction to Contemporary Social Theory. Abingdon: Routledge.

Elster, Jon. 2009. *Alexis de Tocqueville, the First Social Scientist*. New York: Cambridge University Press.

Emirbayer, Mustafa, and Ann Mische. 1998. "What Is Agency?" *American Journal of Sociology* 103:962–1023.

Escarpit, Robert. 1966. *The Book Revolution*. London: Harrap.

Faris, Elsworth. 1936. "Review of *Mind, Self, and Society* by G. H. Mead." *American Journal of Sociology* 41:909–13.

Fast, Howard. 1990. *Being Red: A Memoir*. Boston: Houghton Mifflin.

Fay, Margaret. 1983. "The Influence of Adam Smith on Marx's Theory of Alienation." *Science and Society* 47:129–51.

Feagin, Joe. 1978. *Racial and Ethnic Relations*. Englewood Cliffs: Prentice Hall. Reprinted in 1996, 1999.

Fergerson, Gerard. 1999. Introduction to *Marie: Or Slavery in the United States*, by Gustave de Beaumont, ix–xxii. Baltimore: Johns Hopkins University Press.

Fernandes, Teresa Sousa. 2008. "Chemical Metaphors in Sociological Discourse: Durkheim Through the Imagery of Rousseau." *Journal of Classical Sociology* 8:447–66.

Fields, Karen E. 1995. "Translator's Introduction: Religion as an Eminently Social Thing." In *The Elementary Forms of Religious Life*, xvii–lxxiii. New York: Free Press.

———. 2005. "Translating Durkheim." In *The Cambridge Companion to Durkheim*, edited by Jeffrey C. Alexander and Philip Smith, 160–80. Cambridge: Cambridge University Press.

Filloux, Jean-Claude. 1977. *Durkheim et le socialism*. Geneva: Librairie Droz.

Fine, Gary Alan. 1993. "The Sad Demise, Mysterious Disappearance, and Glorious Triumph of Symbolic Interactionism." *Annual Review of Sociology* 19:61–87.

———. 1979. "George Herbert Mead and the Chicago Tradition of Sociology." *Symbolic Interaction* 2:9–26.

Fisher, Berenice, and Anselm Strauss. 1978. "The Chicago Tradition and Social Change: Thomas, Park and Their Successors." *Symbolic Interaction* 1:5–23.

Foucault, Michel. 1983. "On the Genealogy of Ethics: An Overview of the Work in Progress." In *Michel Foucault: Beyond Structuralism and Hermeneutics*, edited by Hubert L. Dreyfus and Paul Rabinow, 229–69. Chicago: University of Chicago Press.

———. 1991. "Nietzsche, Genealogy, History." In *The Foucault Reader*, edited by Paul Rabinow, 76–100. London: Penguin. First published 1971.

Fournier, Marcel. 2014. "*Les Formes Élémentaires* Comme Oeuvre Collective: Les Contributions d'Henri Hubert et de Marcel Mauss à la Sociologie de la Religion Tardive d'Émile Durkheim." *Canadian Journal of Sociology* 39:523–46.

Frank, Jerome N. 1945. "Review of *Democracy in America*, Phillips Bradley." *Federal Bar Journal* 6:455–66.

Frazer, James. 1887. *Totemism*. Edinburgh: Adam and Charles Black.

Fromm, Erich. 1964. Foreword to *Karl Marx: Early Writings*, edited by Tom Bottomore, i–vi. New York: McGraw-Hill Paperbacks.

Gans, Herbert J. 1998. "Best-Sellers by American Sociologists: An Exploratory Study." In *Required Reading: Sociology's Most Influential Books*, edited by Dan Clawson, 19–27. Amherst: University of Massachusetts Press.

Gardiner, Juliet. 2000. "Recuperating the Author: Consuming Fictions of the 1990s." *The Papers of the*

*Bibliographical Society of America* 94:255–74.
Garvin, Tom, and Hess, Andreas. 2008. "Tocqueville's Dark Shadow: Gustave Beaumont as Public Sociologist and Intellectual *Avant la Lettre*." In *Intellectuals and Their Publics Perspectives from the Social Sciences*, edited by Christian Fleck, Andreas Hess, and E. Stina Lyon, 157–72. Farnham: Ashgate.
Gates, Henry Louis, Jr., ed. 1984. *Black Literature and Literary Theory*. New York: Methuen.
———, ed. 1989. Introduction to *The Souls of Black Folk*, by W. E. B. Du Bois. Reprint of 1903 ed. New York: Bantam Books.
———. 1992. *Loose Canons*. Oxford: Oxford University Press.
———, ed. 1999. Introduction to *The Souls of Black Folk*, by W. E. B. Du Bois. Reprint of 1903 ed., edited by Henry Louis Gates Jr. and Terri Hume Oliver. New York: Norton Critical Editions.
———. 2006. "A Debate on Activism in Black Studies." In *A Companion to African American Studies*, edited by Lewis R. Gordon and Janne Anna Gordon, 96–98. Malden, MA: Blackwell.
———. 2007. *Black Folk Then and Now*. Oxford: Oxford University Press.
Gates, Henry Louis, Jr., and Valerie Smith, eds. 1996. *Norton Anthology of African American Literature*. New York: Norton.
Gehlen, Arnold. 1988. *Man: His Nature and Place in the World*. New York: Columbia University Press. First published 1940.
Genette, Gerard. 1997. *Paratexts: Thresholds of Interpretation*. Cambridge: Cambridge University Press.
Gerhardt, Uta. 2011. *The Social Thought of Talcott Parsons*. Farnham: Ashgate.
Ghosh, Peter. 1994. "Some Problems with Talcott Parsons' Version of the 'Protestant Ethic.'" *Archives Européenes de Sociologie* 35:104–23.
———. 2001. "Translation as a Conceptual Act." *Max Weber Studies* 2:59–63.
———. 2014. *Max Weber and the Protestant Ethic: Twin Histories*. Oxford: Oxford University Press.
Gibson, Donald B. 1989. Introduction to *The Souls of Black Folk*, by W. E. B. Du Bois. Reprint of 1903 ed. New York: Penguin.
Giddens, Anthony. 1971. *Capitalism and Modern Social Theory: An Analysis of the Writings of Marx, Durkheim and Max Weber*. Cambridge: Cambridge University Press.
———. 1972. *Émile Durkheim: Selected Writings*. Cambridge: Cambridge University Press.
———. 1979. *Émile Durkheim*. New York: Viking.
Gilkeson, John S. 2010. *Anthropologists and the Rediscovery of America, 1886–1965*. Cambridge: Cambridge University Press.
Gilroy, Paul. 1993. *The Black Atlantic: Modernity and Double Consciousness*. Cambridge: Harvard University Press, 1993.
Glassman, E. H. 1981. *The Translation Debate: What Makes a Bible Translation Good?* Downers Grove: Intervarsity.
Goffman, Erving. 1974. *Frame Analysis*. Cambridge: Harvard University Press.
Goldhammer, Arthur. 2003. "Remarks on the Mansfield-Winthrop Translation." *French Politics, Culture and Society* 21:110–19.
Gooding-Williams, Robert. 2005. "Du Bois, Politics, Aesthetics: An Introduction." In *100 Years of "The Souls of Black Folk": A Celebration of W. E. B. Du Bois*, edited by Robert Gooding-Williams and Dwight A. McBride, 203–16. Durham: Duke University Press.
———. 2009. *In the Shadow of Du Bois: Afro-modern Political Thought in America*. Cambridge: Harvard University Press.

Goodwin, Glenn A., and Joseph A Scimecca. 2005. *Classical Sociological Theory*. Belmont: Thomson.

Gouldner, Alvin. 1970. *The Coming Crisis of Western Sociology*. New York: Basic Books.

Graham, S. 1953. "Comments." In *The Souls of Black Folk*, xiii–xv. New York: Blue Heron.

Green, Dan S., and Edwin D. Driver. 1976. "W. E. B. Du Bois: A Case in the Sociology of Sociological Negation." *Phylon* 37:308–33.

———, ed. 1978. *W. E. B. Du Bois on Sociology and the Black Community*. Chicago: University of Chicago Press.

Greene, Lancaster M. 1945. "Review: Tocqueville on Democracy." *American Journal of Economics and Sociology* 4:556–58.

Griffin, Erica L., compiler. 2003. "Reviews of *The Souls of Black Folk*." In *The Souls of Black Folk: One Hundred Years Later*, edited by Dolan Hubbard, 18–33. Columbia: University of Missouri Press.

Guillory, John. 1994. *Cultural Capital: The Problem of Literary Canon Formation*. Chicago: University of Chicago Press.

Habermas, Jürgen. 1971. *Knowledge and Human Interests*. Boston: Beacon. First published 1968.

———. 1984. *The Theory of Communicative Action: Reason and the Rationalization of Society*. Vol. 1. Translated by Thomas McCarthy. Cambridge: Polity. First published 1981.

———. 1985. "A Philosophico-political Profile." *New Left Review* 151:76–77.

———. 1987. *The Theory of Communicative Action: Lifeworld and System; A Critique of Functionalist Reason*. Vol. 2. Cambridge: Polity. First published 1981.

Hacker, Andrew, ed. 1964. *Democracy in America*. New York: Washington Square.

Hall, Stuart. 1967. *The Young Englanders*. London: Community Relations Commission.

———. 1996. "New Ethnicities." In *Stuart Hall: Critical Dialogues in Cultural Studies*, edited by David Morley and Kwon-Hsing Chen, 441–49. New York: Routledge. First published 1988.

———. 1997. "Race, the Floating Signifier." Transcript by Media Education Foundation, pp. 1–17. http://www.mediaed.org/transcripts/Stuart-Hall-Race-the-Floating-Signifier-Transcript.pdf.

Hamilton, Nora. 1992. "The Cuban Economy: Dilemmas of Socialist Construction." In *Cuba: A Different America*, edited by Wilber A. Chaffee Jr. and Gary Prevost, 36–54. Lanham: Rowman and Littlefield.

Hamilton, Richard F. 2003. "American Sociology Rewrites Its History." *Sociological Theory* 21:281–97.

Hare, Nathan. 1969. "Questions and Answers About Black Studies." *The Massachusetts Review* 10:727–36.

Healey, Joseph. 1995. *Race, Ethnicity, Gender and Class*. Thousand Oaks: Pine Forge.

Hecker, Rolf. 1997. "Rjazanovs Editionsprinzipien der ersten MEGA." In *David Borisovič und die erste MEGA*, edited by Carl-Erich Vollgraf, Richard Sperl, and Rolf Hecker, 7–27. Berlin: Argument-Verlag.

———. 2002. "La seconda sezione della MEGA2 verso il completamento." In *MEGA2: Marx ritrovato*, edited by Alessandro Mazzone, 49–67. Rome: Mediaprint.

Heffner, Richard D., ed. 1956. *Democracy in America, Specially Edited and Abridged for the Modern Reader*. New York: Signet.

Hegel, Georg W. F. 1923. *Jenenser Logik: Metaphysik und Naturphilosophie*. Edited by Georg Lasson. Leipzig: Felix Meiner.

———. 1931. *Jenenser Realphilosophie*. Edited by Johannes Hoffmeister. Leipzig: Felix Meiner.

Henslin, James M. 2014. *Sociology: A Down-to-Earth Approach*. 12th ed. Hoboken, NJ: Pearson Education. First published 1992.

Holmwood, John. 2007. "Sociology as Public Discourse and Professional Practice: A Critique of Michael Burawoy." *Sociological Theory* 25:46–66.

Holub, Robert C. 1984. *Reception Theory. A Critical Introduction*. London: Methuen.

Hommes, Jakob. 1955. *Der technische Eros Das Wesen der materialistischen Geschichtsauffassung*. Freiburg: Herder.

Honneth, Axel, and Hans Joas. 1988. *Social Action and Human Nature*. Cambridge: Cambridge University Press.

Hook, Sidney. 1994. *From Hegel to Marx: Studies in the Intellectual Development of Karl Marx*. New York: Columbia University Press. First published 1936.

hooks, bell. 1990. "Postmodern Blackness." *Postmodern Culture* 1:1–7.

Horowitz, David, ed. 1971. *Radical Sociology: An Introduction*. San Francisco: CanField.

How, Alan R. 2007. "The Author, the Text and the Canon." *Journal of Classical Sociology* 7:5–22.

———. 2016. *Restoring the Classic in Sociology: Traditions, Texts and the Canon*. London: Palgrave Macmillan.

Hubert, Henri. 1904. "Étude sommaire de la représentation du temps dans la religion et la magie." *Annuaire de l'Ecole Pratique des Hautes Etudes Section des Sciences Religieuses*: 1–39.

Huebner, Daniel R. 2012. "The Construction of *Mind, Self, and Society*: The Social Process Behind G. H. Mead's Social Psychology." *Journal of the History of the Behavioral Sciences* 48:134–53.

———. 2014. *Becoming Mead The Social Process of Academic Knowledge*. Chicago: University of Chicago Press.

Hughes, Elaine. 2003. "Selected Publication History." In *The Souls of Black Folk: One Hundred Years Later*, 323–25. Columbia: University of Missouri Press.

Hunter, Marcus Anthony. 2013. *Black Citymakers: How "The Philadelphia Negro" Changed Urban America*. New York: Oxford University Press.

Hyppolite, Jean. 1969. *Studies on Marx and Hegel*. New York: Harper and Row.

Itzigsohn, Jose, and Karida Brown. 2015. "Sociology and the Theory of Double Consciousness: W. E. B. Du Bois's Phenomenology of Racialized Subjectivity." *Du Bois Review: Social Science Research on Race* 12:231–48.

Jacobs, Paul, and Saul Landau. 1966. *The New Radicals: A Report with Documents*. New York: Random House.

James, C. L. R. 1963. *Black Jacobins: Toussaint L'Ouverture and the San Domingo Revolution*. New York: Vintage Books. First published in 1938.

———. 1965. Introduction to *The Souls of Black Folk*, by W. E. B. Du Bois, vii–xx. Reprint of 1903 ed. London: Longmans.

Janara, Laura. 2004. "Brothers and Others. Tocqueville and Beaumont, U.S. Genealogy, Democracy, and Racism." *Political Theory* 32:773–800.

Jauss, Hans-Robert. 1970. "Literary History as a Challenge to Literary Theory." *New Literary History* 2:7–37.

Joas, Hans. 1985. *G. H. Mead: A Contemporary Re-examination of His Thought*. Translated by Raymond Meyer. Cambridge: MIT Press.

———. 1987. "Symbolic Interactionism." In *Social Theory Today*, edited by Anthony Giddens and Jonathan Turner, 82–115. Cambridge: Polity.

———. 1993. *Pragmatism and Social Theory*. Chicago: University of Chicago Press.

———. 1996. *The Creativity of Action*. Cambridge: Polity.

———. 2015. Foreword to *Mind, Self, and Society: "The Definitive Edition,"* edited by Charles Morris and annotated by Hans Joas and Daniel R.

Huebner, ix–xii. Chicago: University of Chicago Press.

Joas, Hans, and Daniel R. Huebner, eds. 2016. *The Timeliness of George Herbert Mead*. Chicago: University of Chicago Press.

Jones, Robert Alun. 1977. "On Understanding a Sociological Classic." *American Journal of Sociology* 83:279–319.

———. 2001. "Pragmatism and Protestantism in the Development of Durkheim's Sociology of Religion." In *Reappraising Durkheim for the Study and Teaching of Religion Today*, edited by Thomas A. Idinopulos and Brian C. Wilson, 45–58. Leiden: Brill.

Jones, Susan Stedman. 2001. *Durkheim Reconsidered*. Cambridge: Polity.

Kahn, Jonathon. 2009. "The Pragmatic Religious Naturalism of W. E. B. Du Bois." In *The Souls of W. E. B. Du Bois*, edited by Edward J. Blum and Jason R. Young, 41–65. Macon: Mercer University Press.

Kammen, Michael. 1998. *Alexis de Tocqueville and "Democracy in America."* Washington, DC: Library of Congress.

Kasinitz, Philip. 2006. "Missing Tocqueville?" *Sociological Forum* 21:693–94.

Keen, Mike. 1999. *Stalking the Sociological Imagination: J. Edgar Hoover's FBI Surveillance of American Sociology*. Westport, CT: Greenwood.

Kelsey, Carl. 1903. "Review of *The Souls of Black Folk*, by W. E. Burghardt Du Bois (Chicago: A. C. McClurg, 1903). Pp. x, 264." *Annals of the American Academy of Political and Social Sciences* 22:230–32.

Kendall, Diana. 2011. *Sociology in Our Times*. Belmont: Wadsworth.

King, Richard. 2008. "The Place of W. E. B. Du Bois in American and European Intellectual History." In *The Cambridge Companion to W. E. B. Du Bois*, edited by Shamoon Zamir, 131–44. Cambridge: Cambridge University Press.

Kiniery, Paul. 1945. "*Democracy in America* by Alexis de Tocqueville, Phillips Bradley." *Catholic Historical Review* 31:345–47.

Kramnick, Isaac. 2003. Introduction to *Democracy in America and Two Essays on America*, by Alexis de Tocqueville, ix–xlviii. Translated by Gerald E. Bevan. London: Penguin.

Kuehnelt-Leddihn, Erik von. 1966. *Democracy in America*. Translated by Henry Reeve. Classics of Conservatism. New Rochelle: Arlington House.

Labedz, Leopold, ed. 1962. Introduction to *Revisionism: Essays on the History of Marxist Ideas*, 9–27. London: George Allen and Unwin.

Lacroix, Bernard. 1981. *Durkheim et le politique*. Paris: Presses de la Fondation Nationale des Sciences Politiques.

Lamberti, Jean-Claude. 1989. *Tocqueville and the Two Democracies*. Translated by Arthur Goldhammer. Cambridge: Harvard University Press.

Lamont, Michele. 1988. "How to Become a Dominant French Philosopher: The Case of Jacques Derrida." *American Journal of Sociology* 93:584–622.

Landshut, Siegfried, and J.-P. Mayer. 1932. "Einleitung, 'Die Bedeutung der Fruheschriften von Marx fuer ein neues Verstaendnis." In *Fruhe Schriften*, 1. Leipzig: Alfred Kröner.

Laski, Harold. 1945. 1945. Foreword to *Democracy in America*. Edited by Phillips Bradley. Based on the Henry Reeve translation as revised by Francis Bowen. 2 vols. New York: Vintage Books.

———. 1948. *The American Democracy: A Commentary and an Interpretation*. New York: Viking.

———. 1966. Introduction to *Democracy in America*, by Alexis de Tocqueville. Edited by J.-P. Mayer and Max Lerner. Translated by George Lawrence. New York: Harper and Row.

———. 1997. *The Rise of European Liberalism*. New Brunswick: Transaction. First published 1936.

Latour, Bruno, and Peter Weibel. 2005. *Making Things Public: Atmospheres of Democracy*. Cambridge: MIT Press.

Leckey, Colum. 1995. "David Riazanov and Russian Marxism." *Russian History / Histoire Russe* 22:127–53.

Lefevere, André. 1985. "Why Waste Our Time on Rewrites? The Trouble with Interpretation and the Role of Rewriting in an Alternative Paradigm." In *The Manipulation of Literature: Studies in Literary Translation*, edited by Theo Hermans, 215–43. London: Croom Helm.

———, ed. 1990. *Translation/History/Culture: A Sourcebook*. New York: Routledge.

———. 1992. *Translation, Rewriting, and the Manipulation of Literary Fame*. London: Routledge.

———. 1999. "Composing the Other." In *Post-colonial Translation*, edited by Susan Bassnett and Harish Trivedi, 75–94. London: Routledge.

Lejeune, Philippe. 1975. *Le pacte autobiographique*. Paris: Seuil.

Lemert, Charles. 1994. "A Classic from the Other Side of the Veil: Du Bois's *Souls of Black Folk*." *Sociological Quarterly* 35:383–96.

———. 1995. *Sociology After the Crisis*. Boulder: Westview.

———. 1997. *Social Things: An Introduction to the Sociological Life*. Lanham: Rowman and Littlefield.

———. 2004. *Social Theory: The Multicultural and Classical Readings*. Boulder: Westview.

———. 2006. "Cultural Politics in the Negro Soul." In *The Souls of W. E. B. Du Bois: New Essays and Reflections*, edited by Alford A. Young, 73–98. Boulder: Paradigm.

———. 2007. *Thinking the Unthinkable*. Boulder: Paradigm.

Leopold, David. 2007. *The Young Karl Marx*. Cambridge: Cambridge University Press.

Lerner, Max. 1957. *America as a Civilization*. New York: Simon and Schuster.

———. 1966. Introduction to *Democracy in America*, by Alexis de Tocqueville. Edited by J.-P. Mayer and Max Lerner. Translated by George Lawrence. New York: Harper and Row.

Levine, Donald N. 1995. *Visions of the Sociological Tradition*. Chicago: University of Chicago Press.

———. 2015. "The Variable Status of the Classics in Differing Narratives of the Sociological Tradition." *Journal of Classical Sociology* 15:305–20.

Lewis, David Levering. 1993. *W. Du Bois: Biography of a Race, 1868–1919*. New York: Holt.

Lewis, J. David. 1979. "A Social Behaviorist Interpretation of the Meadian 'I.'" *American Journal of Sociology* 85:261–87.

———. 1981. "A Social Behaviorist Interpretation of the Meadian 'I.'" In *Philosophy, Social Theory and the Thought of George Herbert Mead*, edited by Mitchel Aboulafia, 109–35. Albany: SUNY Press.

Lewis, J. David, and Richard L. Smith. 1980. *American Sociology and Pragmatism*. Chicago: University of Chicago Press.

Lichtblau, Klaus, and Johannes Weiss, eds. 1993. "Einleitung der Herausgeber." In *Max Weber: Die protestantische Ethik und der "Geist" des Kapitalismus. Textausgabe auf der Grundlage der Fassung von 1904/5*. Bodenheim: Athenaeum-Hain-Hanstein.

Lichtenstein, Nelson. 2005. "Pluralism, Postwar Intellectuals and the Demise of the Union Idea." In *The Great Society and the High Tide of Liberalism*, edited by S. M. Milkis and J. M. Mileur, 83–114. Amherst: University of Massachusetts Press.

Lidz, Victor. 2010. "Talcott Parsons and the Transatlantic Voyages of Weberian and Durkheimian Theories." In *Transatlantic Voyages: The Migration and Development of Ideas*, edited by

Cherry Schrecker, 39–51. Avebury: Ashgate.

Lipset, Seymour Martin, Martin Trow, and James S. Coleman. 1956. *Union Democracy: The Internal Politics of the International Typographical Union*. New York: Free Press.

Locke, John. 1707. *An Essay for the Understanding of St. Paul's Epistles: By Consulting St. Paul Himself*. London: Printed by J. H. for Awnsham and John Churchill. Accessed December 1, 2016. http://teleiosministries.com/pdfs/Misc/understanding-st-paul%27s-epistles-by-john-locke.pdf.

Loughran, Kevin. 2015. "The Philadelphia Negro and the Canon of Classical Urban Theory." *Du Bois Review: Social Science Research on Race* 12:249–67.

Luhmann, Niklas. 1995. *Social Systems*. Stanford: Stanford University Press. First published 1984.

Lukács, Georg. 1971. *History and Class Consciousness*. Translated by Rodney Livingstone. Cambridge: MIT Press. First published 1923.

———. 1975. *The Young Hegel: Studies in the Relations Between Dialectics and Economics*. London: Merlin Press. First published 1938.

———. 1983. "Lukács on His Life and Work." In *Record of a Life*, edited by István Eorsi, 171–82. London: Verso. First published 1971.

Lukes, Stephen. 1973. *Émile Durkheim, His Life and Work: A Historical and Critical Study*. London: Allen Lane.

Macionis, John J. 2016. *Sociology*. 16th ed. Hoboken, NJ: Pearson Education. First published 1987.

Maidan, Michael. 1990. "The Rezeptionsgeschichte of the Paris Manuscripts." *History of European Ideas* 12:767–81.

Man, H. de. 1932. "Der neu entdeckte Marx." *Der Kampf* 25:224.

Mancini, Mathew. 2006. *Alexis de Tocqueville and American Intellectuals: From His Times to Ours*. Lanham: Rowman and Littlefield.

Mansfield, Harvey C., Jr. 2010. *Tocqueville: A Very Short Introduction*. Oxford: Oxford University Press.

Mansfield, Harvey C., Jr., and Delba Winthrop. 2000. "Translating Tocqueville's *Democracy in America*." *La Revue Tocqueville / The Tocqueville Review* 21:153–63.

Manza, Jeff, and Michael McCarthy. 2011. "The Neo-Marxist Legacy in American Sociology." *Annual Review of Sociology* 37:155–83.

Marable, Manning. 2006. "Celebrating Souls: Deconstructing the Du Boisian Legacy." In *The Souls of W. E. B. Du Bois: New Essays and Reflections*, edited by Alford A. Young, 7–28. Boulder: Paradigm.

Marcuse, Herbert. 1941. *Reason and Revolution: Hegel and the Rise of Social Theory*. New York: Oxford University Press.

———. 1956. *Eros and Civilization: A Philosophical Inquiry into Freud*. Boston: Beacon.

———. 1972a. *Counterrevolution and Revolt*. Boston: Beacon.

———. 1972b. *Studies in Critical Philosophy*. London: New Left Books.

———. 1985. *Soviet Marxism: A Critical Analysis*. New York: Columbia University Press. First published 1958.

———. 2002. *One-Dimensional Man: Studies in the Ideology of Advanced Industrial Society*. London: Routledge. First published 1964.

———. 2007. "The Foundations of Historical Materialism." In *The Essential Marcuse: Selected Writings of Philosopher and Social Critic Herbert Marcuse*, edited by Andrew Feenberg and Andrew Leiss, 72–114. Boston: Beacon. First published 1932.

Marshall, Lynn L. 1967. "Review of *Democracy in America*, by Alexis de Tocqueville." *Journal of American History* 54:378–80.

Martindale, Don. 1981. *The Nature and Types of Sociological Theory*. Prospect Heights: Waveland. First published 1960.

Marx, Karl. 1844. *Manuskripte*: References (divided by a slash) are to *Ökonomisch-philosophische Manuskripte aus dem Jahre 1844*, MEW, Ergänzungsband, volume 1, pp. 465–588 / *Economic and Philosophic Manuscripts of 1844*, MECW, volume 3, pp. 229–346 / and *Economic and Philosophical Manuscripts*, EW, pp. 279–400, respectively.

———. 1927–37. *Oeuvres Philosophiques*. Edited by Jules Molitor. 6 vols. Paris: Alfred Costes.

———. 1932. "Nationalökonomie und Philosophie: Über den Zusammenhang der Nationalökonomie mit Staat, Recht, Moral, und bürgerlichem Leben (1844)." In *Karl Marx, Der historische Materialismus: Die Frühschriften*, edited by Siegfried Landshut and Jacob Peter Mayer, 283–375. Leipzig: Alfred Kröner.

———. 1956. *Economic and Philosophical Manuscripts of 1884*. Translated by Martin Milligan. Moscow: Foreign Languages Pub. House. Reprint, Moscow: Progress, 1957, 1970, 1974, 1977; London: Lawrence and Wishart, 1959, 1981; New York: Prometheus Books, 1988; Mineola, NY: Dover 2007; Blacksburg, VA Wilder, 2011. Reprinted in *The Marx-Engels Reader*, edited by Robert C. Tucker, 66–125. New York: W. W. Norton, 1972.

———. 1964. *Economic and Philosophic Manuscripts of 1844*. Edited and introduced by Dirk J. Struik. Translated by Martin Milligan. New York: International Publishers.

———. 1967. *Capital, Volume I*. New York: International Publishers. First published 1867.

———. 1973. *Grundrisse*. Translated by Martin Nicolaus. New York: Vintage Books. First published 1858.

———. 1982. *Marx-Engels-Gesamtausgabe*. Abteilung I. Bd. 2, Berlin: Dietz Verlag, 187–322; 323–438, 685–917.

Mattson, Kevin. 2002. *Intellectuals in Action*. University Park: Pennsylvania State University Press.

Mauss, Marcel. 1906. "Essai sur les variations saisonnières des sociétés eskimo: Étude de morphologie sociale." *L'Année sociologique* 9:39–132.

Mayer, Carl. 2008. "In Memoriam Albert Salomon." In *Albert Salomon Werke*. Vol. 1, *Biographische Materialien and Schriften, 1921–1933*, edited by Peter Gostmann and Peter Wagner, 59–73. Wiesbaden: Verlag für Sozialwissenschaften.

Mayer, Jacob-Peter. 1939. *The Prophet of the Mass Age: A Study of Alexis de Tocqueville*. London: J. M. Dent and Sons. Reprinted as *Alexis de Tocqueville: A Biographical Essay in Political Science*, with a new commemorative essay. New York: Harper, 1960.

———. 1946. *Sociology of Film: Studies and Documents*. London: Faber and Faber.

———. 1949. *The Recollections of Alexis de Tocqueville*. Edited by J.-P. Mayer. Translated by Alexander Teixeira de Mattos. New York: Columbia University Press.

———. 1951. "Preface to *Démocratie en Amérique*." In *Alexis de Tocqueville, Oeuvres, Papiers et Correspondances*, edited by J.-P. Mayer. Paris: Gallimard.

———. 1957. *Les voyages de Tocqueville et la genèse de sa sociologie politique*. Commentary by J.-P. Mayer. Paris: Corbeil.

———. 1958. *Journeys to England and Ireland*. By Alexis de Tocqueville. Edited by J.-P. Mayer. Translated by George Lawrence and K. P. Mayer. New Haven: Yale University Press.

———. 1959. "Alexis de Tocqueville: A Commentated Bibliography."

*Revue Internationale de Philosophie* 13:350–53.

———. 1960. *Alexis de Tocqueville: A Biographical Essay in Political Science.* New York: Harper.

———. 1966. Foreword to *Democracy in America*, by Alexis de Tocqueville. Edited by J.-P. Mayer and Max Lerner. Translated by George Lawrence. New York: Harper and Row.

———. 1968. Preface to *De la démocratie en Amérique: Les grands themes.* Paris: Gallimard.

Mayer, Michael S. 2009. *The Eisenhower Years.* New York: Infobase.

McAdam, Doug. 2007. "The Impact of the Sixties on Public Sociology." In *Sociology in America*, edited by Craig Calhoun, 411–26. Chicago: University of Chicago Press.

McKenzie, Donald F. 1985. *Bibliography and the Sociology of Texts.* London: British Library.

McKinnon, Andrew. 2014. "Elementary Forms of the Metaphorical Life: Tropes at Work in Durkheim's Theory of the Religious." *Journal of Classical Sociology* 14:203–21.

McPhail, Clark, and Cynthia Rexroat. 1979. "Mead vs. Blumer: The Divergent Methodological Perspectives of Social Behaviorism and Symbolic Interactionism." *American Sociological Review* 44:449–67.

Mead, George Herbert. 1934. *Mind, Self, and Society: From the Standpoint of a Social Behaviorist.* Edited by Charles Morris. Chicago: University of Chicago Press.

———. 2001. *Essays in Social Psychology.* Edited and introduced by Mary Jo Deegan. New Brunswick: Transaction.

———. 2011. *G. H. Mead: A Reader.* Edited and introduced by Filipe Carreira da Silva. London: Routledge.

———. 2015. *Mind, Self, and Society.* Edited by Charles Morris. Annotated by Hans Joas and Daniel R. Huebner. Chicago: University of Chicago Press.

Mehring, Franz, ed. 1902. *Aus dem literarischen Nachlass von Karl Marx, Friedrich Engels und Ferdinand Lassalle.* Stuttgart: J. H. W. Dietz.

Menand, Louis. 2001. *The Metaphysical Club: A Story of Ideas in America.* New York: Farrar, Straus, and Giroux.

Merleau-Ponty, Maurice. 1964. *Sense and Non-sense.* Evanston: Northwestern University Press.

Merton, Robert King. 1968. *Social Theory and Social Structure.* New York: Free Press.

———. 1972. "Insiders and Outsiders: A Chapter in the Sociology of Knowledge." *American Journal of Sociology* 78:9–47.

Miller, Joseph Hillis. 1979. "The Critic as Host." In *Deconstruction and Criticism*, 217–53. New York: Seabury.

Miller, William Watts. 2012. *A Durkheimian Quest: Solidarity and the Sacred.* New York: Berghahn.

Mills, Charles Wright. 1942. "The Professional Ideology of Social Pathologists." *American Journal of Sociology* 49:165–80.

———. 1959. *The Sociological Imagination.* New York: Oxford University Press.

———, ed. 1960a. *Images of Man: The Classic Tradition in Sociological Thinking.* New York: Georges Braziller.

———. 1960b. "Letter to the New Left." *New Left Review* I/5:18–23.

———. 1962. *The Marxists.* New York: Dell.

———. 2000. *The Sociological Imagination.* Oxford: Oxford University Press. First published 1959.

———. 2002. *White Collar: The American Middle Classes.* Oxford: Oxford University Press. First published 1951.

Mommsen, Wolfgang. 1959. *Max Weber und die deutsche Politik, 1890–1920.* Tübingen: Mohr.

———. 1963. "Zum Begriff der 'plebiszitaren Führerdemokratie' bei Max Weber." *Kölner Zeitschrift für Soziologie und Sozialpsychologie* 15:295–322.

Morrione, Thomas J., ed. 2004. "Appendix III. Herbert Blumer: A Biography." In Herbert Blumer, *George Herbert Mead and Human Conduct*, edited and introduced by Thomas J. Morrione. Walnut Creek, CA: Altamira.

Morris, Aldon D. 2007. "Sociology of Race and W. E. B. Du Bois." In *Sociology in America*, edited by Craig Calhoun, 503–34. Chicago: University of Chicago Press.

———. 2015. *The Scholar Denied: W. E. B Du Bois and the Birth of Modern Sociology*. Berkeley: University of California Press.

Morris, Charles W. 1934. Preface to *Mind, Self, and Society: From the Standpoint of a Social Behaviorist*, edited by Charles Morris, v–xxxvi. Chicago: University of Chicago Press.

———. 1970. *The Pragmatic Movement in American Philosophy*. New York: Georges Braziller.

Morrison, Ken. 2003. "Book Reviews: *The Elementary Forms of Religious Life*, Free Press, 1995 and Oxford University Press, 2001." *Social Forces* 82:399–404.

Moses, Wilson J. 2004. *Creative Conflict in African American Thought*. Cambridge: Cambridge University Press.

Mouzelis, Nikos. 1997. "In Defense of the Sociological Canon: A Reply to David Parker." *Sociological Review* 45:244–53.

Muirhead, John Henry. 1892. *The Elements of Ethics: An Introduction to Moral Philosophy*. New York: Charles Scribner's Sons.

Mumford, Lewis. 1944. *The Condition of Man*. New York: Holt.

Musto, Marcello. 2009. "Marx in Paris: Manuscripts and Notebooks of 1844." *Science and Society* 73:386–402.

———. 2015. "The 'Young Marx' Myth in Interpretations of the Economic-Philosophic Manuscripts of 1844." *Critique: Journal of Socialist Theory* 43:233–60.

Nation. 1903. "Review of *The Souls of Black Folk* by W. E. B. Du Bois." 76:481–82.

Neal, Larry. 2000. "And Shine Swam On: An Afterword." In *African American Literary Theory: A Reader*, edited by Winston Napier, 69–80. New York: NYU Press.

Nelson, Benjamin. 1974. "Max Weber's Author's Introduction (1920): A Master Clue to His Main Aims." *Sociological Inquiry* 44:269–78.

Nisbet, Robert A. 1993. "Still Questing." *Intercollegiate Review* 29:41–45.

———. 2002. *Sociology as an Art Form*. New Brunswick: Transaction. First published 1976.

———. 2004. *The Sociological Tradition*. New Brunswick: Transaction. First published 1966.

Nolla, Eduardo. 1990. *De la démocratie en Amérique*. Paris: J. Vrin.

Offe, Claus. 2005. *Reflections on America: Tocqueville, Weber and Adorno in the United States*. Cambridge: Polity.

Ollman, Bertell. 1971. *Alienation: Marx's Conception of Man in Capitalist Society*. New York: Cambridge University Press

Ollman, Bertell, and Edward Vernoff, eds. 1982. *The Left Academy: Marxist Scholarship on American Campuses*. New York: McGraw-Hill.

Orbach, Harold. 1983. "The Genesis of *Mind, Self and Society*: Mead's Social Psychology and Charles Morris' Presentation of It." Paper presented at the Society for the Study of Symbolic Interaction Annual Meeting, Detroit, September 1–2.

Orgel, Stephen. 1981. "What Is a Text?" *Research Opportunities in Renaissance Drama* 26:3–6.

Outhwaite, William. 2009. "Canon Formation in Late 20th-Century British Sociology." *Sociology* 43:1029–45.

Palonen, Kari. 2003. "Translation, Politics and Conceptual Change." In *Redescriptions: Yearbook of Political*

*Thought and Conceptual History*, 7:15–35. Jyväskylä, Finland: University of Jyväskylä.

Park, Robert E., and Ernest Burgess. 1921. *Introduction to the Science of Sociology*. Chicago: University of Chicago Press.

Parker, David. 1997. "Why Bother with Durkheim? Teaching Sociology in the 1990s." *Sociological Review* 45:122–46.

Parsons, Talcott. 1927. *Der Kapitalismus bei Sombart und Max Weber: Inaugural-Dissertation zur Erlangung der Doktorwürde*. Harvard University Archives, Parsons Papers, HUGFP 42.8.2, box 1.

———. 1930. "Translator's Preface." In *The Protestant Ethic and the Spirit of Capitalism*, ix–xi. London: Allen and Unwin.

———. 1958. "Preface to New Edition." In *The Protestant Ethic and the Spirit of Capitalism*, xii–xvii. New York: Scribner's.

———. 1965. "Full Citizenship for the Negro American?" In *The Negro American*, edited by Talcott Parsons and K. B. Clark, 709–54. Boston: Beacon.

———. 1967. *Sociological Theory and Modern Society*. New York: Free Press.

———. 1968. *The Structure of Social Action*. New York: Free Press. First published 1937.

———. 1970. "On Building Social System Theory: A Personal History." *Daedalus* 99:826–81.

———. 1971a. "Comparative Studies and Evolutionary Change." In *Comparative Methods in Sociology*, edited by I. Vallier, 97–139. Berkeley: University of California Press.

———. 1971b. *The System of Modern Societies*. Englewood Cliffs: Prentice Hall.

———. 1975. "On 'De-Parsonizing Weber.'" *American Sociological Review* 40:666–70.

———. 1977. *Social Systems and the Evolution of Action Theory*. New York: Free Press.

———. 1980. "The Circumstances of My Encounter with Max Weber." In *Sociological Traditions from Generation to Generation*, edited by Robert K. Merton and Matilda Riley, 37–43. Norwood, NJ: Ablex.

———. 1991. "'Capitalism' in Recent German Literature: Sombart and Weber." *Journal of Political Economy* 36–37:641–44; 31–51, 1928–29. Reprinted in *Talcott Parsons: The Early Essays*, edited with an introduction by Charles Camic, 3–37. Chicago: University of Chicago Press.

Parsons, Talcott, Edward Shils, Kaspar D. Naegele, and Jesse R. Pitts, eds. 1961. *Theories of Society: Foundations of Modern Sociological Theory*. Vol. 2. New York: Free Press.

Pickering, W. S. F., ed. 1975. *Durkheim on Religion*. Translated by Jacqueline Redding. London: Routledge.

———. 1984. *Durkheim's Sociology of Religion: Themes and Theories*. London: Routledge.

———. 2002. *Durkheim and Representations*. London: Routledge.

Pierson, George Wilson. 1996. *Tocqueville in America*. Baltimore: Johns Hopkins University Press. Originally published as *Tocqueville and Beaumont in America*, 1938.

Platt, Jennifer. 1998. "A Brief History of the ISA: 1948–1997." International Sociological Association. Accessed December 1, 2016. http://www.isa-sociology.org/uploads/files/histoy-of-isa-1948-1997(1)(1).pdf.

Poggi, Gianfranco. 1972. *Images of Society: Essays on the Sociological Theories of Tocqueville, Marx, and Durkheim*. Stanford: Stanford University Press.

Pope, Whitney. 1986. *Tocqueville: His Social and Political Theory*. Beverly Hills, CA: Sage.

Popitz, Heinrich. 1953. *Der entfremdete Mensch: Zeitkritik und Geschichtsphilosophie des jungen*

Marx. Basle: Verlag fur Recht und Gesellschaft.

Poster, Mark. 1975. *Existentialist Marxism in Post-war France*. Princeton: Princeton University Press.

Poussaint, Alvin, 1969. "*The Souls of Black Folk*: A Critique." In *The Souls of Black Folk*, by W. E. B. Du Bois. Reprint of 1903 ed., edited by Nathan Hare and Alvin Poussaint, xxviii–xlii. New York: Signet / New American Library.

Putnam, Robert D. 1993. *Making Democracy Work: Civic Traditions in Modern Italy*. Princeton: Princeton University Press.

———. 2001. *Bowling Alone*. New York: Simon and Schuster.

Rabaka, Reiland. 2007. *W. E. B. Du Bois and the Problems of the Twenty-First Century: An Essay on Africana Critical Theory*. Lanham: Lexington.

———. 2008. *Du Bois's Dialectics: Black Radical Politics and the Reconstruction of Critical Social Theory*. Lanham: Lexington.

———. 2010a. *Against Academic Apartheid*. Lanham: Lexington.

———, ed. 2010b. Introduction to *W. E. B. Du Bois*, xii–xlviii. Farnham: Ashgate.

Rampersad, Arnold. 1985. "W. E. B. Du Bois as a Man of Literature." In *Critical Essays on W. E. Du Bois*, edited by William L. Andrews, 57–72. Boston: G. K. Hall.

———. 1990. *The Art and Imagination of W. E. B. Du Bois*. New York: Schocken. First published 1976.

Rancière, Jacques. 2009. *Hatred of Politics*. London: Verso.

Redding, Saunders. 1961. Introduction to *The Souls of Black Folk*, by W. E. B. Du Bois. Reprint of 1903 ed. Premier Americana. Greenwich, CT: Fawcett.

Redlich, Norman. 1958. "Review of *America as Civilization*." *The Nation* 186:95–97.

Reed, Adolph. 1997. *W. E. B. Du Bois and American Political Thought*. Oxford: Oxford University Press.

Reed, Isaac, and Jeffrey C. Alexander. 2009. "Social Science as Reading and Performance: A Cultural-Sociological Understanding of Epistemology." *European Journal of Social Theory* 12:21–41.

Reinhold, Robert. 1973. "A Mentor of Sociologists Retires After 42 Years at Harvard Post." *New York Times*, June 14, 1973.

Resh, Richard W. 1963. "Alexis de Tocqueville and the Negro: *Democracy in America* Reconsidered." *Journal of Negro History* 48:251–59.

Rex, John. 1974. Introduction to *Approaches to Sociology: An Introduction to Major Trends in British Sociology*, 1–11. London: Routledge and Kegan Paul.

Riazanov, David. 1927. *Arkhiv K. Marksa i F. Engelsa*. Vol. 3. Moscow: Gosudarstvennoe izdatel'stvo.

———. 1929. "Einleitung." In *MEGA1/1.2*, ix–xlv. Berlin: Marx-Engels-Verlag.

Ricoeur, Paul. 1981. *Hermeneutics and the Human Sciences: Essays on Language, Action and Interpretation*. Edited and translated by John B. Thompson. Cambridge: Cambridge University Press.

———. 2006. *On Translation*. London: Routledge.

Riesebrodt, Martin. 2005. "Dimensions of the Protestant Ethic." In *The Protestant Ethic Turns 100: Essays on the Centenary of the Weber Thesis*, edited by William H. Swatos Jr. and Lutz Kaelber, 23–51. Boulder: Paradigm.

Riesman, David. 1993. "The Oral Tradition, the Written Word, and the Screen Image." In *Abundance for What?*, 418–41. New Brunswick: Transaction. First published 1955.

———. 2001. "Twenty Years After—a Second Preface." In *The Lonely Crowd: A Study of the Changing American Character*. Abr. and rev. ed. New Haven: Yale University Press.

Riesman, David, Nathan Glazer, and Reuel Denney. 2001. *The Lonely Crowd: A Study of the Changing American*

*Character*. Abr. and rev. ed. New Haven: Yale University Press. First published 1950. Reprinted with new prefaces in 1961, 1969.

Ritzer, George, ed. 2008. *The New Blackwell Companion to Social Theory*. Oxford: Blackwell.

Rogers, Melvin. 2012. "The People, Rhetoric, and Affect: On the Political Force of Du Bois' 'The Souls of Black Folk.'" *American Political Science Review* 106:188–203.

Rojahn, Jürgen. 2002. "The Emergence of a Theory: The Importance of Marx's Notebooks Exemplified by Those from 1844." *Rethinking Marxism* 14:29–46.

Rosenberger, Coleman. 1945. "Review of *Democracy in America*, by Alexis de Tocqueville." *New Mexico Quarterly Review* 15:364–68.

Roth, Guenther. 1999. "Max Weber at Home and in Japan: On the Troubled Genesis and Successful Reception of His Work." *International Journal of Politics, Culture and Society* 12:515–25.

Rubel, Maximilien. 1957. *Karl Marx: Essai de biographie intellectuelle*. Paris: Rivière.

Rudwick, Elliott M. 1957. "W. E. B. Du Bois and the Atlanta University Studies on the Negro." *Journal of Negro Education* 26:466–76.

———. 1974. "W. E. B. Du Bois as Sociologist." In *Black Sociologists: Historical and Contemporary Perspectives*, edited by James E. Blackwell and Morris Janowitz, 25–55. Chicago: University of Chicago Press.

Salomon, Albert. 1935a. *Alexis de Tocqueville, Autorität und Freiheit: Schriften, Reden und Briege*. Edited and introduced by Albert Salomon. Zurich: Praschau.

———. 1935b. "Tocqueville: Moralist and Sociologist." *Social Research* 2:405–27.

———. 1939. "Tocqueville's Philosophy of Freedom." *The Review of Politics* 1:400–431.

———. 1959. "Tocqueville, 1959." *Social Research* 36:449–70.

Sartre, Jean-Paul. 1958. *Being and Nothingness*. Translated by Hazel E. Barnes. London: Routledge. First published 1943.

Satterwhite, James H. 1992. *Varieties of Marxist Humanism*. Pittsburgh: University of Pittsburgh Press.

Scaff, Lawrence. 2005. "The Creation of the Sacred Text: Talcott Parsons Translates *The Protestant Ethic and the Spirit of Capitalism*." *Max Weber Studies* 6:205–28.

———. 2006. "Max Weber's Reception in the United States." In *Das Faszinosum Max Weber. Die Geschichte seiner Geltung*, edited by Karl-Ludwig Ay and Knut Borchardt, 55–89. Konstanz: UVK.

———. 2014. "Max Weber in the United States." *SocietàMutamentoPolitica: Rivista Italiana di Sociologia* 5:271–91.

Schaefer, Richard T. 2011. *Sociology*. 13th ed. New York: McGraw-Hill.

Schleifer, James T. 2012. *The Chicago Companion to Tocqueville's "Democracy in America."* Chicago: University of Chicago Press.

Schneidermann, Howard G. 2001. Introduction to *The Protestant Establishment Revisited*, edited by E. Digby Baltzell, ix–xxxii. Boulder: Transaction.

Searle, John. 1969. *Speech Acts: An Essay in the Philosophy of Language*. Cambridge: Cambridge University Press.

Seidman, Stephen. 2008. *Contested Knowledge: Social Theory Today*. Oxford: Blackwell.

Shalin, Dmitri. 1986. "Pragmatism and Social Interactionism." *American Sociological Review* 51:9–29.

———. 2011. *Pragmatism and Democracy: Studies in History, Social Theory, and Progressive Politics*. New Brunswick: Transaction.

Sherman, Lawrence W. 1974. "Uses of the Masters." *The American Sociologist* 9:176–81.

Sica, Alan, and Stephen Turner, eds. 2005. *The Disobedient Generation: Social Theorists in the Sixties*. Chicago: University of Chicago Press.

Silva, Filipe Carreira da. 2007. "Re-examining Mead: G. H. Mead on the Material Reproduction of Society." *Journal of Classical Sociology* 7:291–313.

———. 2008. *Mead and Modernity: Science, Selfhood and Democratic Politics*. Lanham: Lexington.

———. 2009. "Bringing Republican Ideas Back Home: The Dewey-Laski Connection." *History of European Ideas* 35:360–68.

Simmel, Georg. 1978. *The Philosophy of Money*. Translated by Tom Bottomore and David Frisby. London: Routledge and Kegan Paul. First published 1907.

Skinner, Quentin. 1969. "Meaning and Understanding in the History of Ideas." *History and Theory* 8:3–53.

Skocpol, Theda. 1996. "Unraveling from Above." *The American Prospect* 25:20–25.

Smith, Philip, and Jeffrey C. Alexander. 1996. "Review Essay: Durkheim's Religious Revival." *American Journal of Sociology* 102:585–92.

Smith, Robertson. 1889. *Lectures on the Religion of the Semites: Fundamental Institutions*. First Series. London: Adam and Charles Black.

Sorokin, Pitirim. 1928. *Contemporary Sociological Theories*. New York: Harper and Brothers.

———. 1966. *Sociological Theories of Today*. New York: Harper and Row.

Spencer, Baldwin, and Francis J. Gillen. 1899. *The Native Tribes of Central Australia*. London: Macmillan.

Spivak, Gayatri. 1988. "Can the Subaltern Speak?" In *Marxism and the Interpretation of Culture*, edited by Cary Nelson and Lawrence Grossberg, 271–313. Urbana: University of Illinois Press.

Stanfield, John H. 2010. "Du Bois on Citizenship." *Journal of Classical Sociology* 10:171–88.

Stauth, Georg, and Bryan Turner. 1988. *Nietzsche's Dance: Resentment, Reciprocity and Resistance in Social Life*. Oxford: Blackwell.

Steber, Martina. 2015. "'The West,' Tocqueville and West German Conservatism from the 1950s to the 1970s." In *Germany and "the West": The History of a Modern Concept*, edited by Riccardo Bavaj and Martina Steber, 230–45. New York: Berghahn.

Stedman Jones, Gareth. 2007. "Marx's Critique of Political Economy: A Theory of History or a Theory of Communism?" In *Marxist History-Writing for the Twenty-First Century*, edited by Chris Wickham, 140–57. Oxford: Oxford University Press.

Strauss, Leo. 1952. *Persecution and the Art of Writing*. New York: Free Press.

Struik, Dirk J., ed. 1964. *Economic and Philosophic Manuscripts of 1844*, by Karl Marx. Translated by Martin Milligan. New York: International Publishers.

Sullivan, Shannon. 2003. "Remembering the Gift." *Transactions of the Charles Sanders Peirce Society* 39:205–25.

Swatos, William H., and Peter Kivisto. 2005. "The Contexts of the Publication and Reception of *The Protestant Ethic*." In *The Protestant Ethic Turns 100: Essays on the Centenary of the Weber Thesis*, edited by William H. Swatos Jr. and Lutz Kaelber, 111–37. Boulder: Paradigm.

Swedberg, Richard. 2009. *Tocqueville's Political Economy*. Princeton: Princeton University Press.

Sydnor, Charles S. 1945. "Review of *Democracy in America*, by Alexis de Tocqueville." *Political Science Quarterly* 60:457–59.

Tedman, Gary. 2004. "Marx's 1844 Manuscripts as a Work of Art: A Hypertextual Reinterpretation." *Rethinking Marxism* 16:427–41.

Thier, Erich. 1957. *Das Menschenbild des jungen Marx*. Göttingen: Vandenhoeck and Ruprecht.

Tillery, Alvin, Jr. 2009. "Tocqueville as Critical Race Theorist." *Political Research Quarterly* 62:639–52.

Tocqueville, Alexis de. 1848. *De la Démocratie en Amérique: Revue et corrigée, et augmenté d'un Avertissement et d'un Examen comparatif de la Démocratie aux États-Unis et en Suisse*. 4 vols. Paris: Pagnerre.

———. 1951. *Oeuvres Complètes*. Edited by J.-P. Mayer and G. Rudler. *Correspondance Anglaise*. Vol. 6, *Correspondance D'Alexis de Tocqueville avec Henry Reeve et John Stuart Mill*. Paris: Gallimard.

———. 1956. *Democracy in America, Specially Edited and Abridged for the Modern Reader*. Edited by Richard D. Heffner. New York: Signet. (Most recent reedition is *Democracy in America: Specially Edited and Abridged for the Modern Reader* by Richard D. Heffner, with a new afterword by Vartan Gregorian [New York: New American Library, 2010].)

———. 1966. *Democracy in America*. Edited by J.-P. Mayer and Max Lerner. Translated by George Lawrence. New York: Harper and Row.

———. 1980. *Alexis de Tocqueville on Democracy, Revolution, and Society*. Edited by John Torpey and Stephen Mennell. Chicago: University of Chicago Press.

———. 2000. *Democracy in America*. Translated, edited, and with an introduction by Harvey C. Mansfield and Delba Winthrop. Chicago: University of Chicago Press.

Torpey, John. 2006. "Alexis de Tocqueville, Forgotten Founder." *Sociological Forum* 21:695–707.

Trevino, A. Javier, ed. 2001. *Talcott Parsons Today: His Theory and Legacy in Contemporary Sociology*. Lanham: Rowman and Littlefield.

Tribe, Keith. 2007. "Talcott Parsons as Translator of Max Weber's Basic Sociological Categories." *History of European Ideas* 33:212–33.

———. 2014. *The Economy of the Word: Language, History, and Economics*. Oxford: Oxford University Press.

———. 2015. *The Economy of the Word: Language, History and Economics*. New York: Oxford University Press.

Tucker, Charles. 1988. "Herbert Blumer: A Pilgrimage with Pragmatism." *Symbolic Interaction* 11:99–124.

Tucker, Robert C. 2000. *Philosophy and Myth in Karl Marx*. Boulder: Transaction. First published 1961.

Tugendhat, Ernst. 1991. *Self-Consciousness and Self-Determination*. Cambridge, MA: MIT Press.

Turner, Bryan S. 2008. *The New Blackwell Companion to Social Theory*. Oxford: Blackwell.

Turner, Jonathan H. 2002. *The Structure of Sociological Theory*. 7th ed. Belmont: Wadsworth. First published 1974.

Turner, Stephen. 2014. *American Sociology: From Pre-disciplinary to Post-normal*. Basingstoke: Palgrave Macmillan.

Vatter, Miguel. 2012. "The Quarrel Between Populism and Republicanism: Machiavelli and the Antinomies of Plebeian Politics." *Contemporary Political Theory* 11:242–63.

Vieira, Mónica Brito. 2009. *The Elements of Representation in Hobbes: Aesthetics, Theatre, Law, and Theology in the Construction of Hobbes's Theory of the State*. Leiden: Brill.

Vogt, W. Paul. 1993. "Durkheim's Sociology of Law: Morality and the Cult of the Individual." In *Emile Durkheim: Sociologist and Moralist*, edited by Stephen Turner, 71–94. New York: Routledge.

Waples, Douglas. 1931. "The Graduate Library School at Chicago." *The Library Quarterly* 1:26–36.

Ward, John William. 1966. "The Democratic Animal." Review of *Democracy in America*, by Alexis de Tocqueville. *Book Week*, December 25, 1966, 1, 10.

Wearne, Bruce C. 1989. *The Theory and Scholarship of Talcott Parsons to 1951*. Cambridge: Cambridge University Press.

Webb, Robert Kiefer. 1955. *The British Working Class Reader, 1790–1848* New York: George Allen and Unwin.

Weber, Max. 1930. "Author's Introduction." In *The Protestant Ethic and the Spirit of Capitalism*, translated by Talcott Parsons, 13–31. London: Allen and Unwin. First published 1920.

———. 1946. *From Max Weber: Essays in Sociology*. Edited and translated by Hans H. Gerth and C. Wright Mills. New York: Oxford University Press.

———. 1978. *Economy and Society*. Edited and translated by Guenther Roth and Claus Wittich. Berkeley: University of California Press.

Weber, Max, Alfred Ploetz, and W. E. B. Du Bois. 1973. "Max Weber on Race and Society II." *Sociological Analysis* 34:308–12.

West, Cornel. 1982. *Prophesy Deliverance*. Philadelphia: Westminster.

———. 1989. *The American Evasion of Philosophy: A Genealogy of Pragmatism*. Madison: University of Wisconsin Press.

———. 1994. *Race Matters*. New York: Vintage Books.

Winant, Howard. 2000. "Race and Race Theory." *Annual Review of Sociology* 26:169–85.

———. 2004. "Dialectics of the Veil." In *The New Politics of Race: Globalism, Difference, Justice*, edited by Howard Winant, 25–38. Minneapolis: University of Minnesota Press.

———. 2007. "The Dark Side of the Force." In *Sociology in America*, edited by Craig Calhoun, 535–71. Chicago: University of Chicago Press.

Woelfel, Joseph. 1967. "Comment on the Blumer-Bales Dialogue Concerning the Interpretation of Mead's Thought." *American Journal of Sociology*, 72:409.

Wolin, Sheldon. 1981. "Max Weber: Legitimation, Method, and the Politics of Theory." *Political Theory* 9:401–24.

Wright, Benjamin F. 1946. "Of *Democracy in America*." *American Political Science Review* 40:52–61

Wright, Earl. 2002. "Why Black People Tend to Shout." *Sociological Spectrum* 22:335–61.

———. 2006. "W. E. B. Du Bois and the Atlanta University Studies on the Negro, Revisited." *Journal of African American Studies* 9:3–17.

Zamir, Shamoon. 1995. *Dark Voices: W. E. B. Du Bois and American Thought, 1888–1903*. Chicago: University of Chicago Press.

Zeitlin, Irving. 1968. *Ideology and the Development of Sociological Theory*. Englewood Cliffs: Prentice Hall.

Zerubavel, Eviatar. 1981 *Hidden Rhythms*. Chicago: University of Chicago Press.

Ziegler, Benjamin Munn. 1958. "Review of *America as a Civilization*, by Max Lerner." *Yale Law Journal* 67:1513–15.

LIST OF EDITIONS CONSULTED

**Durkheim's *Elementary Forms***
1915. *The Elementary Forms of the Religious Life: A Study in Religious Sociology*. Translated by Joseph Ward Swain. London: George Allen and Unwin; New York: Macmillan. xi, 456 pages, 23 cm. Reprinted 1926, 1954, 1957, 1964.

1965. *The Elementary Forms of the Religious Life*. First paperback ed. Translated by Joseph Ward Swain. Glencoe: Free Press.

1975. *Durkheim on Religion*. Translated by Jacqueline Redding. Edited by W. S. F. Pickering. London: Routledge. Abr. ed. Reprint, Atlanta: Scholars, 1994.

1976. *The Elementary Forms of the Religious Life: A Study in Religious Sociology.* Translated by Joseph Ward Swain. London: George Allen and Unwin; 2nd ed., New York: Macmillan; reprint, New York: Dover, 2008.

1995. *The Elementary Forms of Religious Life.* Translated by Karen Fields. Glencoe: Free Press.

2001. *The Elementary Forms of Religious Life.* Edited by Mark S. Cladis. Translated by Carol Cosman. Oxford: Oxford World's Classics. Reprinted 2008 (abridged version).

2012. *The Elementary Forms of the Religious Life.* Translated by Joseph Ward Swain, with an introduction by Steven Alan Childress. Centennial Edition. New Orleans: Quid Pro Books.

### Marx's *1844 Manuscripts*

1932. "Nationalökonomie und Philosophie: Über den Zusammenhang der Nationalökonomie mit Staat, Recht, Moral, und bürgerlichem Leben (1844)." In *Karl Marx, Der historische Materialismus: Die Frühschriften*, edited by Siegfried Landshut and Jacob Peter Mayer, 285–375. Leipzig: Alfred Kröner.

1932. "Ökonomisch-philosophische Manuskripte aus dem Jahre 1844." In *MEGA I/3*, 29–172. Berlin: Marx-Engels-Verlag.

1956. *Economic and Philosophical Manuscripts of 1884.* Translated by Martin Milligan. Moscow: Foreign Languages Pub. House. Reprint, Moscow: Progress, 1967, 1970, 1974, 1977; London: Lawrence and Wishart, 1959, 1981; New York: Prometheus Books, 1988; Mineola, NY: Dover, 2007; Blacksburg, VA: Wilder, 2011. Reprinted in *The Marx-Engels Reader*, edited by Robert C. Tucker, 66–125. New York: W. W. Norton, 1972.

1964. *Economic and Philosophic Manuscripts of 1884.* Edited and introduced by Dirk J. Struik. Translated by Martin Milligan. New York: International Publishers. Reprinted 1969. Reprint, London: Lawrence and Wishart, 1970. ("Translated from the complete German text as first published in Marx-Engels, *Gesamtausgabe*, Abt. I, Bd. 3 [*Collected Works*, sec. I, vol. 3]—Berlin, 1932 . . . Included as an appendix is Frederick Engels 'Outlines of a critique of political economy,' which was translated from the German text contained in *Gesamtausgabe*, Abt. I, Bd. 2, Berlin, 1930." 255 pages 21 cm.)

1964. *Karl Marx: Early Writings.* Edited by T. B. Bottomore. Foreword by Erich Fromm. London: McGraw-Hill.

1974. *Karl Marx: Early Writings.* New York: Random House / London and Harmondsworth: Penguin and New Left Review. *Economic and Philosophical Manuscripts* (279–400) translated by Gregor Benton. Introduction by Lucio Colletti. Reprint, London: Penguin Classics, 1992, 2000.

1975. *Marx-Engels Collected Works.* London: Lawrence and Wishart.

1982. *Marx-Engels-Gesamtausgabe.* Abteilung I. Bd. 2, Berlin: Dietz Verlag, 187–322; 323–438, 685–917.

*Physical Copy of the Manuskripte*

Marx, Karl. 1844. *Nationalökonomie und Philosophie.* A. Manuskripte von Karl Marx, 7–9. International Institute for Social History, Amsterdam. http://hdl.handle.net/10622/ARCH00860.

### Du Bois's *The Souls of Black Folk*

1903. *The Souls of Black Folk: Essays and Sketches.* Chicago: A. C. McClurg.

1953. *The Souls of Black Folk.* New York: Blue Heron.

1953. *The Souls of Black Folk*. Reprint of 1903 ed., with an introduction by Saunders Redding. Greenwich, CT: Fawcett.

1961. *The Souls of Black Folk*. Reprint of 1903 ed., with an introduction by Saunders Redding. Premier Americana. Greenwich, CT: Fawcett.

1965. *The Souls of Black Folk*. Reprint of 1903 ed., in *Three Negro Classics*, edited and introduced by John Hope Franklin. New York: Avon.

1965. *The Souls of Black Folk*. Reprint of 1903 ed., with an introduction by C. L. R. James. London: Longmans.

1968. *The Souls of Black Folk*. New York: Magnavision Large Print Books.

1968. *The Souls of Black Folk*. Reprint of 1903 ed., in the *Basic Afro-American Reprint Library Series*. New York: Johnson Reprint Corporation.

1969. *The Souls of Black Folk*. Reprint of 1903 ed., edited and introduced by Nathan Hare and Alvin Poussaint. New York: Signet / New American Library.

1973. *The Souls of Black Folk*. Reprint of 1953 ed., in *Collected Published Works of W. E. B. Du Bois*, edited by Herbert Aptheker. Millwood, NY: Kraus-Thomson.

1979. *The Souls of Black Folk*. Fisk Diamond Jubilee edition, with an introduction by L. M. Collins. Nashville: Fisk University Press.

1989. *The Souls of Black Folk*. Reprint of 1903 ed., with an introduction by Henry Louis Gates Jr. New York: Bantam Books.

1989. *The Souls of Black Folk*. Reprint of 1903 ed., with an introduction by Donald B. Gibson. New York: Penguin.

1990. *The Souls of Black Folk*. Reprint of 1903 ed., with an introduction by John Edgar Wideman. New York: Vintage/Library of America.

1990. *The Souls of Black Folk*. Partial reprint of 1903 ed., with an introduction by Kwame Anthony Appiah, in *Early African-American Classics*. New York: Bantam Books.

1993. *The Souls of Black Folk*. Reprint of 1903 ed., with an introduction by Arnold Rampersad. New York: Knopf.

1997. *The Souls of Black Folk*. Reprint of 1903 ed., edited with an introduction by David W. Blight and Robert Gooding-Williams. Bedford Cultural Editions. Boston: Bedford/St. Martin's.

1999. *The Souls of Black Folk*. Reprint of 1903 ed., edited by Henry Louis Gates Jr. and Terri Hume Oliver. New York: Norton Critical Editions.

2003. *The Souls of Black Folk*. Reprint of 1903 ed. New York: Barnes and Noble Classics.

2003. *The Souls of Black Folk*. Reprint of 1953 ed., with an introduction by David Levering Lewis. New York: Modern Library.

2003. *Die Seelen der Schwarzen*. Translated by Hans Jürgen Meyer-Wendt and Barbara Meyer-Wendt. Freiburg: Orange Press.

2004. *The Souls of Black Folk*. With an introduction by Manning Marable. Foreword by Charles Lemert. 100th Anniversary ed. Boulder: Paradigm.

Weber's *The Protestant Ethic*

1930. *The Protestant Ethic and the Spirit of Capitalism*. Translated by Talcott Parsons, with a foreword by R. H. Tawney. London: George Allen and Unwin. New York: Charles Scribner's Sons. Reprinted 1948, 1950, 1952, 1956, 1958 (paperback), 1960.

1930. *The Protestant Ethic and the Spirit of Capitalism, and, the Evolution of the Capitalistic Spirit*. Translated by Talcott Parsons. Includes "The Evolution of the Capitalistic Spirit," from *General Economic History*, translated by Frank H. Knight. Chicago: University of Chicago Bookstore. Reprinted 1946.

1958. *The Protestant Ethic and the Spirit of Capitalism*. "Preface to New Edition" by Talcott Parsons. Translated by Talcott Parsons, with a foreword by

R. H. Tawney. London: George Allen and Unwin. First paperback edition, New York: Charles Scribner's Sons Library Edition. Latest reprint by Mineola, NY: Dover, 2003.

1958. *The Protestant Ethic and the Spirit of Capitalism*. Upper Saddle River: Pearson Education.

1976. *The Protestant Ethic and the Spirit of Capitalism: A Classic Study of the Fundamental Relationships Between Religion and the Economic and Social Life in Modern Culture*. 2nd ed. Translated by Talcott Parsons, with a foreword by Anthony Giddens. London: George Allen and Unwin; New York: Charles Scribner's Sons.

1977. *The Protestant Ethic and the Spirit of Capitalism*. Upper Saddle River: Pearson.

1985. *The Protestant Ethic and the Spirit of Capitalism*. Translated by Talcott Parsons, with an introduction by Anthony Giddens. London: Unwin Hyman. (Routledge edited this version from 1992 and included it in Routledge Classics series in 2001; repr., London: Harper Collins Academic, 1991).

1996. *The Protestant Ethic and the Spirit of Capitalism*. Translated by Talcott Parsons, with a foreword by Randall Collins. Los Angeles: Roxbury. Reprinted in revised form in 1998.

2001. *The Protestant Ethic and the Spirit of Capitalism*. 3rd ed. Translated, introduced, and edited by Stephen Kalberg. Includes Weber's essays "The Protestant Sects and the Spirit of Capitalism" and "Prefatory Remarks" to *Collected Essays in the Sociology of Religion*. Los Angeles: Roxbury. (Also issued by Fitzroy Dearborn, 2001; Wiley/Blackwell, 2001.)

2002. *The Protestant Ethic and the Spirit of Capitalism and Other Writings*. Translated and edited by Peter Baehr and Gordon C. Wells. London: Penguin.

2009. *The Protestant Ethic and the Spirit of Capitalism: The Talcott Parsons Translation Interpretations*. Edited by Richard Swedberg. New York: W. W. Norton.

2009. *The Protestant Ethic and the Spirit of Capitalism with Other Writings on the Rise of the West*. Translated and introduced by Stephen Kalberg. Oxford: Oxford University Press.

2010. *The Protestant Ethic and the Spirit of Capitalism: The Revised 1920 Edition*. Translated and introduced by Stephen Kalberg. Oxford: Oxford University Press.

**Tocqueville's *Democracy in America***

1912. *Democracy in America*. Translated by Henry Reeve, with a critical and biographical introduction by John Bigelow. 2 vols. New York: D. Appleton. 3rd reprint.

1945. *Democracy in America*. Edited by Phillips Bradley. Based on the Henry Reeve translation as revised by Francis Bowen. 2 vols. New York: Vintage Books. (The 1990 edition has a new introduction by Daniel J. Boorstin.)

1946. *Democracy in America*. Edited and introduced by Henry Steele Commager. Translated by Henry Reeve. Abr. ed. London: Oxford University Press.

1956. *Democracy in America, Specially Edited and Abridged for the Modern Reader*. Edited by Richard D. Heffner. New York: Signet. (Most recent reedition is *Democracy in America: Specially Edited and Abridged for the Modern Reader by Richard D. Heffner*, with a new afterword by Vartan Gregorian [New York: New American Library, 2010].)

1961–62. *Democracy in America*. Translated by Henry Reeve, with a critical appraisal of each volume by John Stuart Mill. 2 vols. New York: Schocken.

1964. *Democracy in America.* Abridged, edited, and introduced by Andrew Hacker. New York: Washington Square.

1966. *Democracy in America.* Edited by Erik von Kuehnelt-Leddihn. Translated by Henry Reeve. Classics of Conservatism. New Rochelle: Arlington House.

1966. *Democracy in America.* Edited by J.-P. Mayer and Max Lerner. Translated by George Lawrence. New York: Harper and Row.

1980. *Democracy in America.* The Henry Reeve text as revised by Francis Bowen and further corrected by Phillips Bradley. Abridged with an introduction by Thomas Bender. New York: Modern Library.

1990. *Democracy in America.* Chicago: Encyclopædia Britannica.

1994. *Democracy in America.* Everyman's Library series, with an introduction by Alan Ryan. New York: Knopf.

1998. *Democracy in America.* Translated by Henry Reeve. Revised by Francis Bowen. Abridged and with an introduction by Patrick Renshaw. London: Wordsworth Classics in World Literature.

2000. *Democracy in America.* Translated by Henry Reeve, with an introduction by Joseph Epstein. New York: Bantam Classics.

2000. *Democracy in America.* Abridged, with introduction, by Sanford Kessler. Translated and annotated by Stephen D. Grant. Indianapolis: Hackett.

2000. *Democracy in America.* Translated, edited, and with an introduction by Harvey C. Mansfield and Delba Winthrop. Chicago: University of Chicago Press.

2003. *Democracy in America and Two Essays on America.* Translated by Gerald E. Bevan, with an introduction and notes by Isaac Kramnick. London: Penguin.

2004. *Democracy in America.* Translated by Arthur Goldhammer. New York: Library of America.

2007. *Democracy in America.* Edited by Isaac Kramnick. New York: W. W. Norton.

2008. *Democracy in America.* Translated by Elizabeth Trapnell Rawlings. Abridged with an introduction by Michael Kammen. Boston: Bedford/St. Martin's.

2010. *Democracy in America.* Memphis: General Books.

2010. *Democracy in America: Historical-Critical Edition of De la démocratie en Amérique.* Edited by Eduardo Nolla. Translated by James T. Schleifer. Bilingual French-English ed. 4 vols. Indianapolis: Liberty Fund.

# INDEX

Abbott, James R., 190
Adams, Henry, 184
Addams, Jane, 192, 198
Adoratskii, Viktor, 78
Adorno, Theodor, 128
Alcan, Félix, 17, 29, 31, 34
Alexander, Jeffrey C., 40, 42, 45, 198, 215 n. 30
  canon, shaping sociological, 198, 208 n 7, 208 n. 9
  "cultural" Durkheim, 12, 21–26, 32, 36, 38, 210 n. 26
  iconic consciousness, 210 n. 29 (Chapter 1), 210 n. 1 (Chapter 2)
  "materialist" Durkheim, 24, 32, 38
  "two Durkheims," 24
Ali, Muhammad, 117
Almond, Gabriel, 188
Alpert, Harry, 19
Althusser, Louis, 86–87
Anagnos, George, 47
Anderson, William, 177
Andrews, William, 117
Apel, Karl-Otto, 55
Appelrouth, Scott, 191
Aptheker, Herbert, 102–3, 105, 111, 217 n. 17, 217 n. 25
  Du Bois, complete works edition, 119, 217 n. 23
Aristotle, 189
Aron, Raymond, 221 n. 21
  canon, creating sociological, 20, 167
  and Durkheim as classic of sociology, 20

  and Tocqueville
    anti-Marx, 164
    as classic of sociology, 167, 184, 189–90
    rebirth, 160, 164
Arunta, Australian aboriginal people, 27
Ashley, David, 191
Audier, Serge, 164, 167, 220 n. 6
authorial angst, 113
authorial control, 12, 22, 48, 56, 103, 172
authorial meaning and intentions, 6, 65, 76
authorial-textual achievement, 43–44
Ayres, Clarence, 139

Baehr, Peter, 44, 51, 58, 135
Baert, Patrick, 54, 191
Baltzell, Edward Digby, 159–60, 188, 221 n. 23
Barnes, Harry Elmer, 144
Baudrillard, Jean, 169
Bauman, Zygmunt, 92
Beard, Charles A., 184
Beaumont, Gustave de, 176, 182
Becker, Herman, 71
Becker, Howard S., 44, 211 n. 17
Bell, Daniel, 86, 184–85, 214 n. 20, 214 n. 25
Bell, Monica, 134
Bellah, Robert, 37, 191, 208 n. 5
Below, Georg von, 140, 149, 210 n. 3
Bendix, Reinhard, 88–89, 188
Benjamin, Walter, 96
Benoit-Smullyan, Emile, 19
Berman, Marshall, 63–64
Besnard, Philippe, 26, 37

Bhambra, Gurminder K., 132
Binkley, W. E., 177
Birnbaum, Pierre, 37
Blau, Peter M., 18
Blight, David W., 106
Blumer, Herbert, 48, 51–55, 211 n. 14, 211 n. 16
  and Mead as classic of sociology, 46, 59
  symbolic interactionism, representative of, 44, 58–59
Booth, Charles, 98
Borlandi, Massimo, 29, 37, 208 n. 12
Bottomore, Tom, 84–85, 97–90, 214 n. 18, 215 n. 29
Boudon, Raymond, 191
Bouglé, Célestin, 184, 209 n. 16
Bourdieu, Pierre, 25, 90, 198
Brentano, Lujo, 140, 149
Brick, Howard, 154, 214 n. 25
Browne, Francis Fisher, 100, 216 nn. 4–5, 216–17 n. 14
Bulmer, Martin, 132
Burawoy, Michael, 89, 108, 120, 190, 215 n. 30
Burckhardt, Carl J., 165, 169
Burgess, Ernest, 18

Camic, Charles, 44, 137–38, 207–8 n. 1, 211 n. 21
Cannan, Edwin, 139
canon, sociological, 6, 20, 44–45
canonization, within sociology, 4, 13–15, 44–45, 198, 203
  Du Bois, 119–21, 127, 131–33
  marginalization within the canon, 99, 119
  Durkheim, 12, 36–37, 54, 120, 190, 198
  Marx, 84, 88, 93, 120, 198
  late, 88, 215 nn. 27–28
  Mead, 13, 43–44, 46, 50, 53–56, 59
  Tocqueville, 14, 166–67, 181–90, 199
  decanonization, 14, 190–93, 199
  Weber, 13, 54, 120, 135–38, 154, 190
Carus, Alwin C., 47
Chartier, Roger, 14–15
Cladis, Mark S., 39–40
Clark, Terry N., 37
Coleman, James S., 188
Collins, Randall, 26, 88, 190, 198, 220 n. 21, 221 n. 12
Colwell, James L., 181, 221 n. 18

Commager, Henry Steele, 157, 177–80, 184, 187
Comte, Auguste, 198
conflict theory, 88–91
Connell, R. W., 120, 198, 215 n. 28, 218 n. 3
contextualism, 18, 31, 36, 75
Cook, Gary Alan, 59, 211 n. 6
Cooley, Charles H., 156, 184, 198
Coser, Lewis A., 20, 59, 82, 88–90, 215 n. 29
Cosman, Carol, 36, 39–40
Côté, Jean François, 59–60
Crain, Caleb, 194
Crenshaw, Kimberlé, 126

Dahl, Robert, 184
Dahrendorf, Ralf, 88–89
Darwinism, 55
Dawson, Matthew, 108
Derrida, Jacques, 128–29
Dewey, John, 58, 210 n. 4, 212 n. 23
Dhanagare, Dinesh N., 85
Drescher, Seymour, 188, 197
Driver, Edwin D., 121, 217 n. 24
Du Bois, Shirley Graham, 97–98, 112–14
Du Bois, William Edward Burghardt
  African American studies movement, 98, 115–16, 126–27, 131–32
  alienation of blacks, 106–7, 119, 123
  black Atlantic, 125
  black canon, 126, 131–32
  black power movement, 115–18, 122
  black self-determination, 119
  black separatism, 119
  civil rights movement, 98, 111, 114–16, 130
  double consciousness, 13, 98, 107–8, 118–19, 123–26, 134
  multicultural interpretations, 13, 98, 100, 128
  *Philadelphia Negro. A Social Study, The* (1899), 98–100, 102–3, 120, 133
  relationship with Booker T. Washington, 101, 106, 110, 116, 216 n. 6
  sociology of blackness, 131
  *Suppression of the African Slave Trade to America* (1896), 100
  veil, separating the lives of black and whites, 104, 107–8
  whiteness, hegemonic conceptions of, 123, 126

See also Aptheker, Herbert; canonization, within sociology; paratext; Parsons, Talcott
Durkheim, Émile
  conservatism, 18
  cultural Durkheim, 12, 21–26, 32, 36, 38
  *Division of Labor in Society* (1893), 24
  effervescence, 28–29, 208 n. 10
  marginal in the canon, 38
  materialist Durkheim, 24, 32, 38
  rationalism, 20, 27
  scholarship, new, 36–41
  See also Alexander, Jeffrey C.; Aron, Raymond; canonization, within sociology; paratext; Parsons, Talcott; translator as editor
Dwiggins, William Addison, 173, 176, 220 n. 10

Echeverria, Durand, 183
editorial intervention, 4, 8–11, 15, 22
editorial landscape, 182
editors-cum-commentators, 5, 14, 89, 156 158, 204
editors-*cum*-translators, 14, 158, 204
Edles, Laura, 191
Edwards, Barrington S., 132
Edwards, Breanna, 123
Elazar, Daniel J., 188
Elias, Norbert, 120, 198
Elliott, Anthony, 192
Elster, Jon, 191, 220 n. 24
Engels, Friedrich, 64, 71–73, 84, 212 n. 2, 213 n. 11
epitext, 5, 12
Escarpit, Robert, 174

Faris, Ellsworth, 51, 211 n. 5
Fast, Howard, 97, 112–13, 217 n. 21
Fay, Margaret, 68–70, 81, 213 nn. 5–6, 214 n. 18
Feuerbach, Ludwig, 80, 212 n. 2, 213–14 n. 17
Fichte, Johann Gottlieb, 54
Fields, Karen E., 23, 35–40, 208 n. 13, 205 n. 17
Filloux, Jean-Claude, 37
Foucault, Michel, 65
Fournier, Marcel, 26, 37
Frank, Jerome N., 177

Franklin, Benjamin, 142
Franklin, John Hope, 114, 120
Frazer, James, 27–28, 35
Freud, Sigmund, 93, 113, 156, 211 n. 14
Fromm, Erich, 85–87, 91, 170

Gallimard, Gaston, 182
Gans, Herbert J., 170
Garvey, Marcus, 122, 125
Garvin, Tom, 176
Gates, Henry Louis, Jr., 100, 123, 126–28, 131–32, 217 n. 29, 218 n. 31
Geertz, Clifford, 40, 42
Gehlen, Arnold, 55, 212 n. 24
Genette, Gerard, 5, 6, 207 n. 2
Gerhardt, Uta, 137–38, 140, 218 nn. 5–6, 219–20 n. 17
Ghosh, Peter, 6–7, 137, 146–47, 218 n. 2
Gibson, Donald B., 126–27, 217–18 n. 30
Giddens, Anthony, 190, 198, 209 n. 25
  Parsons, dispute with, 138, 156, 220 n. 19, 220 n. 21
Gilkeson, John S., 185
Gillen, Francis, 26–27, 29
Gilroy, Paul, 124–25, 217 n. 29
Gingrich, Newton Leroy, 180
Goethe, Johann Wolfgang von, 165, 217 n. 29
Goffman, Erving, 44, 211 n. 17
Goldhammer, Arthur, 196–97, 221–22 n. 26
Gooding-Williams, Robert, 103, 106
Goodwin, Glenn A., 191
Gosselin, Charles, 157
Gouldner, Alvin, 18
Gramsci, Antonio, 91, 123
Green, Dan S., 121, 217 n. 24
Greene, Lancaster M., 176
Griffin, Erica L., 105, 110–11
Groethuysen, Bernard, 182
Guevara, Ernesto "Che," 91
Guillory, John, 198

Habermas, Jürgen, 21, 46, 55–59, 198, 212 n. 22
Hacker, Andrew, 180
Hall, Stuart, 123–24, 128, 217 n. 27
Hamilton, Nora, 91
Hamilton, Richard F., 191
Hamilton, Walton, 139
Hare, Nathan, 114–18, 120, 131
Heffner, Richard D., 180

INDEX | 253

Hegel, Georg W. F., 54, 125, 128–29, 140
  Marx, and, 69, 74–77, 80–83, 87–88, 94–95, 213–14 n. 17
Henslin, James M., 191
Hess, Andreas, 176
Hill Collins, Patricia, 134
Hobhouse Leonard T., 139
Holub, Robert C., 130
Hommes, Jakob, 83
Hook, Sidney, 82
Hoover, J. Edgar, 90
Hubert, Henri, 28, 208 n. 12, 209 n. 16
Huebner, Daniel R., 43, 58–61, 210 n. 3
Humboldt, Wilhelm von, 54
Hunter, Marcus Anthony, 132
Hyppolite, Jean, 83

intertextual analysis, 29–30
Intichiuma, ritual practice of Arunta, Australian aboriginal people, 27
Itzigsohn, Jose, and Karida Brown, 132

Jacobs, Paul, 63
James, C. L. R., 114, 121–23
James, William, 55, 212 n. 23, 217 n. 29
Jaspers, Karl, 139
Jauss, Hans-Robert, 51, 130
Joas, Hans, 43, 55, 58–60, 207–8 n. 1, 212 nn. 24–25
Johnson, James Weldon, 128
Jones, Robert Alun, 17, 28, 37

Kalberg, Stephen, 135
Kammen, Michael, 192
Kant, Immanuel, 30–31, 80, 154, 208 nn. 14–15
Kasinitz, Philip, 192
Kautsky, Karl, 72
Keen, Mike, 90
Kelsey, Carl, 105, 111
Kendall, Diana, 191
Khrushchev, Nikita, 63
King, Martin Luther, Jr., 98, 114
Kiniery, Paul, 177
Kołakowski, Leszek, 92
Kramnick, Isaac, 177, 192, 221–22 n. 26
Kuehnelt-Leddihn, Erik von, 180

Labedz, Leopold, 72
Lafargue, Laura, 71

Lafargue, Paul, 71
Landau, Saul, 63
Landshut, Siegfried, 62, 74–79, 85, 160, 213 n. 12
Laski, Harold, 164, 173–75, 177, 181, 184–85, 221 n. 13
Lawrence, George, 157, 178, 183–84, 194, 197, 199
Lefevere, André, on the politics of translation, 7
Lejeune, Philippe, 6
Lemert, Charles, 134, 192, 215–16 n. 1, 217 n. 29
Leopold, David, 64
Lerner, Max, 177, 181, 183–87, 193, 199, 221 n. 21
Levine, Donald N., 17, 19, 207 n. 1, 208 n. 7, 211 n. 14
Liber, Francis, 184
license
  editorial, 48
  interpretative, 85, 194
  translator's, 38
Lichtenstein, Nelson, 188
Lidz, Victor, 138, 153
Lillie, W. T., 46–47, 60
Lippmann, Walter, 91
Lipset, Seymour Martin, 187–88
Locke, John, 4–5, 207 n. 3
Lockwood, David, 88
Loughran, Kevin, 132
Luhmann, Niklas, 49
Lukács, Georg, 56, 82–83, 91–92
Lukes, Stephen, 24, 26, 37

Machiavelli, Niccolò, 176
Macionis, John J., 191
Maidan, Michael, 84
Malcolm X, 119
Man, Henri De, 79–80
Mancini, Mathew, 160, 173, 178, 180, 193
Mannheim, Karl, 139, 143
Mansfield, Harvey C., Jr., 160, 193–200, 221–22 n. 26, 222 n. 27
Marcuse, Herbert, 68, 79–81, 83, 87, 93–96, 214 n. 18
  and Marxist humanism, 80–81, 85, 91
Marshall, Lynn L., 183
Martindale, Don, 19, 189, 207 n. 1

Martineau, Harriet, 192, 198
Marx, Karl
  alienation, 13, 63, 65, 68–89 92–95, 213–14 n. 17
  as humanist, 79–80, 84–86, 91–95
  materialism, historical and philosophical, 18, 79–80, 84, 142
  mature Marx, 79, 86, 90, 95
  scientific, 79, 86–87, 91
  young Marx, 62–63, 73, 81, 86–87, 90, 92–93
  *See also* canonization, within sociology; Hegel, Georg W. F.; Marcuse, Herbert; paratext; Parsons, Talcott translator as editor
Marxism, 78–80, 83, 90
  orthodox, 72–73, 81–84, 88, 90, 94
  Soviet, 78–80, 94
  Western, 78–80, 83, 215 n. 27, 215 n. 30
Mattson, Kevin, 91
Mauss, Marcel, 28, 30, 208–9 n. 16
Mayer, Jacob-Peter, 62, 74–75, 85, 160, 213 n. 12
Mayhew, Henry, 98
McCarthyism, 85, 93, 97, 112, 114, 130, 187
McClurg, A. C., 97, 100–101, 112, 216–17 n. 14
McPhail, Clark, 53
Mead, George Herbert, 51
  as idealist thinker, 58
  *Mind, Self, and Society*
    artificially fabricated, 13, 43–44, 46–50, 60–61
    reception in the United States, 51–54; in Germany, 55–59
  in social behaviorism, 48, 56, 211 n. 11
  *See also* Blumer, Herbert; canonization, within sociology; paratext; Parsons, Talcott
Mead, Henry Tufts, 47
Mead, Irene Tufts, 47
Mehring, Franz, 72
Meissner, Otto, 71
Menand, Louis, 55
Mennell, Stephen, 192
Merleau-Ponty, Maurice, 83
Merton, Robert King, 52, 102, 119–20, 198, 212 n. 26
Miller, Joseph Hillis, 5
Milligan, Martin, 63, 84, 214 n. 22
Mills, Charles Wright, 53, 59, 63, 91–92, 198

Mommsen, Wolfgang, 138
Montesquieu, 199
Morris, Aldon D., 119, 132–34
Morris, Charles W., 43–48, 53, 55, 57, 60–61, 210 n. 4
Morrison, Ken, 37
Morrison, Toni, 128
Muirhead, John Henry, 35, 209 n. 23
Mumford, Lewis, 172
Musto, Marcello, 76, 78, 80, 213 n. 14

Napoleon III, 168
Neal, Larry, 119
Nelson, Benjamin, 149
Nietzsche, Friedrich, 154, 165, 219 n. 15
Nisbet, Robert, 20, 159–60, 172–73, 188–91

Obama, Barack, 25
Offe, Claus, 165
Ollman, Bertell, 92, 215 n. 27
Orenstein, David, 191

Palonen, Kari, on the politics of translation, 7
Pan-Africanism, 113, 122, 132–33
paratext, 6–7, 10, 12, 203–4, 207 n. 5
  Du Bois, 103–4, 107
  Durkheim, 32, 38–39, 209 n. 25
  Marx, 84, 215 nn. 27–28
  Mead, 61
  Tocqueville, 158, 174, 188, 194
  Weber, 144, 146–47
Pareto, Vilfredo, 154, 198, 209 n. 25
Park, Robert E., 18
Parsons, Talcott, 25, 51, 54, 88–91, 198, 218 nn. 4–9
  and Du Bois, 119–20
  and Durkheim, 18, 21–23
  and Marx, 89, 215 n. 28
  and Mead, 212 n. 27
  *See also* Giddens, Anthony; Weber, Max
Pascal, Blaise, 199
Passow, Richard, 140, 149
Peirce, Charles Sanders, 55, 58, 212 n. 23
peritext, 5, 115
Pickering, W. S. F., 37, 208 n. 14, 209 n. 25
Pierson, George Wilson, 160–63, 166–68, 172–76, 183–84, 200
Poggi, Gianfranco, 190
Pope, Whitney, 191

Popitz, Heinrich, 83
Poussaint, Alvin, 114–15, 118
Proudhon, Pierre-Joseph, 165
Putnam, Robert D., 191

Rabaka, Reiland, 115, 119, 132, 134
Rampersad, Arnold, 126, 216 n. 10, 217 n. 29
Redding, Saunders, 114–16, 127
Rédier, Antoine, 163–64, 182
Redlich, Norman, 187
Reed, Adolph, 128
Reeve, Henry, 157, 183
Rex, John, 88, 215 n. 28
Rexroat, Cynthia, 53
Reynolds, Cecil A., 22, 33–34
Riazanov, David, 72–74, 78, 82, 212 n. 3, 213 n. 11
Ricoeur, Paul, 49, 137, 210 n. 27, 218 n. 3
Riesebrodt, Martin, 148, 219 n. 11
Riesman, David, 169–72, 184, 187–88
Rogers, Melvin, 102–3
Rojahn, Jürgen, 76
Ropke, Wilhelm, 169
Rosenberger, Coleman, 176
Roth, Guenther, 155
Rousseau, Jean Jacques, 176, 199
Rubel, Maximilien, 83–85
Rudwick, Elliott M., 121, 217 n. 26

Salin, Edgar, 140, 143
Salomon, Albert, 159, 175–76, 181–82, 188, 220 n. 2, 221 n. 18
Sartre, Jean-Paul, 83
Satterwhite, James H., 92
Scaff, Lawrence, 136, 138, 144–47, 154, 219 n. 12
Schaefer, Richard T., 191
Schelsky, Helmut, 169
Schelting, Alexander von, 139
Schneidermann, Howard G., 159
Schoeps, Hans-Joachim, 169
Scimecca, Joseph A., 191
Seidman, Stephen, 120, 191
Shakespeare, William, 45
Shalin, Dmitri, 52, 60
Shils, Edward, 37, 189
Siebeck, Mohr, 135, 219 n. 16
Siebeck, Oskar, 135, 145–46, 219 n. 12

Silva, Filipe Carreira da, 58–59, 191, 208 n. 4, 210 n. 2, 211 n. 6, 221 n. 13
Simmel, Georg, 82, 89, 198, 209 n. 25
Skinner, Quentin, 46, 78
Skocpol, Theda, 191
Smith, Adam, 69–70, 77, 81, 189, 213 n. 5, 213–14 n. 17
Smith, Philip, 25, 37, 40, 210 n. 26
Smith, Richard L., 211 n. 8, 211 n. 21
Smith, Robertson, 27
Smith, Valerie, 126
Socrates, 49–50
Solomon, Friedrich, 75
Sombart, Werner, 23, 137, 139–41, 143, 150
Sorel, Georges, 165–66, 220 n. 4, 220 n. 6
Sorokin, Pitirim, 19, 189, 207 n. 1, 208 n. 3
Spencer, Baldwin, 26–29
Spencer, Herbert, 198, 209 n. 25
Stalin, I. V., 63, 73, 94
Stalinism, 92, 214 n. 20
Stanfield, John H., 113
Stauth, Georg, 125, 219 n. 15
Stedman Jones, Gareth, 76
Stedman Jones, Susan, 27
Strauss, Leo, 193, 195–96, 199–200
Sumner, Graham, 198
Swain, Joseph Ward, 22–23, 32–36, 38–40, 209 nn. 17–23, 210 n. 28
Swedberg, Richard, 191
Sydnor, Charles S., 176

Tarde, Gabriel, 184
Tawney, Richard Henry, 139, 146–47, 219 n. 12
textual criticism, 64
textual exegesis, 6–7, 20, 32
Thier, Erich, 83
Tillery, Alvin, Jr., 193
Tiryakian, Edward, 37
Tocqueville, Alexis de
  analyst of mass society, 166–70, 182, 186–87
  centralization, administrative, 162, 168, 188, 190
  conservative appropriations, 157–58, 169, 192–94, 197, 199–200
  ideal types, Weberian, anticipation of, 199
  liberal, 163, 182, 188, 200
  Marx, complementary to, 163–65
  Marx, in opposition to, 160, 164, 177, 180

nonliberal, 163–64, 174
*Old Regime and the Revolution, The*, 159, 167–68, 190
political theorist, 193, 199
*See also* Aron, Raymond; canonization, within sociology; paratext; translator as editor
Tönnies, Ferdinand, 198
Torpey, John, 192
translation, politics of, 6–8
translator as editor, 7–9, 11–14, 156, 197, 204
 Durkheim, 22–23, 38
 Marx, 84, 89
 Tocqueville, 158, 160–61, 193–97
 Weber, 136–38, 150, 156
Trevino, A. Javier, 136
Tribe, Keith, 70, 77, 147, 213 n. 6
Trow, Martin A., 188
Tucker, Charles, 52
Tucker, Robert C., 92
Tugendhat, Ernst, 56, 212 n. 22
Turner, Bryan S., 125, 219 n. 15
Turner, Jonathan H., 191
Turner, Stephen, 136, 215 n. 30

Verba, Sydney, 188
Villard, Oswald Garrison, 110
Vogt, Paul, 22
*Voynich Manuscript, The*, 203

Ward, John William, 183
Ward, William Hayes, 110
Washington, Booker T., 101–4, 106, 110–11, 116, 128, 216 n. 6
Watts Miller, William, 27–29
Wearne, Bruce C., 137, 151, 154, 219 n. 14

Weber, Alfred, 139
Weber, Marianne, 139, 143–46, 165, 218 n. 9, 219 n. 12
Weber, Max
 bureaucratic rationalization, 56, 133, 141–2, 148
 capitalism, dual conception of, 140–43, 151–52
 charisma and routine, 151, 153
 ideal type, 14, 143, 150–53, 167, 199
 Parsons, Talcott, as translator, editor, and scholar of, 13–14, 135–56, 219 n. 12, 219 n. 14, 220 n. 19
 *Protestant Ethic and the Spirit of Capitalism, The*
  nonmaterialistic, 149
  origin, convoluted, 135
  value-free science, 142
 *See also* canonization, within sociology; paratext; translator as editor
Weber circle, 139
Wells, Gordon, 135
West, Cornel, 119, 125
Wetham, Frederic, 168
Wideman, John Edgar, 126
Winant, Howard, 112, 119, 132, 216 n. 12
Winthrop, Delba, 193–200, 221–22 n. 26, 222 n. 27
Wittgenstein, Ludwig, 55
Wright, Benjamin F., 177
Wright, Earl, 119, 217 n. 26

Zamir, Şhamoon, 105, 216 n. 11
Zbinden, Hans, 169
Zeitlin, Irving, 18
Ziegler, Benjamin Munn, 184

THE PENN STATE SERIES IN THE HISTORY OF THE BOOK
James L. W. West III, General Editor

*Editorial Board*
Robert R. Edwards (Pennsylvania State University)
Paul Eggert (Loyola University Chicago)
Simon Eliot (University of London)
William L. Joyce (Pennsylvania State University)
Beth Luey (Massachusetts Historical Society)
Willa Z. Silverman (Pennsylvania State University)

PREVIOUSLY PUBLISHED TITLES IN THE PENN STATE SERIES IN THE HISTORY OF THE BOOK

Peter Burke, *The Fortunes of the "Courtier": The European Reception of Castiglione's "Cortegiano"* (1996)

Roger Burlingame, *Of Making Many Books: A Hundred Years of Reading, Writing, and Publishing* (1996)

James M. Hutchisson, *The Rise of Sinclair Lewis, 1920–1930* (1996)

Julie Bates Dock, ed., *Charlotte Perkins Gilman's "The Yellow Wall-Paper" and the History of Its Publication and Reception: A Critical Edition and Documentary Casebook* (1998)

John Williams, ed., *Imaging the Early Medieval Bible* (1998)

Ezra Greenspan, *George Palmer Putnam: Representative American Publisher* (2000)

James G. Nelson, *Publisher to the Decadents: Leonard Smithers in the Careers of Beardsley, Wilde, Dowson* (2000)

Pamela E. Selwyn, *Everyday Life in the German Book Trade: Friedrich Nicolai as Bookseller and Publisher in the Age of Enlightenment* (2000)

David R. Johnson, *Conrad Richter: A Writer's Life* (2001)

David Finkelstein, *The House of Blackwood: Author-Publisher Relations in the Victorian Era* (2002)

Rodger L. Tarr, ed., *As Ever Yours: The Letters of Max Perkins and Elizabeth Lemmon* (2003)

Randy Robertson, *Censorship and Conflict in Seventeenth-Century England: The Subtle Art of Division* (2009)

Catherine M. Parisian, ed., *The First White House Library: A History and Annotated Catalogue* (2010)

Jane McLeod, *Licensing Loyalty: Printers, Patrons, and the State in Early Modern France* (2011)

Charles Walton, ed., *Into Print: Limits and Legacies of the Enlightenment; Essays in Honor of Robert Darnton* (2011)

James L. W. West III, *Making the Archives Talk: New and Selected Essays in Bibliography, Editing, and Book History* (2012)

John Hruschka, *How Books Came to America: The Rise of the American Book Trade* (2012)

A. Franklin Parks, *William Parks: The Colonial Printer in the Transatlantic World of the Eighteenth Century* (2012)

Roger E. Stoddard, comp., and David R. Whitesell, ed., *A Bibliographic Description of Books and Pamphlets of American Verse Printed from 1610 Through 1820* (2012)

Nancy Cervetti, *S. Weir Mitchell: Philadelphia's Literary Physician* (2012)

Karen Nipps, *Lydia Bailey: A Checklist of Her Imprints* (2013)

Paul Eggert, *Biography of a Book: Henry Lawson's "While the Billy Boils"* (2013)

Allan Westphall, *Books and Religious Devotion: The Redemptive Reading of an Irishman in Nineteenth-Century New England* (2014)

Scott Donaldson, *The Impossible Craft: Literary Biography* (2015)

John Bidwell, *Graphic Passion: Matisse and the Book Arts* (2015)

Peter L. Shillingsburg, *Textuality and Knowledge: Essays* (2017)

Steven Carl Smith, *An Empire of Print: The New York Publishing Trade in the Early American Republic* (2017)

Colm Tóibín, Marc Simpson and Declan Kiely, *Henry James and American Painting* (2017)

www.ingramcontent.com/pod-product-compliance
Lightning Source LLC
Chambersburg PA
CBHW021939290426

44108CB00012B/893